W9-BSU-511

Policy Documents
&
Reports

AAUP

AMERICAN ASSOCIATION
OF
UNIVERSITY PROFESSORS

Policy Documents
&
Reports

NINTH
EDITION

Published by the American Association of University Professors
Washington, D.C.
Distributed by The Johns Hopkins University Press
Baltimore and London

American Association of University Professors
1012 Fourteenth Street, NW
Washington, DC 20005

First published   1968
Ninth edition   2001
ISSN 0897-1595
ISBN 0-9649548-1-8

Editor: B. Robert Kreiser
Production Editor: Wendi Maloney
Editorial Assistant: Nanette Crisologo

CONTENTS

PROFESSIONAL ETHICS

RESEARCH AND TEACHING

DISTANCE EDUCATION AND INTELLECTUAL PROPERTY

DISCRIMINATION

COLLEGE AND UNIVERSITY GOVERNMENT

COLLECTIVE BARGAINING

STUDENT RIGHTS AND FREEDOMS

COLLEGE AND UNIVERSITY ACCREDITATION

COLLATERAL BENEFITS

CONSTITUTION

APPENDICES

INDEX

INTRODUCTION

For eighty-five years the American Association of University Professors has been engaged in developing standards for sound academic practice and in working for the acceptance of these standards by the community of higher education. The Association has long been viewed as the authoritative voice of the academic profession in this regard.

This volume presents in convenient format a wide range of policies as they have been formulated by standing and special committees, at times in cooperation with other organizations, and adopted by the Association's national Council and by the annual meeting of the membership. Included also are a number of reports on significant topics that have been approved for publication. Additional policy documents and reports have been published periodically in *Academe: Bulletin of the American Association of University Professors*. Statements of official policy are also found in the published reports of relevant committees and the published record of meetings of the Council and the annual meeting. Those interested are invited to consult with the Association's Washington office staff about policies on particular subjects that are not included in this volume but may be published elsewhere.

The names of the Association's staff and Association committees and their membership are listed annually in *Academe*, usually in the last issue of the year. The Association's Constitution (which is reprinted in this volume), together with the staff and committee rosters, provides an outline of the Association's structure.

Active membership in the AAUP is open to teachers and research scholars holding faculty status in accredited institutions, or in institutions that are candidates for accreditation. Academic librarians are eligible, as are counselors holding faculty status and other professional appointees included with the faculty in a collective bargaining unit.

Graduate Student membership is open to persons who are currently, or within the past five years have been, enrolled in graduate studies in accredited institutions, and who are not eligible for active membership.

Associate membership is reserved for persons serving in accredited institutions whose work is primarily administrative. *Retired* membership is open to *active* members retired for reasons of age. *Public* membership is open to all persons not eligible for *active, graduate student, associate,* or *retired* membership. Inquiries concerning membership should be addressed to the Association's Washington office.

The Washington office staff, as one of its key functions, is available to provide interpretations of Association policies and to advise as to their applicability in particular situations. This service is offered to members and nonmembers alike, to faculty members, to administrators, and to others who may be interested. Leaders of local AAUP chapters and state conferences can also be approached for advice on matters of concern. A major responsibility of a chapter or conference is to seek the adoption or retention of local institutional regulations that comport with Association policies.

The nature and value of Association policy documents are explained in detail in an article, "The Usefulness of AAUP Policy Statements," by Ralph S. Brown and Matthew W. Finkin.[1] Each author served the Association as general counsel and as chair of its Committee on Academic Freedom and Tenure (Committee A). The following text is excerpted from their article.

[1] *AAUP Bulletin* 64 (1978): 5–11.

The policy documents of the American Association of University Professors may be used in one of three ways. First, they offer guidance to all components of the academic community either for the development of institutional policy or for the resolution of concrete issues as they arise. Second, some documents, like the *Recommended Institutional Regulations on Academic Freedom and Tenure*, are fashioned in a form that is explicitly adaptable as official institutional policy, and they formalize particular advice the AAUP staff gives in recurring situations. Only recently, and thus far to a limited extent, has a third use developed: parties to lawsuits—both administrations and faculty—have begun to invoke AAUP standards to buttress their cases, either because these standards express academic custom generally or because they serve as an aid to the interpretation of institutional regulations or policies that derive from AAUP sources.[2] The value of AAUP standards in litigation depends, however, on their intrinsic persuasiveness and the degree to which they enjoy widespread acceptance. Their usefulness in litigation is directly proportional to their usefulness in other settings.

THE FORMATION OF AAUP POLICY

For more than three decades now, AAUP documents that appear to merit continuing reference have been collected for convenience in a single compilation entitled *Policy Documents and Reports*, familiarly known as the "Redbook." However, this compendium is neither the exclusive source of AAUP policy, nor does it, standing alone, at all reflect the elaborate and often time-consuming process by which policy is proposed, tested, reshaped, and, finally, adopted. Notably, the published reports of ad hoc investigating committees on conditions of academic freedom and tenure, approved for publication by the Association's Committee A, develop a species of common law that guides Committee A's deliberations and is often of wider interest. The contents of these reports are shared in advance with the affected institutional administrations to ensure their factual accuracy; comments of the administration on issues of policy or interpretation are noted so that the reader may make an independent judgment of the situation.

Proposed policies, like the *Recommended Institutional Regulations*, that interpret the broad language of the 1940 *Statement of Principles on Academic Freedom and Tenure* are published first for the comment of the academic community. Criticism and suggestions are frequently submitted by college and university administrators and by the national organizations that represent them. The soundness and phrasing of proposed policy statements are then reviewed in the light of these remarks as well as comments from the AAUP's membership and other interested persons. A revised text might then be published for comment once more, an amended text proposed for final adoption, or no action taken, thereby holding a particular formulation in abeyance pending further experience with the problem.

The policy statements of the Association enjoy varying levels of organizational endorsement. Some are in tentative form and are designed to generate further discussion within the academic community; some bear the imprimatur of one or another standing committee; some are officially adopted by the governing Council; and some are endorsed by the annual meeting of members and chapter representatives. This variety is not inadvertent. The percipient reader will regard this disparity not as a defect but as a testimonial. It is precisely because the Association generates policy through deliberation rather than through pronouncement—because it prefers the slow crystallization of opinion in the academic community to the instantaneous response of elected or appointed leaders—that it publishes proposed standards before it votes on them and that it lets them pass through various stages of ratification, assessing their worth and reliability by a slow and careful means.

A practice recommended with diffidence by Committee A (or another of AAUP's standing committees)[3] may constitute the closest approximation to wisdom on the subject for the time

---

[2] Some legal decisions that have relied on AAUP policy statements, and some scholarly writings referring to AAUP standards, are listed in an appendix at the end of this volume. References to legal decisions and/or to federal or state legislation have been updated throughout the volume.

[3] In order to clarify the AAUP's structure and activities, the Association's governing Council has decided to discontinue the tradition of listing the organization's standing committees—save for the best known among them, Committee A on Academic Freedom and Tenure—by alphabetical designations. The committees will hereafter be listed by their subject titles in all AAUP publications, including this edition of *Policy Documents and Reports*.

being; it would be needlessly impoverishing to cast it aside until it was moved along for superior endorsement. Such endorsement is not automatically forthcoming. Committee reports on a knotty issue may be rejected by the Council or the annual meeting, sometimes more than once. Such reports are not printed in *Policy Documents and Reports*. We have tried to clarify the internal processes that affect the presentation of AAUP policy statements. We naturally believe that their value reflects the anxious care that has gone into their preparation. But many of the key statements are not simply the AAUP's own, the pronouncements of professors only. The AAUP has a long history of collaboration with other organizations that speak for college and university presidents, who have views that sometimes diverge from those of the academy of teachers.

The conspicuous example of the collaborative statement is, of course, the fundamental 1940 *Statement of Principles on Academic Freedom and Tenure*, a joint enterprise with the Association of American Colleges (now the Association of American Colleges and Universities) that has been endorsed by 170 other organizations in higher education. The substantial number of endorsing organizations stands as ample testimony to the normative value of the 1940 *Statement*.

ADOPTING OR DISCLAIMING AAUP POLICIES

Probably hundreds of colleges and universities have invoked the 1940 *Statement* in their regulations or handbooks. Adoption of or reference to the 1940 *Statement* does not necessarily entail a commitment to the many AAUP policy statements that the Association has derived from the 1940 *Statement* and from its own evolving ideas of good practice. Surely no one would contend that adherence in 1950 to the 1940 *Statement*, without more, "binds" an institution to AAUP interpretations of 2000, in the sense that the later interpretations become an amendment to the institution's regulations. Similarly, if a college incorporates parts of the *Recommended Institutional Regulations* in its own regulations, later revision by AAUP will not alter what the institution has adopted, except on those few occasions when the college's rules express an intent to submit to AAUP revisions, sight unseen.

We do not mean to say that later views will or should have no influence. The advantage of using the language of something as familiar as the 1940 *Statement* is that one has access to a good deal of commentary, to a body of custom—to be sure, far from monolithic—in the academic community, and to a growing number of judicial decisions. All these familiar aids to interpretation help one understand what one is getting into and initially to avoid undesired consequences. A possible disadvantage is that new interpretations will later appear—with the AAUP only one of many sources—that may not be wanted. If the new interpretation is persuasive to an authoritative decision maker, like a judge or an arbitrator, one will be stuck with it in the particular case. And what then? If those with a voice in framing rules concur, then the rule can be changed. That, in a simple-minded way, is how institutions adapt to a changing scene.

If an institution resolutely tries to wall itself off from such outside influences, it loses the good along with the bad. In the case of AAUP policies, it is a gross error to regard them as altogether bestowing privileges on faculty. The 1940 *Statement* and attendant glosses can be positively helpful to administrators in rejecting unfounded faculty grievances.[4]

---

[4] For example, in *Korf v. Ball State University*, 726 F.2d 1222, 1227 (7th Cir. 1984), the federal appellate court cited the prohibition in the Association's *Statement on Professional Ethics* against exploitation of students in upholding the dismissal of a professor charged with having made repeated sexual advances to students. In another case, a federal district court, in holding that certain language used by a faculty member was not protected by the First Amendment, referred to the requirement of "appropriate restraint" contained in the 1940 *Statement* (*Starsky v. Williams*, 353 F. Supp. 900 [D. Ariz. 1972], *aff'd in part, rev'd in part*, 512 F. 2d 109 [9th Cir. 1975]). In a third case, a federal appellate court reversed a lower-court decision holding that a university regulation was unconstitutionally vague and overbroad. The appellate court took notice that the university regulation "was adopted almost verbatim from the 1940 *Statement of Principles* of the American Association of University Professors" (*Adamian v. Jacobsen*, 523 F.2d 929 [9th Cir. 1975]). On remand, the district court sustained the dismissal of the faculty member under this regulation.

AAUP STANDARDS IN THE COURTS

We do not unreservedly admire the increasing resort to the courts in academic disputes. Even aside from the burden of "seven-figure lawyers' fees"—burdens which fall on both sides in litigation—the rising tide of litigation shows that we have failed to keep our disputes within the academic family.

But let us take the scene as it is. There are more and more court cases because faculty members, when they believe that they have been injured, for example, by denial of due process, by an infringement of academic freedom, or by unfair treatment in a retrenchment action, conclude that they will not and should not give up if they can get help from the law. The immediate question, when college administrations and professors do go to court, is how judges view, and how should they view, AAUP policy statements.

Sometimes questions of due process and of academic freedom have constitutional dimensions. Expert though judges may be on the First and Fourteenth Amendments, the application of these broad mandates to a particular case is often not self-evident. Due process is a flexible concept. Academic due process is not the same as due process before a federal regulatory agency. The views of experts are one guide to a decision. We submit that the AAUP has some expertise in academic due process, and, as we suggested earlier, by adhering to a familiar standard, an institution often will save itself from legal sanctions that may attend an unknown standard.

In cases that do not invoke constitutional questions, a court will probably be trying to interpret a university handbook or regulations. The absence of detailed individual contracts, which are not common in the academic world, makes such documents the chief source of guidance toward the rights and duties of all parties. When regulations use terms customary in the academic world like "tenure," it is helpful to look to the academic community's understanding about what the term means, which to a large extent is found in the 1940 *Statement* and the commentary upon it. When regulations explicitly refer to the 1940 *Statement*, it is relevant to consider its history, later bilateral interpretations, and unilateral AAUP refinements as a guide to what the *Statement* means in a particular situation. The weight to be accorded these different kinds of interpretations varies. The AAUP has been at pains to distinguish them. Documents like the 1940 *Statement* that have joint authorship and extensive endorsement represent a consensus that extends beyond the faculty organization. Unilateral AAUP pronouncements, such as the *Recommended Institutional Regulations* or the opinions of an ad hoc investigating committee adopted by Committee A, represent the AAUP's opinion of how the 1940 *Statement* should be read. The AAUP has not argued that adopting the 1940 *Statement* necessarily binds any institution to a unilateral interpretation of it, nor has any court so held. What the AAUP has said in its amicus briefs is that, insofar as the courts are concerned, these documents should be understood as reasoned argument. To the extent that they reflect a reasoned exposition of how the controversy should be resolved, a court may well be persuaded by them—unless, of course, some party makes a better, i.e., a more reasoned argument.

In sum, to the extent that the standards of academic freedom and tenure built up by the AAUP over eighty-five years represent a body of persuasive professional opinion, the courts should give weight to them; if the standards are arbitrary or unreasoned, they should not.

ACADEMIC FREEDOM, TENURE, AND DUE PROCESS

From its inception in 1915, the main work of the Association has been in the area of academic freedom and tenure. Policy in this vital field has evolved gradually but continuously since that time. In the year of its founding the Association formulated a "Declaration of Principles," a statement on academic freedom and tenure and professional responsibility, which concluded with a section enumerating desirable procedures. This statement (to be found in Appendix I in this volume) was put to immediate use by the organization's standing Committee on Academic Freedom and Tenure (Committee A) in dealing with particular cases. Ten years later, the American Council on Education called a conference of a number of its constituent members, among them the AAUP, for the purpose of formulating a shorter statement that would take into account a decade's experience. The product of this effort became known as the 1925 Conference Statement on Academic Freedom and Tenure; it was endorsed by the Association of American Colleges (now the Association of American Colleges and Universities) in 1925 and by this Association in 1926. Beginning in 1934, the two endorsing organizations again joined in a series of conferences. The result was the present policy document, the landmark 1940 Statement of Principles on Academic Freedom and Tenure, which in later years has been further endorsed by 170 additional learned societies and educational associations, and which in 1970 was supplemented by a series of "Interpretive Comments."

Since 1940, the Association has issued other policy statements and reports which explain and develop aspects of the Statement of Principles and which also set forth procedural standards for academic due process in a variety of situations. The most generally used among these statements are the 1958 Statement on Procedural Standards in Faculty Dismissal Proceedings (developed jointly with the Association of American Colleges), the Statement on Procedural Standards in the Renewal or Nonrenewal of Faculty Appointments, and the Recommended Institutional Regulations on Academic Freedom and Tenure.

The Association, also from its inception, has assumed responsibility not only for promulgating principles and standards but also for implementing them in specific situations. Believing that unrectified departures from sound academic standards do injury to the entire academic profession, the Association in addition publishes reports of ad hoc investigating committees on specific cases at colleges and universities that raise issues of academic freedom and tenure. These reports offer helpful guidance for the understanding of later situations confronted by the Association and constitute implementation of Association policy. They also contribute to the ongoing process of education in accepted principles and practice which is the central purpose and the most important activity of the Association.

1940 Statement of Principles on Academic Freedom and Tenure
With 1970 Interpretive Comments

In 1940, following a series of joint conferences begun in 1934, representatives of the American Association of University Professors and of the Association of American Colleges (now the Association of American Colleges and Universities) agreed upon a restatement of principles set forth in the 1925 Conference Statement on Academic Freedom and Tenure. *This restatement is known to the profession as the 1940 Statement of Principles on Academic Freedom and Tenure.*

The 1940 Statement *is printed below, followed by Interpretive Comments as developed by representatives of the American Association of University Professors and the Association of American Colleges in 1969. The governing bodies of the two associations, meeting respectively in November 1989 and January 1990, adopted several changes in language in order to remove gender-specific references from the original text.*

The purpose of this statement is to promote public understanding and support of academic freedom and tenure and agreement upon procedures to ensure them in colleges and universities. Institutions of higher education are conducted for the common good and not to further the interest of either the individual teacher[1] or the institution as a whole. The common good depends upon the free search for truth and its free exposition.

Academic freedom is essential to these purposes and applies to both teaching and research. Freedom in research is fundamental to the advancement of truth. Academic freedom in its teaching aspect is fundamental for the protection of the rights of the teacher in teaching and of the student to freedom in learning. It carries with it duties correlative with rights.[1][2]

Tenure is a means to certain ends; specifically: (1) freedom of teaching and research and of extramural activities, and (2) a sufficient degree of economic security to make the profession attractive to men and women of ability. Freedom and economic security, hence, tenure, are indispensable to the success of an institution in fulfilling its obligations to its students and to society.

ACADEMIC FREEDOM

(a) Teachers are entitled to full freedom in research and in the publication of the results, subject to the adequate performance of their other academic duties; but research for pecuniary return should be based upon an understanding with the authorities of the institution.

(b) Teachers are entitled to freedom in the classroom in discussing their subject, but they should be careful not to introduce into their teaching controversial matter which has no relation to their subject.[2] Limitations of academic freedom because of religious or other aims of the institution should be clearly stated in writing at the time of the appointment.[3]

---

[1] The word "teacher" as used in this document is understood to include the investigator who is attached to an academic institution without teaching duties.

[2] Boldface numbers in brackets refer to Interpretive Comments which follow.

(c) College and university teachers are citizens, members of a learned profession, and officers of an educational institution. When they speak or write as citizens, they should be free from institutional censorship or discipline, but their special position in the community imposes special obligations. As scholars and educational officers, they should remember that the public may judge their profession and their institution by their utterances. Hence they should at all times be accurate, should exercise appropriate restraint, should show respect for the opinions of others, and should make every effort to indicate that they are not speaking for the institution.[4]

ACADEMIC TENURE

After the expiration of a probationary period, teachers or investigators should have permanent or continuous tenure, and their service should be terminated only for adequate cause, except in the case of retirement for age, or under extraordinary circumstances because of financial exigencies.

In the interpretation of this principle it is understood that the following represents acceptable academic practice:

1. The precise terms and conditions of every appointment should be stated in writing and be in the possession of both institution and teacher before the appointment is consummated.
2. Beginning with appointment to the rank of full-time instructor or a higher rank,[5] the probationary period should not exceed seven years, including within this period full-time service in all institutions of higher education; but subject to the proviso that when, after a term of probationary service of more than three years in one or more institutions, a teacher is called to another institution, it may be agreed in writing that the new appointment is for a probationary period of not more than four years, even though thereby the person's total probationary period in the academic profession is extended beyond the normal maximum of seven years.[6] Notice should be given at least one year prior to the expiration of the probationary period if the teacher is not to be continued in service after the expiration of that period.[7]
3. During the probationary period a teacher should have the academic freedom that all other members of the faculty have.[8]
4. Termination for cause of a continuous appointment, or the dismissal for cause of a teacher previous to the expiration of a term appointment, should, if possible, be considered by both a faculty committee and the governing board of the institution. In all cases where the facts are in dispute, the accused teacher should be informed before the hearing in writing of the charges and should have the opportunity to be heard in his or her own defense by all bodies that pass judgment upon the case. The teacher should be permitted to be accompanied by an advisor of his or her own choosing who may act as counsel. There should be a full stenographic record of the hearing available to the parties concerned. In the hearing of charges of incompetence the testimony should include that of teachers and other scholars, either from the teacher's own or from other institutions. Teachers on continuous appointment who are dismissed for reasons not involving moral turpitude should receive their salaries for at least a year from the date of notification of dismissal whether or not they are continued in their duties at the institution.[9]
5. Termination of a continuous appointment because of financial exigency should be demonstrably bona fide.

1940 INTERPRETATIONS

At the conference of representatives of the American Association of University Professors and of the Association of American Colleges on November 7–8, 1940, the following interpretations of the 1940 *Statement of Principles on Academic Freedom and Tenure* were agreed upon:

1. That its operation should not be retroactive.
2. That all tenure claims of teachers appointed prior to the endorsement should be determined in accordance with the principles set forth in the 1925 *Conference Statement on Academic Freedom and Tenure.*

3. If the administration of a college or university feels that a teacher has not observed the admonitions of paragraph (c) of the section on Academic Freedom and believes that the extramural utterances of the teacher have been such as to raise grave doubts concerning the teacher's fitness for his or her position, it may proceed to file charges under paragraph 4 of the section on Academic Tenure. In pressing such charges, the administration should remember that teachers are citizens and should be accorded the freedom of citizens. In such cases the administration must assume full responsibility, and the American Association of University Professors and the Association of American Colleges are free to make an investigation.

1970 INTERPRETIVE COMMENTS

Following extensive discussions on the 1940 Statement of Principles on Academic Freedom and Tenure *with leading educational associations and with individual faculty members and administrators, a joint committee of the AAUP and the Association of American Colleges met during 1969 to reevaluate this key policy statement. On the basis of the comments received, and the discussions that ensued, the joint committee felt the preferable approach was to formulate interpretations of the* Statement *in terms of the experience gained in implementing and applying the* Statement *for over thirty years and of adapting it to current needs.*

The committee submitted to the two associations for their consideration the following "Interpretive Comments." These interpretations were adopted by the Council of the American Association of University Professors in April 1970 and endorsed by the Fifty-sixth Annual Meeting as Association policy.

In the thirty years since their promulgation, the principles of the 1940 *Statement of Principles on Academic Freedom and Tenure* have undergone a substantial amount of refinement. This has evolved through a variety of processes, including customary acceptance, understandings mutually arrived at between institutions and professors or their representatives, investigations and reports by the American Association of University Professors, and formulations of statements by that association either alone or in conjunction with the Association of American Colleges. These comments represent the attempt of the two associations, as the original sponsors of the 1940 *Statement*, to formulate the most important of these refinements. Their incorporation here as Interpretive Comments is based upon the premise that the 1940 *Statement* is not a static code but a fundamental document designed to set a framework of norms to guide adaptations to changing times and circumstances.

Also, there have been relevant developments in the law itself reflecting a growing insistence by the courts on due process within the academic community which parallels the essential concepts of the 1940 *Statement*; particularly relevant is the identification by the Supreme Court of academic freedom as a right protected by the First Amendment. As the Supreme Court said in *Keyishian v. Board of Regents*, 385 U.S. 589 (1967), "Our Nation is deeply committed to safeguarding academic freedom, which is of transcendent value to all of us and not merely to the teachers concerned. That freedom is therefore a special concern of the First Amendment, which does not tolerate laws that cast a pall of orthodoxy over the classroom."

The numbers refer to the designated portion of the 1940 *Statement* on which interpretive comment is made.

1. The Association of American Colleges and the American Association of University Professors have long recognized that membership in the academic profession carries with it special responsibilities. Both associations either separately or jointly have consistently affirmed these responsibilities in major policy statements, providing guidance to professors in their utterances as citizens, in the exercise of their responsibilities to the institution and to students, and in their conduct when resigning from their institution or when undertaking government-sponsored research. Of particular relevance is the *Statement on Professional Ethics*, adopted in 1966 as Association policy. (A revision, adopted in 1987, may be found in AAUP, *Policy Documents and Reports*, 9th ed. [Washington, D.C., 2001], 133–34.)

2. The intent of this statement is not to discourage what is "controversial." Controversy is at the heart of the free academic inquiry which the entire statement is designed to foster. The passage serves to underscore the need for teachers to avoid persistently intruding material which has no relation to their subject.

3. Most church-related institutions no longer need or desire the departure from the principle of academic freedom implied in the 1940 *Statement*, and we do not now endorse such a departure.

4. This paragraph is the subject of an interpretation adopted by the sponsors of the 1940 *Statement* immediately following its endorsement which reads as follows:

> If the administration of a college or university feels that a teacher has not observed the admonitions of paragraph (c) of the section on Academic Freedom and believes that the extramural utterances of the teacher have been such as to raise grave doubts concerning the teacher's fitness for his or her position, it may proceed to file charges under paragraph 4 of the section on Academic Tenure. In pressing such charges, the administration should remember that teachers are citizens and should be accorded the freedom of citizens. In such cases the administration must assume full responsibility, and the American Association of University Professors and the Association of American Colleges are free to make an investigation.

Paragraph (c) of the section on Academic Freedom in the 1940 *Statement* should also be interpreted in keeping with the 1964 "Committee A Statement on Extramural Utterances" (*Policy Documents and Reports*, 32), which states inter alia: "The controlling principle is that a faculty member's expression of opinion as a citizen cannot constitute grounds for dismissal unless it clearly demonstrates the faculty member's unfitness for his or her position. Extramural utterances rarely bear upon the faculty member's fitness for the position. Moreover, a final decision should take into account the faculty member's entire record as a teacher and scholar."

Paragraph 5 of the *Statement on Professional Ethics* also deals with the nature of the "special obligations" of the teacher. The paragraph reads as follows:

> As members of their community, professors have the rights and obligations of other citizens. Professors measure the urgency of other obligations in the light of their responsibilities to their subject, to their students, to their profession, and to their institution. When they speak or act as private persons they avoid creating the impression of speaking or acting for their college or university. As citizens engaged in a profession that depends upon freedom for its health and integrity, professors have a particular obligation to promote conditions of free inquiry and to further public understanding of academic freedom.

Both the protection of academic freedom and the requirements of academic responsibility apply not only to the full-time probationary and the tenured teacher, but also to all others, such as part-time faculty and teaching assistants, who exercise teaching responsibilities.

5. The concept of "rank of full-time instructor or a higher rank" is intended to include any person who teaches a full-time load regardless of the teacher's specific title.*

6. In calling for an agreement "in writing" on the amount of credit given for a faculty member's prior service at other institutions, the *Statement* furthers the general policy of full understanding by the professor of the terms and conditions of the appointment. It does not necessarily follow that a professor's tenure rights have been violated because of the absence of a written agreement on this matter. Nonetheless, especially because of the variation in permissible institutional practices, a written understanding concerning these matters at the time of appointment is particularly appropriate and advantageous to both the individual and the institution.**

7. The effect of this subparagraph is that a decision on tenure, favorable or unfavorable, must be made at least twelve months prior to the completion of the probationary period. If the decision is negative, the appointment for the following year becomes a terminal one. If the decision is affirmative, the provisions in the 1940 *Statement* with respect to the termination of service of teachers or investigators after the expiration of a probationary period should apply from the date when the favorable decision is made.

---

* For a discussion of this question, see the "Report of the Special Committee on Academic Personnel Ineligible for Tenure," *Policy Documents and Reports*, 88–91.

** For a more detailed statement on this question, see "On Crediting Prior Service Elsewhere as Part of the Probationary Period," *ibid.*, 100–101.

The general principle of notice contained in this paragraph is developed with greater specificity in the *Standards for Notice of Nonreappointment*, endorsed by the Fiftieth Annual Meeting of the American Association of University Professors (1964). These standards are:

> Notice of nonreappointment, or of intention not to recommend reappointment to the governing board, should be given in writing in accordance with the following standards:
>
> (a) *Not later than March 1 of the first academic year of service*, if the appointment expires at the end of that year; or, if a one-year appointment terminates during an academic year, at least three months in advance of its termination.
>
> (b) *Not later than December 15 of the second academic year of service*, if the appointment expires at the end of that year; or, if an initial two-year appointment terminates during an academic year, at least six months in advance of its termination.
>
> (c) At least twelve months before the expiration of an appointment after two or more years in the institution.

Other obligations, both of institutions and of individuals, are described in the *Statement on Recruitment and Resignation of Faculty Members*, as endorsed by the Association of American Colleges and the American Association of University Professors in 1961.

8. The freedom of probationary teachers is enhanced by the establishment of a regular procedure for the periodic evaluation and assessment of the teacher's academic performance during probationary status. Provision should be made for regularized procedures for the consideration of complaints by probationary teachers that their academic freedom has been violated. One suggested procedure to serve these purposes is contained in the *Recommended Institutional Regulations on Academic Freedom and Tenure*, prepared by the American Association of University Professors.

9. A further specification of the academic due process to which the teacher is entitled under this paragraph is contained in the *Statement on Procedural Standards in Faculty Dismissal Proceedings*, jointly approved by the American Association of University Professors and the Association of American Colleges in 1958. This interpretive document deals with the issue of suspension, about which the 1940 *Statement* is silent.

The 1958 *Statement* provides: "Suspension of the faculty member during the proceedings is justified only if immediate harm to the faculty member or others is threatened by the faculty member's continuance. Unless legal considerations forbid, any such suspension should be with pay." A suspension which is not followed by either reinstatement or the opportunity for a hearing is in effect a summary dismissal in violation of academic due process.

The concept of "moral turpitude" identifies the exceptional case in which the professor may be denied a year's teaching or pay in whole or in part. The statement applies to that kind of behavior which goes beyond simply warranting discharge and is so utterly blameworthy as to make it inappropriate to require the offering of a year's teaching or pay. The standard is not that the moral sensibilities of persons in the particular community have been affronted. The standard is behavior that would evoke condemnation by the academic community generally.

ENDORSERS

Association of Social and Behavioral Scientists 1968
College English Association 1968
National College Physical Education Association for Men 1969
American Real Estate and Urban Economics Association 1969
History of Education Society 1969
Council for Philosophical Studies 1969
American Musicological Society 1969
American Association of Teachers of Spanish and Portuguese 1969
Texas Junior College Teachers Association 1970
College Art Association of America 1970
Society of Professors of Education 1970
American Anthropological Association 1970
Association of Theological Schools 1970
Association of Schools and Mass Communication of Journalism 1971
American Business Law Association 1971
American Council for the Arts 1972
New York State Mathematics Association of Two-Year Colleges 1972
College Language Association 1973
Pennsylvania Historical Association 1973
Massachusetts Regional Community College Faculty Association 1973
American Philosophical Association*** 1974
American Classical League 1974
American Comparative Literature Association 1974
Rocky Mountain Modern Language Association 1974
Society of Architectural Historians 1975
American Statistical Association 1975
American Folklore Society 1975
Association for Asian Studies 1975
Linguistic Society of America 1975
African Studies Association 1975
American Institute of Biological Sciences 1975
North American Conference on British Studies 1975
Sixteenth-Century Studies Conference 1975
Texas Association of College Teachers 1976
Society for Spanish and Portuguese Historical Studies 1976
Association for Jewish Studies 1976
Western Speech Communication Association 1976
Texas Association of Colleges for Teacher Education 1977
Metaphysical Society of America 1977
American Chemical Society 1977
Texas Library Association 1977
American Society for Legal History 1977
Iowa Higher Education Association 1977
American Physical Therapy Association 1979
North Central Sociological Association 1980
Dante Society of America 1980
Association for Communication Administration 1981
American Association of Physics Teachers 1982
Middle East Studies Association. 1982
National Education Association 1985
American Institute of Chemists 1985

*** Endorsed by the Association's Western Division in 1952, Eastern Division in 1953, and Pacific Division in 1962.

1958 Statement on Procedural Standards in Faculty Dismissal Proceedings

The following statement was prepared by a joint committee representing the Association of American Colleges (now the Association of American Colleges and Universities) and the American Association of University Professors and was approved by these two associations at their annual meetings in 1958. It supplements the 1940 Statement of Principles on Academic Freedom and Tenure by providing a formulation of the "academic due process" that should be observed in dismissal proceedings. The exact procedural standards here set forth, however, "are not intended to establish a norm in the same manner as the 1940 Statement of Principles on Academic Freedom and Tenure, but are presented rather as a guide...."

The governing bodies of the American Association of University Professors and the Association of American Colleges, meeting respectively in November 1989 and January 1990, adopted several changes in language in order to remove gender-specific references from the original text.

INTRODUCTORY COMMENTS

Any approach toward settling the difficulties which have beset dismissal proceedings on many American campuses must look beyond procedure into setting and cause. A dismissal proceeding is a symptom of failure; no amount of use of removal process will help strengthen higher education as much as will the cultivation of conditions in which dismissals rarely if ever need occur.

Just as the board of control or other governing body is the legal and fiscal corporation of the college, the faculty is the academic entity. Historically, the academic corporation is the older. Faculties were formed in the Middle Ages, with managerial affairs either self-arranged or handled in course by the parent church. Modern college faculties, on the other hand, are part of a complex and extensive structure requiring legal incorporation, with stewards and managers specifically appointed to discharge certain functions.

Nonetheless, the faculty of a modern college constitutes an entity as real as that of the faculties of medieval times, in terms of collective purpose and function. A necessary precondition of a strong faculty is that it have first-hand concern with its own membership. This is properly reflected both in appointments to and in separations from the faculty body.

A well-organized institution will reflect sympathetic understanding by trustees and teachers alike of their respective and complementary roles. These should be spelled out carefully in writing and made available to all. Trustees and faculty should understand and agree on their several functions in determining who shall join and who shall remain on the faculty. One of the prime duties of the administrator is to help preserve understanding of those functions. It seems clear on the American college scene that a close positive relationship exists between the excellence of colleges, the strength of their faculties, and the extent of faculty responsibility in determining faculty membership. Such a condition is in no way inconsistent with full faculty awareness of institutional factors with which governing boards must be primarily concerned.

In the effective college, a dismissal proceeding involving a faculty member on tenure, or one occurring during the term of an appointment, will be a rare exception, caused by individual human weakness and not by an unhealthful setting. When it does come, however, the college should be prepared for it, so that both institutional integrity and individual human rights may be preserved during the process of resolving the trouble. The faculty must be willing to recommend the dismissal of a colleague when necessary. By the same token, presidents and governing boards must be willing to give full weight to a faculty judgment favorable to a colleague.

One persistent source of difficulty is the definition of adequate cause for the dismissal of a faculty member. Despite the 1940 *Statement of Principles on Academic Freedom and Tenure* and subsequent attempts to build upon it, considerable ambiguity and misunderstanding persist throughout higher education, especially in the respective conceptions of governing boards, administrative officers, and faculties concerning this matter. The present statement assumes that individual institutions will have formulated their own definitions of adequate cause for dismissal, bearing in mind the 1940 *Statement* and standards which have developed in the experience of academic institutions.

This statement deals with procedural standards. Those recommended are not intended to establish a norm in the same manner as the 1940 *Statement of Principles on Academic Freedom and Tenure*, but are presented rather as a guide to be used according to the nature and traditions of particular institutions in giving effect to both faculty tenure rights and the obligations of faculty members in the academic community.

PROCEDURAL RECOMMENDATIONS

1. Preliminary Proceedings Concerning the Fitness of a Faculty Member

When reasons arise to question the fitness of a college or university faculty member who has tenure or whose term appointment has not expired, the appropriate administrative officers should ordinarily discuss the matter with the faculty member in personal conference. The matter may be terminated by mutual consent at this point; but if an adjustment does not result, a standing or ad hoc committee elected by the faculty and charged with the function of rendering confidential advice in such situations should informally inquire into the situation, to effect an adjustment, if possible, and, if none is effected, to determine whether in its view formal proceedings to consider the faculty member's dismissal should be instituted. If the committee recommends that such proceedings should be begun, or if the president of the institution, even after considering a recommendation of the committee favorable to the faculty member, expresses the conviction that a proceeding should be undertaken, action should be commenced under the procedures which follow. Except where there is disagreement, a statement with reasonable particularity of the grounds proposed for the dismissal should then be jointly formulated by the president and the faculty committee; if there is disagreement, the president or the president's representative should formulate the statement.

2. Commencement of Formal Proceedings

The formal proceedings should be commenced by a communication addressed to the faculty member by the president of the institution, informing the faculty member of the statement formulated, and also informing the faculty member that, at the faculty member's request, a hearing will be conducted by a faculty committee at a specified time and place to determine whether he or she should be removed from the faculty position on the grounds stated. In setting the date of the hearing, sufficient time should be allowed the faculty member to prepare a defense. The faculty member should be informed, in detail or by reference to published regulations, of the procedural rights that will be accorded. The faculty member should state in reply whether he or she wishes a hearing, and, if so, should answer in writing, not less than one week before the date set for the hearing, the statements in the president's letter.

3. Suspension of the Faculty Member

Suspension of the faculty member during the proceedings is justified only if immediate harm to the faculty member or others is threatened by the faculty member's continuance. Unless legal considerations forbid, any such suspension should be with pay.

4. Hearing Committee

The committee of faculty members to conduct the hearing and reach a decision should be either an elected standing committee not previously concerned with the case or a committee established as soon as possible after the president's letter to the faculty member has been sent. The choice of members of the hearing committee should be on the basis of their objectivity and competence and of the regard in which they are held in the academic community. The committee should elect its own chair.

5. Committee Proceeding

The committee should proceed by considering the statement of grounds for dismissal already formulated, and the faculty member's response written before the time of the hearing. If the faculty member has not requested a hearing, the committee should consider the case on the basis of the obtainable information and decide whether the faculty member should be removed; otherwise, the hearing should go forward. The committee, in consultation with the president and the faculty member, should exercise its judgment as to whether the hearing should be public or private. If any facts are in dispute, the testimony of witnesses and other evidence concerning the matters set forth in the president's letter to the faculty member should be received.

The president should have the option of attendance during the hearing. The president may designate an appropriate representative to assist in developing the case; but the committee should determine the order of proof, should normally conduct the questioning of witnesses, and, if necessary, should secure the presentation of evidence important to the case.

The faculty member should have the option of assistance by counsel, whose functions should be similar to those of the representative chosen by the president. The faculty member should have the additional procedural rights set forth in the 1940 *Statement of Principles on Academic Freedom and Tenure*, and should have the aid of the committee, when needed, in securing the attendance of witnesses. The faculty member or the faculty member's counsel and the representative designated by the president should have the right, within reasonable limits, to question all witnesses who testify orally. The faculty member should have the opportunity to be confronted by all adverse witnesses. Where unusual and urgent reasons move the hearing committee to withhold this right, or where the witness cannot appear, the identity of the witness, as well as the statements of the witness, should nevertheless be disclosed to the faculty member. Subject to these safeguards, statements may, when necessary, be taken outside the hearing and reported to it. All of the evidence should be duly recorded. Unless special circumstances warrant, it should not be necessary to follow formal rules of court procedure.

6. Consideration by Hearing Committee

The committee should reach its decision in conference, on the basis of the hearing. Before doing so, it should give opportunity to the faculty member or the faculty member's counsel and the representative designated by the president to argue orally before it. If written briefs would be helpful, the committee may request them. The committee may proceed to decision promptly, without having the record of the hearing transcribed, where it feels that a just decision can be reached by this means; or it may await the availability of a transcript of the hearing if its decision would be aided thereby. It should make explicit findings with respect to each of the grounds of removal presented, and a reasoned opinion may be desirable. Publicity concerning the committee's decision may properly be withheld until consideration has been given to the case by the governing body of the institution. The president and the faculty member should be notified of the decision in writing and should be given a copy of the record of the hearing. Any release to the public should be made through the president's office.

7. Consideration by Governing Body

The president should transmit to the governing body the full report of the hearing committee, stating its action. On the assumption that the governing board has accepted the principle of the faculty hearing committee, acceptance of the committee's decision would normally be expected. If the governing body chooses to review the case, its review should be based on the record of the previous hearing, accompanied by opportunity for argument, oral or written or both, by the principals at the hearing or their representatives. The decision of the hearing committee should either be sustained or the proceeding be returned to the committee with objections specified. In such a case the committee should reconsider, taking account of the stated objections and receiving new evidence if necessary. It should frame its decision and communicate it in the same manner as before. Only after study of the committee's reconsideration should the governing body make a final decision overruling the committee.

8. Publicity

Except for such simple announcements as may be required, covering the time of the hearing and similar matters, public statements about the case by either the faculty member or administrative officers should be avoided so far as possible until the proceedings have been completed. Announcement of the final decision should include a statement of the hearing committee's original action, if this has not previously been made known.

Statement on Procedural Standards in the Renewal or Nonrenewal of Faculty Appointments

The statement which follows, a revision of a statement originally adopted in 1971, was approved by the Association's Committee on Academic Freedom and Tenure (Committee A), adopted by the Association's Council in November 1989, and endorsed by the Seventy-sixth Annual Meeting.

Except for special appointments clearly designated at the outset as involving only a brief association with the institution, all full-time faculty appointments are either with continuous tenure or probationary for tenure. Procedures bearing on the renewal or nonrenewal of probationary appointments are this statement's concern.

THE PROBATIONARY PERIOD: STANDARDS AND CRITERIA

The 1940 *Statement of Principles on Academic Freedom and Tenure* prescribes that "during the probationary period a teacher should have the academic freedom that all other members of the faculty have." The Association's *Recommended Institutional Regulations on Academic Freedom and Tenure* prescribe further that "all members of the faculty, whether tenured or not, are entitled to protection against illegal or unconstitutional discrimination by the institution, or discrimination on a basis not demonstrably related to the faculty member's professional performance. . . ." A number of the rights of nontenured faculty members provide support for their academic freedom and protection against improper discrimination. They cannot, for example, be dismissed before the end of a term appointment except for adequate cause that has been demonstrated through academic due process—a right they share with tenured members of the faculty. If they assert that they have been given notice of nonreappointment in violation of academic freedom or because of improper discrimination, they are entitled to an opportunity to establish their claim in accordance with Regulation 10 of the *Recommended Institutional Regulations*. They are entitled to timely notice of nonreappointment in accordance with the schedule prescribed in the statement on *Standards for Notice of Nonreappointment*.[1]

Lacking the reinforcement of tenure, however, academic freedom and protection against improper discrimination for probationary faculty members have depended primarily upon the understanding and support of their tenured colleagues, the administration, and professional organizations, especially the American Association of University Professors. In the *Statement on Government of Colleges and Universities*, the Association has asserted that "faculty status and related matters are primarily a faculty responsibility; this area includes appointments,

---

[1] The "Standards for Notice" are as follows:
  1. *Not later than March 1 of the first academic year of service*, if the appointment expires at the end of that year; or, if a one-year appointment terminates during an academic year, at least three months in advance of its termination;
  2. *Not later than December 15 of the second academic year of service*, if the appointment expires at the end of that year; or, if an initial two-year appointment terminates during an academic year, at least six months in advance of its termination;
  3. At least twelve months before the expiration of an appointment after two or more years in the institution. (AAUP, *Policy Documents and Reports*, 9th ed. [Washington, D.C., 2001], 31.)

reappointments, decisions not to reappoint, promotions, the granting of tenure, and dismissal." Collegial deliberation of the kind envisioned by the *Statement on Government* will minimize the risk of a violation of academic freedom, of improper discrimination, and of a decision that is arbitrary or based on inadequate consideration.

Frequently, young faculty members have had no training or experience in teaching, and their first major research endeavor may still be uncompleted at the time they start their careers as college teachers. Under these circumstances, it is particularly important that there be a probationary period—a maximum of seven years under the 1940 *Statement of Principles on Academic Freedom and Tenure*—before tenure is granted. Such a period gives probationary faculty members time to prove themselves, and their colleagues time to observe and evaluate them on the basis of their performance in the position rather than on the basis only of their education, training, and recommendations.

Good practice requires that the institution (department, college, or university) define its criteria for reappointment and tenure and its procedures for reaching decisions on these matters. The 1940 *Statement of Principles* prescribes that "the precise terms and conditions of every appointment should be stated in writing and be in the possession of both institution and teacher before the appointment is consummated." Moreover, fairness to probationary faculty members prescribes that they be informed, early in their appointments, of the substantive and procedural standards that will be followed in determining whether or not their appointments will be renewed or tenure will be granted.

The Association accordingly recommends:

1. *Criteria and Notice of Standards.* Probationary faculty members should be advised, early in their appointment, of the substantive and procedural standards generally accepted in decisions affecting renewal and tenure. Any special standards adopted by their particular departments or schools should also be brought to their attention.

THE PROBATIONARY PERIOD: EVALUATION AND DECISION

The relationship of the senior and junior faculty should be one of colleagueship, even though nontenured faculty members know that in time they will be judged by their senior colleagues. Thus the procedures adopted for evaluation and possible notification of nonrenewal should not endanger this relationship where it exists, and should encourage it where it does not. Nontenured faculty members should have available to them the advice and assistance of their senior colleagues; and the ability of senior colleagues to make a sound decision on renewal or tenure will be enhanced if an opportunity is provided for a regular review of the candidate's qualifications. A conjunction of the roles in counseling and evaluation may be productive: for example, an evaluation, whether interim or at the time of final determination of renewal or tenure, should be presented in such a manner as to assist nontenured faculty members as they strive to improve their performance.

Any recommendation regarding renewal or tenure should be reached by an appropriate faculty group in accordance with procedures approved by the faculty. Because it is important to both the faculty member and the decision-making body that all significant information be considered, the candidate should be notified that a decision is to be made regarding renewal of appointment or the granting of tenure and should be afforded an opportunity to submit material that the candidate believes to be relevant to the decision.

The Association accordingly recommends:

2. (a) *Periodic Review.* There should be provision for periodic review of a faculty member's situation during the probationary service.
   (b) *Opportunity to Submit Material.* Probationary faculty members should be advised of the time when decisions affecting renewal and tenure are ordinarily made, and they should be given the opportunity to submit material that they believe will be helpful to an adequate consideration of their circumstances.

Observance of the practices and procedures outlined above should minimize the likelihood of reasonable complaint if nontenured faculty members are given notice of nonreappointment. They will have been informed of the criteria and procedures for renewal and tenure; they will have been counseled by faculty colleagues; they will have been given an opportunity to have all material relevant to their evaluation considered; and they will have a timely decision representing the views of faculty colleagues.

NOTICE OF REASONS

Since 1971 it has been the Association's position, reached after careful examination of advantages and disadvantages, that nontenured faculty members notified of nonreappointment should, upon request, receive a statement of the reasons for the decision. In reaching this position, the Association considered the needs both of the institution and of the individual faculty member.

A major responsibility of the institution is to recruit and retain the best-qualified faculty within its goals and means. In a matter of such fundamental importance, the institution, through the appropriate faculty agencies, must be accorded the widest latitude consistent with academic freedom, equal opportunity, and the standards of fairness. The Association recognized that the requirement of giving reasons could lead, however erroneously, to an expectation that the decision-making body must justify its decision. A notice of nonreappointment could thus become confused with dismissal for cause, and under these circumstances the decision-making body could become reluctant to reach adverse decisions which might culminate in grievance procedures. As a result there was some risk that the important distinction between tenure and probation would be eroded.

Weighed against these important institutional concerns, however, were the interests of the individual faculty members. They could be honestly unaware of the reasons for a negative decision, and the decision could be based on a judgment of shortcomings which they could easily remedy if informed of them. A decision not to renew an appointment could be based on erroneous information which the faculty member could readily correct if informed of the basis for the decision. Again, the decision could be based on considerations of institutional policy or program development which have nothing to do with the faculty member's professional competence, and if not informed of the reasons, the faculty member could mistakenly assume that a judgment of inadequate performance has been made. In the face of a persistent refusal to supply the reasons, a faculty member may be more inclined to attribute improper motivations to the decision-making body or to conclude that its evaluation has been based upon inadequate consideration. If the faculty member wished to request a reconsideration of the decision, or a review by another body, ignorance of the reasons for the decision would create difficulties both in reaching a decision whether to initiate such a request and in presenting a case for reconsideration or review.

The Association's extensive experience with specific cases since 1971 has confirmed its conclusion that the reasons in support of the faculty member's right to be informed outweigh the countervailing risks. Every notice of nonreappointment, however, need not be accompanied by a written statement of the reasons for nonreappointment. It may not always be to the advantage of the faculty member to be informed of the reasons for nonreappointment, particularly in writing. The faculty member may be placed under obligation to divulge them to the appointing body of another institution if it inquired. Similarly, a written record is likely to become the basis for continuing responses by the faculty member's former institution to prospective appointing bodies.

At many institutions, moreover, the procedures of evaluation and decision may make it difficult, if not impossible, to compile a statement of reasons which precisely reflects the basis of the decision. When a number of faculty members participate in the decision, they may oppose a reappointment for a variety of reasons, few or none of which may represent a majority view. To include every reason, no matter how few have held it, in a written statement to the faculty member may misrepresent the general view and damage unnecessarily both the morale and the professional future of the faculty member.

In many situations, of course, a decision not to reappoint will not reflect adversely upon the faculty member. An institution may, for example, find it necessary for financial or other reasons to restrict its offerings in a given department. The acquisition of tenure may depend not only upon satisfactory performance but also upon a long-term opening. Nonrenewal in these cases does not suggest a serious adverse judgment. In these situations, providing a statement of reasons, either written or oral, should pose no difficulty, and such a statement may in fact assist the faculty member in searching for a new position.

Should the faculty member, after weighing the considerations cited above, decide to request the reasons for the decision against reappointment, the reasons should be given. The faculty member also should have the opportunity to request a reconsideration by the decision-making body.

The Association accordingly recommends:

3. *Notice of Reasons*. In the event of a decision not to renew an appointment, the faculty member should be informed of the decision in writing, and, upon request, be advised of the reasons which contributed to that decision. The faculty member should also have the opportunity to request a reconsideration by the decision-making body.

WRITTEN REASONS

Having been given orally the reasons which contributed to the decision against reappointment, the faculty member, to avoid misunderstanding, may request that they be confirmed in writing. The faculty member may wish to petition the appropriate faculty committee, in accordance with Regulation 10 of the Association's *Recommended Institutional Regulations*, to consider an allegation that the reasons given, or that other reasons which were not stated, constitute a violation of academic freedom or improper discrimination. The faculty member may wish to petition a committee, in accordance with Regulation 15 of the *Recommended Institutional Regulations*, to consider a complaint that the decision resulted from inadequate consideration and was therefore unfair. The faculty member may believe that a written statement of reasons might be useful in pursuing a professional career.

If the department chair or other appropriate institutional officer to whom the request is made believes that confirming the oral statement in writing may be damaging to the faculty member on grounds such as those cited earlier in this statement, it would be desirable for that officer to explain the possible adverse consequences of confirming the oral statement in writing. If, in spite of this explanation, the faculty member continues to request a written statement, the request should be honored.

The Association accordingly recommends:

4. *Written Reasons*. If the faculty member expresses a desire to petition the grievance committee (such as is described in Regulations 10 and 15 of the Association's *Recommended Institutional Regulations*), or any other appropriate committee, to use its good offices of inquiry, recommendation, and report, or if the request is made for any other reason satisfactory to the faculty member alone, the reasons given in explanation of the nonrenewal should be confirmed in writing.

REVIEW PROCEDURES: ALLEGATIONS OF VIOLATION OF ACADEMIC FREEDOM OR OF DISCRIMINATION

The best safeguard against a proliferation of grievance petitions on a given campus is the observance of sound principles and procedures of academic freedom and tenure and of institutional government. Observance of the procedures recommended in this statement—procedures which would provide guidance to nontenured faculty members, help assure them of a fair professional evaluation, and enlighten them concerning the reasons contributing to key decisions of their colleagues—should contribute to the achievement of harmonious faculty relationships and the development of well-qualified faculties.

Even with the best practices and procedures, however, faculty members will at times think that they have been improperly or unjustly treated and may wish another faculty group to review a decision of the faculty body immediately involved. The Association believes that fairness to both the individual and the institution requires that the institution provide for such a review when it is requested. The possibility of a violation of academic freedom or of improper discrimination is of vital concern to the institution as a whole, and where either is alleged it is of cardinal importance to the faculty and the administration to determine whether substantial grounds for the allegation exist. The institution should also be concerned to see that decisions respecting reappointment are based upon adequate consideration, and provision should thus be made for a review of allegations by affected faculty members that the consideration has been inadequate.

Because of the broader significance of a violation of academic freedom or of improper discrimination, the Association believes that the procedures to be followed in these two kinds of complaints should be kept separate from a complaint over adequacy of consideration. Regulation 10 of the *Recommended Institutional Regulations* provides a specific procedure for the review of complaints of academic freedom violation or of discrimination:[2]

> If a faculty member on probationary or other nontenured appointment alleges that a decision against reappointment was based significantly on considerations violative of (1) academic freedom or (2) governing policies on making appointments without prejudice with respect to race, sex, religion, national origin, age, disability, marital status, or sexual orientation, the allegation will be given preliminary consideration by the [insert name of committee], which will seek to settle the matter by informal methods. The allegation will be accompanied by a statement that the faculty member agrees to the presentation, for the consideration of the faculty committees, of such reasons and evidence as the institution may allege in support of its decision. If the difficulty is unresolved at this stage, and if the committee so recommends, the matter will be heard in the manner set forth in Regulations 5 and 6, except that the faculty member making the complaint is responsible for stating the grounds upon which the allegations are based, and the burden of proof will rest upon the faculty member. If the faculty member succeeds in establishing a prima facie case, it is incumbent upon those who made the decision against reappointment to come forward with evidence in support of their decision. Statistical evidence of improper discrimination may be used in establishing a prima facie case.

The Association accordingly recommends:

5. *Petition for Review Alleging an Academic Freedom Violation or Improper Discrimination.* Insofar as the petition for review alleges a violation of academic freedom or improper discrimination, the functions of the committee that reviews the faculty member's petition should be the following:
   (a) to determine whether or not the notice of nonreappointment constitutes on its face a violation of academic freedom or improper discrimination;
   (b) to seek to settle the matter by informal methods;
   (c) if the matter remains unresolved, to decide whether or not the evidence submitted in support of the petition warrants a recommendation that a formal proceeding be conducted in accordance with Regulations 5 and 6 of the *Recommended Institutional Regulations*, with the burden of proof resting upon the complaining faculty member.

REVIEW PROCEDURES: ALLEGATIONS OF INADEQUATE CONSIDERATION

Complaints of inadequate consideration are likely to relate to matters of professional judgment, where the department or departmental agency should have primary authority. For this reason, the basic functions of the review committee should be to determine whether the appropriate faculty body gave adequate consideration to the faculty member's candidacy in reaching its decision and, if the review committee determines otherwise, to request reconsideration by that body.

It is easier to state what the standard "adequate consideration" does not mean than to specify in detail what it does. It does not mean that the review committee should substitute its own judgment for that of members of the department on the merits of whether the candidate should be reappointed or given tenure.[3] The conscientious judgment of the candidate's departmental colleagues must prevail if the invaluable tradition of departmental autonomy in professional judgments is to prevail. The term "adequate consideration" refers essentially to procedural rather

---

[2] Faculties processing complaints under Regulations 10 and 15 may wish to secure the further advice of the Association's Washington office.

[3] As used here, "department" may refer to any institutional body or individual responsible for making a recommendation or decision on reappointment.

than to substantive issues: Was the decision conscientiously arrived at? Was all available evidence bearing on the relevant performance of the candidate sought out and considered? Was there adequate deliberation by the department over the import of the evidence in the light of the relevant standards? Were irrelevant and improper standards excluded from consideration? Was the decision a bona fide exercise of professional academic judgment? These are the kinds of questions suggested by the standard "adequate consideration."

If, in applying this standard, the review committee concludes that adequate consideration was not given, its appropriate response should be to recommend to the department that it assess the merits once again, this time remedying the inadequacies of its prior consideration.

An acceptable review procedure, representing one procedural system within which such judgments may be made, is outlined in Regulation 15 of the *Recommended Institutional Regulations*, as follows:

> If any faculty member alleges cause for grievance in any matter not covered by the procedures described in the foregoing regulations, the faculty member may petition the elected faculty grievance committee [here name the committee] for redress. The petition will set forth in detail the nature of the grievance and will state against whom the grievance is directed. It will contain any factual or other data which the petitioner deems pertinent to the case. Statistical evidence of improper discrimination, including discrimination in salary, may be used in establishing a prima facie case. The committee will decide whether or not the facts merit a detailed investigation; if the faculty member succeeds in establishing a prima facie case, it is incumbent upon those who made the decision to come forward with evidence in support of their decision. Submission of a petition will not automatically entail investigation or detailed consideration thereof. The committee may seek to bring about a settlement of the issue satisfactory to the parties. If in the opinion of the committee such a settlement is not possible or is not appropriate, the committee will report its findings and recommendations to the petitioner and to the appropriate administrative officer and faculty body, and the petitioner will, upon request, be provided an opportunity to present the grievance to them. The grievance committee will consist of three [or some other number] elected members of the faculty. No officer of administration will serve on the committee.

The Association accordingly recommends:

6. *Petition for Review Alleging Inadequate Consideration.* Insofar as the petition for review alleges inadequate consideration, the functions of the committee which reviews the faculty member's petition should be the following:
   (a) to determine whether the decision of the appropriate faculty body was the result of adequate consideration, with the understanding that the review committee should not substitute its judgment on the merits for that of the faculty body;
   (b) to request reconsideration by the faculty body when the committee believes that adequate consideration was not given to the faculty member's qualifications (in such instances, the committee should indicate the respects in which it believes that consideration may have been inadequate);
   (c) to provide copies of its report and recommendation to the faculty member, the faculty body, and the president or other appropriate administrative officer.

Recommended Institutional Regulations on Academic Freedom and Tenure

The Recommended Institutional Regulations on Academic Freedom and Tenure *set forth, in language suitable for use by an institution of higher education, rules which derive from the chief provisions and interpretations of the 1940* Statement of Principles on Academic Freedom and Tenure *and of the 1958* Statement on Procedural Standards in Faculty Dismissal Proceedings. *The* Recommended Institutional Regulations *were first formulated by the Committee on Academic Freedom and Tenure (Committee A) in 1957. A revised and expanded text, approved by Committee A in 1968, reflected the development of Association standards and procedures. Texts with further revisions were approved by Committee A in 1972, in 1976, in 1982, in 1990, and in 1999.*

The current text is based upon the Association's continuing experience in evaluating regulations actually in force at particular institutions. It is also based upon further definition of the standards and procedures of the Association over the years. The Association will be glad to assist in interpretation of the regulations or to consult about their incorporation in, or adaptation to, the rules of a particular college or university.

FOREWORD

These regulations are designed to enable the [named institution] to protect academic freedom and tenure and to ensure academic due process. The principles implicit in these regulations are for the benefit of all who are involved with or are affected by the policies and programs of the institution. A college or university is a marketplace of ideas, and it cannot fulfill its purposes of transmitting, evaluating, and extending knowledge if it requires conformity with any orthodoxy of content and method. In the words of the United States Supreme Court, "Teachers and students must always remain free to inquire, to study and to evaluate, to gain new maturity and understanding; otherwise our civilization will stagnate and die."

1. STATEMENT OF TERMS OF APPOINTMENT

(a) The terms and conditions of every appointment to the faculty will be stated or confirmed in writing, and a copy of the appointment document will be supplied to the faculty member. Any subsequent extensions or modifications of an appointment, and any special understandings, or any notices incumbent upon either party to provide, will be stated or confirmed in writing and a copy will be given to the faculty member.

(b) With the exception of special appointments clearly limited to a brief association with the institution, and reappointments of retired faculty members on special conditions, all full-time faculty appointments are of two kinds: (1) probationary appointments; (2) appointments with continuous tenure.

(c) Except for faculty members who have tenure status, every person with a teaching or research appointment of any kind will be informed each year in writing of the renewal of the appointment and of all matters relative to eligibility for the acquisition of tenure.

2. PROBATIONARY APPOINTMENTS

(a) Probationary appointments may be for one year, or for other stated periods, subject to renewal. The total period of full-time service prior to the acquisition of continuous tenure will not exceed ____ years,[1] including all previous full-time service with the rank of instructor or higher in other institutions of higher learning [*except* that the probationary period may extend to as much as four years, even if the total full-time service in the profession thereby exceeds seven years; the terms of such extension will be stated in writing at the time of initial appointment].[2] Scholarly leave of absence for one year or less will count as part of the probationary period as if it were prior service at another institution, unless the individual and the institution agree in writing to an exception to this provision at the time the leave is granted.

(b) The faculty member will be advised, at the time of initial appointment, of the substantive standards and procedures generally employed in decisions affecting renewal and tenure. Any special standards adopted by the faculty member's department or school will also be transmitted. The faculty member will be advised of the time when decisions affecting renewal or tenure are ordinarily made, and will be given the opportunity to submit material believed to be helpful to an adequate consideration of the faculty member's circumstances.

(c) Regardless of the stated term or other provisions of any appointments, written notice that a probationary appointment is not to be renewed will be given to the faculty member in advance of the expiration of the appointment, as follows: (1) not later than March 1 of the first academic year of service if the appointment expires at the end of that year; or, if a one-year appointment terminates during an academic year, at least three months in advance of its termination; (2) not later than December 15 of the second academic year of service if the appointment expires at the end of that year; or, if an initial two-year appointment terminates during an academic year, at least six months in advance of its termination; (3) at least twelve months before the expiration of an appointment after two or more years of service at the institution. The institution will normally notify faculty members of the terms and conditions of their renewals by March 15, but in no case will such information be given later than____.[3]

(d) When a faculty recommendation or a decision not to renew an appointment has first been reached, the faculty member involved will be informed of that recommendation or decision in writing by the body or individual making the initial recommendation or decision; the faculty member will be advised upon request of the reasons which contributed to that decision. The faculty member may request a reconsideration by the recommending or deciding body.

(e) If the faculty member so requests, the reasons given in explanation of the nonrenewal will be confirmed in writing.

(f) Insofar as the faculty member alleges that the decision against renewal by the appropriate faculty body was based on inadequate consideration, the committee[4] which reviews the faculty member's allegation will determine whether the decision was the result of adequate consideration in terms of the relevant standards of the institution. The review committee will not substitute its judgment on the merits for that of the faculty body. If

---

[1] Under the "1940 Statement of Principles on Academic Freedom and Tenure," this period may not exceed seven years.

[2] The exception here noted applies only to an institution whose maximum probationary period exceeds four years.

[3] April 15 is the recommended date.

[4] This committee, which can be the grievance committee noted in Regulation 15, is to be an elected faculty body. Similarly, the members of the committees noted in Regulations 4(c)(2), 4(d)(3), and 10 are to be elected. A committee of faculty members appointed by an appropriate elected faculty body can substitute for a committee that is elected directly.

the review committee believes that adequate consideration was not given to the faculty member's qualifications, it will request reconsideration by the faculty body, indicating the respects in which it believes the consideration may have been inadequate. It will provide copies of its findings to the faculty member, the faculty body, and the president or other appropriate administrative officer.

3. TERMINATION OF APPOINTMENT BY FACULTY MEMBERS

Faculty members may terminate their appointments effective at the end of an academic year, provided that they give notice in writing at the earliest possible opportunity, but not later than May 15, or thirty days after receiving notification of the terms of appointment for the coming year, whichever date occurs later. Faculty members may properly request a waiver of this requirement of notice in case of hardship or in a situation where they would otherwise be denied substantial professional advancement or other opportunity.

4. TERMINATION OF APPOINTMENTS BY THE INSTITUTION

(a) Termination of an appointment with continuous tenure, or of a probationary or special appointment before the end of the specified term, may be effected by the institution only for adequate cause.

(b) If termination takes the form of a dismissal for cause, it will be pursuant to the procedures specified in Regulation 5.

Financial Exigency

(c)(1) Termination of an appointment with continuous tenure, or of a probationary or special appointment before the end of the specified term, may occur under extraordinary circumstances because of a demonstrably bona fide financial exigency, i.e., an imminent financial crisis which threatens the survival of the institution as a whole and which cannot be alleviated by less drastic means.

[NOTE: Each institution in adopting regulations on financial exigency will need to decide how to share and allocate the hard judgments and decisions that are necessary in such a crisis.

As a first step, there should be a faculty body which participates in the decision that a condition of financial exigency exists or is imminent,[5] and that all feasible alternatives to termination of appointments have been pursued.

Judgments determining where within the overall academic program termination of appointments may occur involve considerations of educational policy, including affirmative action, as well as of faculty status, and should therefore be the primary responsibility

---

[5] **See** "The Role of the Faculty in Budgetary and Salary Matters" (AAUP, *Policy Documents and Reports*, 9th ed. [Washington, D.C., 2001], 232–35), especially the following passages:

The faculty should participate both in the preparation of the total institutional budget and (within the framework of the total budget) in decisions relevant to the further apportioning of its specific fiscal divisions (salaries, academic programs, tuition, physical plant and grounds, etc.). The soundness of resulting decisions should be enhanced if an elected representative committee of the faculty participates in deciding on the overall allocation of institutional resources and the proportion to be devoted directly to the academic program This committee should be given access to all information that it requires to perform its task effectively, and it should have the opportunity to confer periodically with representatives of the administration and governing board. . . .

Circumstances of financial exigency obviously pose special problems. At institutions experiencing major threats to their continued financial support, the faculty should be informed as early and specifically as possible of significant impending financial difficulties. The faculty—with substantial representation from its nontenured as well as its tenured members, since it is the former who are likely to bear the brunt of the reduction—should participate at the department, college or professional school, and institution-wide levels in key decisions as to the future of the institution and of specific academic programs within the institution. The faculty, employing accepted standards of due process, should assume primary responsibility for determining the status of individual faculty members.

of the faculty or of an appropriate faculty body.[6] The faculty or an appropriate faculty body should also exercise primary responsibility in determining the criteria for identifying the individuals whose appointments are to be terminated. These criteria may appropriately include considerations of length of service.

The responsibility for identifying individuals whose appointments are to be terminated should be committed to a person or group designated or approved by the faculty. The allocation of this responsibility may vary according to the size and character of the institution, the extent of the terminations to be made, or other considerations of fairness in judgment. The case of a faculty member given notice of proposed termination of appointment will be governed by the following procedure.]

(2) If the administration issues notice to a particular faculty member of an intention to terminate the appointment because of financial exigency, the faculty member will have the right to a full hearing before a faculty committee. The hearing need not conform in all respects with a proceeding conducted pursuant to Regulation 5, but the essentials of an on-the-record adjudicative hearing will be observed. The issues in this hearing may include:

(i) The existence and extent of the condition of financial exigency. The burden will rest on the administration to prove the existence and extent of the condition. The findings of a faculty committee in a previous proceeding involving the same issue may be introduced.

(ii) The validity of the educational judgments and the criteria for identification for termination; but the recommendations of a faculty body on these matters will be considered presumptively valid.

(iii) Whether the criteria are being properly applied in the individual case.

(3) If the institution, because of financial exigency, terminates appointments, it will not at the same time make new appointments except in extraordinary circumstances where a serious distortion in the academic program would otherwise result. The appointment of a faculty member with tenure will not be terminated in favor of retaining a faculty member without tenure, except in extraordinary circumstances where a serious distortion of the academic program would otherwise result.

(4) Before terminating an appointment because of financial exigency, the institution, with faculty participation, will make every effort to place the faculty member concerned in another suitable position within the institution.

(5) In all cases of termination of appointment because of financial exigency, the faculty member concerned will be given notice or severance salary not less than as prescribed in Regulation 8.

(6) In all cases of termination of appointment because of financial exigency, the place of the faculty member concerned will not be filled by a replacement within a period of three years, unless the released faculty member has been offered reinstatement and a reasonable time in which to accept or decline it.

Discontinuance of Program or Department Not Mandated by Financial Exigency[7]

(d) Termination of an appointment with continuous tenure, or of a probationary or special appointment before the end of the specified term, may occur as a result of bona fide formal discontinuance of a program or department of instruction. The following standards and procedures will apply.

---

[6] See "Statement on Government of Colleges and Universities" (*Policy Documents and Reports*, 217–23), especially the following passage:

Faculty status and related matters are primarily a faculty responsibility; this area includes appointments, reappointments, decisions not to reappoint, promotions, the granting of tenure, and dismissal. The primary responsibility of the faculty for such matters is based upon the fact that its judgment is central to general educational policy.

[7] When discontinuance of a program or department is mandated by financial exigency of the institution, the standards of Regulation 4(c) above will apply.

(1) The decision to discontinue formally a program or department of instruction will be based essentially upon educational considerations, as determined primarily by the faculty as a whole or an appropriate committee thereof.

[NOTE: "Educational considerations" do not include cyclical or temporary variations in enrollment. They must reflect long-range judgments that the educational mission of the institution as a whole will be enhanced by the discontinuance.]

(2) Before the administration issues notice to a faculty member of its intention to terminate an appointment because of formal discontinuance of a program or department of instruction, the institution will make every effort to place the faculty member concerned in another suitable position. If placement in another position would be facilitated by a reasonable period of training, financial and other support for such training will be proffered. If no position is available within the institution, with or without retraining, the faculty member's appointment then may be terminated, but only with provision for severance salary equitably adjusted to the faculty member's length of past and potential service.

[NOTE: When an institution proposes to discontinue a program or department of instruction, it should plan to bear the costs of relocating, training, or otherwise compensating faculty members adversely affected.]

(3) A faculty member may appeal a proposed relocation or termination resulting from a discontinuance and has a right to a full hearing before a faculty committee. The hearing need not conform in all respects with a proceeding conducted pursuant to Regulation 5, but the essentials of an on-the-record adjudicative hearing will be observed. The issues in such a hearing may include the institution's failure to satisfy any of the conditions specified in Regulation 4(d). In such a hearing a faculty determination that a program or department is to be discontinued will be considered presumptively valid, but the burden of proof on other issues will rest on the administration.

Termination Because of Physical or Mental Disability

(e) Termination of an appointment with tenure, or of a probationary or special appointment before the end of the period of appointment, because of physical or mental disability, will be based upon clear and convincing medical evidence that the faculty member, even with reasonable accommodation, is no longer able to perform the essential duties of the position. The decision to terminate will be reached only after there has been appropriate consultation and after the faculty member concerned, or someone representing the faculty member, has been informed of the basis of the proposed action and has been afforded an opportunity to present the faculty member's position and to respond to the evidence. If the faculty member so requests, the evidence will be reviewed by the Faculty Committee on Academic Freedom and Tenure [or whatever title it may have] before a final decision is made by the governing board on the recommendation of the administration. The faculty member will be given severance salary not less than as prescribed in Regulation 8.

Review

(f) In cases of termination of appointment, the governing board will be available for ultimate review.

5. DISMISSAL PROCEDURES

(a) Adequate cause for a dismissal will be related, directly and substantially, to the fitness of faculty members in their professional capacities as teachers or researchers. Dismissal will not be used to restrain faculty members in their exercise of academic freedom or other rights of American citizens.

(b) Dismissal of a faculty member with continuous tenure, or with a special or probationary appointment before the end of the specified term, will be preceded by: (1) discussions between the faculty member and appropriate administrative officers looking toward a mutual settlement; (2) informal inquiry by the duly elected faculty committee [insert name of committee] which may, failing to effect an adjustment, determine whether in its opinion dismissal proceedings should be undertaken, without its opinion being binding upon the president; (3) a statement of charges, framed with reasonable particularity by the president or the president's delegate.

(c) A dismissal, as defined in Regulation 5(a), will be preceded by a statement of reasons, and the individual concerned will have the right to be heard initially by the elected faculty hearing committee [insert name of committee].[8] Members deeming themselves disqualified for bias or interest will remove themselves from the case, either at the request of a party or on their own initiative. Each party will have a maximum of two challenges without stated cause.[9]

(1) Pending a final decision by the hearing committee, the faculty member will be suspended, or assigned to other duties in lieu of suspension, only if immediate harm to the faculty member or others is threatened by continuance. Before suspending a faculty member, pending an ultimate determination of the faculty member's status through the institution's hearing procedures, the administration will consult with the Faculty Committee on Academic Freedom and Tenure [or whatever other title it may have] concerning the propriety, the length, and the other conditions of the suspension. A suspension which is intended to be final is a dismissal, and will be treated as such. Salary will continue during the period of the suspension.

(2) The hearing committee may, with the consent of the parties concerned, hold joint prehearing meetings with the parties in order to (i) simplify the issues, (ii) effect stipulations of facts, (iii) provide for the exchange of documentary or other information, and (iv) achieve such other appropriate prehearing objectives as will make the hearing fair, effective, and expeditious.

(3) Service of notice of hearing with specific charges in writing will be made at least twenty days prior to the hearing. The faculty member may waive a hearing or may respond to the charges in writing at any time before the hearing. If the faculty member waives a hearing, but denies the charges or asserts that the charges do not support a finding of adequate cause, the hearing tribunal will evaluate all available evidence and rest its recommendation upon the evidence in the record.

(4) The committee, in consultation with the president and the faculty member, will exercise its judgment as to whether the hearing should be public or private.

(5) During the proceedings the faculty member will be permitted to have an academic advisor and counsel of the faculty member's choice.

(6) At the request of either party or the hearing committee, a representative of a responsible educational association will be permitted to attend the proceedings as an observer.

(7) A verbatim record of the hearing or hearings will be taken and a typewritten copy will be made available to the faculty member without cost, at the faculty member's request.

(8) The burden of proof that adequate cause exists rests with the institution and will be satisfied only by clear and convincing evidence in the record considered as a whole.

(9) The hearing committee will grant adjournments to enable either party to investigate evidence as to which a valid claim of surprise is made.

(10) The faculty member will be afforded an opportunity to obtain necessary witnesses and documentary or other evidence. The administration will cooperate with the hearing committee in securing witnesses and making available documentary and other evidence.

---

[8] This committee should not be the same as the committee referred to in Regulation 5(b)(2).

[9] Regulations of the institution should provide for alternates, or for some other method of filling vacancies on the hearing committee resulting from disqualification, challenge without stated cause, illness, resignation, or other reason.

(11) The faculty member and the administration will have the right to confront and cross-examine all witnesses. Where the witnesses cannot or will not appear, but the committee determines that the interests of justice require admission of their statements, the committee will identify the witnesses, disclose their statements, and, if possible, provide for interrogatories.

(12) In the hearing of charges of incompetence, the testimony will include that of qualified faculty members from this or other institutions of higher education.

(13) The hearing committee will not be bound by strict rules of legal evidence, and may admit any evidence which is of probative value in determining the issues involved. Every possible effort will be made to obtain the most reliable evidence available.

(14) The findings of fact and the decision will be based solely on the hearing record.

(15) Except for such simple announcements as may be required, covering the time of the hearing and similar matters, public statements and publicity about the case by either the faculty member or administrative officers will be avoided so far as possible until the proceedings have been completed, including consideration by the governing board of the institution. The president and the faculty member will be notified of the decision in writing and will be given a copy of the record of the hearing.

(16) If the hearing committee concludes that adequate cause for dismissal has not been established by the evidence in the record, it will so report to the president. If the president rejects the report, the president will state the reasons for doing so, in writing, to the hearing committee and to the faculty member, and provide an opportunity for response before transmitting the case to the governing board. If the hearing committee concludes that adequate cause for a dismissal has been established, but that an academic penalty less than dismissal would be more appropriate, it will so recommend, with supporting reasons.

6. ACTION BY THE GOVERNING BOARD

If dismissal or other severe sanction is recommended, the president will, on request of the faculty member, transmit to the governing board the record of the case. The governing board's review will be based on the record of the committee hearing, and it will provide opportunity for argument, oral or written or both, by the principals at the hearings or by their representatives. The decision of the hearing committee will either be sustained or the proceeding returned to the committee with specific objections. The committee will then reconsider, taking into account the stated objections and receiving new evidence if necessary. The governing board will make a final decision only after study of the committee's reconsideration.

7. PROCEDURES FOR IMPOSITION OF SANCTIONS
OTHER THAN DISMISSAL

(a) If the administration believes that the conduct of a faculty member, although not constituting adequate cause for dismissal, is sufficiently grave to justify imposition of a severe sanction, such as suspension from service for a stated period, the administration may institute a proceeding to impose such a severe sanction; the procedures outlined in Regulation 5 will govern such a proceeding.

(b) If the administration believes that the conduct of a faculty member justifies imposition of a minor sanction, such as a reprimand, it will notify the faculty member of the basis of the proposed sanction and provide the faculty member with an opportunity to persuade the administration that the proposed sanction should not be imposed. A faculty member who believes that a major sanction has been incorrectly imposed under this paragraph, or that a minor sanction has been unjustly imposed, may, pursuant to Regulation 15, petition the faculty grievance committee for such action as may be appropriate.

8. TERMINAL SALARY OR NOTICE

If the appointment is terminated, the faculty member will receive salary or notice in accordance with the following schedule: at least three months, if the final decision is reached by March 1 (or three months prior to the expiration) of the first year of probationary service; at least six months, if the decision is reached by December 15 of the second year (or after nine months but prior to eighteen months) of probationary service; at least one year, if the decision is reached after eighteen months of probationary service or if the faculty member has tenure. This provision for terminal notice or salary need not apply in the event that there has been a finding that the conduct which justified dismissal involved moral turpitude. On the recommendation of the faculty hearing committee or the president, the governing board, in determining what, if any, payments will be made beyond the effective date of dismissal, may take into account the length and quality of service of the faculty member.

9. ACADEMIC FREEDOM AND PROTECTION AGAINST DISCRIMINATION

(a) All members of the faculty, whether tenured or not, are entitled to academic freedom as set forth in the 1940 *Statement of Principles on Academic Freedom and Tenure*, formulated by the Association of American Colleges and the American Association of University Professors.

(b) All members of the faculty, whether tenured or not, are entitled to protection against illegal or unconstitutional discrimination by the institution, or discrimination on a basis not demonstrably related to the faculty member's professional performance, including but not limited to race, sex, religion, national origin, age, disability, marital status, or sexual orientation.

10. COMPLAINTS OF VIOLATION OF ACADEMIC FREEDOM OR OF DISCRIMINATION IN NONREAPPOINTMENT

If a faculty member on probationary or other nontenured appointment alleges that a decision against reappointment was based significantly on considerations violative of (a) academic freedom or (b) governing policies on making appointments without prejudice with respect to race, sex, religion, national origin, age, disability, marital status, or sexual orientation, the allegation will be given preliminary consideration by the [insert name of committee], which will seek to settle the matter by informal methods. The allegation will be accompanied by a statement that the faculty member agrees to the presentation, for the consideration of the faculty committees, of such reasons and evidence as the institution may allege in support of its decision. If the difficulty is unresolved at this stage, and if the committee so recommends, the matter will be heard in the manner set forth in Regulations 5 and 6, except that the faculty member making the complaint is responsible for stating the grounds upon which the allegations are based, and the burden of proof will rest upon the faculty member. If the faculty member succeeds in establishing a prima facie case, it is incumbent upon those who made the decision against reappointment to come forward with evidence in support of their decision. Statistical evidence of improper discrimination may be used in establishing a prima facie case.

11. ADMINISTRATIVE PERSONNEL

The foregoing regulations apply to administrative personnel who hold academic rank, but only in their capacity as faculty members. Administrators who allege that a consideration violative of academic freedom, or of governing policies against improper discrimination as stated in Regulation 10, significantly contributed to a decision to terminate their appointment to an administrative post, or not to reappoint them, are entitled to the procedures set forth in Regulation 10.

12. POLITICAL ACTIVITIES OF FACULTY MEMBERS

Faculty members, as citizens, are free to engage in political activities. Where necessary, leaves of absence may be given for the duration of an election campaign or a term of office, on timely application, and for a reasonable period of time. The terms of such leave of absence will be set forth in writing, and the leave will not affect unfavorably the tenure status of a faculty member, except that time spent on such leave will not count as probationary service unless otherwise agreed to.[10]

[NOTE: Regulations 13, 14, and 15 are suggested in tentative form, and will require adaptation to the specific structure and operations of the institution; the provisions as recommended here are intended only to indicate the nature of the provisions to be included, and not to offer specific detail.]

13. GRADUATE STUDENT ACADEMIC STAFF

(a) The terms and conditions of every appointment to a graduate or teaching assistantship will be stated in writing, and a copy of the appointment document will be supplied to the graduate or teaching assistant.

(b) In no case will a graduate or teaching assistant be dismissed without having been provided with a statement of reasons and an opportunity to be heard before a duly constituted committee. (A dismissal is a termination before the end of the period of appointment.)

(c) A graduate or teaching assistant who establishes a prima facie case to the satisfaction of a duly constituted committee that a decision against reappointment was based significantly on considerations violative of academic freedom, or of governing policies against improper discrimination as stated in Regulation 10, will be given a statement of reasons by those responsible for the nonreappointment and an opportunity to be heard by the committee.

(d) Graduate or teaching assistants will have access to the faculty grievance committee, as provided in Regulation 15.

14. OTHER ACADEMIC STAFF

(a) In no case will a member of the academic staff[11] who is not otherwise protected by the preceding regulations which relate to dismissal proceedings be dismissed without having been provided with a statement of reasons and an opportunity to be heard before a duly constituted committee. (A dismissal is a termination before the end of the period of appointment.)

(b) With respect to the nonreappointment of a member of such academic staff who establishes a prima facie case to the satisfaction of a duly constituted committee that a consideration violative of academic freedom, or of governing policies against improper discrimination as stated in Regulation 10, significantly contributed to the nonreappointment, the academic staff member will be given a statement of reasons by those responsible for the nonreappointment and an opportunity to be heard by the committee.

15. GRIEVANCE PROCEDURE

If any faculty member alleges cause for grievance in any matter not covered by the procedures described in the foregoing regulations, the faculty member may petition the elected faculty grievance committee [here name the committee] for redress. The petition will set forth in detail the nature of the grievance and will state against whom the grievance is directed. It will

---

[10] See "Statement on Professors and Political Activity," *Policy Documents and Reports*, 33–34.
[11] Each institution should define with particularity who are members of the academic staff.

contain any factual or other data which the petitioner deems pertinent to the case. Statistical evidence of improper discrimination, including discrimination in salary, may be used in establishing a prima facie case. The committee will decide whether or not the facts merit a detailed investigation; if the faculty member succeeds in establishing a prima facie case, it is incumbent upon those who made the decision to come forward with evidence in support of their decision. Submission of a petition will not automatically entail investigation or detailed consideration thereof. The committee may seek to bring about a settlement of the issue(s) satisfactory to the parties. If in the opinion of the committee such a settlement is not possible or is not appropriate, the committee will report its findings and recommendations to the petitioner and to the appropriate administrative officer and faculty body, and the petitioner will, upon request, be provided an opportunity to present the grievance to them. The grievance committee will consist of three [or some other number] elected members of the faculty. No officer of administration will serve on the committee.

NOTE ON IMPLEMENTATION

The *Recommended Institutional Regulations* here presented will require for their implementation a number of structural arrangements and agencies. For example, the *Regulations* will need support by:

(a) channels of communication among all the involved components of the institution, and between them and a concerned faculty member;
(b) definitions of corporate and individual faculty status within the college or university government, and of the role of the faculty in decisions relating to academic freedom and tenure; and
(c) appropriate procedures for the creation and operation of faculty committees, with particular regard to the principles of faculty authority and responsibility.

The forms which these supporting elements assume will of course vary from one institution to another. Consequently, no detailed description of the elements is attempted in these *Recommended Institutional Regulations*. With respect to the principles involved, guidance will be found in the Association's 1966 *Statement on Government of Colleges and Universities*.

Standards for Notice of Nonreappointment

The statement which follows was adopted by the Association's Council in October 1963 and endorsed by the Fiftieth Annual Meeting in 1964. In 1989 and 1990, the appropriate Association bodies adopted several changes in language in order to remove gender-specific references from the original text.

Because a probationary appointment, even though for a fixed or stated term, carries an expectation of renewal, the faculty member should be explicitly informed of a decision not to renew an appointment, in order that the faculty member may seek a position at another college or university.[1] Such notice should be given at an early date, since a failure to secure another position for the ensuing academic year will deny the faculty member the opportunity to continue in the profession. The purpose of this statement is to set forth in detail, for the use of the academic profession, those standards for notice of nonreappointment which the Association over a period of years has actively supported and which are expressed as a general principle in the 1940 *Statement of Principles on Academic Freedom and Tenure*.

THE STANDARDS FOR NOTICE

Notice of nonreappointment, or of intention not to recommend reappointment to the governing board, should be given in writing in accordance with the following standards:

1. *Not later than March 1 of the first academic year of service*, if the appointment expires at the end of that year; or, if a one-year appointment terminates during an academic year, at least three months in advance of its termination.
2. *Not later than December 15 of the second academic year of service*, if the appointment expires at the end of that year; or, if an initial two-year appointment terminates during an academic year, at least six months in advance of its termination.
3. At least twelve months before the expiration of an appointment after two or more years in the institution.

---

[1] For renewable term appointments not specifically designated as probationary for tenure, see "The Applicability of the 'Standards for Notice of Nonreappointment' to All Full-Time Faculty on Renewable Term Appointments," *Academe: Bulletin of the AAUP* 81 (September–October 1995): 51–54.

Committee A Statement on Extramural Utterances

The statement which follows was approved by the Association's Committee on Academic Freedom and Tenure (Committee A) in October 1964. Its purpose is to clarify those sections of the 1940 Statement of Principles on Academic Freedom and Tenure *relating to the faculty member's exercise of freedom of speech as a citizen. In 1989, Committee A approved several changes in language in order to remove gender-specific references from the original text.*

The 1940 *Statement of Principles* asserts the right of faculty members to speak or write as citizens, free from institutional censorship or discipline. At the same time it calls attention to the special obligations of faculty members arising from their position in the community: to be accurate, to exercise appropriate restraint, to show respect for the opinions of others, and to make every effort to indicate that they are not speaking for the institution. An interpretation of the 1940 *Statement*, agreed to at a conference of the Association of American Colleges and the AAUP held on November 8, 1940, states that an administration may file charges in accordance with procedures outlined in the *Statement* if it feels that a faculty member has failed to observe the above admonitions and believes that the professor's extramural utterances raise grave doubts concerning the professor's fitness for continuing service.

In cases involving such charges, it is essential that the hearing should be conducted by an appropriate—preferably elected—faculty committee, as provided in Section 4 of the 1958 *Statement on Procedural Standards in Faculty Dismissal Proceedings*.[1] The controlling principle is that a faculty member's expression of opinion as a citizen cannot constitute grounds for dismissal unless it clearly demonstrates the faculty member's unfitness to serve. Extramural utterances rarely bear upon the faculty member's fitness for continuing service. Moreover, a final decision should take into account the faculty member's entire record as a teacher and scholar. In the absence of weighty evidence of unfitness, the administration should not prefer charges; and if it is not clearly proved in the hearing that the faculty member is unfit to continue, the faculty committee should make a finding in favor of the faculty member concerned.

Committee A asserts that it will view with particular gravity an administrative or board reversal of a favorable faculty committee hearing judgment in a case involving extramural utterances. In the words of the 1940 *Statement of Principles*, "the administration should remember that teachers are citizens and should be accorded the freedom of citizens." In a democratic society freedom of speech is an indispensable right of the citizen. Committee A will vigorously uphold that right.

---

[1] Section 4 provides:

> The committee of faculty members to conduct the hearing and reach a decision should either be an elected standing committee not previously concerned with the case or a committee established as soon as possible after the president's letter to the faculty member has been sent. The choice of members of the hearing committee should be on the basis of their objectivity and competence and of the regard in which they are held in the academic community. The committee should elect its own chair. (AAUP, *Policy Documents and Reports*, 9th ed. [Washington, D.C., 2001], 13.)

Statement on Professors and Political Activity

The statement which follows was prepared by a subcommittee of the Association's Committee on Academic Freedom and Tenure (Committee A) and approved by Committee A. It was adopted by the Association's Council in May 1969, and endorsed by the Fifty-fifth Annual Meeting. It was endorsed in 1970 by the Association of American Colleges (now the Association of American Colleges and Universities). The governing bodies of the two associations, meeting respectively in November 1989 and January 1990, eliminated five introductory paragraphs that were no longer applicable and adopted several changes in language in order to remove gender-specific references from the original text.

INTRODUCTION

The institutional regulations of many colleges and universities govern the participation of professors in political activity and public office holding. These regulations vary from absolute prohibitions against holding public office, campaigning for public office, or participating in the management of political campaigns, to requirements that professors engaging in such political activities merely inform administrative authorities in the college or university of their activities.

In view of the range and variety of institutional and legislative restrictions on political activities of professors, the American Association of University Professors and the Association of American Colleges believe there is a need for a definition of rights and obligations in this area. The following statement is offered as a guide to practice. It is hoped that colleges and universities will formulate and publish regulations consistent with these principles.

STATEMENT

1. College and university faculty members are citizens, and, like other citizens, should be free to engage in political activities so far as they are able to do so consistently with their obligations as teachers and scholars.
2. Many kinds of political activity (e.g., holding part-time office in a political party, seeking election to any office under circumstances that do not require extensive campaigning, or serving by appointment or election in a part-time political office) are consistent with effective service as members of a faculty. Other kinds of political activity (e.g., intensive campaigning for elective office, serving in a state legislature, or serving a limited term in a full-time position) will often require that professors seek a leave of absence from their college or university.
3. In recognition of the legitimacy and social importance of political activity by professors, universities and colleges should provide institutional arrangements to permit it, similar to those applicable to other public or private extramural service. Such arrangements may include the reduction of the faculty member's workload or a leave of absence for the duration of an election campaign or a term of office, accompanied by equitable adjustment of compensation when necessary.
4. Faculty members seeking leaves should recognize that they have a primary obligation to their institution and to their growth as educators and scholars; they should be mindful of the problem which a leave of absence can create for their administration, their colleagues, and their students; and they should not abuse the privilege by too frequent or too late application or too extended a leave. If adjustments in their favor are made, such as reduction of workload, they should expect the adjustments to be limited to a reasonable period.

5. A leave of absence incident to political activity should come under the institution's normal rules and regulations for leaves of absence. Such a leave should not affect unfavorably the tenure status of a faculty member, except that time spent on such leave from academic duties need not count as probationary service. The terms of a leave and its effect on the professor's status should be set forth in writing.

Academic Freedom and Artistic Expression

The statement which follows was adopted by the participants in the 1990 Wolf Trap Conference on Academic Freedom and Artistic Expression, sponsored by the American Association of University Professors, the American Council on Education, the Association of Governing Boards of Universities and Colleges, and the Wolf Trap Foundation. The statement was endorsed by AAUP's Committee on Academic Freedom and Tenure (Committee A) and by its Council at their meetings in June 1990.

Attempts to curtail artistic presentations at academic institutions on grounds that the works are offensive to some members of the campus community and of the general public occur with disturbing frequency. Those who support restrictions argue that works presented to the public rather than in the classroom or in other entirely intramural settings should conform to their view of the prevailing community standard rather than to standards of academic freedom. We believe that, "essential as freedom is for the relation and judgment of facts, it is even more indispensable to the imagination."[1] In our judgment academic freedom in the creation and presentation of works in the visual and the performing arts, by ensuring greater opportunity for imaginative exploration and expression, best serves the public and the academy.

The following proposed policies are designed to assist academic institutions to respond to the issues that may arise from the presentation of artistic works to the public and to do so in a manner which preserves academic freedom:

1. *Academic Freedom in Artistic Expression*

Faculty members and students engaged in the creation and presentation of works of the visual and the performing arts are as much engaged in pursuing the mission of the college or university as are those who write, teach, and study in other academic disciplines. Works of the visual and the performing arts are important both in their own right and because they can enhance our understanding of social institutions and the human condition. Artistic expression in the classroom, the studio, and the workshop therefore merits the same assurance of academic freedom that is accorded to other scholarly and teaching activities. Since faculty and student artistic presentations to the public are integral to their teaching, learning, and scholarship, these presentations merit no less protection. Educational and artistic criteria should be used by all who participate in the selection and presentation of artistic works. Reasonable content-neutral regulation of the "time, place, and manner" of presentations should be developed and maintained. Academic institutions are obliged to ensure that regulations and procedures do not impair freedom of expression or discourage creativity by subjecting artistic work to tests of propriety or ideology.

2. *Accountability*

Artistic performances and exhibitions in academic institutions encourage artistic creativity, expression, learning, and appreciation. The institutions do not thereby endorse the specific artistic presentations, nor do the presentations necessarily represent the institution. This principle of institutional neutrality does not relieve institutions of general responsibility for maintaining professional and educational standards, but it does mean that institutions are not responsible

---

[1] Helen C. White, "Our Most Urgent Professional Task," *AAUP Bulletin* 45 (March 1959): 282.

for the views or the attitudes expressed in specific artistic works any more than they would be for the content of other instruction, scholarly publication, or invited speeches. Correspondingly, those who present artistic work should not represent themselves or their work as speaking for the institution and should otherwise fulfill their educational and professional responsibilities.

3. The Audience

When academic institutions offer exhibitions or performances to the public, they should ensure that the rights of the presenters and of the audience are not impaired by a "heckler's veto" from those who may be offended by the presentation. Academic institutions should ensure that those who choose to view an exhibition or attend a performance may do so without interference. Mere presentation in a public place does not create a "captive audience." Institutions may reasonably designate specific places as generally available or unavailable for exhibitions or performances.

4. Public Funding

Public funding for artistic presentations and for academic institutions does not diminish (and indeed may heighten) the responsibility of the university community to ensure academic freedom and of the public to respect the integrity of academic institutions. Government imposition on artistic expression of a test of propriety, ideology, or religion is an act of censorship which impermissibly denies the academic freedom to explore, to teach, and to learn.

On Freedom of Expression and Campus Speech Codes

The statement which follows was approved by the Association's Committee on Academic Freedom and Tenure (Committee A) in June 1992 and adopted by the Association's Council in November 1994.

Freedom of thought and expression is essential to any institution of higher learning. Universities and colleges exist not only to transmit knowledge. Equally, they interpret, explore, and expand that knowledge by testing the old and proposing the new.

This mission guides learning outside the classroom quite as much as in class, and often inspires vigorous debate on those social, economic, and political issues that arouse the strongest passions. In the process, views will be expressed that may seem to many wrong, distasteful, or offensive. Such is the nature of freedom to sift and winnow ideas.

On a campus that is free and open, no idea can be banned or forbidden. No viewpoint or message may be deemed so hateful or disturbing that it may not be expressed.

Universities and colleges are also communities, often of a residential character. Most campuses have recently sought to become more diverse, and more reflective of the larger community, by attracting students, faculty, and staff from groups that were historically excluded or underrepresented. Such gains as they have made are recent, modest, and tenuous. The campus climate can profoundly affect an institution's continued diversity. Hostility or intolerance to persons who differ from the majority (especially if seemingly condoned by the institution) may undermine the confidence of new members of the community. Civility is always fragile and can easily be destroyed.

In response to verbal assaults and use of hateful language some campuses have felt it necessary to forbid the expression of racist, sexist, homophobic, or ethnically demeaning speech, along with conduct or behavior that harasses. Several reasons are offered in support of banning such expression. Individuals and groups that have been victims of such expression feel an understandable outrage. They claim that the academic progress of minority and majority alike may suffer if fears, tensions, and conflicts spawned by slurs and insults create an environment inimical to learning.

These arguments, grounded in the need to foster an atmosphere respectful of and welcoming to all persons, strike a deeply responsive chord in the academy. But, while we can acknowledge both the weight of these concerns and the thoughtfulness of those persuaded of the need for regulation, rules that ban or punish speech based upon its content cannot be justified. An institution of higher learning fails to fulfill its mission if it asserts the power to proscribe ideas—and racial or ethnic slurs, sexist epithets, or homophobic insults almost always express ideas, however repugnant. Indeed, by proscribing any ideas, a university sets an example that profoundly disserves its academic mission.

Some may seek to defend a distinction between the regulation of the content of speech and the regulation of the manner (or style) of speech. We find this distinction untenable in practice because offensive style or opprobrious phrases may in fact have been chosen precisely for their expressive power. As the United States Supreme Court has said in the course of rejecting criminal sanctions for offensive words:

> [W]ords are often chosen as much for their emotive as their cognitive force. We cannot sanction the view that the Constitution, while solicitous of the cognitive content of individual speech, has little or no regard for that emotive function which, practically speaking, may often be the more important element of the overall message sought to be communicated.

The line between substance and style is thus too uncertain to sustain the pressure that will inevitably be brought to bear upon disciplinary rules that attempt to regulate speech.

Proponents of speech codes sometimes reply that the value of emotive language of this type is of such a low order that, on balance, suppression is justified by the harm suffered by those who are directly affected, and by the general damage done to the learning environment. Yet a college or university sets a perilous course if it seeks to differentiate between high-value and low-value speech, or to choose which groups are to be protected by curbing the speech of others. A speech code unavoidably implies an institutional competence to distinguish permissible expression of hateful thought from what is proscribed as thoughtless hate.

Institutions would also have to justify shielding some, but not other, targets of offensive language—proscribing uncomplimentary references to sexual but not to political preference, to religious but not to philosophical creed, or perhaps even to some but not to other religious affiliations. Starting down this path creates an even greater risk that groups not originally protected may later demand similar solicitude—demands the institution that began the process of banning some speech is ill equipped to resist.

Distinctions of this type are neither practicable nor principled; their very fragility underscores why institutions devoted to freedom of thought and expression ought not adopt an institutionalized coercion of silence.

Moreover, banning speech often avoids consideration of means more compatible with the mission of an academic institution by which to deal with incivility, intolerance, offensive speech, and harassing behavior:

1. Institutions should adopt and invoke a range of measures that penalize conduct and behavior, rather than speech—such as rules against defacing property, physical intimidation or harassment, or disruption of campus activities. All members of the campus community should be made aware of such rules, and administrators should be ready to use them in preference to speech-directed sanctions.
2. Colleges and universities should stress the means they use best—to educate—including the development of courses and other curricular and co-curricular experiences designed to increase student understanding and to deter offensive or intolerant speech or conduct. These institutions should, of course, be free (indeed encouraged) to condemn manifestations of intolerance and discrimination, whether physical or verbal.
3. The governing board and the administration have a special duty not only to set an outstanding example of tolerance, but also to challenge boldly and condemn immediately serious breaches of civility.
4. Members of the faculty, too, have a major role; their voices may be critical in condemning intolerance, and their actions may set examples for understanding, making clear to their students that civility and tolerance are hallmarks of educated men and women.
5. Student personnel administrators have in some ways the most demanding role of all, for hate speech occurs most often in dormitories, locker rooms, cafeterias, and student centers. Persons who guide this part of campus life should set high standards of their own for tolerance and should make unmistakably clear the harm that uncivil or intolerant speech inflicts.

To some persons who support speech codes, measures like these—relying as they do on suasion rather than sanctions—may seem inadequate. But freedom of expression requires toleration of "ideas we hate," as Justice Holmes put it. The underlying principle does not change because the demand is to silence a hateful speaker, or because it comes from within the academy. Free speech is not simply an aspect of the educational enterprise to be weighed against other desirable ends. It is the very precondition of the academic enterprise itself.

On Collegiality as a Criterion for Faculty Evaluation

The statement which follows was approved by the Association's Committee on Academic Freedom and Tenure (Committee A) and adopted by the Association's Council in November 1999.

In evaluating faculty members for promotion, renewal, tenure, and other purposes American colleges and universities have customarily examined faculty performance in the three areas of teaching, scholarship, and service, with service sometimes divided further into public service and service to the college or university. While the weight given to each of these three areas varies according to the mission and evolution of the institution, the terms are themselves generally understood to describe the key functions performed by faculty members.

In recent years, Committee A has become aware of an increasing tendency on the part not only of administrations and governing boards but also of faculty members serving in such roles as department chairs or as members of promotion and tenure committees to add a fourth criterion in faculty evaluation: "collegiality."[1] For the reasons set forth in this statement, we view this development as highly unfortunate, and we believe that it should be discouraged.

Few if any responsible faculty members would deny that collegiality, in the sense of collaboration and constructive cooperation, identifies important aspects of a faculty member's overall performance. A faculty member may legitimately be called upon to participate in the development of curricula and standards for the evaluation of teaching, as well as in peer review of the teaching of colleagues. Much research, depending on the nature of the particular discipline, is by its nature collaborative and requires teamwork as well as the ability to engage in independent investigation. And committee service of a more general description, relating to the life of the institution as a whole, is a logical outgrowth of the Association's view that a faculty member is an "officer" of the college or university in which he or she fulfills professional duties.[2]

Understood in this way, collegiality is not a distinct capacity to be assessed independently of the traditional triumvirate of scholarship, teaching, and service. It is rather a quality whose value is expressed in the successful execution of these three functions. Evaluation in these three areas will encompass the contributions that the virtue of collegiality may pertinently add to a faculty member's career. The current tendency to isolate collegiality as a distinct dimension of evaluation, however, poses several dangers. Historically, "collegiality" has not infrequently been associated with ensuring homogeneity, and hence with practices that exclude persons on the basis of their difference from a perceived norm. The invocation of "collegiality" may also threaten academic freedom. In the heat of important decisions regarding promotion or tenure, as well as other matters involving such traditional areas of faculty responsibility as curriculum or academic hiring, collegiality may be confused with the expectation that a faculty member

---

[1] At some institutions, the term "collegiality" or "citizenship" is employed in regulations or in discussions of institutional practice as a synonym for "service." Our objection is to the use of the term "collegiality" in its description of a separate and additional area of performance in which the faculty member is to be evaluated.

[2] The locus classicus for this term is the "1940 Statement of Principles on Academic Freedom and Tenure": "College and university teachers are citizens, members of a learned profession, and officers of an educational institution." (AAUP, *Policy Documents and Reports*, 9th ed. [Washington, D.C., 2001], 3.)

display "enthusiasm" or "dedication," evince "a constructive attitude" that will "foster harmony," or display an excessive deference to administrative or faculty decisions where these may require reasoned discussion. Such expectations are flatly contrary to elementary principles of academic freedom, which protect a faculty member's right to dissent from the judgments of colleagues and administrators.

A distinct criterion of collegiality also holds the potential of chilling faculty debate and discussion. Criticism and opposition do not necessarily conflict with collegiality. Gadflies, critics of institutional practices or collegial norms, even the occasional malcontent, have all been known to play an invaluable and constructive role in the life of academic departments and institutions. They have sometimes proved collegial in the deepest and truest sense. Certainly a college or university replete with genial Babbitts is not the place to which society is likely to look for leadership. It is sometimes exceedingly difficult to distinguish the constructive engagement that characterizes true collegiality from an obstructiveness or truculence that inhibits collegiality. Yet the failure to do so may invite the suppression of dissent. The very real potential for a distinct criterion of "collegiality" to cast a pall of stale uniformity places it in direct tension with the value of faculty diversity in all its contemporary manifestations.

Relatively little is to be gained by establishing collegiality as a separate criterion of assessment. A fundamental absence of collegiality will no doubt manifest itself in the dimensions of scholarship, teaching, or, most probably, service, though here we would add that we all know colleagues whose distinctive contribution to their institution or their profession may not lie so much in service as in teaching and research. Professional misconduct or malfeasance should constitute an independently relevant matter for faculty evaluation. So too should efforts to obstruct the ability of colleagues to carry out their normal functions, to engage in personal attacks, or to violate ethical standards. The elevation of collegiality into a separate and discrete standard is not only inconsistent with the long-term vigor and health of academic institutions and dangerous to academic freedom, it is also unnecessary.

Committee A accordingly believes that the separate category of "collegiality" should not be added to the traditional three areas of faculty performance. Institutions of higher education should instead focus on developing clear definitions of scholarship, teaching, and service, in which the virtues of collegiality are reflected. Certainly an absence of collegiality ought never, by itself, to constitute a basis for nonreappointment, denial of tenure, or dismissal for cause.

Access to Faculty Personnel Files

*The report which follows, approved in 1999 jointly by the Association's Committee on Academic Free-
dom and Tenure (Committee A) and its Committee on the Status of Women in the Academic Profession
(Committee W), is a briefer version of a report initially approved by the two committees in 1992, adopted by the Association's Council in June of that year, and endorsed by the Seventy-eighth Annual Meeting.*

Access by faculty members to their own personnel files and to the files of colleagues has
been a significant issue for the academic profession. The long-standing practice on
many campuses of confidentiality of such files has been tested by state "sunshine" laws,
by court decisions requiring disclosure of personnel files in certain litigation situations, and by
concern about racial and gender discrimination in faculty personnel decisions. The issue of confidentiality was perhaps most significantly highlighted in the 1990 decision of the United States
Supreme Court in *University of Pennsylvania v. EEOC*, 493 U.S. 182. There, the Court unanimously held that the Equal Employment Opportunity Commission, investigating a charge of
employment discrimination in violation of Title VII of the 1964 Civil Rights Act, is entitled to
secure, through the issuance of a subpoena, faculty personnel files relevant to the case, including files of faculty members other than the complaining party. (The Court left unresolved the
question whether the personnel files to be turned over to the agency might be in redacted form,
i.e., edited so as to avoid disclosure of the identity of the evaluator.)

The Court in *University of Pennsylvania* rejected the university's claim that it had a privilege,
rooted in the First Amendment and in more general notions of academic freedom, to shield
such files against the agency's demands for disclosure. It held that the only limitations upon
what had to be disclosed were those that usually obtain when enforcing administrative sub-
poenas, i.e., the relevance of the requested material and the burden to the defendant. Lower
courts appear to agree that the same scope of discovery granted to the EEOC applies to actions
brought under Title VII by private litigants.

In view of the ability of faculty members in many personnel disputes to have access to personnel files, through judicial or administrative directives, colleges and universities should give
further attention to the question whether they should voluntarily make such files available
through their own internal regulations, particularly those setting forth procedures for peer
review by faculty committees. Committees A and W of the American Association of University Professors have considered the circumstances and conditions under which faculty members
should be afforded access to their own personnel records and to the records of others. The
attentions of the two committees were focused upon four questions. Although issues of access
to personnel files may be raised in other situations, we believe that the answers to these questions deal with the central issues and provide guidance for other situations that might arise.
This report, after recounting the four questions, will set forth "the case for openness" and "the
case for confidentiality," and will summarize the conclusions of Committees A and W on each
of the questions.

1. When, and in what form, should faculty members have access to materials in their own
   personnel files?
2. When, and in what form, should faculty members have access to general information
   about other faculty members, such as is normally contained in a curriculum vitae?
3. When, and in what form, should faculty peer review committees have access to the files
   of faculty complainants and of other faculty members whose files are relevant for
   comparison?
4. When, and in what form, should faculty peer review committees make available to a faculty
   complainant the personnel files of other faculty members?

THE CASE FOR OPENNESS

A central argument in support of greater access to faculty personnel files is that knowledge that one's evaluation of the work of a faculty member—whether at one's own institution or at another institution—might be accessible to that person will induce greater care and responsibility on the part of the commentator. The knowledge that one's assessment will be shielded from the scrutiny of the faculty member being discussed could encourage careless and unsubstantiated commentary. In too many instances, confidentiality has been known to foster invidiously discriminatory assessments. AAUP's tradition of academic freedom and faculty governance relies upon a standard of professionalism that should enable faculty members to be willing to be held accountable for their judgments. To suggest that collegiality requires total secrecy would undermine this concept.

It can also be argued that affording a faculty member access to evaluations of his or her work is further justified by the great professional and personal consequences of decisions about reappointment, promotion, or tenure. Quite apart from cases of suspected discrimination, access could be a means of ensuring not only greater care in evaluation but also simple fairness to the faculty member being assessed, for that person is commonly in the best position to comment upon or to rebut the critical comments of others, whose judgment may be a product of misinformation, misunderstanding, or disciplinary bias.

Proponents of openness assert that the benefits of access to personnel files are particularly great in situations in which a faculty member claims to have been the victim of invidious discrimination in violation of law. The same would be true when a claim is made that norms of the academy have been violated because a faculty member has been punished for exercising academic freedom or because procedures have not afforded thorough or fair consideration of the faculty member's status.

Another important reason for greater openness derives from long-standing AAUP policies relating to the providing of reasons and peer review in certain cases of challenged personnel decisions. The AAUP has long supported the right of a faculty member to receive, upon request, a written statement of reasons for the denial of reappointment or tenure. AAUP policy has also long endorsed intramural review by an independent faculty body of allegations that a decision on faculty status has been tainted by violations of academic freedom or by invidious discrimination or resulted from inadequate consideration.

Thus proponents of openness argue that a faculty member's right to reasons is surely vacuous if there is no effective correlative right to ascertain whether those reasons are substantiated by materials in the faculty member's personnel file, including the assessments of faculty peers. Just as surely, it would seem, the role of peer review is undermined if a faculty committee impaneled to assess a colleague's claims relating to academic freedom, discrimination, or inadequate consideration—or institutional claims of inferior performance in teaching or scholarship—cannot have full access to relevant personnel information. In many such cases, relevant information will include not only assessments of the faculty complainant but also assessments of his or her colleagues, particularly those in the same discipline who are alleged by the complainant to have received preferential treatment.

Another basis for increased access is the decision of the Supreme Court in *University of Pennsylvania v. EEOC*. Faculty complainants have recourse to the courts and to administrative agencies for legal redress on a variety of contractual, statutory, and constitutional theories, and the likelihood is great that they will be able through litigation to secure discovery of relevant personnel materials, their own and in many cases those of faculty colleagues. The institution should therefore be willing to make such materials available voluntarily through intramural procedures. Doing so would help ensure that faculty grievances may be resolved fairly, expeditiously, and inexpensively without the felt necessity of initiating legal proceedings. Coincidentally, doing so would allow for primary emphasis upon resolution of such disputes, best suited to internal collegial assessment, where the AAUP would have them resolved—before faculty peer review committees rather than before a judicial or administrative decision maker lacking in understanding of the values and criteria intrinsic to the academy.

Those who emphasize the values of confidentiality of faculty files argue that the objectives just articulated may be all but fully achieved by providing a faculty complainant or a faculty appeals committee with personnel information in either summary or redacted form. Summaries, however, will typically fail to capture the detail, nuance, and tone that are often of the greatest importance in conveying the writer's views and that must, in the interests of fairness and accuracy, be communicated to faculty members as well. Moreover, a serious issue may well arise as to the scholarly competence or objectivity of the person assigned the task of reducing personnel assessments to summary form.

Similar flaws, although perhaps of a somewhat lesser order of magnitude, may obtain when material is made accessible only in redacted form. Very often, the probative force of evaluative comments may be either enhanced by the scholarly credentials of the evaluator, or diluted or indeed altogether discredited by that individual's known scholarly (and in some cases even personal) biases. To delete information about the source of evaluative comments may serve to deprive an aggrieved faculty member and peer review panels of much that might bear upon the weight of the faculty member's claim—that might show in some instances that the claim is particularly weak, but in others that it is quite credible.

THE CASE FOR CONFIDENTIALITY

Perhaps the most weighty argument in support of confidentiality of faculty personnel files is that such confidentiality is the only way to ensure complete candor in the evaluation of candidates for appointment, reappointment, promotion, and tenure. Honest evaluations are at the core of the personnel decision-making process and are indispensable to the quality of an academic institution. Evaluators, whether internal or external, who know that the faculty candidate (or contentious third parties) will have relatively unfettered access to evaluations are likely to be a good deal less candid in their assessments. Revealing the identity of evaluators along with their critical comments may bias the process toward letters of appraisal that are less reliable, and thus less useful.

Proponents of confidentiality see no justification for providing fewer safeguards of confidentiality to the comments of internal reviewers than to the comments of those at other institutions. The adverse impact of open access would be at least as great. Evaluations from within departments may be most seriously affected. Lack of confidentiality may either result in less-than-candid assessments, as already noted, or create the risk, at least as discomfiting, that candidly critical assessments will strain internal collegial relationships and seriously undermine morale and community.

Confidentiality as a safeguard for candid assessments of quality is not unique to personnel files; it characterizes other pertinent processes within the academy. For example, reputable university presses and peer-reviewed journals routinely rely upon confidential processes of evaluation. Even more pertinently, faculty deliberations that culminate in personnel decisions are all but universally conducted in private; and many institutions have secret ballots on such matters as a further means of ensuring uninhibited assessments.

The advocates of open access to personnel files, particularly for the aggrieved faculty member, must conclude that any sacrifice of candor is outweighed by a more urgent and pervasive need to uncover distortions and biases, whether intentional or inadvertent, by colleagues and extramural evaluators. The advocates of confidentiality, however, challenge this assumption of distortion and bias. They view it as incompatible with a paradigm of faculty professionalism that relies instead on faculty integrity, respect, collegiality, and self-discipline. Indeed, they view the AAUP's traditional commitment to academic freedom and faculty self-governance as ultimately founded upon such a paradigm.

This is not to say that confidentiality cannot be abused. Of course it can. It is only to argue that, on the whole, faculty members can and should be trusted to discharge their evaluative responsibilities with integrity and seriousness of purpose, that confidentiality will contribute to a freer, franker, and better process of evaluation, and that in the long run this benefit will outweigh the predictable costs of abuse.

It can be argued that even if this benign paradigm of professionalism is thought naive—or, more pertinently, even if it has unquestionably been shown to fail in particular instances of demonstrable discrimination (or violation of academic freedom)—it does not follow that we must discard all restraints upon disclosure of faculty personnel files. Although openness is a value, it is not an absolute value. Its desirability depends upon its impact on other significant values, such as privacy, collegiality, and the promotion of the general academic enterprise. The question, therefore, is one of balance. A far better balance might be struck through the endorsement of intermediate levels of disclosure. Such a balance would recognize the need to root out distortion and bias but would also honor traditional attributes of faculty professionalism.

Some advocates of confidentiality assert that most of the benefits of openness recounted above can be attained—without undue sacrifice of the benefits that derive from confidentiality—if faculty files were to be made available in redacted form. Others would go further and claim that the benefits of openness could be attained even if faculty files were to be made available not at any time on demand, but only in the case of an adverse personnel decision, and, in those cases in which it would suffice and can be done readily and fairly, through the preparation of summaries. Such forms of intermediate levels of disclosure would enable faculty members independently to review the basis for, and if desired to comment upon, personnel decisions that affect them.

Although proponents of confidentiality would concede that special situations arise in which claims of discrimination cannot be sustained without access to unredacted files, they would argue that these situations are infrequent when measured against the thousands of personnel decisions made on college and university campuses each year, and that these relatively rare occasions can in any event be easily accommodated by creating mechanisms to grant unredacted access in appropriate circumstances.

In keeping with the idea that confidentiality of files should be compromised only sparingly, and only in a manner carefully tailored to the exigencies of the case, one can surely make a stronger claim for access, in summary or redacted form, to the files of an aggrieved faculty member than for access to the files of third persons. Access by a faculty complainant to the files of colleagues presents the problems relating to candor and collegiality noted above, and it also creates new problems by impairing the colleagues' interests in privacy and by possibly engendering intramural divisiveness.

CONCLUSIONS

1. Committees A and W have concluded that faculty members should, at all times, have access to their own files, including unredacted letters, both internal and external.

The committees determined that, for the reasons elaborated above in the section titled "The Case for Openness," such access promotes care and accuracy in evaluations, and also provides faculty members a fair opportunity to learn of and respond to critical evaluations. Such access is therefore likely to discourage evaluations that are based upon improper disciplinary, gender, or racial bias, and to facilitate access to proof of such bias. The identity of the writer should be known, because this information will be of pervasive importance in assessing the weight to be given to such evaluations. An individual who is uncertain whether grounds exist for contesting an adverse personnel decision cannot know if there is a basis for appeal unless he or she knows not only the official stated reasons for such a decision but also the substance of the letters of evaluation, internal and external, as well as their authorship.

2. Committees A and W have concluded that a faculty member should be afforded access upon request to general information about other faculty members such as is normally contained in a curriculum vitae.

The members of the two committees believe that faculty members should surely know as much about their colleagues as does the general public. Institutions of higher education gather curricula vitae from faculty members at regular intervals, often in the context of yearly salary reviews as well as in reviews for reappointment, tenure, and promotion. There is little reason not to share this information within the university community when it is generally available. A wider distribution of this kind of material could benefit those who are unsure of how their work compares with that of others, and it could serve the larger good of keeping faculty members abreast of each other's work.

3. Committees A and W have concluded that, for purposes of comparison, files of a faculty complainant and of other faculty members should be available in unredacted form to faculty appeals committees to the extent that such committees deem the information relevant and necessary to the fair disposition of the case before them.

At the heart of AAUP policies regarding such core issues as academic freedom, due process, antidiscrimination, and faculty governance is the role of peer review committees in the appeal of adverse personnel decisions. It is essential that such committees, initially in deciding whether a faculty claim has sufficient merit to warrant a formal hearing, and subsequently in deciding at a hearing the relevance and weight to be given to various materials in faculty personnel files, be permitted to examine all materials that might arguably be relevant.

Those essential powers of faculty appeals committees would be untenably hobbled if an administrative official could unilaterally determine that certain materials are not relevant to a faculty claim, or that relevant materials are too sensitive to be reviewed by the committee in unedited form. Although there is always a risk that unedited sensitive material might be improperly "leaked" to the aggrieved faculty member or to others, Committees A and W believe that AAUP-recommended policies on disclosure should be shaped by an assumption of responsible and professional behavior by peer-review committee members.

Because relevance is the central criterion for access by a peer review committee, it follows that in appropriate cases the committee should be afforded access to materials contained in the personnel files of faculty members other than the complainant. Such recourse to third-party files, however, is likely to be the exception rather than the rule; it will not likely be relevant in a wide variety of faculty grievances, including cases in which violation of academic freedom or inadequate consideration is alleged.

Committees A and W recognize that the practice on a significant number of campuses relating to disclosure to peer review committees is considerably more restrictive than that advocated here. Nonetheless, the recommendation of the committees is thought particularly warranted, for two reasons.

First, as already noted, a movement toward access for such committees is very much consistent with, if not indeed dictated by, core AAUP-recommended policies on faculty governance and peer review. Second, a faculty member whose appeal is markedly hampered by the committee's inability to secure meaningful access to materials (including relevant third-party materials) will often be able to secure such materials by pressing his or her case in an administrative or judicial forum; all parties would be better served—as would the concept of peer review—if comparable access could be secured through more expeditious and less expensive intramural procedures. (Relatedly, given the fact that personnel files are subject to discovery in formal legal proceedings, it is unlikely that their availability to peer review committees under limited circumstances, as an effective alternative to or precursor of formal legal proceedings, would materially increase any inclination on the part of peer evaluators to be less than candid or to refrain from commenting altogether.)

4. Committees A and W have concluded that a faculty appeals committee should make available to the aggrieved faculty member, in unredacted form and without prejudging the merits of the case, all materials the appeals committee deems relevant to the complaint, including personnel files of other faculty members, having due regard for the privacy of those who are not parties to the complaint.

If a faculty appeals committee determines that certain material, even from third-party files, is relevant to the claims made by an aggrieved faculty member, there would normally be little or no justification for withholding that material from the faculty complainant pursuing intramural procedures. Indeed, it is difficult to contemplate a system of academic due process and peer review in which a faculty complainant should be required to present his or her case while being denied an opportunity to examine material that the faculty hearing body has determined to be relevant to the case.

The wisdom of providing access in intramural proceedings is reinforced by the likelihood that most such material, because of the determination of relevance by a peer review panel, would ultimately be discoverable in any event by the faculty complainant in a formal legal proceeding. Because the scrutiny of third-party files will ordinarily be regarded as relevant only in those cases in which discrimination is alleged, such cases are the most likely to generate agency or court directives to disclose such material.

Moreover, because Committees A and W also believe that such discrimination cases tend particularly to call for disclosure of the source of evaluations in order to assess the credibility or bias of the evaluator, they believe that such evaluations—including those relating to relevant faculty members other than the complainant—should be communicated to the complainant unedited and unredacted.

Given the importance of the privacy interests of the faculty members whose files might be turned over to an aggrieved colleague, Committees A and W emphasize that a claim of privacy for such files should be honored, barring a strong reason to the contrary. The only legitimate reason for not doing so is the need to use those files as comparators when judging whether a faculty complainant has been discriminated against or otherwise unfairly treated. The faculty appeals committee should have the authority to make the determination of reasonable need to disclose such information to a faculty complainant, and to take steps to minimize the risks of further disclosure.

*   *   *   *   *

Committees A and W recognize that some colleges and universities, while willing to abide by most of the principles suggested in this report, would prefer to carve out an exception with regard to the disclosure of evaluations in unredacted form, especially if the evaluations were originally solicited under an explicit or implicit assurance of confidentiality. Even apart from the issue of redaction, we appreciate that the recommendations made here go beyond the practices regarding access to personnel files that are common in many colleges and universities. We believe, however, that the AAUP can make a contribution by setting forth the strong affirmative reasons that warrant such openness while urging institutions to move forthrightly in that direction.

On the Imposition of Tenure Quotas

The statement which follows was approved by the Association's Committee on Academic Freedom and Tenure (Committee A) and adopted by the Association's Council in October 1973.

Many institutions of higher education have had to consider ways of accommodating the number and composition of their faculty to a static or declining financial situation. The Association has developed criteria applicable where a reduction in faculty positions is contemplated because of financial exigency or discontinuance of a program.[1] This statement will concern itself with institutional policies designed to shape the overall composition of the faculty by limiting the number of tenured positions, and especially with those policies which establish a fixed maximum percentage of faculty who may possess tenure at a given time.[2]

The Association, while recognizing the concerns that motivate such quotas, opposes them. They are an unwise solution to the problem they purport to solve, and can have grave consequences for the institutions that adopt them. Moreover, they are not compelled, for other more nearly satisfactory alternatives are available.

Recognizing that tenure best protects academic freedom, but that it is usually undesirable to afford tenure automatically upon an individual's joining a faculty, the American Association of University Professors has supported the employment of a stated maximum probationary period, of sufficient but not excessive length, during which the academic qualifications and performance of newer faculty members can be evaluated in terms of institutional standards and expectations. Indeed, it is principally to provide each institution with a reasonable opportunity of assessing the skills of probationary appointees in terms of its tenure standards (and the availability of others whom it may also desire to consider for tenured appointment) that this Association has not favored policies of automatic tenure. However, to continue the service of faculty members beyond the maximum probationary period, while withholding tenure, presents an unwarranted hazard to their academic freedom.

Accordingly, institutions may properly set high standards for tenure, but they subvert the functions of tenure standards if they provide that, no matter how clearly nontenured faculty members meet any stated academic standard (and no matter how well they compare with the tenured faculty and all others whom the institution is able to attract to that faculty), the system is such as to require their release from the very positions in which they have served with unqualified distinction. Holding faculty members in nontenured service, and then releasing them because a numerical limit on tenured positions prohibits their retention, has the effect of nullifying probation. All full-time appointments, excepting only special appointments of specified brief duration and reappointments of retired faculty members on special conditions,

---

[1] See Regulations 4(c) and 4(d) of the Association's "Recommended Institutional Regulations on Academic Freedom and Tenure," AAUP, *Policy Documents and Reports*, 9th ed. (Washington, D.C., 2001), 23–25. See also the Association's statement on "The Role of the Faculty in Budgetary and Salary Matters," *ibid.*, 232–35, and "On Institutional Policies Resulting from Financial Exigency: Some Operating Guidelines," *ibid.*, 230–31.

[2] The report and recommendations of the Commission on Academic Tenure in Higher Education, published in 1973, called for "policies relating to the proportion of tenured and nontenured faculty that will be compatible with the composition of [the institution's] present staff, its resources, and its future objectives." See *Faculty Tenure* (San Francisco: Jossey-Bass, 1973), 45–51, particularly the commission's recommendation on pages 50–51.

should be either probationary relating to continuous tenure or with continuous tenure.[3] To make appointments which are destined to lead to nonretention because of a fixed numerical quota of tenured positions, obviating any realistic opportunity for the affected individuals to be evaluated for tenure on their academic record, is to depart from a basic feature of the system of tenure and thus to weaken the protections of academic freedom.

A variation to nonretention because of a tenure quota, one which Committee A finds wholly inimical to the principles of academic freedom which tenure serves, is the policy adopted at a few institutions of withholding tenure from admittedly qualified candidates who have completed the maximum probationary period but retaining them in a kind of holding pattern, perpetually more vulnerable than their tenured colleagues to termination of services, unless and until the quota eases for them and they too are granted tenure. If they have fully earned an entitlement to tenure, there can be no justification for continuing them in a less favorable and more vulnerable status than their tenured colleagues.

Committee A, accordingly, opposes the adoption of tenure quotas for the following reasons:

1. If combined with the possibility of additional term contracts beyond the period of maximum probationary service plainly adequate to determine the individual's entitlement to tenure, the system indefensibly extends conditions of jeopardy to academic freedom.
2. Probation with automatic termination of appointment is not probation; those whom quotas affect by automatically excluding them from consideration for tenure essentially are reduced to a terminal class of contract workers rendered incapable of full and equal faculty membership irrespective of the nature of the service they have given and irrespective of the professional excellence of that service.
3. In designating a portion of the probationary regular faculty as ineligible to continue, in order to cope with needs of staff flexibility and financial constraints, a quota system is a crude and unjust substitute for more equitable methods of academic planning.

Committee A, in registering its concern over the fixing of a maximum numerical percentage of tenured faculty, does not suggest that an institution should be unconcerned with appointment policies which will permit it to bring new members into its faculty with some regularity. A sound academic program needs elements not only of continuity but also of flexibility, which is served by the continuing opportunity to recruit new persons and to pursue new academic emphases. It is desirable for a faculty to include those recently arrived from the seminars of our graduate schools as well as those who are well established as scholars and teachers.

Such considerations of flexibility are often adduced in support of tenure quotas. But this misses two central points. First, the system of tenure does not exist as subordinate to convenience and flexibility. The protection of academic freedom must take precedence over the claimed advantages of increased flexibility.

Second, imposing a numerical limit on the percentage of tenured faculty disregards a range of other ways to attain a desired mix of senior and junior faculty. Indeed, it imposes an inequitable burden on a vulnerable portion of the faculty in a facile response to issues of academic staffing that should reflect far more comprehensive planning. Establishing fixed quotas may deprive the profession of a large part of the generation of scholars and teachers who currently populate the nontenured positions at our colleges and universities. It would be preferable by far to employ a variety of other measures—some affecting tenured faculty, others affecting probationary and nontenured faculty, and still others affecting prospective faculty members—to ensure that the necessary burdens of financial stringency and lack of growth are shared to some extent by all academic generations.

While opposing the imposition of tenure quotas, Committee A recognizes that the general proportion of a faculty on tenure can have an important long-range bearing on the nature and quality of an institution of higher education. Given a situation in which there is small prospect for significant growth in the total size of the faculty, considerations which merit attention include:

---

[3] See "Recommended Institutional Regulations on Academic Freedom and Tenure," Regulation 1(b), *Policy Documents and Reports*, 21.

1. The desired distribution of tenured and nontenured faculty should be viewed as a long-term goal rather than a short-term solution. The ratio of tenured to nontenured faculty is itself the dynamic consequence of a complex of academic decisions and developments, each of which can be reconsidered. These include: (a) the rate of growth of the institution and its faculty; (b) the fraction of those appointed initially to tenured or probationary positions; (c) the use of visiting faculty members; (d) the use of graduate assistants; (e) the average length of the probationary period of nontenured faculty members who ultimately achieve tenure; (f) the fraction of nontenured faculty members who ultimately achieve tenure; (g) the institutional policy on retirement; and (h) the age distribution of the total faculty.

2. A satisfactory long-range plan may well imply that, along the way, the proportion of the faculty on tenure will at first increase and then, as the force of the plan takes effect, decrease. Just as the end of growth in the size of the faculty leads to a gradual increase in the proportion of those tenured, so the gradual aging of the present faculty will ultimately lead to a tendency for the proportion to decline. Most changes in academic personnel policies require some lag in time before full implementation and impact, and there is nothing disastrous in a temporary bulge in the percentage of faculty members on tenure. On the other hand, long-range injury to an institution may result from rigid and hasty application of any single presumed remedy, such as the imposition of a fixed quota.

3. It should be recognized that, in the short run, reducing the proportion of a faculty on tenure produces very little benefit by way of flexibility. It is only over a period of several years that a change in the proportion acquires pertinency. If an institution finds itself, at the beginning of development of a long-range plan, at or near a preferred distribution which it wishes generally to maintain, it may well be sensible to choose consciously to exceed the desired distribution temporarily while the steps necessary to return to that distribution take effect.

4. Equity and institutional morale demand that the probationary faculty not be made to bear all or almost all of the burden of satisfying the desired tenure ratio. Attractive accelerated retirement opportunities for senior tenured faculty present one possible alternative. Additionally, consideration may be given to planning carefully the proportion of teaching and research done by full-time and part-time tenured and probationary faculty, teaching assistants, and temporary appointees.

Foreclosing promotion to a tenured position because of a numerical quota is unacceptable. Stricter standards for the awarding of tenure can be developed over the years, with a consequent decrease in the probability of achieving tenure. But it is essential to distinguish a deliberate change in standards, retaining a positive probability of an individual's achieving tenure pursuant to well-defined criteria and adequate procedures for evaluation and review, from a situation in which the granting of tenure, for reasons unrelated to the individual's merits, is never a realistic possibility.

Post-Tenure Review: An AAUP Response

The following report, approved in June 1999 by the Association's Committee on Academic Freedom and Tenure (Committee A), was adopted that month by the Council and endorsed by the Eighty-fifth Annual Meeting. It is a briefer version of a report that was published in the September–October 1998 issue of Academe: Bulletin of the AAUP.

INTRODUCTION

The Association's existing policy on post-tenure review, approved by Committee A and adopted by the Council in November 1983, is as follows:

> The Association believes that periodic formal institutional evaluation of each postprobationary faculty member would bring scant benefit, would incur unacceptable costs, not only in money and time but also in dampening of creativity and of collegial relationships, and would threaten academic freedom.

> The Association emphasizes that no procedure for evaluation of faculty should be used to weaken or undermine the principles of academic freedom and tenure. The Association cautions particularly against allowing any general system of evaluation to be used as grounds for dismissal or other disciplinary sanctions. The imposition of such sanctions is governed by other established procedures, enunciated in the 1940 *Statement of Principles on Academic Freedom and Tenure* and the 1958 *Statement on Procedural Standards in Faculty Dismissal Proceedings* that provide the necessary safeguards of academic due process.

By the mid-1990s, new forms of post-tenure review were appearing: a significant number of legislatures, governing boards, and university administrators were making such reviews mandatory; others were in various stages of consideration. For this reason it has become necessary not only to *reaffirm* the principles of the 1983 statement, but also to provide standards which can be used to assess the review process when it is being considered or implemented. This report accordingly offers practical recommendations for faculty at institutions where post-tenure review is being considered or has been put into effect.

The principles guiding this document are these: Post-tenure review ought to be aimed not at accountability, but at faculty development. Post-tenure review must be developed and carried out by faculty. Post-tenure review must not be a reevaluation of tenure, nor may it be used to shift the burden of proof from an institution's administration (to show cause for dismissal) to the individual faculty member (to show cause why he or she should be retained). Post-tenure review must be conducted according to standards that protect academic freedom and the quality of education.

DEFINITION OF TERMS

Because post-tenure review is used to mean many things, it is important to define our understanding of the term. Lurking within the phrase are often two misconceptions: that tenured faculty are not already recurrently subject to a variety of forms of evaluation of their work, and that the presumption of merit that attaches to tenure should be periodically cast aside so that the faculty member must bear the burden of justifying retention. Neither assumption is true. Although it would perhaps be best to utilize a term other than post-tenure review, most alternative expressions (such as periodic evaluation of tenured faculty) do not clearly enough dispel the misconceptions, and the more familiar term has become so widely adopted in academic parlance that it would only create additional confusion were it not used here.

Post-tenure review is a system of periodic evaluation that goes beyond the many traditional forms of continuous evaluation utilized in most colleges and universities. These traditional forms of evaluation vary in their formality and comprehensiveness. They include annual reports for purposes of determining salary and promotion, reviews for the awarding of grants and sabbaticals, and reviews for appointment to school and university committees, graduate faculties, interdisciplinary programs, and professorial chairs and learned societies. More narrowly focused reviews include course-by-course student teaching evaluations, peer review and wider public scrutiny of scholarly presentations and publications, and both administrative and collegial observation of service activities. Faculty members are also evaluated in the course of the program reviews required for regional or specialized accreditation and certification of undergraduate and graduate programs.

What post-tenure review typically adds to these long-standing practices is a formalized additional layer of review which, if it is not simply redundant, may differ in a number of respects: the frequency and comprehensiveness of the review, the degree of involvement by faculty peers, the use of self-evaluations, the articulation of performance objectives, the extent of constructive "feedback," the application of innovative standards and principles, and the magnitude of potential sanctions. At its most draconian, post-tenure review aims to reopen the question of tenure; at its most benign, it formalizes and systematizes long-standing practices. In this report, we use the term post-tenure review to refer to the variety of practices that superimpose a more comprehensive and systematic structure on existing processes of evaluation of tenured faculty.

POST-TENURE REVIEW AND ACADEMIC FREEDOM: A GENERAL CAUTION

Post-tenure review should not be undertaken for the purpose of dismissal. Other formal disciplinary procedures exist for that purpose. If they do not, they should be developed separately, following generally accepted procedures.[1]

Even a carefully designed system of post-tenure review may go awry in a number of ways of serious concern to the Association. Many, though not all, proponents of post-tenure review purportedly seek to supplement preexisting ways of reviewing the performance of tenured faculty with a system of managerial accountability that could ensure faculty productivity, redirect faculty priorities, and facilitate dismissal of faculty members whose performance is deemed unsatisfactory. Despite assurances by proponents that they do not so intend, the substitution of managerial accountability for professional responsibility characteristic of this more intrusive form of post-tenure review alters academic practices in ways that inherently diminish academic freedom.

The objectionable change is not that tenured faculty would be expected to undergo periodic evaluation. As noted here, they generally do—and they should. Nor is there any claim that tenure must be regarded as an indefinite entitlement. Tenured faculty are already subject to dismissal for incompetence, malfeasance, or failure to perform their duties, as well as on grounds of bona fide financial exigency or program termination. Nor is the issue, as many faculty imagine, simply who controls the evaluation. Faculty members as well as administrators can and do err.

Rather, the most objectionable feature of many systems of post-tenure review is that they ease the prevailing standards for dismissal and diminish the efficacy of those procedures

---

[1] These procedures are set forth in the "1940 Statement of Principles on Academic Freedom and Tenure," the "1958 Statement on Procedural Standards in Faculty Dismissal Proceedings," and the Association's "Recommended Institutional Regulations on Academic Freedom and Tenure." These documents appear in AAUP, *Policy Documents and Reports*, 9th ed. (Washington, D.C., 2001), 3–10, 11–14, 21–30.

that ensure that sanctions are not imposed for reasons violative of academic freedom. Some proponents of post-tenure review, motivated by a desire to facilitate the dismissal of tenured faculty, seek to substitute less protective procedures and criteria at the time of post-tenure review. But demanding procedures and standards are precisely what prevent dismissal for reasons violative of academic freedom.

If the standard of dismissal is shifted from "incompetence" to "unsatisfactory performance," as in some current proposals, then tenured faculty must recurrently "satisfy" administrative officers rather than the basic standards of their profession. In addition, some forms of post-tenure review shift the burden of proof in a dismissal hearing from the institution to the tenured faculty member by allowing the institution to make its case simply by proffering the more casually developed evaluation reports from earlier years. Effectively the same concerns arise when the stipulated channel for challenging substantively or procedurally unfair judgments in the course of post-tenure review is through a grievance procedure in which the burden of proving improper action rests with the faculty member.

Academic freedom is not adequately protected in any milieu in which most faculty members bear the burden of demonstrating a claim that their dismissal is for reasons violative of their academic freedom. The heightened protection of the tenured faculty is not a privilege, but a responsibility earned by the demonstration of professional competence in an extended probationary period, leading to a tenured position with its "rebuttable presumption of professional excellence."[2] It chills academic freedom when faculty members are subjected to revolving contracts or recurrent challenge after they have demonstrated their professional competence.

When post-tenure review substitutes review procedures for adversarial hearing procedures, or diverse reappointment standards for dismissal standards, it creates conditions in which a host of plausible grounds for dismissal may cloak a violation of academic freedom. Innovative research may be dismissed as unproven, demanding teaching as discouraging, and independence of mind as a lack of collegiality. The lengthy demonstration of competence that precedes the award of tenure is required precisely so that faculty are not recurrently at risk and are afforded the professional autonomy and integrity essential to academic quality.

We recognize that some tenured faculty members may, nonetheless, fail to fulfill their professional obligations because of incompetence, malfeasance, or simple nonperformance of their duties. Where such a problem appears to exist, "targeted" review and evaluation should certainly be considered, in order to provide the developmental guidance and support that can assist the faculty member to overcome those difficulties. Should it be concluded, however, that such developmental assistance is (or is likely to be) unavailing, the remedy lies not in a comprehensive review of the entire faculty, nor in sacrificing the procedural protections of the tenured faculty member, but in an orderly application of long-standing procedures such as those in the Association's *Recommended Institutional Regulations on Academic Freedom and Tenure* (Regulations 5–8) for the imposition of sanctions up to and including dismissal.

In other cases, faculty members may voluntarily agree to redirect their work or to accept early-retirement incentives as a consequence, for example, of a decision to redirect departmental priorities. But the use of sanctions pursuant to individual reviews to induce the resignation of programmatically less "desirable" faculty members or to redirect otherwise competent faculty endeavors may well have deleterious consequences for academic freedom. The prohibition of the use of major sanctions to redirect or reinvigorate faculty performance without a formal finding of inadequacy does not mean that administrators and colleagues have no less demanding recourse to bring about improvement. Although academic acculturation will ordinarily have provided a sufficient incentive, the monetary rewards or penalties consequent on salary, promotion, and grant reviews can and do encourage accommodation to institutional standards and professional values.

---

[2] See William Van Alstyne, "Tenure: A Summary, Explanation, and 'Defense,'" *AAUP Bulletin* 57 (1971): 328–33, and Matthew W. Finkin, "The Assault on Faculty Independence," *Academe: Bulletin of the AAUP* 83 (July–August 1997): 16–21.

Even on campuses where there is not thought to be a problem with so-called "deadwood" or incompetent faculty members, many proponents of post-tenure review, as well as those who adopt it in the hope of forestalling more comprehensive and blatant attacks on tenure, sometimes envision such review as a means for achieving larger management objectives such as "downsizing," "restructuring," or "reengineering." Individual faculty reviews should, however, focus on the quality of the faculty member's work and not on such larger considerations of programmatic direction. Downsizing may be properly accomplished through long-term strategic planning and, where academically appropriate, formal program discontinuance (with tenured faculty subject to termination of appointment only if reasonable efforts to retrain and reassign them to other suitable positions are unsuccessful).

It might be thought that the untoward impact on academic freedom and tenure may thus be eliminated by implementing a system of post-tenure review that has no explicit provision for disciplinary sanctions. Even here, however, where the reviews are solely for developmental ends, there is a natural expectation that, if evidence of deficiency is found, sanctions of varying degrees of subtlety and severity will indeed follow, absent prompt improvement. Hence, even the most benign review may carry a threat, require protections of academic due process, and inappropriately constrain faculty performance. This point warrants further elaboration.

A central dimension of academic freedom and tenure is the exercise of professional judgment in such matters as the selection of research projects, teaching methods and course curricula, and evaluations of student performance. Those who have followed recent attacks on faculty workloads know that the issue rapidly shifted from the allegation that faculty did not work enough (which, it turned out, they plainly did) to the allegation that faculty did not do the right sort of work. Some proponents of post-tenure review will thus not be content with the identification of the few "slackers" already known to their colleagues by other means, nor even with the imposition of a requirement of faculty cooperation and institutional loyalty. They also want faculty members to give back some portion of their ability to define their own work and standards of performance. For example, increased emphasis on students' evaluations of teaching may lead to the avoidance of curricular experimentation or discourage the use of more demanding course materials and more rigorous standards. Periodic review that is intended not only to ensure a level of faculty performance (defined by others than faculty) but also to shape that performance accordingly, and regardless of tenure, is a most serious threat to academic freedom.

Another consequence of the misapplication of the managerial model to higher education is the ignoring of another important dimension of academic freedom and tenure: time, the time required to develop and complete serious professional undertakings. Shortening the time horizon of faculty, so as to accord with periodic reviews, will increase productivity only artificially, if at all. More frequent and formal reviews may lead faculty members to pick safe and quick, but less potentially valuable, research projects to minimize the risk of failure or delayed achievement.

By way of summary, then, of the Association's principal conclusions, well-governed universities already provide a variety of forms of periodic evaluation of tenured faculty that encourage both responsible performance and academic integrity. Those forms of post-tenure review which diminish the protections of tenure also unambiguously diminish academic freedom, not because they reduce job security but because they weaken essential procedural safeguards. The only acceptable route to the dismissal of incompetent faculty is through carefully crafted and meticulously implemented procedures that place the burden of proof on the institution and that ensure due process. Moreover, even those forms of post-tenure review which do not threaten tenure may diminish academic freedom when they establish a climate that discourages controversy or risk-taking, induces self-censorship, and in general interferes with the conditions that make innovative teaching and scholarship possible. Such a climate, although frequently a product of intervention by trustees or legislators, may instead regrettably flow on occasion from unduly intrusive monitoring by one's faculty peers.

Comprehensive post-tenure review is thus a costly and risky innovation, which may fail either to satisfy ill-informed critics on the one hand or to protect professional integrity on the other. If managerially imposed, it may be a poor substitute for the complex procedures colleges and universities have crafted over the years to balance professional responsibility and autonomy. On the other hand, if designed and implemented by the faculty in a form that properly safeguards academic freedom and tenure and the principle of peer review, and if funded at a meaningful level, it may offer a way of evaluating tenured faculty which supports professional development as well as professional responsibility. To that end, we offer the following guidelines and standards.

GUIDELINES FOR DECIDING WHETHER OR NOT TO ESTABLISH A FORMAL SYSTEM OF POST-TENURE REVIEW

1. It is the obligation of the administration and governing board to observe the principle, enunciated in the Association's *Statement on Government of Colleges and Universities*, that the faculty exercises primary responsibility for faculty status and thus the faculty is the appropriate body to take a leadership role in designing additional procedures for the evaluation of faculty peers. Faculty representatives involved in the development of those procedures should be selected by the faculty according to procedures determined by the faculty.[3]

2. Any discussion of the evaluation of tenured faculty should take into account procedures that are already in place for that purpose: e.g., annual merit reviews of teaching, scholarly productivity, and service; comprehensive consideration at the time of promotion to professor and designation to professorial chairs; and programmatic and accreditation reviews that include analyses of the qualifications and performance of faculty members in that program. The discussion should elicit convincing data on what it is that existing procedures fail to address. The questions for faculty bodies include:

   (a) What are the problems that are calling for this particular solution? Are they of a degree that requires more elaborate, or more focused, procedures for enhancing faculty performance?

   (b) If the answer to the latter question is yes, would it be possible to devise a system of post-tenure review on the basis of existing procedures—for example, a five-year review that is "piggybacked" onto the annual reviews? It should be noted that this system may serve a constructive purpose for those departments that do not do an adequate job in their annual review.

   (c) Is the projected post-tenure review confined to developmental purposes, or is it being inappropriately projected as a new and easier way of levying major sanctions up to and including dismissal?

3. If the institution does not already have in place standards for dismissal-for-cause proceedings, it should adopt such procedural standards as are set forth in existing Association policy statements rather than move to post-tenure review as an alternative dismissal route.[4]

4. Just as the Association has never insisted on a single model of faculty governance but only on the underlying premises that should guide a college or university in respect to that governance, so here any particular form of post-tenure review will depend on the characteristics of the institution: its size, its mission, and the needs and preferences of the faculty, as well as on the resources that the institution can bring to bear in the area of faculty development. Again, the questions to be asked include, but are not necessarily limited to:

   (a) whether the review should be "blanket" for all tenured faculty or focused on problematic cases;

---

[3] Here, and in other guidelines and standards set forth below, the procedures, in addition to conforming with established AAUP-supported standards, should also conform to the applicable provisions of any collective bargaining agreement.

[4] Again, the applicable policy statements are the "1940 Statement of Principles," the "1958 Statement on Procedural Standards," and the "Recommended Institutional Regulations."

(b) whether a review can be activated at the request of an individual faculty member for purposes that he or she would regard as constructive;

(c) whether a cost-benefit analysis shows that institutional resources can adequately support a meaningful and constructive system for post-tenure review without damage to other aspects of the academic program and to the recognition of faculty merit, since the constructiveness of such a system depends not only on the application of these standards but also on the ability to support and sustain faculty development.

5. Any new system of post-tenure review should initially be set up on a trial basis and, if continued, should itself be periodically evaluated with respect to its effectiveness in supporting faculty development and redressing problems of faculty performance, the time and cost of the effort required, and the degree to which in practice it has been effectively cordoned off—as it must be if it is to be constructive—from disciplinary procedures and sanctions.

MINIMUM STANDARDS FOR GOOD PRACTICE IF A FORMAL SYSTEM OF POST-TENURE REVIEW IS ESTABLISHED

1. Post-tenure review must ensure the protection of academic freedom as defined in the 1940 *Statement of Principles*. The application of its procedures, therefore, should not intrude on an individual faculty member's proper sphere of professional self-direction, nor should it be used as a subterfuge for effecting programmatic change. Such a review must not become the occasion for a wide-ranging "fishing expedition" in an attempt to dredge up negative evidence.

2. Post-tenure review must not be a reevaluation or revalidation of tenured status as defined in the 1940 *Statement*. In no case should post-tenure review be used to shift the burden of proof from the institution's administration (to show cause why a tenured faculty member should be dismissed) to the individual faculty member (to show cause why he or she should be retained).

3. The written standards and criteria by which faculty members are evaluated in post-tenure review should be developed and periodically reviewed by the faculty. The faculty should also conduct the actual review process. The basic standard for appraisal should be whether the faculty member under review discharges conscientiously and with professional competence the duties appropriately associated with his or her position, not whether the faculty member meets the current standards for the award of tenure as those might have changed since the initial granting of tenure.

4. Post-tenure review should be developmental and supported by institutional resources for professional development or a change of professional direction. In the event that an institution decides to invest the time and resources required for comprehensive or "blanket" review, it should also offer tangible recognition to those faculty members who have demonstrated high or improved performance.

5. Post-tenure review should be flexible enough to acknowledge different expectations in different disciplines and changing expectations at different stages of faculty careers.

6. Except when faculty appeals procedures direct that files be available to aggrieved faculty members, the outcome of evaluations should be confidential, that is, confined to the appropriate college or university persons or bodies and the faculty member being evaluated, released otherwise only at the discretion or with the consent of the faculty member.

7. If the system of post-tenure review is supplemented, or supplanted, by the option of a formal development plan, that plan cannot be imposed on the faculty member unilaterally, but must be a product of mutual negotiation. It should respect academic freedom and professional self-direction, and it should be flexible enough to allow for subsequent alteration or even its own abandonment. The standard here should be that of good faith on both sides—a commitment to improvement by the faculty member and to the adequate support of that improvement by the institution—rather than the literal fulfillment of a set of nonnegotiable demands or rigid expectations, quantitative or otherwise.

8. A faculty member should have the right to comment in response to evaluations, and to challenge the findings and correct the record by appeal to an elected faculty grievance committee.[5] He or she should have the same rights of comment and appeal concerning the manner in which any individualized development plan is formulated, the plan's content, and any resulting evaluation.
9. In the event that recurring evaluations reveal continuing and persistent problems with a faculty member's performance that do not lend themselves to improvement after several efforts, and that call into question his or her ability to function in that position, then other possibilities, such as a mutually agreeable reassignment to other duties or separation, should be explored. If these are not practicable, or if no other solution acceptable to the parties can be found, then the administration should invoke peer consideration regarding any contemplated sanctions.[6]
10. The standard for dismissal or other severe sanction remains that of adequate cause, and the mere fact of successive negative reviews does not in any way diminish the obligation of the institution to show such cause in a separate forum before an appropriately constituted hearing body of peers convened for that purpose. Evaluation records may be admissible but rebuttable as to accuracy. Even if they are accurate, the administration is still required to bear the burden of proof and demonstrate through an adversarial proceeding not only that the negative evaluations rest on fact, but also that the facts rise to the level of adequate cause for dismissal or other severe sanction. The faculty member must be afforded the full procedural safeguards set forth in the 1958 *Statement on Procedural Standards in Faculty Dismissal Proceedings* and the *Recommended Institutional Regulations on Academic Freedom and Tenure*, which include, among other safeguards, the opportunity to confront and cross-examine adverse witnesses.

---

[5] See Regulation 15, "Recommended Institutional Regulations," *Policy Documents and Reports*, 29–30.
[6] See Regulations 5–7, "Recommended Institutional Regulations," *ibid.*, 25–27.

The Status of Part-Time Faculty

The report which follows was prepared by a subcommittee of the Association's Committee on Academic Freedom and Tenure (Committee A). It was approved for publication by Committee A in November 1980.

Consistent with the 1940 *Statement of Principles on Academic Freedom and Tenure*, which calls for academic freedom for everyone engaged in teaching or research, Committee A, through successive editions of the *Recommended Institutional Regulations on Academic Freedom and Tenure*, has set forth safeguards for the academic freedom of all teachers and researchers, full time or part time, tenured or nontenured, regular faculty or graduate assistants. The *Recommended Institutional Regulations* contain provisions for academic due process for all teachers and researchers, again including those who serve less than full time; these provisions recognize, as do the courts, that due process is a flexible concept and that the extent of procedural protections depends, in part, upon the magnitude of the contemplated abridgment of rights.[1] Additional policies applicable to faculty members serving less than full time are developed in the statement, *Senior Appointments with Reduced Loads*, approved by Committee A and by the Association's Committee on the Status of Women in the Academic Profession. In 1979, Committee A authorized the publication of a statement, *Academic Freedom and Due Process for Faculty Members Who Serve Less Than Full Time*, which is a compilation of existing policies relating to part-time service.[2] This subcommittee's task has been to expand upon that statement and to offer new propositions, consistent with Association principles, to address some of the continuing problems concerning part-time faculty members.

While the Association has long recognized that part-time service has a place on a college or university faculty and that certain rights ought to be afforded to faculty members serving less than full time, it has not addressed itself comprehensively to the status, role, rights and privileges, and responsibilities of part-time members of a faculty. The role of part-time faculty members in institutional life, their participation in academic governance, their entitlement to particular provisions of academic due process, and their eligibility for tenure in part-time positions, all need to be discussed. Guidelines are needed to assist colleges and universities in setting appropriate standards for the employment of part-time faculty members. The treatment of part-time faculty members, in terms of salary and fringe benefits and of security of employment, also deserves examination. This report is designed to address these issues and to offer propositions and guidelines to assist colleges and universities in formulating policy relating to part-time members of the faculty.

BACKGROUND

1. The Increasing Use of Part-Time Faculty in the 1970s

The last decade has seen a dramatic growth, in both relative and absolute terms, in the use of part-time faculty members in higher education. Figures provided by the National Center for

---

[1] Regulation 1(a) specifies that "the terms and conditions of every appointment to the faculty will be stated or confirmed in writing, and a copy of the appointment document will be supplied to the faculty member. Any subsequent extensions or modifications of an appointment, and any special understandings, or any notices incumbent upon either party to provide, will be stated or confirmed in writing and a copy will be given to the faculty member." Regulation 14(a), which would be applicable to part-time faculty in any case where Regulations 5 and 6 (which deal with dismissal for cause) may not be, calls for "a statement of reasons and an opportunity to be heard before a duly constituted committee" prior to involuntary termination before the end of the period of appointment. Regulation 14(b) and Regulation 15 afford part-time faculty members access to grievance committees under certain stipulated conditions. (AAUP, *Policy Documents and Reports*, 9th ed. [Washington, D.C., 2001], 21–30.)

[2] *Academe: Bulletin of the AAUP* 65 (September 1979): 294.

Education Statistics indicate that part-time faculty members now comprise 32 percent of the total teaching force in higher education.[3] Between the years 1972 and 1977, the rate of faculty growth was 50 percent for part-time staff and 9 percent for full-time staff. The most widespread use of part-time teachers is in two-year community colleges, where they now constitute 51 percent of the faculty.[4] Approximately 24 percent of the faculty at four-year liberal arts colleges are part-time faculty members,[5] as are approximately 20 percent of the faculty at research universities.[6] In the last few years, the rate of growth of part-time faculty members in liberal arts colleges seems to have been decreasing, but the increase in the growth rate of this population in community colleges continues. At some community colleges, almost the entire faculty serves on a part-time basis.

The growth of part-time service in higher education has brought with it a host of problems. They involve the rights, privileges, and economic welfare of this category of faculty members, most of whom currently enjoy only marginal status. The problems also involve the relationship with full-time faculty within their institution and the institution's responsibilities to students in programs which are staffed largely or wholly by part-time faculty members. Who are these part-time faculty? What do they do? What skills do they possess? This knowledge should assist in determining what legitimate expectations part-time service engenders and how they can be met. There are, in addition, legitimate concerns relating to the expectations of students and flexibility in institutional staffing.

2. The Present Statement

This report is concerned with all categories of part-time faculty members, irrespective of the proportion of service they provide, their official status at the institution that employs them, or the specific nature of their service. Only two categories of part-time faculty will be excluded from consideration: (a) graduate assistants who are teaching part time at the university where they are students, and (b) teachers who hold "part-time" positions but, in fact, have a load equivalent to that of a full-time faculty position. In the first instance, the dual role of faculty and student raises problems which should be considered separately. In the second case, exclusion is warranted because the Association's position is that the part-time faculty member who performs the duties and has the teaching load equal to those of a full-time faculty member at the institution is entitled, regardless of his or her specific title, to the rights and privileges of a full-time faculty member.[7]

The basic concerns are two-fold: (a) that part-time faculty members not be exploited, and (b) that they not be engaged to replace full-time faculty members with a result that would undermine the protection of academic freedom which faculty tenure provides and the amount of just compensation which faculty members have achieved. The common concern for academic quality should encompass provision for appropriate review of the qualifications of part-time faculty members, their participation in the planning and implementation of the curriculum, their availability to students for advice and counseling, their ability to keep current in their respective fields,[8] and the chilling effect on their teaching which lack of the protections of academic

---

[3] The total number of faculty members in higher education is reported to be 675,000, with 32 percent of them serving part time. The figure does not include graduate assistants. [The overreliance on part-time faculty has increased since this report was first published. In 1997, about 43 percent of all faculty (approximately 990,000) held part-time appointments.]

[4] "The Loneliness of the Part-Time Lecturer," *The Times Higher Education Supplement*, 3 March 1980.

[5] *Ibid.*

[6] David W. Leslie and Ronald B. Head, "Part-Time Faculty Rights," *Educational Record* 10 (winter 1979): 46.

[7] Also excluded from this report are issues relating to those who have full-time appointments with the institution but whose faculty responsibilities are less than full time. See 1970 Interpretive Comment Number 5 of the "1940 Statement of Principles" (*Policy Documents and Reports*, 6).

[8] Owing to other commitments, to high teaching loads carried perhaps simultaneously at several institutions, to lack of access to laboratories, libraries, and computers, and to lack of a reward system, many part-time faculty members report difficulty in keeping up with their field.

due process may engender. A balance must be struck if the long-term interests of full-time and part-time faculty members, of students, and of higher education and research in general are to be served.

3. Part-Time Service Viewed in the Context of the 1940 Statement of Principles

Although the Association has concerned itself with the academic freedom of all faculty members, part time as well as full time, it has not advocated extending the system of academic tenure so broadly. The 1940 *Statement of Principles on Academic Freedom and Tenure* refers, with respect to tenure, only to those appointed to full-time service. It mentions only full-time service in defining the probationary years preceding the attainment of tenure. The underlying concept is that responsibility for academic quality falls upon those who, fully committed to academic life, have shaped and taught the courses central to the academic mission of their institution.

This concept has rested on a view of the academic profession in which part-time service has been occasional and on an ad hoc basis. It provided a way to staff classes in response to temporary or emergency needs; it offered apprentice training to graduate students; and it allowed adjunct professors with highly specialized training to be engaged to teach an occasional course. It was also viewed as allowing an institution economic as well as academic flexibility. lt was cost effective. It was not seen as entailing an ongoing institutional commitment, nor was it viewed as affecting long-term individual interests. The concept assumed that those holding part-time positions were not and should not be a part of the institution in the manner of full-time members of the faculty upon whom rested the responsibility for the quality and character of the institution's academic program.

The subcommittee believes that the propositions to be advanced below on the role and rights of part-time faculty are consonant with the 1940 *Statement of Principles*, responsive to contemporary concerns, and mindful of the needs both of colleges and universities and of the individuals who are directly affected.

WHO ARE THE PART-TIME FACULTY?

While the categories of part-time faculty service are manifold and difficult to classify, we can describe briefly a few "typical" part-time situations.

1. Part-Time Faculty Members Who Would Prefer Full-Time Positions

These individuals, who constitute 30 percent of the part-time faculty,[9] most resemble full-time faculty members in their commitment, in the duties they perform, and, in many cases, in their academic qualifications; they are also the most susceptible to exploitation. They teach part time—sometimes simultaneously at several institutions—only because they cannot get full-time positions. They may have previously taught full time and been denied reappointment or tenure, sometimes at the very institution where they now serve part time. While some may not have met the scholarly requirements for retention, for many there was simply no available full-time position. As part-time faculty, they carry teaching loads which, while primarily if not exclusively in elementary courses, are in some instances heavier in contact hours than those of their full-time colleagues. They are frequently paid a small per-course remuneration and have only those fringe benefits mandated by law. Sometimes they have no office space, no library facilities, no access to laboratories, no secretarial support. Most of them would oppose an "up-or-out" tenure policy for part-time faculty, for they perceive it as likely to end their tenuous hold on the institution. They do want, and by and large they need, increased employment security and better compensation.

2. Those Who Serve Part Time By Choice But Have No Full-Time Employment Outside the Home

These faculty members tend to have a wide range of qualifications, of duties, of commitment to their institutions, and of reasons for preferring part-time status. Some are like full-time faculty

---

[9] Howard P. Tuckman, William D. Vogler, and Jaime Caldwell, *Part-Time Faculty Series* (Washington, D.C.: AAUP, 1978). These empirical studies were made possible by a grant to the AAUP from the Ford Foundation. Six articles were included in the above publication, and a seventh appeared in *Academe* 66 (1980): 71–76.

members in every way except the percentage of time devoted to academic employment; they choose to spend some time with their families, tending to their investments, freelance writing, consulting, painting, or whatever. Many of them want to be evaluated for tenure by the same qualitative standards as are their full-time colleagues so that, since they meet the tests, albeit on a part-time basis, they are entitled to tenure's protections.

Others, however, may be committed primarily to teaching and provide instruction in the basic courses at institutions where full-time faculty members are expected to concentrate on research. Many of these part-time faculty members would welcome the opportunity to participate in faculty government, and in particular in planning the curriculum and advising students. Some would want to be evaluated for tenure, but according to different criteria from those applied to full-time faculty members. Most are not compensated on a basis comparable to full-time faculty at the institution, and most have little security of employment, even after having taught successfully for many years. They often have no access to group insurance plans, retirement plans, or unemployment benefits.

3. Those Who Have Full-Time Employment Elsewhere

While these faculty members tend not to rely on their teaching for security of employment, as teachers they are entitled to protections of academic due process which, more often than not, stated institutional policies fail to assure them. The specialists who teach certain advanced courses which enrich the curriculum may well prefer not to assume any additional institutional responsibilities; others, especially those who teach core courses such as elementary mathematics or accounting, English composition, or clinical law, might improve both the course offerings and their own performance by participating in departmental discussion and planning. For those with full-time positions elsewhere, access to fringe benefits is not generally of significant concern; few, however, would not welcome better pay.

4. The Retirees

Faculty members who retire from full-time service either at the normal age of retirement or at an earlier age sometimes continue to teach part time. Frequently, in surrendering tenure, they are left without any protections of academic due process. Sometimes their fringe benefits are also cut off,[10] and their pay is reduced to a low per-course stipend. They cannot seek tenure once again, but they do seek equitable treatment.

The categorization we have offered is based largely on the part-time faculty member's own commitment. The subcommittee believes that, when a faculty member's primary commitment is to an institution, the institution should make a corresponding commitment, particularly in terms of security of employment and of financial compensation. The difficulties arise in determining the specific circumstances in which the commitment by the university should arise and what form it should take.[11]

Some view the concerns of part-time faculty members as essentially a women's issue. It is true that the interest at some institutions in making part-time faculty members eligible for tenure was generally in response to a perceived need to provide flexibility for women who wanted to devote significant time to their families while pursuing a full-fledged academic career.[12] It is also true that women are, in comparison to their representation among the community of full-time

---

[10] Employers may be restricted in this practice under the Age Discrimination in Employment Act.

[11] That primary economic dependence on the employing institution should be a consideration in determining what degree of protection part-time faculty members should have remains an issue. Typically, such an argument has been made to the disadvantage of two-income families, but not to that, for example, of the medical school faculty member with a private practice or of the independently wealthy. We reject the degree of economic dependence upon a college or university as a consideration in determining faculty status.

[12] Other women have preferred to consider their home commitment as primary; in their cases, the part-time academic employment can be regarded in the same way as it is for those whose primary commitment is to other remunerative employment.

faculty members, disproportionately represented in part-time positions. Many women, how-ever, teach on a part-time basis only because they cannot obtain full-time positions. It is there-fore important to note that colleges and universities cannot meet their obligation to provide equal employment opportunity by having a substantial number of their female appointees on a part-time status which provides them with little or no opportunity for movement to full-time positions. The subcommittee does not view the concerns surrounding part-time faculty mem-bers as generally constituting women's issues. They are concerns which involve faculty mem-bers of both sexes.

POLICY PROPOSALS

1. Tenure for Part-Time Faculty

The 1973 report of the Commission on Academic Tenure in Higher Education discussed part-time faculty service and found merit in the view that individuals who regularly provide part-time service on an institution's faculty should be accorded tenure if they qualify for it. The commission recommended that "institutions consider modifying their tenure arrangements in order to permit part-time faculty service under appropriate conditions to be credited toward the award of tenure, and to permit tenure positions to be held by faculty members who for fam-ily or other appropriate reasons cannot serve on a full-time basis."[13] During the past decade, a number of institutions have modified their tenure regulations so as to permit tenure positions to be held on a part-time basis.[14] From what the subcommittee has been able to discover, the number of faculty members who have actually been granted tenure in a part-time position is very small. Although we recognize that the large majority of part-timers neither need nor desire the privileges of tenure and that for the most part colleges and universities have used part-time faculty service in a manner compatible with the health and quality of the institution,

> WE RECOMMEND that colleges and universities, depending upon the manner in which they utilize part-time faculty service, consider creating a class of regular part-time faculty members, con-sisting of individuals who, as their professional career, share the teaching, research, and adminis-trative duties customary for faculty at their institution, but who for whatever reason do so less than full time. They should have the opportunity to achieve tenure and the rights it confers. The Associ-ation stands ready to provide guidance to institutions wishing to develop such policies.[15]

2. Security of Employment for Part-Time Faculty

The part-time faculty member who is like the full-time faculty member in qualifications and respon-sibilities frequently has a comparable commitment to his or her institution. Many part-time faculty members who teach year in and year out can and should participate in institutional life in a way that is both impracticable and unnecessary for part-time faculty members whose involvement is occasional or peripheral. The part-time faculty member engaged only for highly specialized courses may also have only a modest commitment to the institution. The distinctions in duration of service and in commitment suggest that different types of part-timers are entitled to

---

[13] Commission on Academic Tenure in Higher Education, *Faculty Tenure* (San Francisco: Jossey-Bass, 1973), 78–81. The commission, an independent body, undertook a comprehensive study of the tenure system. The project was sponsored jointly by the AAUP and the Association of American Colleges. Funding was pro-vided by the Ford Foundation.

[14] American, Colgate, Columbia, Cornell, Princeton, Rutgers, Stanford, and Wesleyan Universities, UCLA, and the University of Wisconsin are among the institutions known to us to have developed policies allow-ing tenure for part-time faculty.

[15] These rights do not include entitlement to a full-time position should the part-time faculty member wish to become full-time. Moreover, the class should be defined through the regular procedures of the institu-tion; like the full-time faculty member, the part-time faculty member in this class should not be allowed to waive a decision on tenure.

In addition, we would not insist that part-time faculty members who, for example, teach courses not car-rying academic credit should be included in the tenure system. The centrality of the courses that are taught is a legitimate consideration, but we resist viewing it as a consideration applicable only to part-time faculty. If full-time members of the faculty are to be eligible for certain considerations, so should part-time faculty members who possess the same academic qualifications and teach in the same type of program.

different degrees of security. Some institutions, as we have stated, have acknowledged these distinctions by defining a class of part-time faculty eligible for tenure with attendant rights and responsibilities. Of more concern, however, is minimal employment security for much larger numbers of part-time faculty members, based not on probation and potential tenure but on more careful initial screening and periodic review by faculty colleagues.

We realize that fluctuations in enrollment can create unanticipated staffing needs. In most instances, however, one should be able to anticipate at least a term in advance how many sections of a given course will need to be staffed. In practice, colleges and universities often staff courses at the last minute, and as a consequence part-time appointments are typically made upon the recommendation of a department chair to a dean without benefit of opinion from others in the department. This practice has fostered a two-class system in which part-time faculty members are often isolated from their full-time colleagues. Often they are left out of departmental meetings; they do not participate in curricular planning; they have no vote in departmental affairs; and they are afforded no opportunity for peer review or for advancement through the academic ranks.

WE RECOMMEND that part-time faculty members not be appointed routinely or repeatedly at the last minute. The practice of continually appointing the same part-time faculty member on term-by-term contracts with employment contingent upon enrollment is, in the large majority of cases, callous and unnecessary.

WE RECOMMEND that in those instances when cancellation of a course leaves a part-time faculty member without an expected appointment, financial compensation should be made for the time spent in preparing the course and for dealing with the course prior to its cancellation.

WE RECOMMEND that, where part-time employment is not casual and occasional, colleges and universities should endeavor to regularize their use of part-time faculty members so that they can be appointed in closer conformity to standards and procedures governing full-time faculty members. We hesitate a little in recommending formal notice requirements or a presumption of renewal after a specified period. We have seen such policies lead to subversion of the principle of adequate notice by issuing blanket notification of nonrenewal by the specified date, with the real decision in individual cases held off until later. Part-time as well as full-time faculty members are, however, entitled to individual consideration in the renewal process. Accordingly,

WE RECOMMEND that part-time faculty who have been employed for six or more terms, or consecutively for three or more terms, receive a full term's notice. Any lesser period may prevent their reentry into the part-time market, given the cyclical nature of academic appointments. The issuance of notice should be preceded by a more thorough faculty role in the evaluation process than is customarily the case with part-time faculty members.

WE RECOMMEND that colleges and universities afford part-time faculty members the protections of academic due process summarized in the Association's *Academic Freedom and Due Process for Faculty Members Who Serve Less Than Full Time*. In particular, part-time faculty members should have access to the institution's regular grievance procedure.

3. The Role of Part-Time Faculty in Academic Governance

The differing levels of involvement of part-time faculty members in the life of the institution should be reflected in the degree of their involvement in institutional governance. The occasional part-time faculty member usually has nothing to do with the faculty as a whole, and even his or her participation in departmental committees and curricular planning tends to be negligible. The more considerable commitment of the part-time faculty member whose service is more like that of a full-timer does, however, raise the question of whether these part-time faculty members should have the right or the obligation to participate in governance and departmental decisions; whether, for example, they should have voting rights. Empirical evidence demonstrates that most part-time faculty, even the regular part-time faculty member whose responsibilities include many nonteaching activities, tend to have little formal role in university or departmental governance.[16] As a consequence, their status within the university or college community is diminished.

---

[16] Tuckman, Vogler, and Caldwell, *Part-Time Faculty Series.*

Crucial for the sense of professional pride and responsibility which characterize the academic profession is the central role full-time faculty members traditionally play in the determination of the structure and content of curricula, individual courses, and teaching materials. Similarly, a sense of professionalism is derived from the significant role faculty members play in governing academic departments and in the governance of institutions of higher learning. Without access to the governing bodies, a faculty member's sense of professionalism is impaired, to the potential detriment of the quality of the educational process in which he or she is involved. Faculty members who are treated like "hired hands," with syllabi they have played no role in preparing, may be insufficiently motivated to perform with the care and ingenuity of the faculty member who is actively involved in shaping his or her environment.

When a faculty is organized for purposes of collective bargaining, the appropriate test of inclusion in the bargaining unit that is used by the National Labor Relations Board is whether or not a "community of interest" or a "mutuality of interest" exists among the members of the proposed unit. If there is a category of part-time faculty members composed of those who are eligible for tenure, it appears likely that they would be included in a bargaining unit with full-time faculty members. Indeed, the few part-time faculty members who are in this category are often called "fractional time" or "full time with reduced load" rather than part time. Similar claims for inclusion might be made by part-time faculty members paid on a pro-rata basis,[17] independent of their qualifications or security entitlements. Politically, the inclusion of part-time faculty is often viewed as threatening to the interests of the full-time faculty, and, to the degree that the part-time faculty and full-time faculty have different commitments to the institution, the threat becomes more real. There is a basic problem as to whether a bargaining unit composed primarily of full-time faculty members can fairly represent the part-time faculty if they are included in the bargaining unit. And, if the part-time faculty are excluded from the unit, will the administration exploit them and use them to undercut the full-time faculty?[18] Throughout this statement on part-time faculty problems, we make proposals designed for the better integration of part-time faculty and full-time faculty. We believe that a better integration will improve the quality of education and the academic climate. We also believe that, as institutions move toward improved communication between part-time and full-time faculty members, the likelihood of the difficulties posed above occurring in a collective bargaining situation will be lessened.

Universities and colleges should recognize that participation in academic governance is likely to enhance a faculty member's sense of professionalism and elicit a higher quality of performance than can otherwise be expected. Moreover, the institution would benefit from the part-time faculty member's contributions.

> WE RECOMMEND, whenever possible and erring on the side of inclusion rather than exclusion, that part-time faculty members be involved in the determination of goals, techniques, and schedules for those courses which they teach. Moreover, they should be actively involved in planning the curricula of which their courses are a part. To the extent that other, more general, considerations which are dealt with by departmental or institution-wide committees impinge on these more specific matters relative to courses taught by part-time faculty, these faculty members should serve as participating members on such committees. If part-time faculty members are subject to appropriate review procedures and have, as they should, access to the regular institutional grievance procedure, they should also be represented on the bodies concerned with these matters when cases involving part-time faculty are heard.

[17] A part-time faculty member who receives pro-rata compensation is paid that percentage of the compensation of a similarly qualified full-time faculty member represented by the ratio of the part-time teaching load (measured by contact hours) to the full-time counterpart. Under this arrangement, other responsibilities are not taken into consideration in determining workload.

[18] At some institutions the part-time faculty have a separate bargaining unit; this can also lead to playing off the interests of the two units against one another.

4. Compensation and Fringe Benefits for Part-Time Faculty

Recent studies suggest that most part-time faculty members teach at a per-course rate less than that paid to full-time faculty members.[19] Data also suggest that they receive fewer fringe benefits than their full-time counterparts. This is especially true where the individual part-time faculty member teaches less than half time and does not participate in the range of faculty responsibilities outside the classroom. There is also a small portion of the part-time labor market that is paid on a pro-rata basis and is eligible for cost-of-living and merit increases. One study concludes that a little more than one-quarter of all institutions currently prorate compensation.[20] The practice of paying a flat rate per course or per student hour to part-time faculty does little to relate the part-time salary payment scale to the salary rates paid to full-time faculty. Bearing in mind that part-time faculty members differ widely among themselves in the nature of the duties they perform, the qualifications they possess, and the disciplines in which they work, and appreciating the differences among them in need, expectation, and bargaining power, we believe that simple fairness obligates institutions to rationalize their compensation of part-time faculty members and to develop policies that treat part-time faculty equitably.

WE RECOMMEND that colleges and universities, through their regular procedures, devise equitable scales for paying part-time faculty members.

Although the task is difficult, it is necessary for colleges and universities to develop appropriate criteria for comparing part-time and full-time responsibilities, properly taking into account nonteaching activities and individual qualifications. The criteria would enable an institution to determine which part-time faculty members appropriately should be paid on a pro-rata scale and which should be paid on a per-course or per-student-hour basis. In either case, some provision should be made for merit, seniority, and cost-of-living increases.

Discussion regarding compensation of part-time faculty often proceeds upon the assumption that for many compensation is extra, a component, but not an essential component, of the family income. This appears no longer to be the case for an increasing number of part-time faculty members.[21] Even if it were true, we do not believe that the degree of individuals' financial dependency on their employer should enter significantly into a determination of compensation for part-time faculty. In the past, such considerations contributed unduly to the practice of paying housewives who taught part time appreciably less than their male counterparts.[22] These considerations are often cited in defense of various scales of compensation and of particular salaries as well as to justify other employers' practices. We believe that they should not be relevant to the measurement of the degree of a faculty member's commitment to his or her institution nor of the commitment that the institution should make to the faculty member.

In discussing compensation we must also bear in mind that colleges and universities utilize part-time faculty members in order to effect monetary economies and flexibility in staffing the academic program. What must be guarded against are practices which exploit the part-time faculty, contribute to poor morale, and adversely affect the quality of education. Such practices inevitably injure not only part-time faculty members, but also their full-time colleagues and, most of all, students.

For many part-time faculty, a wage scale based on a per-course rate or a per-hour rate is reasonable. The full-time faculty member who teaches an additional course as an overload may be paid for it on a per-course basis; the business executive, secondary-school teacher, lawyer, or government official who teaches a single course, either occasionally or regularly, does not look to the part-time position as a primary professional commitment. By and large, these part-time faculty teach for stimulation, prestige, and variety, while the pay provided them supplements their basic income. More importantly, most of these part-time faculty members are appointed to teach, and the nonteaching functions performed by full-time faculty are not their concern. Their own professional development is not significantly related to their part-time teaching work. The time they spend on reading and research, on participating in meetings and

---

[19] See Howard P. Tuckman and William D. Vogler, "The 'Part' in Part-Time Wages," and "The Fringes of a Fringe Group: Part-Timers in Academe," *Part-Time Faculty Series*, 1–15, 40–52.

[20] Leslie and Head, "Part-Time Faculty Rights," 60.

[21] Tuckman and Vogler, "The Fringes of a Fringe Group," 50–52.

[22] Barbara H. Tuckman and Howard P. Tuckman, "Part-Timers, Sex Discrimination, and Career Choice at Two-Year Institutions: Further Findings from the AAUP Survey," *Academe* 66 (1980): 71–76.

presenting talks, usually relates to their primary employment and is compensated by that employer. If, in line with our previous recommendations, some of these part-time faculty members do become more involved in advising, departmental and curricular work, and related responsibilities, their compensation should reflect this greater commitment.

Of particular concern to us is the 30 percent of the part-time faculty population who teach one or more courses only because they cannot find a full-time position. Often the income they derive from their teaching—and some piece together two or three part-time positions at different institutions in order to have the equivalent of a full-time position—provides their sole means of support. These faculty members tend to teach the same courses regularly and frequently perform at least part of the range of nonteaching duties of their full-time counterparts. They deserve adequate compensation and security, being peculiarly vulnerable to the exploitation we discussed earlier. These part-time faculty members are also the unwilling subject of the tensions affecting the members of the full-time faculty who have a voice in the establishment of rates of part-time compensation. If a certain amount of highly cost-effective teaching is done by part-time faculty, their own compensation will be higher. On the other hand, this would mean that the out-of-classroom duties associated with the courses and students taught by the part-time faculty must often be performed by the full-time faculty. If the ratio of full-time to part-time faculty becomes small, the full-time faculty can become overburdened and the quality of education will suffer. Moreover, increasing numbers of part-time faculty members are being appointed in an attempt to avoid any institutional commitment to tenure; the presence of large numbers of faculty serving "at will" can have a chilling effect on general conditions of academic freedom at the institution as well as on academic quality. Finally, the presence of a source of cheap substitute labor may well depress the compensation scale of full-time faculty. What is required is a balance between retaining institutional flexibility and avoiding the exploitation of part-time faculty which may lead to the exploitation of full-time faculty as well.

Accrediting bodies have been guided by various ratios to express the desired balance between full-time and part-time faculty in a healthy academic institution. Such ratios grew out of the perception that part-time faculty members, because of their commitment of time to an institution, were unable to provide the amount of administrative service, curricular planning, and service in academic governance considered appropriate to sustain a vigorous academic enterprise. Currently it is more difficult to gauge what proportion of a curriculum in a variety of disciplines can be taught by part-time faculty without endangering the quality of education. Colleges and universities must be mindful of the dangers of misusing part-time faculty members and eroding their academic standards. They must recognize the diverse ways in which part-time service can be used and the variety of needs of the different kinds of part-time faculty members they employ. Where the part-time faculty members function largely as full-time faculty but on reduced time, and where they are similarly qualified, institutions should develop commensurate pay scales and fringe benefit packages. They should consider whether pro-rata compensation would, in the long run, enhance not only the purses of the part-time faculty members but also the health of the institution as a whole.

No overriding legal principle requires that part-time faculty members receive prorated compensation, but considerations of fairness and regard for overall institutional welfare point to an increasing need to identify the part-time faculty members who are carrying workloads that can be legitimately considered comparable to a portion of a full-time workload at the same institution and to compensate them on a pro-rata basis.

> WE RECOMMEND that the part-time faculty member whose contribution to the academic program of the institution and to its academic life is equal to that of a full-timer except for the proportion of time given to the position, and whose qualifications are comparable, receive prorated compensation.[23]

If an equivalency between full-time and part-time workloads is inappropriate, pay scales should be devised which reflect the similarities and differences that distinguish part-time workloads

---

[23] A policy of prorated compensation is often seen as an attempt to eliminate part-time faculty members by making them as expensive to employ as are full-timers. This is not what we propose. We believe there should be the option of part-time employment for those who prefer it and, moreover, that only those whose qualifications and duties are comparable in every way except in amount of time to those of full-time faculty have a claim to pro-rata compensation.

from full-time ones. The criteria should include (a) the nature of the service being performed—whether it includes nonteaching functions such as advising, research, curriculum planning, and participation in governance; (b) the qualifications of the faculty member; (c) the length of time, either continuous or interrupted, served by the part-time faculty member at the particular institution; and (d) the market value of the discipline being taught. These criteria would enable colleges and universities to compare full-time workloads meaningfully and to determine which of their part-time faculty deserve pro-rata compensation, which deserve a salary scale that rewards merit and length of service, and which can be appropriately compensated on a per-course or per-hour basis, and at what rates.

Institutions should also devise ways to reward part-time faculty members who teach continuously over a number of years, whether they carry only one course per term or a heavier load. Career progression is one mechanism to recognize meritorious work; another is to ensure periodic raises for continuing part-time faculty, on either a seniority or a merit basis. This allows a measure of reward for the more senior part-time faculty member and acknowledges the contribution that continuity of instruction makes to academic life. A system of merit pay would also help prevent the lapse in skills which may occur if part-time faculty members continue to be treated as marginal and are given no incentive to maintain or improve their skills.

Fringe benefits are another means by which colleges and universities can offer security and monetary rewards to their part-time faculty. Fringe benefit policies in higher education vary widely and reflect the essentially unplanned and unregulated growth of policies designed to attend to the needs and interests of part-time faculty members. The average part-time faculty member is not likely to receive fringe benefit coverage, other than that mandated by law, from his or her academic appointment. Only a limited number of institutions have developed fringe benefit policies in which the benefits for part-time faculty members are prorated in proportion to their workload.[24] Many colleges and universities make no contributions to the costs of the fringe benefits extended to part-time faculty members, and often they do not even provide part-time faculty members with access to the fringe benefits available to full-time faculty. A substantial number of part-time faculty members have no retirement, disability, health, or life insurance coverage through their employment.[25]

A part-time faculty member's need for fringe benefit coverage varies in accordance with his or her dependence upon the employing institution as the primary source of income and benefits. Nonetheless, we would assert here, too, that need alone should not dictate the liberality of an institution's fringe benefit policy. Rather, such benefits should be viewed in part as a means to grant recognition of the vital services being performed by a faculty member, part time or full time. While remaining mindful of the administrative costs entailed in extending different types of benefit coverage,

> WE RECOMMEND that colleges and universities design policies on fringe benefits which reflect the varying kinds of commitments made by the part-time members of the faculty.

> WE RECOMMEND that the part-time faculty member whose work is indistinguishable from that of the full-timer with the exception of the proportion of time spent in the activity should have the opportunity to participate in nonmandatory fringe benefits on a prorated basis if his or her workload at the institution is continuous over several years. Where institutions have developed tenure policies for part-time faculty members, fairness urges that these institutions provide part-time faculty members who are eligible for tenure with, at a minimum, access to the full range of fringe benefits available to their full-time colleagues. They should also be allowed access to fringe benefits such as group medical or dental programs on a prorated basis.

Institutions which make nonmandatory fringe benefits available to part-time faculty members on a prorated basis will have to establish criteria to compare the workloads of part-time faculty to those of full-time faculty. We realize that this will incur increased administrative costs, and the certification of workload for the purposes of establishing eligibility for fringe benefits can also add to administrative costs.

---

[24] Tuckman and Vogler, "The Fringes of a Fringe Group," 40–42.
[25] *Ibid.*

It should also be noted that because there is a "large and increasing number of part-time faculty who are forced to rely on their earnings from part-time employment as a sole source of income,"[26] we are discussing a group of faculty members whose situation is economically most precarious, and made more so by the lack of such employment security benefits as unemployment insurance, social security, and retirement benefits. An infusion of university funds to enhance their benefit package rather than their salary could well be a more efficient use of funds for employer and employee alike.

In determining which benefits ought to be prorated for part-time faculty, institutions will have to weigh the cost of providing such nonmandatory benefits as life and medical insurance, workers' compensation, and sick leave against the importance of the benefit in relation to the category of part-time faculty member involved. At a minimum, however,

> WE RECOMMEND equal access for all part-time faculty members to such fringe benefits as medical and dental insurance, and, where possible, the prorating of the employer's contribution. Institutions should endeavor to provide part-time faculty members with access to retirement or life insurance coverage which has a vested component[27] as well as a number of fringe benefits, e.g., tuition remission, which are of less out-of-pocket cost to an institution but which may be extremely valuable to the part-time faculty member.

Needed now are clearly articulated individual institutional policies that address which fringe benefits should be made available to part-time faculty members, on what basis, and at what costs. Varying approaches are possible. All, however, should have certain common goals: (a) that part-time faculty members be treated consistently; (b) that part-time faculty members be given access to all fringe benefits; (c) that continuing and substantial service performed by a part-time faculty member entitles the part-time faculty member to a degree of security; (d) that incentives are needed for part-time faculty members to retain and improve their skills; and (e) that a part-time faculty member whose duties and qualifications are essentially equivalent to those of his or her full-time counterpart should receive compensation proportionate to the full-time counterpart.

The implementation of many of the recommendations of this report will inevitably result in increased costs to the college or university employing part-time faculty. Some full-time faculty members, and some who are part time, may view some of these recommendations as antithetical to their interests. To the extent that the result of changes in policies regarding part-time faculty is an improvement in the quality of education, we believe that they should be sought; if, however, they can be shown to diminish flexibility severely, both for the institution in its special staffing needs and for those faculty members who choose for personal reasons a less-than-full-time commitment to teaching, particular changes may not be desirable. Colleges and universities should arrive at an appropriate balance after weighing the various considerations. Ultimately, if part-time faculty can attain a less precarious status, the academic enterprise as a whole should benefit.

---

[26] Tuckman and Vogler, "The Fringes of a Fringe Group," 49.
[27] TIAA-CREF allows a part-time faculty member to participate in its annuity plans, even in the absence of an employer's contribution. This can afford a useful tax shelter to some.

Senior Appointments with Reduced Loads

The statement which follows was approved by the Association's Committee on the Status of Women in the Academic Profession in April 1987 and by the Committee on Academic Freedom and Tenure (Committee A) in June 1987.

In its 1980 report on the *Status of Part-Time Faculty*, Committee A noted that the 1940 *Statement of Principles on Academic Freedom and Tenure* "refers, with respect to tenure, only to those appointed to full-time service." The concept of tenure rested on a view of part-time service as occasional, adjunct, and cost-effective in terms of flexibility; it assumed no ongoing institutional commitment; and it assumed that part-time faculty members were properly relieved of responsibility for the institution's academic program.

Committee A's 1980 report reflected a significant change in perceptions of the nature of part-time service. Citing the 1973 recommendation of the Commission on Academic Tenure in Higher Education, the report agreed that institutions should "consider modifying their tenure arrangements in order to permit part-time faculty service under appropriate conditions to be credited toward the award of tenure, and to permit tenured positions to be held by faculty members who for family or other appropriate reasons cannot serve on a full-time basis." While Committee A recognized that many part-time faculty members are not potential candidates for tenure, it recommended that colleges and universities "consider creating a class of regular part-time faculty members, consisting of individuals who, as their professional career, share the teaching, research, and administrative duties customary for faculty at their institution, but who for whatever reason do so less than full-time." This class of part-time faculty, the report concluded, "should have the opportunity to achieve tenure and the rights it confers."

Additional benefit would be derived from policies and practices that open senior academic appointments to persons with reduced loads and salaries without loss of status.

In the light of Committee A's recommendation, a senior appointee might choose, for whatever reason, to reduce proportionately his or her overall duties at the institution. If the faculty member were tenured, there would be no loss of the protections of due process and the other entitlements that accrue with tenure;[1] if the faculty member were nontenured, the policy might permit continuance with an "opportunity to achieve tenure and the rights it confers."

These appointments would not normally be made available if the individual were seeking reduction of the academic commitment in order to accept a teaching position elsewhere. Criteria for professional advancement, including promotion in rank, should be the same for all faculty appointees, whether they serve full time or with reduced loads. Where there is mutual agreement among the faculty member, the department, and the college or university administration, opportunity should exist for a faculty member to move from a full to a reduced load and back to full-time status, depending on the needs of the individual and the institution.

These modified appointments would help meet the special needs of individual faculty members, especially those with child-rearing and other personal responsibilities, as well as those seeking a reduced workload as a step toward retirement. A more flexible policy for senior appointments (whether tenured or nontenured) would increase the opportunities available both to individuals and to institutions with respect to faculty appointments.

---

[1] Where the action to reduce a full-time tenured faculty member to part-time status is mandated by a declared financial exigency or discontinuance of program, AAUP policy calls for the preservation of the protections of tenure and for continuance of salary on a pro-rata basis. (See Committee A report on "Academic Freedom and Tenure: Eastern Oregon State College," *Academe: Bulletin of the AAUP* 68 [May–June 1982]: 1a–8a, for further discussion of this issue.)

On Full-Time Non-Tenure-Track Appointments

The report which follows, prepared by a subcommittee of the Association's Committee on Academic Freedom and Tenure (Committee A), was approved by Committee A in June 1986.

INTRODUCTION

Regulation 1(b) of the Association's *Recommended Institutional Regulations on Academic Freedom and Tenure* provides that, "with the exception of special appointments clearly limited to a brief association with the institution, and reappointments of retired faculty members on special conditions, all full-time faculty appointments are of two kinds: (1) probationary appointments; (2) appointments with continuous tenure." As the authors of Committee A's 1978 report *On Full-Time Non-Tenure-Track Appointments* concluded,

> We think that the very limited exceptions allowed by Regulation 1(b) are the most that should be allowed. The teacher with tenure is a teacher whose service can be terminated only for adequate cause; and we think that every full-time teacher should either have that status or be a candidate for it—save for those who fall under the exceptions allowed by Regulation 1(b), in particular, those who are visitors, or temporary replacements, or for whose subjects the institution in good faith expects to have only a short-term need.[1]

Since 1978, regularly funded fixed-term, annually renewable, or indefinite full-time tenure-ineligible appointments (some of them with rather eccentric or unorthodox titles), running parallel to, and in many cases replacing, traditional tenure-track positions, have remained a persistent phenomenon in American colleges and universities. At some institutions and in certain disciplinary fields the number of faculty members appointed to such non-tenure-track positions is continuing to grow. The AAUP has recognized that these non-tenure-track appointments do considerable damage both to principles of academic freedom and tenure and to the quality of our academic institutions—not to mention the adverse consequences for the individuals serving in such appointments.

The subcommittee's task has been to examine and assess the current dimensions of this staffing practice and the arguments made in its support; to review the findings and recommendations of the 1978 subcommittee report on this subject; and to analyze the implications which the continuing proliferation of these appointments may have for the future of higher education.

THE SCOPE AND EXTENT OF THE PROBLEM

Informed discussion of the issues raised by the use of non-tenure-track positions must begin with an analysis of the scope and extent of the problem. Looking at the academic profession as a whole, we have examined data on individual faculty *members* as well as on *positions* at institutions which, taken together, provide an overview of the current situation. The data on *persons* come from a sample survey of 5,000 faculty members conducted by the Carnegie Foundation for the Advancement of Teaching in the spring of 1984 (a similar national survey was also conducted in 1975). The data on *positions*, collected in connection with the preparation of the AAUP's Annual Report on the Economic Status of the Profession, comprise some 163,000 full-time appointments for each of the past two academic years (1984–86) at approximately 800 academic institutions that provided tenure information. According to the Carnegie survey, between 10.6 percent

---

[1] *AAUP Bulletin* 64 (1978): 273.

and 12.6 percent of full-time faculty were not on a tenure track (nor "covered for job security" by a collective-bargaining agreement) in the spring of 1984.[2] The AAUP data indicate that nearly 10 percent of all full-time positions included in the surveys were nontenure track.

The data on hand reveal increasing uniformity in the number of non-tenure-track positions across ranks and types of institution, suggesting that the practice may well be on the way toward becoming entrenched. Indeed, according to the most recent available data from the National Research Council, between 25 percent and 40 percent of all first-time junior faculty appointments in 1981 were to non-tenure-eligible positions.[3] In addition, data from the 1975 and 1984 Carnegie surveys suggest that most types of institutions experienced an increase (often quite substantial) in the proportion of nontenured faculty members who were serving in a full-time capacity but were not eligible for tenure.

The available data show that among women included in the 1984–85 AAUP compensation survey, 16.5 percent, or 6,816, served in non-tenure-track positions. These data suggest that between 40 and 45 percent of all non-tenure-track positions surveyed were filled by women—a striking statistic when one considers that women held only 25 percent of the total number of full-time faculty positions covered in the survey. Of the more than 8,000 positions held by women at the instructor and nonprofessorial ranks, more than half were in non-tenure-track positions.

The subcommittee has examined several recent studies which surveyed the incidence of full-time faculty members serving in non-tenure-track appointments. A 1984 American Council on Education survey of full-time faculty in the humanities found that the number and proportion of "core humanities" faculty outside the tenure system has increased, while the proportion eligible for tenure, but not yet tenured, has fallen. Only 40 percent of the new "core humanities" appointments made in the 1982–83 academic year were to tenured or tenure-track positions. In political science, according to an American Political Science Association survey, over 30 percent of all new full-time faculty members during the 1983–84 and 1984–85 academic years received non-tenure-track appointments.

Although data for other fields are hard to come by, the creation and expansion of non-tenure-eligible positions are clearly not limited to faculty in the humanities and social sciences. They are also quite common in the natural sciences and in rapidly expanding fields like computer science. In many professional schools as well, particularly in the health sciences and in schools of law, new appointments to tenure-ineligible clinical positions appear to be the norm rather than the exception.

In sum, the available data support the view that a far-from-negligible class of more or less permanent "temporary" faculty, a disproportionate number of them women, has become an established feature of American higher education.

STATED REASONS FOR THE USE OF NON-TENURE-TRACK APPOINTMENTS

Numerous forms of appointment exist for faculty members who serve in non-tenure-track positions. The authors of the Association's 1978 report usefully distinguished three principal types of non-tenure-track teachers:

> The first hold indefinitely renewable appointments: the faculty members are appointed for one or more years and are told that their appointments may be renewed—no limit is placed on the number of possible renewals. The second hold "limited renewable" appointments: the faculty members are told that their (usually one-year) appointments may be renewed so many times only. . . . The third occupy "folding chairs": the faculty member's initial appointments (usually for two or three years) are explicitly terminal—no renewal is possible under any circumstances.

---

[2] The lower estimate assumes that all faculty members who held an acting or visiting appointment had tenure at the institution from which they were visiting.
[3] *Departing the Ivy Halls* (Washington, D.C.: National Academy of Sciences, 1983).

The data reported in the surveys cited above do not separate out or distinguish among these various kinds of tenure-ineligible appointments. Whatever the type of non-tenure-track position utilized, however—whether renewable indefinitely, renewable until a stated maximum duration is reached, or fixed-term "folding chair"—the same general arguments have been advanced over the years in justification of these appointments, above all the flexibility they afford the institution in terms of financial investment and programmatic commitments.

Faced with the possibility (and the reality) of shifts in student interests and declining enrollments as well as cutbacks in federal, state, and foundation support, colleges and universities have looked to less costly alternatives to traditional staffing patterns and have seized upon the full-time non-tenure-track position as one of the most convenient of these alternatives. The argument is frequently made that, because individuals appointed to such positions are typically engaged only to teach lower-level classes and thus have attenuated responsibilities as compared with tenure-track faculty members who are also expected to do research and institutional service, the institution is justified in paying them lower salaries and/or giving them heavier teaching loads. Additional savings can accrue by not providing non-tenure-track faculty with normal merit pay increases and fringe benefits—such as institutional research grants, travel subsidies, professional meeting allowances, and sabbaticals. In the case of other benefits (e.g., pensions), there may be a waiting period before the individual attains eligibility. Moreover, most non-tenure-track faculty usually do not achieve the higher salaries based on seniority and promotion through the ranks that tenure-track and tenured faculty would; their opportunities for advancement tend to be limited even if they are reappointed for many years. In addition, if the non-tenure-track faculty are not engaged in research, there are significant ancillary cost savings: fewer demands on the institution for secretarial and research assistance, library and computer facilities, equipment, and office and laboratory space.

Along with financial savings, institutions have found the use of full-time non-tenure-track appointments attractive for their promised contribution to administrative and programmatic flexibility. Colleges and universities can cut or transfer positions without conforming with the standards for notice or the normal procedures for evaluation of performance that are required for regular probationary faculty. New programs can be instituted without requiring a long-term commitment to funding a particular faculty member whose skills and expertise may not be needed should the innovation prove to be of only transient interest. An institution thus can explore student demand for a discipline or field not currently represented among the tenured or tenure-track faculty. The classification of positions as tenure ineligible also enables colleges and universities that are concerned that too high a percentage of the faculty holds tenure to keep down the number of those who enter the tenured ranks.

A complementary argument is that as regular full-time positions are vacated in traditional fields, full-time slots should be filled only on a non-tenure-track basis, because either declining enrollments may be expected in the particular field or expanding enrollments may occur in other fields. It is argued that in fields of declining enrollments, especially where an oversupply of potential faculty appointees exists, the institution does not need to offer very attractive positions. Conversely, in fields where there is a shortage of faculty and high student demand, it is argued either that no one in those fields needs long-term security or that no one really qualified is available, and thus that the position should be filled only on a temporary basis with whoever can be found.

Non-tenure-track appointments do indeed appear to afford an institution greater flexibility. They carry no continued institutional commitment to the support of a program or to the employment of an individual, no matter how excellent either might be. Notwithstanding the oft-made assertion that non-tenure-track appointments are being used primarily to enable institutions to hedge their long-term support for certain positions as opposed to particular individuals, however, the subcommittee doubts that "flexibility" is actually an objective in many non-tenure-track appointments which are currently being made. In fact, a substantial proportion of these appointments are being made in fields that are central to the institution's academic program, with assignment to courses in which continued enrollment is virtually guaranteed. In addition, we must question whether any real flexibility is achieved when a significant number of those who serve in non-tenure-track positions are reappointed indefinitely year after year—attaining de facto tenure without a formal judgment about their qualifications ever having been made.

ADVERSE EFFECTS OF THESE APPOINTMENTS

It seems clear that the expanded use of full-time non-tenure-track appointments can be an expedient answer to fiscal and enrollment problems facing colleges and universities—if saving money is the key consideration. But, in the judgment of this subcommittee, the savings realized are at an inordinately high cost to the quality of the entire academic enterprise. In the remainder of this report we turn to an examination of the serious adverse repercussions of non-tenure-track appointments for individual faculty members, for scholarship and learning, for students, and for institutions of higher learning themselves. In the discussion that follows, the subcommittee has relied upon a variety of sources, some more impressionistic than others, but we have confidence in the accuracy of the picture that has emerged.

1. *Effects on the Non-Tenure-Track Faculty Members Themselves*

The most immediate adverse impact of non-tenure-track appointments, of course, is on those occupying these positions. What seems to have developed at many colleges and universities in the United States is a class of insecure full-time faculty members whose status is inferior to that of both their tenure-eligible and their tenured colleagues and whose role in some respects does not differ from that of teaching assistants. They find themselves frequently at the margins of departmental and institutional life. In many cases they are neither required nor expected—and often not permitted—to advise students, to play a role in faculty personnel and budgetary matters, or to participate in the development of curricula and the formulation and implementation of academic policy. They are, as the 1978 report on this subject observed, denied "full and equal faculty membership irrespective of the nature of the service they have given and irrespective of the professional excellence of that service." They tend to receive less desirable teaching assignments, larger classes, and heavier teaching loads. Their compensation tends to remain low, no matter how well they perform their circumscribed role. Indeed, a rigorous periodic review of their performance may not occur at all.

The appointment of full-time faculty members with attenuated responsibilities serves to develop an underclass, precluded from participation in faculty governance by rule and, in too many cases, from scholarly pursuits and other professional activities by necessity. These faculty members are faced with precarious employment prospects, and hence an uncertain professional future, and are generally without the time, status, and opportunity—or the rewards—to develop themselves professionally as teachers and scholars. Because many of them are appointed to "teach-only" positions, they cannot develop the habits of the professional academic, especially the regular and ongoing pursuit of new knowledge and the periodic revision of their courses. They are often forced to endure recurrent slights from their senior colleagues, who, in the words of one non-tenure-track appointee, "seem to take it for granted that people who accept temporary appointments are somehow deficient or suspect academically."[4] They frequently work in unprofessional and "anti-professional" conditions, relatively cut off from collegial stimulation and support, disconnected from other members of the profession (and the discipline) beyond the department, and lacking both access to institutional resources necessary for building a research career and the incentive or the pressure to become productive scholars. Many are overworked and are necessarily distracted by the constant, time-consuming (and expensive) preoccupation of pursuing their next position. Even those with relatively long-term contracts, who stay in one place for an extended period and are thus able to avoid the disruptions in their work and their lives that attend frequent moves, rarely have opportunities for research, because of heavy teaching loads. They have little in the way of research and other assistance, facilities, or travel money; at some institutions they cannot serve as principal investigator or project director on a grant, even in those cases where research is part of their academic responsibilities. They are rarely eligible for sabbaticals or even for leaves without pay for professional development.

---

[4] Barbara K. Townsend, "Outsiders Inside Academe: The Plight of the Temporary Teachers," *Chronicle of Higher Education*, 28 May 1986, 72.

Individuals who hold indefinitely renewable appointments and who function like regular and ongoing full-time faculty members, but who have no prospect of tenure because of the way their position happens to be defined, serve with their academic freedom in continuous jeopardy. As the authors of the Association's 1978 report observed, "The teachers who must go, hat in hand, every year (or every two years, or every three years) indefinitely into the future, to ask if they may stay, are not teachers who can feel free to speak and write the truth as they see it." Not surprisingly, the more cautious among them are likely to avoid controversy in their classes or with the deans and department heads on whose good will they are dependent for periodic reappointment. The institution may express its commitment to protect their academic freedom, but to those whose appointment may not be renewed solely at the administration's discretion such a commitment may seem of little value—and best not tested. Moreover, as the numbers of non-tenure-track faculty members increase, their freedom is placed in greater jeopardy. The contagion of insecurity restricts unorthodox thinking, while the rising number of non-tenure-track faculty reduces the cadre of those faculty members—notably those with tenure—who are uninhibited in advocating changes in accepted ideas and in the policies and programs of the institutions at which they serve.

2. Effects on Students and the Learning Process

As one critic has observed, the extensive use of full-time non-tenure-track appointments "not only compromises individual working lives and individual careers, but [also] contributes to the dysfunctioning of our colleges and universities as organizations."[5] At a time marked by calls for excellence and more rigorous standards in higher education, the abuse of non-tenure-track appointments can undermine academic standards and lead to the erosion of the quality of undergraduate education. It is difficult to develop a coherent curriculum, maintain uniform standards for evaluating students' performance, or establish continuity between and among courses when major academic responsibilities are divided among "transient" and regular faculty, especially when they have relatively little interaction with one another. Students are denied a stable learning environment and consistent quality instruction by continuous "rotating-out" of faculty. Temporary faculty are less likely to be deeply concerned about or interested in the future of the institution that currently employs them, thus contributing to an institutional environment that discourages students' involvement in learning outside the classroom. Even if these faculty members are interested or concerned, and many are, they may not have the time or the opportunity to develop an institutional memory. They are also less likely to have the time—or the inclination—to direct their creative energies into innovative approaches to teaching or to keep abreast of current developments in their field.

Students are likely to be short-changed in still other ways. Non-tenure-track appointees tend to be assigned to lower-division, undergraduate teaching, often in large lecture classes, and consigned to nothing but routine pedagogy, to their systematic or total exclusion from other courses and levels of courses. According to one observer, "assigning [temporary] faculty to introductory-level courses often creates divisions within a department: those who teach low-prestige 'service' courses to freshmen and sophomores, and those who teach high-prestige upper-division and graduate courses. Such a division implies that the professional standing of the [regular] faculty is unnecessary for teaching 'service' courses," that is, courses which introduce students to an academic discipline.[6] This practice denies freshmen and sophomores the best possible instruction from regular faculty members; compromises academic standards; and raises questions about how seriously a particular department or an entire institution views its teaching function. It is also self-defeating, because the service courses often attract (or repel) potential candidates for advanced courses in the discipline. There is a pressing need for energetic,

[5] Martin Finkelstein, "Life on the 'Effectively Terminal' Tenure Track," Academe: Bulletin of the AAUP 72 (January–February 1986): 36.
[6] Maxine Hairston, "We're Hiring Too Many Temporary Instructors," Chronicle of Higher Education, 17 April 1985, 80.

dedicated, and respected teachers to staff introductory classes in which students can learn the critical thinking and writing skills they must have to succeed in college and beyond. According to the report issued by the National Institute of Education (NIE) Study Group on the Conditions of Excellence in American Higher Education, *Involvement in Learning: Realizing the Potential of American Higher Education*, "When most freshmen courses are taught by low-paid, low-status instructors, students quickly get the message that the department cares little about the large and diverse group of students in its lower-division courses." The NIE report goes on to recommend that "colleges assign as many of their finest instructors as possible to courses [that have] large numbers of first-year students."

We question whether the intellectual mission of a college or university is well served when the institution asserts that certain basic courses are indispensable for a liberal education but then assigns responsibility for those courses to faculty members who are deemed replaceable and unnecessary to the institution. Indeed, we believe that an institution reveals a certain indifference to its academic mission when it removes much of the basic teaching in required core courses from the purview of the regular professoriate. Far from "realizing the potential of American higher education" (the goal of the NIE report), this practice is virtually guaranteed to erode the quality and cohesiveness of a college's academic programs and to make the institution less attractive to prospective students.

3. Effects on Institutional Morale and Academic Governance

The presence of large numbers of temporary faculty members who must anxiously concern themselves from year to year with their status within the institution and the profession is hard on morale—theirs and that of everyone around them. In addition, for the institution as a whole the excessive use of non-tenure-track appointments, by creating a divided, two-class faculty, erodes collegiality and sound governance practices. As we have seen, temporary appointees are not fully integrated into the life of the institution: they are often treated like second-class citizens, mere "contract workers," disenfranchised from collegiate and departmental governance and often isolated from their colleagues.

The fact that many of their colleagues are running so fast just to stay in place in dead-end jobs also affects the current generation of tenure-track faculty members. More of the student advising, committee work, and other administrative duties will fall on them if their non-tenure-track colleagues have attenuated responsibilities and are excluded from the governance process. These burdens impinge upon their time for research and professional development. Moreover, the atmosphere will be less generally supportive of scholarly pursuits, to everyone's loss.

4. Effects on the Future of the Profession

Professors Howard R. Bowen and Jack H. Schuster, authors of the recently published book, *American Professors: A National Resource Imperiled*, state that their study was prompted by concern about the ability of "the higher education community . . . to recruit and retain excellent faculty not only in the immediate future but also over the next twenty-five years, when the replacement of the vast majority of the present faculties will be necessary."[7] That task, involving the recruitment of some 500,000 new faculty members, will not be an easy one, if recent experience is any guide. The NIE's report on excellence notes that the proportion of entering college freshmen planning to become college teachers dropped from 1.8 percent in 1966 to .25 percent in 1982, an 89 percent decline that, in the words of the report, "bodes ill for the future of higher education." Bowen and Schuster point to the fact that "an increasing proportion of doctoral candidates are finding employment in nonacademic industries and professions"; in particular, "higher education has become a steadily less attractive magnet . . . [for] exceptionally talented people such as Rhodes Scholars, members of Phi Beta Kappa, and honor graduates of prestigious institutions." Bowen and Schuster also "see great danger of a steady and growing drain of the ablest people now in the profession," for they are finding significantly more lucrative and professionally more

---

[7] "Outlook for the Academic Profession," *Academe* 71 (September–October 1985): 9–15.

rewarding and challenging career options that will utilize their considerable skills to a greater degree.

The increasing incidence and abuse of non-tenure-track appointments, at the very time when many of the brightest and most talented young men and women are abandoning any thought of pursuing a career in higher education, runs counter to efforts to "recruit, encourage, and develop talents of the highest caliber" and may well contribute to the growing flight from the profession of disappointed and frustrated junior faculty and eventually to a critical short-age of qualified college faculty members in the next generation. Given all the other ways in which colleges and universities are gradually losing their power to compete for current and future faculty talent, the continuing proliferation of these temporary positions—filled by underpaid instructors with low status and no job security—seems short-sighted and counter-productive, "undermin[ing] the attractiveness of careers in higher education both to incum-bents and to potential new entrants," who may be irretrievably lost to the professoriate.[8]

Bowen and Schuster have cited the "concern of faculty [with] the tendency of colleges and universities to shift institutional risk to faculty members by resorting to expedients that under-mine faculty career opportunities. One of these is to employ an increasing proportion of non-tenure-track faculty. . . . All of these practices tend to impair the attractiveness of the profession to younger faculty and to prospective faculty members." According to the NIE study, "Faculty are the core of the academic work force, and their status, morale, collegiality, and commitment to their institutions are critical to student learning. When we allow support for such a critical component of the enterprise to erode to the point at which the profession itself has become less attractive to our brightest students, we are compromising the future of higher learning in America."

Institutions of higher education have a responsibility to nurture talent, but the continued widespread use of non-tenure-track appointments may well destroy the careers of young facul-ty members, reduce the attractiveness of the profession for those fortunate enough to be able to enter it in the first place, undermine academic tenure, and threaten academic freedom. The gen-eral academic community—administrators, trustees, and faculty members alike—has a shared responsibility to foster, not to stifle, the development of a new generation of talented young scholars willing and able to fill the positions that will become available in the decades ahead.

CONCLUSIONS

The dangers to academia that were discussed in the Association's 1978 report *On Full-Time Non-Tenure-Track Appointments* have been shown in recent years to be extensive and serious. Higher education has come to rely increasingly on the services of faculty members who hold appointments in full-time, regularly funded positions that may be renewed indefinitely from year to year but provide no expectation of tenure after the successful completion of a fixed peri-od of probationary service. The persistence, and in some cases expansion, of this class of facul-ty members, especially where they have teaching responsibilities at the core of an institution's regular academic program, jeopardizes the foundations upon which the basic 1940 *Statement of Principles on Academic Freedom and Tenure* rests. Individuals who are offered full-time service only on non-tenure-track lines lack the financial, intellectual, and pedagogical security needed for the profession to be an attractive career choice for young scholars. Moreover, and of even greater importance, faculty members who hold such positions lack the security without which academic freedom and the right to pursue one's own contributions in research and teaching are but illusions.

Like the authors of the Association's statement *On the Imposition of Tenure Quotas*, this sub-committee recognizes that a "sound academic program needs elements not only of continuity but also of flexibility, which is served by the continuing opportunity to recruit new persons and

---

[8] Bowen and Schuster, "Outlook for the Academic Profession."

to pursue new academic emphases." At the same time, however, we share the concerns expressed in that statement regarding the too-facile invocation of considerations of flexibility, whether it is in support of tenure quotas or, as in this case, in defense of non-tenure-track appointments: "The system of tenure does not exist as subordinate to convenience and flexibility. The protection of academic freedom must take precedence over the claimed advantages of increased flexibility."[9]

While responsibility for the substantial increase in the extent to which our colleges and universities are staffed by non-tenure-track teachers rests primarily with administrative officers concerned both to save money and to retain a maximum degree of "managerial flexibility," other institutional constituencies must also bear some responsibility for this state of affairs. In particular, at many institutions senior faculty members have acquiesced in and even encouraged the appointment of large numbers of tenure-ineligible faculty members, perhaps out of a desire to free themselves for their own research and for teaching upper-division and graduate courses or in the belief that the resulting savings would leave more funding for their salaries and benefits. Ultimately, however, the general development of a more-or-less permanent two-tier system brings with it a class consciousness that affects the faculty's perception of itself, the students' perception of the faculty, and the outside world's perception of academe. By their relative lack of concern for their temporary colleagues and their tacit approval of the two-class system in hopes of maintaining and enhancing their own positions, these tenure-track and tenured faculty members may eventually bring to an end the cherished characteristics of their way of life.

Unfortunately, the problem as identified and discussed in 1978 has become more serious. In an era of financial stringency and of diminished national commitment to the development and expansion of higher education, the utilization of tenure-ineligible faculty positions has seemed an attractive strategy. Demographic uncertainties about the size of the college-age population in the future, along with uncertainties about which kinds of colleges and universities will be popular choices, reinforce the desire to have a large, insecure, and impermanent academic labor pool. We believe, however, that the reasons which have been advanced for the use of tenure-ineligible full-time faculty appointments are without merit and that, for the sake of higher education, of academic freedom, and of the professional security and future of coming generations of scholars and their students, the abuse of these appointments should be stopped.

[9] AAUP, *Policy Documents and Reports*, 9th ed. (Washington, D.C., 2001), 47–49.

The Status of Non-Tenure-Track Faculty

The report which follows was approved by the Association's Committee on Part-Time and Non-Tenure-Track Appointments and adopted by the Association's Council in June 1993.

Non-tenure-track faculty account for about half of all faculty appointments in American higher education. The nontenure track consists of two major groups: those who teach part time and those who teach full time but are not on tenure-track lines. Part-time faculty now hold 38 percent of faculty appointments, and non-tenure-track, full-time faculty hold 20 percent.[1] The variety of persons and kinds of appointments within these two broad categories was discussed at some length in the 1980 AAUP report on part-time faculty and the 1986 report on full-time non-tenure-track faculty.[2] Since those reports the variety within non-tenure-track, full-time faculty has expanded, as many faculty members who were once on the tenure track have been moved to term contracts. Together these two categories of faculty constitute a growing and critical problem for higher education. The impact of a long-term fiscal crisis that has produced fluctuating funding patterns has exacerbated the problem. Many institutions increasingly relied upon non-tenure-track faculty as a way to staff classes without having to make long-range commitments to faculty. Most of the relative growth in the numbers of part-time faculty occurred during the period from 1972 to 1977, a period often characterized as one of sharply reduced financial strength for both private and public institutions, and increased institutional interest in alternatives to the tenure system. If those events are important causes of the growth of part-time faculty, then the fact that the supposedly temporary situation did not improve after the economic recovery suggests a growing administrative desire for budgetary discretion. The pressure for flexibility also translates as a need to control the size and density of the tenured faculty. In addition to increased use of part-time faculty, administrative strategies to contain tenure have included extending the probationary period until the full seven years for most faculty, moving numerous faculty off the tenure track, and issuing more term contracts to the growing number of full-time non-tenure-track professors.

Public universities, wary of committing themselves to a long-range budget which the state legislature might not sustain, use non-tenure-track faculty members to buffer the strain between fluctuating student demand, on the one hand, and funding constraints for hiring permanent

---

[1] The data in this report are from the survey of institutions as part of the 1988 National Survey of Postsecondary Faculty (NSOPF) conducted by the National Center for Education Statistics of the Department of Education. The discussion of part-time faculty in this report excludes graduate teaching assistants.

[2] A nationwide survey of part-time faculty sponsored by the AAUP in 1977 provided the data for several landmark studies by Barbara H. and Howard P. Tuckman. The Tuckman studies defined seven groups of part-time faculty, each with different career objectives and conditions. They were "full mooners" (part-time faculty who held a full-time job); "hopeful full-timers" (part-time faculty who held two or more jobs that totaled less than a full-time equivalent); "students" (part-time teachers employed in a different department from the one in which they were pursuing a degree); "homeworkers" (those who chose part-time positions in order to have time for home and child care); "semi-retired" (part time because partly retired); and "part-unknowners" (those who do not fit in any of the above categories). See Tuckman and Tuckman, "Who Are the Part-Timers and What Are Colleges Doing for Them?" *Current Issues in Higher Education* (1981), for a summary. These categories, though some objected to their labels, were instrumental in recognizing the complexity of a work force that had radically different ways of defining itself.

faculty, on the other. Non-tenure-track researchers who can be supported by grants directly or through overhead payments allow institutions to augment resources beyond their budgets. Institutions that find themselves in an increasingly competitive market for funding may reward research over teaching and use non-tenure-track faculty members in lower-division courses to fund release time from teaching for senior faculty.

The increase in non-tenure-track appointments affects the quality of education as a whole and the stability of the profession in particular. The growth of non-tenure-track faculty erodes the size and influence of the tenured faculty and undermines the stability of the tenure system. The large numbers of faculty who now work without tenure leave academic freedom more vulnerable to manipulation and suppression. The professional status of faculty suffers when so many are subject to economic exploitation and demeaning working conditions inconsistent with professional standards. And the quality of education is at risk when the curriculum, advising, and instruction are not in the control of faculty to whom the institution has made the kinds of commitments that ensure scholarly development and recognition of performance.

The term "nontenure track" is sometimes used narrowly to refer only to those full-time faculty members who hold positions off the tenure track at institutions with a system of academic tenure. To assess the full scope of the number of faculty who work outside the tenure system, one must combine several categories. Some part-time faculty members never work full time, and some non-tenure-track faculty members are never part time, but for many others, their appointments may vary from full time to part time from semester to semester or year to year, depending on fluctuations in funding and enrollment. Some faculty members in each category are employed exclusively in the classroom, the laboratory, or the clinic. We also eschew the customary term "temporary" faculty, because the data demonstrate that typically such appointments are not temporary but rather continue indefinitely.

The growth of part-time faculty has often come at the cost of stable employment for those who seek full-time careers. Institutions which assign a significant percentage of instruction to faculty members in whom they make a minimal professional investment undercut their own commitment to quality. Academic programs and a tenure system are not stable when institutions rely heavily on non-tenure-track faculty who receive few, if any, opportunities for professional advancement, whose performance may not be regularly reviewed or rewarded, and who may be shut out of the governing structures of the departments and institutions that appoint them. The tendency to use more part-time faculty to meet enrollment pressures in basic courses also makes the academy more vulnerable to critics who charge that universities pursue research at the expense of teaching.

Some community colleges depend on poorly paid, non-tenure-track faculty members to remain in existence. Many of these institutions have no tenure system and appoint only a few full-time faculty members to organize and supervise a large department of part-time faculty. In four-year colleges and universities, large departments that teach many sections of required freshman courses, for example, in mathematics, English, and foreign languages, often have the highest density of non-tenure-track faculty. In some departments, more than half of the course sections are taught by non-tenure-track faculty members and teaching assistants. While graduate-student teaching is increasingly supervised and evaluated, the performance of non-tenure-track faculty members teaching basic courses may not be monitored or reviewed before reappointment.

As the academic programs in community colleges increasingly move toward offering credits transferable to four-year institutions, the need for a wider adoption of the tenure system in these institutions becomes more apparent. Tenure would support a stable faculty and an improved academic reputation. Faculty in these institutions need professional conditions, academic protections, and curricular control similar to those afforded tenure-track faculty in four-year institutions. The continuing increase in the number of students and faculty members in community colleges means that the overall quality of higher education and the profession will be significantly affected by the professional standards that prevail within these institutions. The high percentage of non-tenure-track faculty in community colleges underscores the importance of enhancing conditions for faculty in these institutions for their own benefit as well as for that of the profession as a whole.

The large number of community colleges is indicative of the diverse developments in contemporary American higher education. The range of institutions and the diversity of student needs have resulted in increasingly diverse kinds of faculty positions. Higher education today includes community colleges which offer a mix of vocational training and transferable college credits; private liberal arts colleges; comprehensive colleges and state universities which may have several campuses offering different kinds of degree programs; and the fifty-eight Association of American Universities institutions which comprise the major research universities. Within these institutions individual faculty members may combine teaching and research, do only one or the other, combine one or both with part-time administrative duties, staff clinics, libraries, or laboratories. Given the variety of needs and assignments, institutions should develop more than one model of the tenurable professor. Multiple models for faculty, developed around the kinds of work they do for their institutions, will better serve both the profession and the institutions. The profession and the public need to recognize and reward valued work on its own terms rather than measure faculty against a dominant model of the traditional professor that may be inconsistent with the institution's own mission for instruction, research, and service to a region or local community.

GROWTH AND DISTRIBUTION OF NON-TENURE-TRACK FACULTY

A 1980 study by the National Center for Education Statistics reported that "part-time faculty members now comprise 32 percent of the total teaching force in higher education [excluding graduate students]." In 1986, the AAUP study, *On Full-Time Non-Tenure-Track Appointments*, reported that "between 10.6 and 12.6 percent of full-time faculty were not on a tenure track," that "between 25 percent and 40 percent of all first-time junior faculty appointments in 1981 were to non-tenure-eligible positions," and that "between 40 and 45 percent of all non-tenure-track positions were filled by women. . . ."[3] The above-cited 1988 NSOPF survey, which included more two-year faculty and faculty at institutions without tenure, found 20 percent of full-time faculty were off the tenure track. This increases the urgency of the warning in the 1986 report that the substantial increase of non-tenure-track faculty has created a two-tier system that could alter "the outside world's perception of academe" and undermine the tenure system. The survey results again affirmed the AAUP's position that with few exceptions there should be only two kinds of appointments for full-time faculty: those that are probationary for tenure and those with tenure.

The average of 38 percent of all faculty who are part time reaches 52 percent of the faculty in community colleges. Less than 5 percent of faculty who are part time are on the tenure track. Seventy-nine percent are classified below assistant professor, for example, instructor, lecturer, or reader. About 90 percent of all full-time lecturers and nearly 50 percent of all full-time instructors are non-tenure-track faculty. Less than 20 percent of the total number of part-time faculty apparently seek full-time positions, though two-thirds of recent Ph.D.'s seek such positions.

Perhaps the key factor in the growth of part-time faculty is the economic advantage for institutions that pay them substantially less than the prorated equivalent paid for comparable work by full-time faculty. Three out of eight part-time faculty members, or nearly 38 percent, earned less than $20,000 from all sources in 1987; and fewer than half earned as much as $30,000 in 1987. (At the same time, it should be noted that nearly one-third of part-time faculty earned $40,000 or more from all sources, while more than 20,000 earned at least $75,000.) As a point of reference, the average salary for full-time faculty was $37,000 for the 1987–88 academic year.[4] Some part-time faculty members who combine two or more jobs do so to earn a total salary of two-thirds that of full-time faculty members, but others combine part-time teaching with well-paid careers in other fields. Non-tenure-track faculty are found among the lowest paid and

[3] *Academe: Bulletin of the AAUP* 72 (July–August 1986): 14a.
[4] *Academe* 74 (March–April 1988): 16. Total professional earnings of full-time faculty members are about 20 to 22 percent more than their base salary, but many part-time faculty members do not have access to benefits.

lowest in total earnings of full-time faculty. No survey exists of the stipend paid per course, but the basic academic salary of part-time faculty members is $6,302 of a total income from all sources of $34,275. Our informal soundings found that stipends per course ranged from $900 to $3,500, with $1,500 per course the most common figure.

On the average, part-time faculty members spent 6.5 years at the same institution in comparison with 11.6 years for full-time faculty. Still, more than 62 percent of part-time faculty reported that their appointments did not last beyond the current term. More than half (52 percent) of part-time faculty had other full-time employment. Part-time faculty averaged fourteen hours per week for the academic institution but had a combined workload of forty-four hours from all jobs compared to fifty-three hours per week averaged by regular, full-time faculty.

Although part-time faculty are employed at institutions of all types, the greater the emphasis the institution places on research, the smaller the percentage of part-time faculty it is likely to employ. These figures conceal within them, however, the reliance of research institutions on graduate student assistants to teach introductory courses. About 17 percent of the total faculty in the prestigious research universities are part-time faculty. At doctoral and comprehensive universities combined, the percentage of part-time faculty goes up to 26.4; at comprehensive institutions alone, part-time teachers constitute 29.8 percent of the entire faculty.[5] At liberal arts colleges, the part-time figure rises to 32.6 percent. At the two-year institutions, the percentage of part-time faculty reaches 52.1 percent of the total faculty. Public research universities employ proportionately fewer part-time faculty than private research universities, though the actual numbers are greater in the public than in the private universities, because the public universities are so much larger. Of the 119,000 faculty members at public research universities, only 14.4 percent are part time; of the 53,000 faculty members at private research universities, 21.7 percent are part time. Although university faculties may have lighter teaching loads and a heavier research emphasis, the data indicate that an institution's commitment to graduate programs and research is likely to reduce the institution's reliance on non-tenure-track faculty. These universities utilize graduate students as teachers, but the ratio of tenure-track to non-tenure-track faculty suggests that public research universities are more likely to have a stable faculty of full-time professors than are institutions in other categories.

The distribution of full-time non-tenure-track appointments also varies significantly by type of institution. Private research and comprehensive universities lead with about 13 percent and 12 percent, respectively, in full-time positions classified as nontenure track or for which tenure is not available. Public doctoral and comprehensive universities are close behind with 10.4 and 10 percent, respectively.

Liberal arts colleges, a category that includes most of the four-year institutions that lack tenure systems, have 11.4 percent of faculty in full-time non-tenure-track appointments. Almost 13 percent of liberal arts faculty are at institutions that do not have systems of tenure; 25 percent of the public two-year faculty and 71 percent of the relatively small number of private two-year faculty are at colleges that do not offer tenure. Almost 90 percent of all faculty members are at institutions that have tenure policies.

Almost all non-tenure-track faculty are in the lowest ranks. About 90 percent of all full-time lecturers and nearly 50 percent of all full-time instructors are nontenure track. Among part-time faculty, slightly more than half (52.7 percent) are employed at the instructor rank, while another quarter (27.6 percent) are employed either as lecturers or with miscellaneous titles or none at all. More than 27,000 part-time faculty members are employed at the senior ranks of associate or full professor, and almost 10 percent are full professors.

---

[5] The categories of institutions used in the 1988 NSOPF survey include "the 100 leading universities in federal research funds" awarding "substantial numbers of doctorates across many fields"; all other doctoral-granting institutions; comprehensive colleges and universities offering the M.A. degree as the highest degree in liberal arts and professional programs; liberal arts colleges which are "smaller and generally more selective than comprehensive colleges and universities" and offer primarily the bachelor's degree; and two-year institutions.

Part-time faculty are disproportionately female. Although men are the majority of part-time faculty in all categories of institutions, women constitute about 42 percent of the part-time faculty compared to 27 percent of full-time faculty. Viewed from another perspective, 43.2 percent of women faculty members work on a part-time basis, while just under 30 percent of male faculty do so.[6] Between 1975 and 1985 the percentage of women on the tenure track went from 18.3 to 20.7 percent, while the percentage of women in non-tenure-track positions rose from 33.6 to 40.3 percent.[7] The gender disparity is greater, fully two to one, for non-tenure-track positions, where 29.4 percent of female full-time faculty members hold positions off the tenure track compared to only 14.7 percent of men. The number of male part-time faculty rose 10.3 percent between 1975 and 1985; the number of female part-time faculty rose by 54.1 percent during that same period.[8] The rapid growth in non-tenure-track appointments of women has had little if any effect on the number of full-time women on the tenure track. It is also disturbing to find that, although similar proportions of white and African-American faculty members are found at institutions without tenure systems (9.1 and 10.2 percent, respectively), the proportion of African-Americans in non-tenure-track positions (15.2 percent) is more than 50 percent greater than that of whites (9.6 percent).

Degree status is an important factor in part-time employment. Overall, part-time faculty are much less likely than full-time faculty to hold doctoral degrees (29 percent vs. 67 percent). In four-year institutions, 55 percent of part-time faculty hold a doctorate in comparison to 89 percent of the full-time faculty. Similarly, fewer than 25 percent of those faculty off the tenure track hold Ph.D.'s compared to 60 percent of tenure-track faculty. Doctoral or professional degrees are held by 28.6 percent of the part-time faculty, while 48.9 percent either have master's degrees or have taken other graduate study. In public two-year institutions, fewer than 20 percent of either full- or part-time faculty have a doctorate or comparable professional degree.

Full-time and tenure-track faculty are also substantially more likely to have published in the two years preceding the survey. Some 21 percent of part-time faculty and 53 percent of full-time faculty reported publishing at least one refereed article, chapter, or book over the preceding two years. The difference in expectations regarding publication and publication rates is substantial between research and doctoral institutions, where publication may be a professional expectation, and two-year colleges, where it may not be.

Recent trends indicate that some tenure-track faculty are being moved to non-tenure-track positions. This shift is especially prevalent in medical colleges and other areas in which clinical and research faculty are employed.[9] Numerous institutions have moved toward the use of five-year renewable contracts to replace tenure-track appointments for faculty members who are not primarily classroom teachers, such as researchers, clinicians, laboratory managers, and librarians. The growth of outside grants to fund research has also produced an increasingly

[6] The increase in the number of part-time faculty members and the disproportionate number who are women are similar in Great Britain. Temporary and part-time faculty are now 42 percent of the academic work force. Fifty-three percent of part-time faculty members are female, although only 20 percent of full-time academics are women. The relationship of the growth of part-time and temporary faculty to declining full-time permanent positions is evident in the Universities' Statistical Records (USR). USR figures show that since 1980 British universities have lost one in ten full-time academic staff. See Amanda Hart and Tom Wilson, "The Politics of Part-Time Staff," *AUT Bulletin* 116 (January 1992): 8–9, and Amanda Hart, "The Changing Profile of University Staff," *ibid.*, 115 (October 1991): 4–5. The *AUT Bulletin* is the publication of the Association of University Teachers, which includes members from England, Northern Ireland, Scotland, and Wales.
[7] Ana María Turner Lomperis, "Are Women Changing the Nature of the Academic Profession?" *Journal of Higher Education* 61 (1990): 669.
[8] This may understate the growth in both male and female part-time faculty, since 132 fewer institutions responded in 1985 than in 1975.
[9] The case of the College of Medicine at the University of Cincinnati seems typical of the pattern. According to Howard Tolley, Jr., "The Medical Center makes five-year renewable faculty appointments in both a 'Clinical Practice' and a 'Research' track while maintaining a traditional tenure-track system for others" ("'Qualified' and Non-Tenurable at U.C.: The AAUP's Second-Class Members," *Focus* 1 [autumn 1990]. Publication of University of Cincinnati AAUP).

large number of faculty members whose appointments are tied to the duration of the grant and who are not eligible for tenure in their institutions.

Appointing nonteaching clinical and research faculty to non-tenure-track positions is often justified by an institution on the grounds that nonclassroom personnel do not need academic freedom. The AAUP's Special Committee on Academic Personnel Ineligible for Tenure considered this matter and determined that all full- and part-time faculty who are employed by the institution (in contrast to those doing contract work sponsored by an outside agency), including those whose responsibilities include only research and not instruction, have academic freedom and should receive the protection of the Association. Only researchers housed in universities but funded by outside agencies may fall outside the protections of tenure. The growing trend to place research and clinical faculty of the institution on temporary contracts weakens academic freedom. The public suffers accordingly.

Job security, benefits, and opportunity to advance are the three working conditions that most divide non-tenure-track faculty from their tenure-track colleagues. Fully half of the full-time non-tenure-track faculty expressed dissatisfaction with their job security, compared to 34 percent of tenure-track and 3.5 percent of tenured faculty. Satisfaction with job security fell to 43 percent for part-time faculty. Almost 80 percent of part-time faculty were satisfied with their assigned workload in comparison to 73 percent of full-time faculty. Only 24 percent of part-time faculty were satisfied with their opportunities to advance as compared to 58 percent of full-time faculty. Women were less satisfied than men in all categories, and markedly more dissatisfied in their sense of the opportunity to advance (38 percent and 51 percent, respectively). Lomperis's study found that among recent Ph.D.'s (those received between 1981 and 1986) in the 1987 labor market, two-thirds were seeking full-time work. Her study indicates that new Ph.D.'s are much less satisfied to be part time than is the group as a whole, which includes all age brackets and types of degrees.

Many institutions prorate benefits for faculty members who have, at least, half-time (twenty hours) appointments. Forty-two percent of part-time faculty who worked more than twenty hours a week reported that the benefits surveyed were available to them, compared to only 11 percent of those who worked fewer than twenty hours a week.[10] The figure fell from the overall average of 42 percent for faculty members working more than twenty hours a week in two-year public institutions. Only 16 percent of faculty members working more than twenty hours a week at two-year public institutions have access to medical insurance, and only 12 percent have access to life insurance.

Many non-tenure-track faculty members labor under conditions that hinder the professional quality of their work. Lack of office space or basic equipment is a common problem that plagues their efforts to prepare course materials and meet with students. Non-tenure-track faculty are typically ineligible for research or travel funds, and those who are part time substantially more so. Many institutions that require regular evaluation of tenure-track faculty lack any process for reviewing the performance of part-time and full-time non-tenure-track faculty members. This absence of incentives or rewards for performance speaks bluntly to the marginal status of non-tenure-track faculty within these institutions.

To be off the tenure track in an institution that has a tenure system also usually means being outside the structure of faculty governance and, for most part-time faculty, outside the bargaining unit in those institutions where there are faculty unions. Only 10 percent of part-time faculty are protected by collective bargaining, as opposed to 23 percent of full-time faculty. The

---

[10] The NSOPF selected for its survey medical and life insurance, retirement plans to which the employer made contributions, tuition remission plans, and institutional funds for professional association memberships and travel (p. 199). Only 60 percent of full-time faculty had tuition remission benefits, however, and only 34 percent of full-time faculty could obtain institutional funds for membership in professional associations.

majority of faculty union contracts cover only full-time faculty.[11] Not surprisingly, the exclusion of non-tenure-track faculty members from the rewards system and the governance structure leaves non-tenure-track faculty powerless and isolated. Since their attainments and abilities do not accrue toward promotion or tenure, non-tenure-track faculty are often invisible within their departments.

There is little evidence to support those who hope that their accomplishments off the tenure track will result in consideration for a tenure-eligible appointment. Part-time positions are not regularly converted to full time, and non-tenure-track faculty seldom receive any priority consideration when their positions are upgraded. Typically, when a non-tenure-track position is converted to the tenure track, the department advertises nationally. The teaching experience of non-tenure-track faculty members in the pool of local applicants may be interpreted as evidence of failed promise when measured against new Ph.D.'s who are just entering the market. Indeed, some part-time faculty who continue to teach in an effort to sustain a professional life while seeking full-time employment are bitterly disappointed to find that the fact of working part time may be taken as a sign that they are not serious about their careers.

It is essential that the extent and nature of non-tenure-track instruction be a central consideration in reviews by accrediting bodies. Some accrediting agencies do recognize the connection between the professional conditions for faculty members and the quality of education offered by the institution. The Middle States Association of Colleges and Schools now urges that "criteria for the appointment of part-time or adjunct faculty and their supervision should be comparable as far as possible to the full-time faculty," and that "provisions for review of teaching and opportunities for professional development should be available."[12] The Western Association of Schools and Colleges (WASC) requires "a core of full-time faculty to support each program."[13] The influence of accrediting agencies, professional associations, and collective bargaining agreements can strengthen efforts to improve the stability and professional development of part-time faculty.

The AAUP is concerned about institutions which persist in practices that undermine or destroy the stability of tenure and academic freedom, including practices that exploit non-tenure-track faculty. Institutions that rely heavily on non-tenure-track faculty members to teach undergraduate students undermine the institution's respect for teaching and the reputation of higher education in the larger society. Institutions exploit faculty members when they appoint numerous part-time faculty in a single department or renew "temporary" faculty members year after year without offering them raises in pay, access to benefits, opportunities for promotion, or eligibility for tenure.

There are legitimate uses of part-time appointments, for example, to meet unexpected increases in enrollment or faculty vacancies, to provide service in a specialized field, or to develop a new academic program. However, the extensive use of part-time positions or extended "temporary" appointments has become habitual in too many institutions. Basic instructional responsibilities should never depend on faculty who are denied professional consideration and who are exempted from the evaluations that are essential for maintaining academic standards.

[11] The exceptions are most often found in community college systems, especially in California and Washington. On many of these campuses, the part-time faculty outnumber the full-time faculty in the unit. (See *Directory of Faculty Contracts and Bargaining Agents in Institutions of Higher Education* 14 [January 1988] for complete listings.)

[12] *Characteristics of Excellence in Higher Education Standards for Accreditation* (Middle States Association of Colleges and Schools, 1989), 25.

[13] Letter from Stephen S. Weiner, Executive Director, WASC, to Ernst Benjamin (July 9, 1991).

GUIDELINES FOR IMPROVEMENT

Improving the professional status of the growing number of non-tenure-track faculty members is difficult in financially hard times and unpopular with most administrations and many faculty members. Still, the AAUP believes that the long-range health of higher education requires that institutions greatly reduce their reliance upon non-tenure-track faculty members, and that faculty members who are appointed to part-time positions should be extended the benefits and privileges of the academic profession. The AAUP's position about full-time faculty is clear: "With the exception of special appointments clearly limited to a brief association with the institution, and reappointments of retired faculty members on special conditions, all full-time faculty appointments are of two kinds: (1) probationary appointments; (2) appointments with continuous tenure."[14] The possibility of tenure for part-time faculty should also be an option when the need for less-than-full-time work extends indefinitely. Administrators often oppose tenure for part-time faculty because it constrains the budgetary flexibility that makes non-tenure-track appointments attractive to them. Some part-time faculty members oppose tenure for part-time faculty because they fear it would eventually result in the termination of their own services. Non-tenure-track faculty members who usually lack research support often worry about standards of judgment that measure them against tenure-track faculty members who engage in research.

The 1980 AAUP report on part-time faculty recommended: (1) that some part-time faculty members should be eligible for tenure; (2) that security of employment for part-time faculty include regularized appointment practices, reasonable notice, and access to the institution's regular grievance procedure; (3) that part-time faculty should participate in academic governance; and (4) that the compensation and fringe benefits of part-time faculty should be equitable, perhaps including prorated compensation and equal access to benefits. The report's recommendation, that "those individuals who, as their professional career, share the teaching, research, and administrative duties customary for faculty at their institution, but who for whatever reason do so less than full-time . . . should have the opportunity to achieve tenure and the rights it confers,"[15] echoes that of the 1973 report of the Commission on Academic Tenure in Higher Education, a study jointly sponsored by the AAUP and the Association of American Colleges.

Although some institutions have moved in the direction of tenure for part-time faculty, and several are negotiating tenure eligibility as part of collective bargaining agreements, others have developed long-term contract arrangements. Extended term appointments or seniority-based security gives part-time faculty members greater appointment stability. Stability of appointment opens the way for the fuller integration of part-time faculty into the academic profession. Only 6 percent of institutions offer tenure to any part-time faculty, but 22 percent of research universities and 17 percent of doctoral universities report having some tenured part-time faculty. Institutions need continuity in their faculty, and contract arrangements that provide security to part-time faculty ameliorate the problems inherent in an unstable work force.

Institutions which habitually employ many part-time and "temporary" full-time faculty members should calculate how many full-time faculty equivalents they routinely need and begin converting their non-tenure-track positions to full-time tenure-track lines. Whenever possible, the regular academic instruction of students should be the responsibility of faculty members who are responsible for the curriculum and participate in the governance of the institution, and to whom the institution is willing to make the commitment of tenure.

In order to address the growing use of non-tenure-track faculty, the AAUP calls on institutions to work toward achieving the following goals:

---

[14] "Recommended Institutional Regulations on Academic Freedom and Tenure," Regulation 1(b), AAUP, *Policy Documents and Reports*, 9th ed. (Washington, D.C., 2001), 21.
[15] "The Status of Part-Time Faculty," *ibid.*, 61.

1. Institutions should limit reliance on non-tenure-track faculty. We recommend as guidelines that institutions limit the use of special appointments and part-time non-tenure-track faculty to no more than 15 percent of the total instruction within the institution, and no more than 25 percent of the total instruction within any given department.
2. In circumstances in which an institution has legitimate needs for a specialized class of faculty in part-time or fractional-time positions, the institution should have policies that provide for their long-term contract stability and for tenure.

The consolidation of non-tenure-track faculty, full and part time, into full-time tenure-track positions requires a long-term commitment of institutional dollars, but failure to make such a commitment will perpetuate the steady erosion of the quality of education in our colleges and universities. Institutions that fail to preserve and advance the quality of education, especially undergraduate education, undermine public confidence in higher education. Accreditation agencies should also regard the growing use of non-tenure-track faculty as a sign of weakness in the health of academic programs. An immediate commitment to equitable professional treatment of non-tenure-track faculty combined with a reduced reliance on part-time faculty is necessary to halt the deleterious effects on the profession that this report identifies.

The alarming extent to which many colleges and universities rely on non-tenure-track faculty means that even institutions which make an immediate commitment to curtail their use of part-time faculty may face an extended period of transition. Institutions should develop plans for a period of transition that project a timetable and numbers for consolidating part-time assignments into full-time tenure-track lines.

Institutions may also need to assess more carefully the cost efficiency of part-time faculty members when their status is subject to change from semester to semester. Institutions face "the growing cost of unemployment benefits for part-time faculty who file and receive these benefits when their services are no longer needed."[16] Nance and Culverhouse found that "at a few urban institutions the money being paid out in unemployment benefits is beginning to approach the total money being paid in compensation for part-time faculty who are teaching. Part-time faculty members have to be employed for only one quarter to be eligible for unemployment checks for up to twenty-six weeks of the rest of the year." Many institutions are likely to be better served economically by long-term appointments that reduce frequent turnover in their faculty.

Reasonable assurance of continued employment, following successful completion of a probationary period, makes the profession more attractive to men and women of ability and provides for a better-qualified professoriate. Above all, security of employment for qualified faculty safeguards the academic freedom essential to the integrity of teaching and scholarship. The best way to achieve these protections in institutions that rely heavily on part-time faculty is to combine part-time non-tenure-track positions to form full-time tenure-track positions.

To the limited extent that part-time positions cannot be replaced with full-time ones because of the need for part-time expertise or because of unexpected fluctuations in enrollment or funding, the institution should provide continued employment to those remaining part-time faculty found qualified for recurrent appointment. Such assurance may include lengthening the term of appointment and the notice required for nonreappointment, and offering continuing part-time appointments. Such continuing appointments would protect part-time faculty members except from demonstrable declines in enrollment and funding that necessitated reductions in courses and sections offered, and would help to stabilize the faculty, protect academic freedom, and enhance the status of those who work part time.

[16] Guinevera Nance and Renee Culverhouse, "The Hidden Costs of Part-Time Faculty," *Planning for Higher Education* 20 (winter 1991–92): 30, 31. Institutions with adverse experience with unemployment benefits must pay higher payroll taxes on all employees.

PROFESSIONAL STANDARDS

Many non-tenure-track faculty, especially those who work part time, express uncertainty about what rights and privileges they are due as faculty members. The AAUP seeks to ensure academic freedom and professional protection for all faculty whether full or part time, tenured or nontenured. To that end we offer the following additional recommendations in an effort to set minimum standards designed to protect the professional standing of all faculty:

1. All appointments, including part-time appointments, should have a description of the specific professional duties required. Complex institutions may require multiple models of faculty appointments consistent with the diverse contributions appropriate to the institution's needs.

2. The performance of faculty members on renewable term appointments, full time and part time, should be regularly evaluated with established criteria appropriate to their positions. Failure to evaluate professional appointments diminishes the institution and the professional standing of the faculty. Evaluation of performance provides essential information for sound and fair institutional decisions regarding compensation, promotion, and tenure. Each institution should define the credentials and the quality of scholarship it requires of faculty members in different academic positions and then should make appointments and decisions regarding compensation and advancement based on the criteria specific to the position. Institutions faced with emergency appointments sometimes employ faculty members whose qualifications fall short of those normally required for tenure-track appointments. In general, institutions should avoid appointing, and should certainly not reappoint, faculty members whose qualifications or performance are so far below the prevailing institutional standard as to make tenure eligibility an impossibility. Any lesser standard shortchanges the students and erodes support for academic standards in the institution and the wider community.

3. Decisions on compensation, promotion, and tenure should be based on the specified duties of the position. Faculty members appointed to teach entry-level courses should have the opportunity to enhance their professional status and receive rewards based on performance of their defined responsibilities and should not be held to expectations which may prevail for other positions.

4. Compensation for part-time employment should be the corresponding fraction for a full-time position having qualitatively similar responsibilities and qualifications. Compensation should include such essential fringe benefits as health insurance, life insurance, and retirement contributions.

5. Timely notice of nonreappointment should be extended to all faculty regardless of length of service. The AAUP's 1980 report on part-time faculty recommends that part-time faculty "who have been employed for six or more terms, or consecutively for three or more terms," should receive at least a full term's notice of nonreappointment. Although it may be impossible to give a full term of notice to faculty members employed for less than three terms, we recommend that every effort be made to notify faculty at the earliest possible opportunity, but in no case later than four weeks prior to the commencement of the next term. Similarly, all faculty members should have reasonable advance notice of course assignments to allow adequate preparation.

6. Institutions should provide the conditions necessary to perform assigned duties in a professional manner, including such things as appropriate office space and necessary supplies, support services, and equipment.

7. Non-tenure-track faculty should be included in the departmental and institutional structures of faculty governance.

8. Part-time faculty should be given fair consideration when part-time positions are converted to full-time positions. The evidence suggests that part-time employment often works as a disadvantage on the job market when applicants are considered for full-time tenure-track positions. Departments should be as scrupulous to avoid this type of discrimination as they are required to be in avoiding other forms of discrimination.

As the number of non-tenure-track faculty appointments grows, the base of the tenure system erodes. The treatment of non-tenure-track faculty appointments is the barometer whereby the general status of the profession may be measured. While the colleague whose performance is undervalued or whose potential is blighted by underemployment bears the personal brunt of the situation, the status of all faculty is undermined by the degree of exploitation the profession allows of its members. Institutions that rely heavily on part-time faculty marginalize the faculty as a whole. Failure to extend to all faculty reasonable professional commitments compromises quality and risks the stability of the profession and the integrity of our standing with the public.

Report of the Special Committee on Academic Personnel Ineligible for Tenure

The report which follows was approved by the Association's Committee on Academic Freedom and Tenure (Committee A) in October 1969. In November 1989, Committee A approved several changes in language in order to remove gender-specific references from the original text.

PREAMBLE

The special committee considered problems with regard to nontenured positions, particularly as they concern three categories of academic people: (1) part-time teachers, (2) full-time teachers who are not considered regular members of faculties, and (3) persons who are appointed to full-time research positions. The special committee's first effort has been to survey and analyze the policies and practices of reputable universities with regard to nontenured positions, reports of which were previously made to the Council and Committee A. Its second concern has been to examine these practices in relation to the 1940 *Statement of Principles on Academic Freedom and Tenure* of the Association of American Colleges and the American Association of University Professors. Its third and final effort has been to formulate an interpretation of the 1940 *Statement* that might serve to guide the latter association in advising interested persons about problems and disputes involving nontenured appointments.

The special committee soon concluded that the 1940 *Statement* could not be interpreted as guaranteeing tenure rights to part-time teachers. Its provisions for a probationary period apply explicitly to ". . . appointment to the rank of full-time instructor or higher rank." The special committee believes, however, that the Association should continue to be actively concerned with cases belonging to this category and should use its influence to persuade institutions to adopt and utilize suitable grievance procedures, so that disputes involving part-time teachers can be judiciously resolved within the institutions. Where such procedures are inadequate or lacking, the Association should vigorously uphold the right of part-time teachers to the same academic freedom that teachers with tenure have. This policy should of course apply equally to full-time teachers during their probationary period.

There has been much discussion by the special committee, as there has been among other organs of the Association, of the question whether the increasing use of people without doctoral degrees as full-time teachers calls for clarification of the probationary requirements set forth in the 1940 *Statement*. That is, does an educational institution have to count years of full-time service accumulated by a tenure candidate before receipt of the doctorate in determining when the decision to grant or not grant tenure must be made? Or, conversely, is it legitimate for an institution to appoint a doctoral candidate as a full-time teacher, in a rank below, or different from, that of instructor, and consider that the term of probation for tenure begins only if and when the candidate receives the doctorate? The 1940 *Statement*, whether intentionally or not, appears to leave room for the second interpretation by saying that the probationary period should begin with appointment at the rank of instructor or a higher rank. It does not, however, say at what rank a full-time teacher with the doctorate must be appointed. After full discussion, the special committee is unanimously agreed that the first interpretation should be Association policy; that is, any person whom an institution appoints to a full-time teaching position should be treated as a candidate for tenure under the requirements of the 1940 *Statement*, no matter what rank or title that person may be given by the institution. If an institution wants to exclude a doctoral candidate (or any other person whom it considers inadequately qualified for regular faculty membership and status) from tenure candidacy, it should not appoint that person as a full-time teacher. The special committee believes that less injustice will be done, both to teachers and to institutions, if this policy is enforced than if the apparent loophole is left open.[1] The special committee also believes that anyone who does an instructor's work should be given appropriate rank and privileges. In short, the special committee wishes to eliminate the second problem category by refusing to grant that, for purposes of the 1940 *Statement*, there is any such thing as a full-time teacher at a rank below that of instructor.

The third problem category, that of research people who are not teachers, is relatively new to higher education. It was not foreseen, and its full effect on the regulation and conduct of academic institutions is not yet foreseeable. In particular, it seems clear to the special committee that the two associations had no major category of such academic people in mind when they formulated the 1940 *Statement*. A question may be, therefore, whether it is possible for the special committee to apply the 1940 *Statement* to this category. Its deliberations may in fact have led to another question: does the 1940 *Statement* itself need some revision, amendment, or supplement in order to provide proper guidance for Association policy in this area? The 1940 *Statement* plainly assumes that the normal basic activity of university professors is teaching and that research is a functionally related activity by means of which teaching is enriched and extended. On this assumption it is entirely reasonable and proper to maintain, as the 1940 *Statement* evidently does, that researchers are the same as teachers insofar as their right to academic freedom, their status as faculty members, and their entitlement to tenure are concerned. In 1940, with negligible exceptions, researchers in universities were teachers, part of whose teaching was by word of mouth and part by the medium of print. The two parts served the same purpose of transmitting the teacher's individual ideas into the arena of public discussion, and the same principles of freedom and of responsibility applied to both.

Now, however, many researchers are working in universities and university-operated agencies to whom this assumption does not so clearly apply. Workers on Department of Defense projects offer the extreme example; but those who work on a project which is defined by a contract between the employing institution and a sponsoring agency, government, industry, or foundation are likely to be more or less limited in their freedom to decide for themselves what line of investigation they will pursue. The question arises whether universities ought to be engaged in this kind of contract research at all. The special committee regards this as an important question, but not one that can be settled at this time by a component of the AAUP. The fact is that many of the best universities are so engaged, and the question to be answered is what the AAUP policy should be toward the people involved, particularly concerning the conditions of academic freedom and tenure under which they work.

The special committee recognizes that many and perhaps most of the researchers doing contract work are qualified by education and training to be members of teaching faculties. What makes them different is their function. A related consideration, which administrators are quick to point out, is that the shifting character of the financial support for contract work imposes a special problem in relation to tenure. It is not so much a matter of the total amount of money available as it is of the fact that individual research contracts run for limited terms, and that researchers are not always transferable from one contract project to another within the same institution. Administratively, the logical solution is to let the individual researcher's contract run for not longer than the term of the project contract. The situation is roughly parallel to that which arises when an institution decides to discontinue a course or department or college. The AAUP recognizes that legitimate academic reasons may require such a change, and that it is not always possible for the institution to retain all the people whose positions are eliminated. Such a situation, rare in teaching faculties, is normal and frequent in contract research.

---

[1] Several sentences, which appeared here in the original report of the special committee and alluded to employment conditions then current, are omitted as being no longer applicable.

These problems are closely related to the fact that many research projects are carried out by teams of researchers under the supervision of project directors. The director of a project, often a faculty member with tenure, and very often a kind of entrepreneur in proposing the project and attracting financial support for it from sources outside the institution, has a legitimate need for freedom in the selection and rejection of team members, and for adequate authority to assign their tasks and coordinate their activities. Furthermore, individual team members are not free to publish results of work they have done on the project without the consent of other members and especially of the director. For these reasons, traditional concepts of academic freedom and tenure do not apply to the activities of contract research teams. The special committee has gone as far as it believes possible, under the circumstances, in asserting and defending in the statement which follows such academic freedom and job security as can be had. Its members feel that an effort to go beyond the limits imposed by the facts of the situation would make the statement weaker, not stronger.

The special committee is by no means indifferent to the conditions under which members of contract research project teams have to work, nor does it advocate indifference on the part of the AAUP. It believes that good administrative and personnel policies ought to operate in this area as in all other areas of academic life, and that the AAUP should try to define good policies and encourage institutions to apply them. It also believes that, whenever academic institutions designate full-time researchers as faculty members, either by formal appointment or by conferring the titles of instructor, assistant or associate professor, or professor, those researchers should have all the rights of other faculty members, and that the AAUP should apply the 1940 *Statement of Principles* to them as strictly as to anyone else.

STATEMENT OF THE SPECIAL COMMITTEE ON ACADEMIC PERSONNEL INELIGIBLE FOR TENURE

A clear definition of acceptable academic practice in American colleges and universities requires some amplification and interpretation of the 1940 *Statement of Principles on Academic Freedom and Tenure*. Most of the 1940 *Statement* applies without change to the operation of universities today. The academic freedom statement, however, leaves some question about the freedom of research for the secondary staff of large research projects restricted by government or industrial support and security. The academic tenure provisions leave some doubt about the tenure rights of part-time teachers and of persons appointed with titles other than those of the four ranks of instructor to professor.

To make quite clear that the policy of the Association provides protection in matters of academic freedom to all teachers at all ranks and on any fractional appointment and to all investigators with university appointments, the following amplifying statement is proposed:

1. The academic freedom of all teachers and investigators with full-time or part-time appointments in a university should have the full protection of the Association.

The committee recognizes that it is appropriate to have, within the university, faculty members who are exclusively investigators. These individuals should be selected by the faculty and should have the full privileges of other professors. The following statement is within the 1940 *Statement* but more directly describes the status of the research faculty member with an academic appointment:

2. Full-time teachers and investigators who are appointed to the rank of instructor, assistant professor, associate professor, and professor should have the rights and privileges appropriate to their rank, including tenure or the eligibility for tenure after the appropriate probationary period.

Acceptable academic practice for tenure is described in the 1940 *Statement of Principles* only for full-time appointments beginning with the rank of instructor. The special committee recommends that these provisions be extended to include all full-time teaching appointments in the university. Part-time appointments are often given to scholars who are still working on their advanced degree programs. If, however, a full-time appointment can be made as a lecturer or acting instructor, without obligating the institution to a limited probationary period, it will diminish the protection of the Association's statement of policy on tenure. To provide for protection of the young teacher's tenure rights, the committee proposes:

3. All full-time teachers, but not investigators, regardless of their titles should acquire tenure after a probationary period as provided for appointments to the rank of full-time instructor or a higher rank in the 1940 *Statement*.

The Association extends the full protection of academic freedom to all teachers and investigators on full-time or part-time university appointments. The policy for the tenure of investigators with full-time university appointments without one of the usual academic ranks has not been adequately determined. Most of these investigator appointments are made from research grants of short duration that are subject to frequent and uncertain renewal. The selection and termination of appointees is made by the project director without the usual procedures of review involved in departmental academic appointments. Until the funds for the support of investigators are assured for substantial periods, and until the university determines policies for the distribution and use of these funds, it will be difficult for the university to assume the obligation for appointments with continuous tenure. The committee makes no recommendation for a tenure policy for investigators who do not have regular academic appointments.

Arbitration in Cases of Dismissal

The report which follows was approved for publication by the Council of the American Association of University Professors in June 1983.

In 1973, the Association's Committee on Academic Freedom and Tenure (Committee A) and the Committee on Representation of Economic and Professional Interests approved publication in the *AAUP Bulletin* of a report which was addressed to the topic, "Arbitration of Faculty Grievances."[1] That report, prepared by a joint subcommittee, was viewed by the committees as a first statement on the relationship of arbitration of faculty grievances to established Association policies. The present report amplifies on the development of arbitral practices in higher education, with particular emphasis on the question of arbitration of dismissal cases.[2] Consistent with the Association's long-standing obligations to the profession to define sound academic practice, this report was prepared after analysis of collective bargaining agreements reached by agents, AAUP and otherwise, and of the relationship of contractual provisions for dismissal to the 1940 *Statement of Principles on Academic Freedom and Tenure*, the 1958 *Statement on Procedural Standards in Faculty Dismissal Proceedings*, and the 1966 *Statement on Government of Colleges and Universities*. It should be added parenthetically that arbitration of faculty status disputes is not limited to institutions with collective bargaining agreements. Members of the subcommittee were aware of one large public system and one large private university which do not have collective bargaining, but which do have faculty regulations that provide for arbitration of certain faculty status matters.

As was noted in the 1973 report, the *Statement on Government of Colleges and Universities* gives to the faculty primary responsibility for making decisions on faculty status and related matters. The *Statement on Government* asserts, "The governing board and president should, on questions of faculty status, as in other matters where the faculty has primary responsibility, concur with the faculty judgment except in rare instances and for compelling reasons which should be stated in detail."

Any discussion of Association policy on dismissals should, of course, begin with the provisions of the 1940 *Statement of Principles on Academic Freedom and Tenure* and the 1958 *Statement on Procedural Standards in Faculty Dismissal Proceedings*. Both documents are joint policies of the AAUP and the Association of American Colleges. The "Academic Tenure" section of the 1940 *Statement* includes a basic outline of the procedural steps necessary for review of the termination for cause of a teacher previous to the expiration of a term appointment. The 1958 *Statement* supplements the 1940 *Statement* by describing the academic due process that should be observed in dismissal proceedings. The Association has also provided a fuller codification of appropriate dismissal procedures in Regulations 5 and 6 of its *Recommended Institutional Regulations on Academic Freedom and Tenure*.

COLLECTIVE BARGAINING MODIFICATION

Collective bargaining normally results in a formally negotiated contract governing terms and conditions of employment; the provisions of the collective agreement define the legal rights and duties of faculty, administrators, and trustees. Customarily, the collective agreement

---

[1] *AAUP Bulletin* 59 (1973): 163–67.
[2] The comments on arbitration of dismissal cases are also applicable to those instances in which an administration seeks not to dismiss, but to impose a severe sanction; cf. the Association's "Recommended Institutional Regulations on Academic Freedom and Tenure," Regulation 7(a), AAUP, *Policy Documents and Reports*, 9th ed. (Washington, D.C., 2001), 27.

authorizes a neutral third party, an arbitrator, to resolve disputes which arise under it. In contrast to most litigation, negotiated arbitration clauses afford the administration and the faculty opportunity to prescribe the procedures and standards which apply and, most important, jointly to select the decision maker.

It is appropriate to restate here the four factors which the 1973 subcommittee noted as essential for the effective use of arbitration:

1. sound internal procedures preliminary to arbitration which enjoy the confidence of both faculty and administration;
2. careful definition of both arbitral subjects and standards to be applied by arbitration;
3. the selection of arbitrators knowledgeable in the ways of the academic world, aware of the institutional implications of their decisions, and, of course, sensitive to the meaning and critical value of academic freedom; and
4. the assurance that the hearing will include evidence relating to the standards and expectations of the teaching profession in higher education and that appropriate weight will be given to such evidence.

This subcommittee concludes that in cases of dismissal the faculty member may properly be given the right, following a proceeding in accordance with the 1958 *Statement on Procedural Standards in Faculty Dismissal Proceedings* and the *Recommended Institutional Regulations*, to appeal a negative decision to an arbitrator. The subcommittee believes that the 1958 *Statement* provides the most appropriate model for faculty dismissal proceedings. However, where alternatives are implemented, it urges that they should at least make provision for meaningful faculty participation in the dismissal process and for compliance with the requirements of academic due process in the formal dismissal hearing.

ESSENTIAL PRELIMINARY FACULTY PARTICIPATION

Before any formal procedures are invoked, the subcommittee believes that the essential faculty procedures preliminary to any contemplated dismissal, already set forth in Association policy statements,[3] should be followed. The subcommittee is particularly disturbed by contractual dismissal procedures which do not provide in any way for formal faculty participation in a mediative effort prior to the formulation of dismissal charges. It is the subcommittee's opinion that such participation is necessary both to resolve disputes short of formal proceedings and to advise the administration on the wisdom of further pursuit of a particular matter.

In the event that an administration, after receiving faculty advice, chooses to formulate charges for dismissal of a tenured member of an institution's faculty or a non-tenured faculty member during the term of appointment, a hearing on the charges should be held, whether or not the faculty member exercises the right to participate in the hearing. A dismissal is not simply a grievance which may not be pursued. A dismissal is a sanction of the highest order requiring a demonstration of cause regardless of the faculty member's individual action or inaction in contesting the charge.

ARBITRATION FOLLOWING A FACULTY HEARING

It is common practice within the profession that, following a hearing before a faculty committee, the hearing committee presents a report to the president who, in turn, either accepts the report or returns it to the committee with reasons for its rejection prior to transmittal of the report to the governing board. The governing board, in turn, has traditionally made the final decision after study of the recommendations presented to it. In the event that the board disagrees with the faculty committee's recommendations, the board should remand the matter to

---

[3] See "1958 Statement on Procedural Standards in Faculty Dismissal Proceedings," *Policy Documents and Reports*, 11–14; and "Recommended Institutional Regulations on Academic Freedom and Tenure," Regulation 5(b), *ibid.*, 25.

the committee and provide an opportunity for reconsideration. This subcommittee recommends that, after the board's ruling, a faculty member who has pursued these traditional procedures should be given the right to proceed to arbitration. If the collective bargaining agreement provides for arbitration of faculty status disputes, it would be anomalous to deny the right to arbitrate a dismissal, while lesser matters dealing with faculty status may be arbitrated. More important, arbitration in this setting is not a substitute for unfettered trustee judgment, but for the courts; thus, it is not a question of whether institutional officers will be subject to external review, but of what forum is best equipped to perform the task.

It is normally the collective bargaining representative's responsibility to control access to arbitration. The subcommittee believes, however, that the issue of dismissal is of such magnitude that an individual against whom dismissal charges have been sustained by the institutional review processes up to and including the institution's board of trustees should have an unfettered right to seek arbitral review. Moreover, the nature of a dismissal charge against an individual is such, with each case standing on its own merits, that arbitration decisions in dismissal cases should not be considered to have created precedent for other arbitrations dealing with dismissals.

Thus, the subcommittee recommends that, in cases where the collective bargaining representative decides not to appeal a dismissal to arbitration, the individual be given the right to seek arbitral review independently. In that event, the individual would be expected to bear those costs of the arbitration normally assumed by the collective bargaining representative.

As the 1973 subcommittee noted, it is of critical importance ". . . that in the agreement to arbitrate any matter affecting faculty status, rights, and responsibilities, the judgment of the faculty as a professional body properly vested with the primary responsibility for such determinations be afforded a strong presumption in its favor." This subcommittee agrees and accordingly recommends that, particularly on questions of academic fitness and the norms of the profession, the arbitrator should give great weight to the findings and recommendations of the faculty hearing committee.

The subcommittee recommends that the collective bargaining agreement not limit the scope of the issues which may come to an arbitrator in a dismissal case. The arbitration decision should, of course, be based on the record. The subcommittee recommends that the collective bargaining agent have the right to participate in the proceedings in order to inform the arbitrator fully about the standards applicable to the case under review. The recommendation to permit the arbitrator to examine the procedures leading to the dismissal charges, the procedures for review of the charges, and the substance of the record developed in the hearings before the faculty committee as well as the arbitration is based on the expectation that the parties will select an arbitrator sensitive to the standards and practices of the local and national academic communities.

The procedures of the actual arbitration proceeding should be codified in advance and either spelled out in the collective bargaining agreement or, if there is a known policy which would guide the proceeding, referred to in the agreement. One policy often referred to in agreements at private institutions is the Voluntary Labor Arbitration Rules of the American Arbitration Association; agreements at public institutions often cite the arbitration rules of the agency which administers the state's collective bargaining statute.

ALTERNATIVE ARBITRATION PROCEDURES

The above proposal contemplates the addition of arbitration to procedures already required by the 1958 *Statement on Procedural Standards* and the *Recommended Institutional Regulations*. The proposal does no violence to the basic fabric of the 1940 *Statement*, for the basic dismissal decision is arrived at with full due process within the local academic community. Arbitration merely substitutes an expert neutral—jointly selected—for the judiciary in any subsequent contest over whether the decision was procedurally deficient or substantially in error under standards widely recognized in the academic world.

The subcommittee recognizes that, in the interest of expeditious adjudication of dismissal charges, some institutions in collective bargaining have devised alternative dismissal procedures.

Such procedures range from direct arbitration of dismissal cases to modifications of the 1958 *Statement* procedures which incorporate arbitration as part of the formal hearing process, thereby obviating the need for an additional arbitration step upon completion of the internal institutional process.

The subcommittee cannot embrace a position that abandons a model of the faculty as a professional body passing judgment upon its members. Thus, it must reject resort to arbitration as a permissible alternative to the 1958 *Statement* procedures unless certain additional requirements are met. Alternative procedures, designed to comply with the spirit of the 1958 *Statement*, would have to be examined on a case-by-case basis. At a minimum, the subcommittee would expect such procedures to comply with the 1958 *Statement on Procedural Standards* in the following respects:

1. There should be specific provision for faculty participation in a mediative effort prior to the formulation of dismissal charges.
2. There should be significant faculty representation on the hearing panel in a formal hearing of any charges.
3. The formal hearing procedures should comply with the requirements of academic due process as outlined in the *Recommended Institutional Regulations*.

SUMMARY

In summary, the subcommittee has concluded that it is permissible to have the potential dismissal of a faculty member subject to review by an outside arbitrator who may make a binding decision. Disputes concerning the dismissal of a faculty member from a tenured position or of a nontenured faculty member during the term of appointment require faculty participation in an effort to mediate the dispute and require a formal hearing.

Consistent with the 1958 *Statement on Procedural Standards* and the *Recommended Institutional Regulations*, we believe arbitral review may be appropriate after presidential and board review. Alternate procedures providing for arbitration at an earlier stage may be acceptable, provided they ensure faculty participation in a mediative effort prior to formulation of dismissal charges, significant faculty participation in a hearing of such charges, and adherence in the formal hearing to the procedural requirements of academic due process.

The "Limitations" Clause in the 1940 Statement of Principles on Academic Freedom and Tenure: Some Operating Guidelines

The following report, approved in 1999 by the Committee on Academic Freedom and Tenure (Committee A), is a revision of a report initially approved for publication in November 1996.

Committee A reported in 1988[1] on the interpretive difficulty surrounding the provision in the 1940 *Statement of Principles*, that "[l]imitations of academic freedom because of religious or other aims of the institution should be clearly stated in writing at the time of the appointment." This provision is commonly known as the "limitations" clause. In 1970, a set of Interpretive Comments on the 1940 *Statement* was adopted as Association policy, including the interpretive comment that "most church-related institutions no longer need or desire the departure from the principle of academic freedom implied in the 1940 *Statement*, and we do not now endorse such a departure." That interpretive comment left it unclear how the Association is to respond to an institution which does invoke the limitations clause in defense of a departure from the principles of academic freedom. In its 1988 report, Committee A held that the interpretive comment did not read the limitations clause out of the 1940 *Statement*, and thus did not imply that the Association would henceforth regard every resulting departure from the principles of academic freedom as by itself warranting Association censure. Committee A held that an institution that commits itself to a predetermined truth, and that binds its faculty accordingly, is not subject to censure on that ground alone. But Committee A also held that such an institution must not represent itself, without qualification, as an institution freely engaged in higher education: the institution must in particular disclose its restrictions on academic freedom to prospective members of the faculty. Committee A held, finally, that an institution is not subject to the academic freedom provisions of the 1940 *Statement*—a breach of which may issue in censure—unless it does represent itself as an institution freely engaged in higher education.

Various sectarian institutions have been founded and are supported by sponsoring religious denominations for the training of their laity and clergy in the faith. So too have a number of institutions been established that are dedicated to the propagation of particular beliefs or schools of thought—in political economy (the Rand School was singled out for mention by Committee A in the 1920s), in clinical psychology, in early childhood pedagogy, and in the education and training of future leaders of the labor movement, to mention only a few. Institutions of this character function within a set of doctrines or beliefs, and they usually do not affirm a recognition of academic freedom, even subject to restriction. They unquestionably contribute to the pluralistic richness of the American intellectual landscape, but they are usually not institutions of a kind to

---

[1] "The 'Limitations' Clause in the 1940 *Statement of Principles*," *Academe: Bulletin of the AAUP* 74 (September–October 1988): 52–58.

which the academic freedom provisions of the 1940 *Statement* apply, and hence imposing censure on their administrations would usually not be appropriate.[2]

The usual is not the universal, however. When institutions dedicated to these or similar limited aims gain, or seek, broader recognition as seats of higher learning—e.g., by expanding their curricula, by identifying themselves as universities or colleges of liberal education, by awarding secular academic degrees, by securing regional or specialized accreditation, and by appealing to the public for support on those grounds—then we believe they are subject to the academic freedom provisions of the 1940 *Statement*, a breach of which may result in censure.

A further consideration is that somewhere between an institution committed to academic freedom and one that pervasively restricts its exercise lies an institution that provides academic freedom in most respects save for a carefully crafted core (or pocket) of credal or doctrinal conformity. This taxonomy corresponds roughly to the one used by the Danforth Commission on Church Colleges and Universities in 1965, distinguishing among the "non-affirming college," the "defender-of-the-faith college," and—between them—the "free Christian (or Jewish) college" that may attach a religious preference in faculty appointment but that gives the faculty "wide freedom consistent with law and good taste." If "law and good taste" are taken to refer to ecclesiastical as well as civil law restrictions, we believe that such an institution is appropriately viewed as subject to the academic freedom provisions of the 1940 *Statement*, and thus as one to which the limitations clause in particular was intended to apply.

As the Danforth Commission report also noted, many "non-affirming" institutions were originally created on strong doctrinal foundations; and, indeed, the prospect of movement from constraint to freedom pervades the Association's engagement with the issue. The 1922 Association of American Colleges proposal, cited in Committee A's 1988 report, referred to the toleration of restrictions as a "temporary concession." The 1970 interpretive comment quoted above spoke of change in the perceived needs and desires of church-related institutions; and it may be worthy of note that the Association did not investigate issues of academic freedom at an institution devoted to clerical education until the Concordia Seminary (Missouri) case in 1975, where, prior to the event under investigation, the institution had come to allow a good deal of academic freedom to flourish.[3]

In other words, movement from constraint to freedom is a historical characteristic of many church-related institutions, and a thoughtful argument could be made for the proposition that, as a pervasively sectarian or proprietary institution ordinarily outside the ambit of the Association's concern moves toward becoming more open, it moves as well toward bringing itself within the compass of the 1940 *Statement*; and that when it has done so to such an extent as to be considered primarily as a seat of unfettered learning, such limited restrictions as the institution retains will be subject to the 1940 *Statement*'s prescriptive requirements, including the limitations clause.

Accordingly, Committee A offers the following set of operating guidelines for Association treatment of a complaint: (1) at the outset by the Association's staff; (2) by the ad hoc committee of investigation, if one is appointed; and (3) by Committee A in considering the ad hoc committee's report.

Guideline One

When a complaint is received from a faculty member alleging a restriction on academic freedom because of a religious or other aim, the staff should decide whether, in its view, the

---

[2] From its inception, the American Association of University Professors has found it necessary to distinguish between institutions of higher learning that are committed to academic freedom and those institutions where free inquiry is subordinated to a religious (or some other) mission. Committee A's seminal 1915 *Declaration of Principles on Academic Freedom and Academic Tenure*, commenting on these latter institutions, stated that

> They do not, at least as regards one particular subject, accept the principles of freedom of inquiry, of opinion, and of teaching; and their purpose is not to advance knowledge by the unrestricted research and unfettered discussion of impartial investigators, but rather to subsidize the promotion of the opinions held by the persons, usually not of the scholar's calling, who provide the funds for their maintenance. . . . Genuine boldness and thoroughness of inquiry, and freedom of speech, are scarcely reconcilable with the prescribed inculcation of a particular opinion upon a controverted question. (AAUP, *Policy Documents and Reports* [Washington, D.C., 2001], 293.)

[3] "Academic Freedom and Tenure: Concordia Seminary," *AAUP Bulletin* 61 (1975): 49–59.

institution is one at which adherence to the academic freedom provisions of the 1940 *Statement* is to be expected. Factors that the staff should consider include the institution's stated mission; its curriculum; its accreditation; its eligibility for tax support; its criteria for selection of its governing body, faculty, students, staff, and administration; and the ways in which it represents itself to the public in bulletins, catalogues, and other pronouncements.

If the staff concludes that the institution is not one at which adherence to the academic freedom provisions of the 1940 *Statement* is to be expected, the general secretary should decline to authorize an investigation.

Comment

The Association already draws an analogous distinction in the applicability of its provisions in that it declines to pursue cases arising at unaccredited institutions. No good reason exists, apart from ease of application, to permit determinations made by accreditation organizations, on which the Association has relatively little influence, to drive Association policy. (This is emphasized, perhaps, by the inclusion of proprietary and vocational "postsecondary education" within the realm of regional accreditation. Nor is state licensure by itself determinative, since the Association would not apply its processes to a "degree mill" authorized to award degrees under applicable state law.) It is only a next step to say that, despite regional accreditation and legal degree-granting authority, the Association's independent assessment of an institution may lead it to conclude that the institution does not purport to provide academic freedom and is not subject to the 1940 *Statement*.

It should be stressed in any event that if an institution is one at which adherence to the academic freedom provisions of the 1940 *Statement* is to be expected, the institution's invocation of the limitations clause does not absolve it of an obligation to afford due process in dismissal and nonreappointment actions as provided for in Association policies. On the contrary, the scope of the institution's limitation and the reasonable expectations of faculty members subject to it, the application of the limitation in the past, and the question whether it is being selectively applied for ulterior purposes are, among others, potential questions that may require a full hearing.

Guideline Two

Where the general secretary has authorized an investigation, the ad hoc committee should be charged with assessing whether or not the institution is subject to the provisions of the 1940 *Statement* in light of considerations of the kind pointed to in Guideline One. If it concludes that the institution is subject to those provisions, and if, further, the institution invoked the limitations clause, then the committee should assess how the limitation applies to the facts as found. Thus the ad hoc committee should consider the degree of specificity of the limitation and whether or not the institution afforded sufficient procedural safeguards to ensure that the application of its rules was adequately cabined.

Comment on the Clarity of the Proscription

It could be argued that an exact limitation is a practical impossibility; that no restrictive language could be devised that would at the same time anticipate future credal constraints or doctrinal disputes and meet a requirement that it be absolutely explicit.

Committee A sees the appropriate standard as not "absolutely explicit" (it is not even absolutely clear what that standard might require), but rather "adequately explicit." Thus, for example, a college's statement that it is "truly religious, but never denominational," that it is "positively and distinctly Christian in its influence, discipline, and instruction," is too broad, too inexact to constitute an acceptable limit on freedom of teaching. It does not provide a reasonable faculty member with clear enough information about—that is, fair warning of—what conduct is proscribed, and hence is not adequately explicit.

By contrast, a restriction on any teaching or utterance that "contradicts *explicit* principles of the [Church's] faith or morals," for example, is adequately explicit. It would, however, be incumbent on an institution adopting such a restriction to show that at the time of appointment, the institution and the faculty member knew precisely what those principles were. In a recent case, the institution required prospective faculty members to subscribe to a set of religious tenets, none of which explicitly proscribed conduct that could be taken as sympathetic to the civil rights of homosexuals; in taking action against a faculty member on grounds of conduct that was perceived as sympathetic to the civil rights of homosexuals, the governing board was bringing to bear on her a restriction of which she had not been given fair warning at the time of appointment.[4]

Adequate explicitness is plainly a matter of degree. Some institutions demand faithfulness to future teachings or doctrines that may be unascertained or unascertainable at the time and which may depart, subtly or radically, from those in effect at the time of appointment. A limitation drafted so broadly as to include any teaching, doctrine, or constraint subsequently promulgated would fail to meet the standard of adequate explicitness. But cases may arise where a restriction not imposed in express terms at the time of appointment can be viewed as covered by a broadly drafted rule because the restriction was reasonably anticipated.[5]

Guideline Three

Committee A is the body that decides, on the basis of the ad hoc committee's report, whether to recommend censure.

1. If Committee A concludes that the institution is not subject to the 1940 *Statement's* requirement to afford academic freedom, it should not recommend censure.
2. If Committee A concludes that the institution is subject to the 1940 *Statement* but has not adhered to the terms of the limitations clause, then Committee A should presumably recommend censure.
3. If Committee A concludes that the institution is subject to the 1940 *Statement* and has adhered to the terms of the limitations clause, then Committee A should not recommend censure unless it concludes that the institution has failed to afford academic due process, or has violated some other key provision of the 1940 *Statement* or of derivative Association-supported standards.

Comment on Institutions for Clerical Education

Committee A said in its 1988 report: "Higher education is not catechesis, and this is no less true for professional clerical education than for any other professional calling." The committee may conclude, however, that a particular institution that is dedicated to training members of the clergy in the faith is outside the ambit of the Association's censure process, in light of Committee A's assessment of considerations of the kind pointed to in Guideline One.

If such an institution was one at which adherence to the academic freedom provisions of the 1940 *Statement* was to be expected, but has now ceased to be one—perhaps because of action by its governing board—the Association may wish to give notice to the profession and the public that the change has taken place.

---

[4] "Academic Freedom and Tenure: Nyack College," *Academe* 80 (September–October 1994): 73–79.
[5] For example, Professor Ehlen at Concordia Seminary (Missouri) in 1975 could reasonably plead lack of adequate notice. But Professor Schmidt's claim at Concordia Theological Seminary (Indiana) in 1989 proved more troublesome; see "Academic Freedom and Tenure: Concordia Theological Seminary," *ibid.*, 75 (May–June 1989): 57–67.

On Crediting Prior Service Elsewhere as Part of the Probationary Period

The statement which follows was approved by the Association's Committee on Academic Freedom and Tenure (Committee A) and adopted by the Council of the American Association of University Professors in June 1978.

The 1940 *Statement of Principles on Academic Freedom and Tenure* defines the probationary period for faculty members as follows:

> Beginning with appointment to the rank of full-time instructor or a higher rank, the probationary period should not exceed seven years, including within this period full-time service in all institutions of higher education; but subject to the proviso that when, after a term of probationary service of more than three years in one or more institutions, a teacher is called to another institution, it may be agreed in writing that the new appointment is for a probationary period of not more than four years, even though thereby the person's total probationary period in the academic profession is extended beyond the normal maximum of seven years. Notice should be given at least one year prior to the expiration of the probationary period if the teacher is not to be continued in service after the expiration of that period.[1]

The underlying objective of the foregoing provision is to recognize university teaching as a profession in which, after a limited probationary period to demonstrate professional competence in their positions, faculty members achieve tenure in order to protect academic freedom and provide a reasonable degree of economic security. Tenure in the profession as a whole, rather than at a particular institution, is not a practical possibility, since a faculty appointment is at a given institution. Nevertheless, to the extent that experience anywhere provides relevant evidence about competence, excessive probation can occur not only at one institution but also through failure to grant any probationary credit for service at one or more previous institutions.

The 1940 *Statement* recognizes, however, that, because there is great diversity among institutions, not all experience is interchangeable, and that an institution may properly wish to determine whether an individual meets its standards for permanent appointment by on-the-spot experience. Thus a minimum probationary period, up to four years, at a given institution is a reasonable arrangement in appointing a person with prior service. It meets a reasonable demand of institutions which wish to make considered decisions on tenure based on performance at those institutions, and the needs of individuals who wished to obtain appointments that might not otherwise have been available to them because of insufficient time for evaluation.

The Association has long had complaints, primarily from research-oriented institutions, that the mandated counting of prior service elsewhere made it risky for them to offer appointments to unproved persons whose teaching experience was in a nonresearch setting or incidental to completion of graduate degree requirements. The Association's response has been to insist that the institutions and the individuals concerned should bear these risks, rather than allow for probationary service which exceeds four years at the current institution with the total probationary years in excess of seven.

---

[1] According to the 1970 Interpretive Comment Number 5: "The concept of 'rank of full-time instructor or a higher rank' is intended to include any person who teaches a full-time load regardless of the teacher's specific title" (AAUP, *Policy Documents and Reports*, 9th ed. [Washington, D.C., 2001], 6).

One consequence of the above, however, is that if an institution adheres to the provision for crediting prior service it is less likely to appoint persons with countable prior service but without demonstrated competence in their current position. Thus avoidance of excessive probation may result, particularly in a "buyer's" market, in unemployability. A second consequence is that institutions sometimes simply disassociate themselves from the 1940 *Statement* in the matter. Each consequence is unfortunate, and either suggests that departures from the existing proviso, to adjust to its changed impact, be allowed under certain circumstances

Nevertheless, the Association continues to take the position that the 1940 *Statement*'s provision for crediting prior service is sound, and it urges adherence to this position. It is particularly opposed to belated arrangements not to count prior service which are made in order to avoid an impending decision on tenure. The Association recognizes, however, that in specific cases the interests of all parties may best be served through agreement at the time of initial appointment to allow for more than four years of probationary service at the current institution (but not exceeding seven years), whatever the prior service elsewhere. Significantly different current responsibilities or a significantly different institutional setting can be persuasive factors in deciding that it is desirable to provide for a fuller current period of probation. In these specific cases, if the policy respecting the probationary period has been approved by the faculty or a representative faculty body, the Association will not view an agreement not to credit prior service as a violation of principles of academic freedom and tenure warranting an expression of Association concern.

In dealing with previous service, the 1940 *Statement*'s admonition that "the precise terms and conditions of every appointment should be stated in writing and be in the possession of both institution and teacher before the appointment is consummated" is particularly important. The years of previous service to be credited should be determined and set forth in writing at the time of initial appointment.

The previous service which should be taken into account is full-time faculty service at an institution of higher education that was accredited or was an official candidate for accreditation by a recognized United States accrediting agency.

Questions on whether to take into account previous service which occurred many years in the past, or previous service in a distinctly different area, should be referred to an appropriate faculty committee at the time of initial appointment.

Faculty Tenure and the End of Mandatory Retirement

The statement which follows was approved by the Association's Committee on Academic Freedom and Tenure (Committee A), adopted by the Association's Council in June 1989, and endorsed by the Seventy-fifth Annual Meeting.

The 1940 *Statement of Principles on Academic Freedom and Tenure* declares that tenure shall continue, absent financial exigency, dismissal for cause, or retirement for age. Since January 1, 1994, however, mandatory retirement for age is prohibited under the federal Age Discrimination in Employment Act. Thus the 1940 *Statement* must be read to mean that retirement terminates tenure, but retirement cannot be "for age."

What does tenure mean in the age of no mandatory retirement? It means that faculty members have tenure until they choose to retire, absent cause for dismissal or financial exigency. But it means, moreover, that by law their terms and conditions of employment cannot be different, because of their age, from those of their younger colleagues. They cannot be singled out for periodic review—no matter how such review is characterized. If there is periodic review for all tenured professors, such review cannot, of course, imply a potential termination of tenure without the safeguards of dismissal-for-cause procedures; it can, on the other hand, determine salary raises for faculty members of all ages.[1]

Contributions to pension plans cannot be terminated nor scaled back on the basis of age.[2] Other benefits, such as life insurance, can be based on age if justified by costs. Faculty members may not be singled out on the basis of age to be urged to cut back to part-time appointments. Office and laboratory facilities cannot be reduced only for faculty members of a certain age.

The abolition of mandatory retirement recognizes that faculty members are individuals whose productivity is not necessarily linked with age. It makes possible judgments based on individual characteristics, not on stereotypes. Some faculty members will choose to retire long before age seventy, particularly if they are assured an adequate retirement income and appropriate treatment by their institution; others will choose to reduce their commitments to part time as they grow older. These will be their choices based on their own circumstances, taking into account the best interests of their students, their colleagues, and their institution, in the best tradition of faculty responsibility.

---

[1] See "Post-Tenure-Review: An AAUP Response," AAUP, *Policy Documents and Reports*, 9th ed. (Washington, D.C., 2001), 50–56.

[2] Limits based on length of service can, however, be built into defined-benefit plans consistent with the Age Discrimination in Employment Act.

Tenure in the Medical School

The report which follows, approved in 1999 by the Association's Committee on Academic Freedom and Tenure (Committee A), is a revision of a report approved for publication by Committee A in November 1995.

INTRODUCTION AND BACKGROUND[1]

This report and proposed policy statement result from ongoing concerns within the American Association of University Professors regarding the changing nature of academic medical centers in American higher education and the impact, evident or potential, of those changes on questions of faculty status and academic freedom within such centers.

Until the early twentieth century, few medical schools were affiliated with universities, most being freestanding proprietary schools of varying standards. The faculty were largely physicians whose income was derived from the private practice of medicine and fees from students. Reforms in medical education early in this century were influenced by the Flexner report and fostered by the American Medical Association, and required the affiliation of medical schools with universities along European (particularly German) lines, with the concurrent establishment of basic-science departments for research and teaching.[2] The new university-affiliated medical schools developed full-time, salaried faculty, some of whom were not physicians but basic scientists by training, and their arrival coincided with the formation of the American Association of University Professors and the development of policies and standards relating to academic freedom and tenure.

The rapid post–World War II growth of medical schools resulted in major changes, including the increase in the number of medical students, curricular revision, augmented postgraduate medical training in clinical specialties (residency programs), greater emphasis on research and patient care, and the creation of non-tenure-track lines of full-time as well as part-time faculty. These expanded responsibilities required an expansion in the total number of faculty as well, and altered the relationship between the faculty and the medical school and also between the medical school and the university. Faculty salaries have become increasingly dependent on income from outside sources (e.g., research grants for faculty in basic-science departments and for nonphysician scientists in clinical department and fees from patient-care activities for physician faculty). Academic advancement and tenure have become increasingly based on scholarly research and publications, and less on teaching and service.

Medical schools have a unique status among institutions of higher learning. Whether state or private, they are large institutions which, with few exceptions, are part of or affiliated with universities. They encompass diverse educational and research interests ranging from molecular biology to preventive medicine. They rely on affiliated hospitals and clinics for patients for medical practice and teaching of students, postgraduates (residents), and fellows.

If medical schools are very different from the universities with which they are affiliated, they are also very different institutions from what they were three decades ago. Then a medical school looked a lot more like the rest of the university. Its revenues came from the same combination

---

[1] Much of the background section of this report has been adopted freely (and with thanks) from a 1994 report by an AAUP Task Force on Medical Schools.

[2] Abraham Flexner, *Medical Education in the United States and Canada* (Boston: Merrymount Press, 1910; Carnegie Foundation for the Advancement of Teaching, Bulletin #4); Lester S. King, *American Medicine Comes of Age, 1840–1920* (Chicago: American Medical Association, 1984); Paul Starr, *The Social Transformation of American Medicine* (New York: Basic Books, 1982).

of sources, but the proportions of that income were very different from what they are now. Revenue now comes from tuition and fees, state and local governments, federal funds (research and other income), endowment, contract research, and medical services.

The number of medical students has not grown in recent years[3] but that number is about double that of thirty-five years ago. The number of faculty members, however, has grown dramatically over that period of time. Today there are about 75,000 faculty members in medical schools. A very substantial number of the newly added faculty members are appointed to full-time positions in clinical departments, but most of their responsibilities are in billable patient care and clinical teaching (supervising medical students in practice settings). The balance between income-generating patient services and the teaching of students weighs heavily on the side of the former. The rapid growth in the number of clinical faculty members, a number about ten times as large as thirty-five years ago, is almost entirely due to its role in producing revenue, as the number of students has only doubled since then.

Because of the volatility of the environment in which medical schools function, now and in the future, it is especially appropriate that the role of tenure as the guarantor of academic freedom in these institutions receive examination. Faculty members in medical schools face problems with respect to tenure different from those faced by faculty members in other parts of the university. The expectation that tenured faculty members create their own salaries from the provision of medical services or research grants will cause increasing problems as resources become scarcer. For example, reliance on external funding for salary support poses special problems for nonphysician tenured and tenure-track faculty researchers in clinical departments. If these faculty members lose research grant support, they cannot turn to medical practice to earn a salary. Their vulnerability is greater than that of tenured physician faculty members who can teach medical specialties and who can earn income by medical practice, as well as that of tenured faculty members in basic-science departments who can teach in their academic specialties.

As a provider of health care, a medical school needs income derived from the clinical services to provide a large share of the salaries of the physician faculty. Physicians who provide patient care include tenure-track and tenured faculty, non-tenure-track faculty, and resident and subspecialty physicians in training. The non-tenure-track physician faculty, who are not necessarily required to be scholars and may do little teaching, provide much of the care of patients, whose fees add to the income of the medical school.

The modern medical school, in short, has the attributes of a business enterprise with largely individual entrepreneurial activities in both patient care and research. Those faculty members so involved are counted on to bring in funds not only to underwrite salaries for supporting personnel, laboratory equipment and supplies, and those indirect costs necessary to maintain the infrastructure of the enterprise, but also to underwrite faculty salaries, including in many cases a portion of the salaries of tenured faculty members. Academic advancement of faculty in basic-science departments and nonphysician faculty in clinical departments is disproportionately dependent upon scholarly research as compared with teaching and service, and the research in turn is disproportionately dependent on salary support from research grants. The heavy dependence on external funding for salary support can divert faculty dedication and effort away from teaching and university service toward research or patient care to maintain their income and status.

The challenges facing the medical school have been succinctly stated by the president of the Association of American Medical Colleges (AAMC), Dr. Jordan J. Cohen:

[3] Robert F. Jones, *American Medical Education: Institutions, Programs, and Issues* (Washington, D.C.: Association of American Medical Colleges, 1992), 10.

The existence of tenure in medical schools represents a linkage to the broader academic culture of the university, with its traditional devotion to a free exchange of ideas without threat of economic penalty. Yet medical schools, because of their increased involvement n the real world of health-care delivery, are also linked to the corporate culture, with its brutal devotion to productivity without guarantees of economic security. The clash of these cultures is reaching deafening proportions and will challenge the most adroit academic administrators. If medical schools are to succeed, they must avoid the Scylla of an ivory-tower disregard of new competitive realities and the Charybdis of a corporate sellout of academic values.[4]

In this report Committee A has attempted to maintain an awareness of precisely those twin dangers.

ISSUES WITH RESPECT TO ASSOCIATION POLICY

The general concern of Committee A is whether medical schools support, or are prepared in the near and long-term future to support, the policies and procedures relating to academic freedom, tenure, and due process that have been promulgated by the AAUP since its founding. The need for a review of Association policy is suggested by the questions raised by some medical school administrators and faculty about the validity of and need for tenure, along with instances of abridgment of academic freedom and due process in medical schools. Among the issues we have noted are: (1) the appearance of de facto departures from standards, for example, in regard to the application of the probationary period; (2) the increasing use of non-tenurable full-time as well as part-time faculty; (3) in some, though not all, medical schools, an apparently inadequate role for medical school faculty in institutional governance, particularly in terms of faculty status, working conditions, and curriculum; and (4) a concern about possible intrusion by outside agents (e.g., state legislatures, Congress, licensing authorities) on governance and curriculum.

Although there is no doubt that the intensity of debate regarding the future of tenure in medical schools is considerably heightened as a result of the pressures we have been outlining, recent studies indicate that tenure in some form remains at the core of the faculty staffing policies of such schools.[5] The issue of tenure is more dramatically highlighted in the drop in the proportion of clinical faculty with tenure or on the tenure track.[6] Within the tenure track, there is growing belief that a six-year probationary period may be inadequate "for basic-science faculty to establish themselves as independent investigators, especially given the competition for research funding." If tenure is suffering erosion, it has not yet endured a frontal attack.

But even where the presence of tenure suggests the reassuring persistence of the system, there is solid evidence that the financial assurances of that system are being defined in a more limited way: that is, in connection with the percentage of institutional "hard money" in the tenure line. Unlike the situation in other academic units in modern American colleges and universities, it is not uncommon in medical schools to have tenure guarantees attached to, say, 20 or 30 percent of a faculty member's full-time appointment, with the remainder of the salary dependent on the procurement of external funding. Inasmuch as the 1940 *Statement of Principles*

[4] Jordan J. Cohen, "Academic Medicine's Tenuous Hold on Tenure," *Academic Medicine* 70 (1995): 294.
[5] The conclusion of Robert F. Jones and Susan C. Sanderson, "Tenure Policies in U.S. and Canadian Medical Schools" (*ibid.*, 69 [1994]: 772–78), is that "medical schools have adapted tenure policies to allow themselves flexibility in meeting their academic and clinical missions. The forces driving schools to fashion unique faculty appointment arrangements are not dissipating. Tenure is likely to continue in the academic medical center of the future but to play a diminished role."
[6] "In 1983, 30,856 clinical faculty were listed on the FRS [Association of American Medical Colleges Faculty Roster System], with 59 percent in tenure streams. . . . By 1993, the number of clinical faculty listed on the FRS had nearly doubled, to 58,607. Only 47 percent were in tenure streams: 26 percent with tenure and 21 percent on track" (*ibid.*, 773).

on *Academic Freedom and Tenure,* drafted and endorsed by the AAUP and the Association of American Colleges and Universities and carrying the endorsement of 170 educational and professional associations, links tenure not only to "freedom of teaching and research and of extramural activities," but also to "a sufficient degree of economic security to make the profession attractive to men and women of ability," there would seem to be involved in appointments of the sort just described a very real question as to precisely what tenure means under conditions that protect only a portion of the faculty member's income. A reasonable interpretation of the 1940 *Statement* would seem to imply that the ability of the faculty member to defend academic freedom, his or her own or the principle in general, is linked to whether the salary is adequate to the maintenance of financial independence.[7]

At the same time, the enormous diversity of medical school programs and of the variety of faculty who teach in them suggests that certain kinds of appointments were not foreseen by, and in any case not intended to fall within the ambit of, the 1940 *Statement*. In contrast to academic faculty of the sort envisioned by that statement, academic physicians deal directly with the general public (patients) in an income-producing environment. Their relationship to the institution with which they are affiliated is therefore fundamentally unlike that of the full-time teachers and investigators who are described in the statement. We acknowledge that no policy adopted by the Association with respect to the academic culture of medical schools can command the adherence of those schools without taking into account the nature of the medical enterprise. Nonetheless, we believe that existing Association policy can convincingly address many of those realities.[8]

The subcommittee acknowledges that medical schools to some extent, and increasingly, partake of the nature of corporate as well as academic enterprise. (Here we would content ourselves with noting that corporations are not by definition incapable of offering appropriate guarantees of appointment.) Association policy must be flexible enough to address this question in a principled manner while being persuasive in terms of policy guidance to those engaged in the daily work of medical education. We also believe, however, that the presence of income-generating activities in no way weakens the claim of faculty members in those schools to the protections of academic freedom and tenure consistent with the particular role that a given faculty member plays. To the extent that medical schools, and academic health centers, are academic institutions, and that an appointment in them is subject to those expectations which apply to

---

[7] Practices vary widely with respect to the percentage of clinical appointments that may be tenured, and in some cases the tenured portion may be so negligible as to be of little concern to the clinical faculty member. The situation has become much more complex since the time of the 1940 *Statement*, and its framers doubtless would not have envisioned the complexities that have emerged. We suggest using a basic-science salary line as a guidepost for determining salary guarantees for clinical faculty members. The faculty of the particular school should be involved in arriving at a specific recommendation. Creative approaches not overtly at odds with existing Association policy seem possible. Thus, one school represented on the subcommittee has adopted a commitment to support such a faculty member at the fiftieth percentile at his or her academic rank as reported annually by the AAMC, or the present salary of the individual, whichever is less.

[8] Although dealing primarily with term contracts in the area of sponsored research, the Association's 1969 "Report of the Special Committee on Academic Personnel Ineligible for Tenure" (AAUP, *Policy Documents and Reports*, 9th ed. [Washington, D.C., 2001], 88–91) acknowledges a category of employment, "contract research teams," to which "traditional concepts of academic freedom and tenure do not apply." It also argues, however, that "whenever academic institutions designate full-time researchers as faculty members, either by formal appointment or by conferring the titles of instructor, assistant or associate professor, or professor, those researchers should have all the rights of other faculty members." In the case of faculty members whose title is modified by the designation "clinical," this issue now presents itself in a new light which we believe needs to be addressed here. More reluctantly, but with the awareness that the Association must nonetheless take account of changing realities, AAUP's Committee on Part-Time and Non-Tenure-Track Appointments has developed, and the Association's Council (1993) approved, a document setting forth the basic protections that should be applied to non-tenure-track faculty: "The Status of Non-Tenure-Track Faculty" (*ibid.*, 77–87; see Statement of Policy below, point 2).

tenured and tenure-track appointments in other disciplinary areas of the university, we see no basis for conceding that such appointments are immune from the application of Association standards. To the extent that an appointment in, for example, a teaching hospital, with perhaps peripheral instructional duties and the expectation of the generation of clinical income, is essentially that of a practitioner, we do not assert that the award of tenure is necessarily appropriate. Rather, we would argue that such classes of faculty should enjoy academic freedom, including, but not restricted to, the right to speak on institutional policy, and that they should be provided with protections against the application of unreasonable or capricious sanctions, such as precipitate dismissal, without the opportunity for a hearing, during a stated term of appointment. An important part of the responsibility for ensuring these conditions lies with the tenured faculty of the institution, in the context of a sound system of shared governance.

For the goal of quality to be implemented in a qualitatively sound way, the faculty members who offer medical education under substantially the same expectations of performance applicable to tenure-track faculty in other disciplines at that institution must have the same opportunity to benefit from freedom of inquiry, in teaching, research, and clinical practice, that ensures high quality in other areas of the academic enterprise. This includes the customary assurances of peer review and the right of appeal (rather than the mere delegation of review to officers of the medical school administration), a probationary period consonant with AAUP standards, a level of participation in the governance of the medical school appropriate to the particular kind of faculty appointment, and sufficient economic security to provide a safeguard for the exercise of academic freedom by all faculty.[9] There should be collegial development of policies regarding laboratory space, clinical and other work assignments, research and space resources, and procedures which encourage the resolution of differences through peer review. In short, after giving all due allowance to the specific realities of the teaching and research environment in medical schools, we do not believe that they are so peculiar as to warrant placing all faculty in such schools beyond the academic pale, that is, outside the generally accepted standards set forth in the 1940 *Statement* and derivative policies of this Association.

STATEMENT OF POLICY

1. The multiple purposes of an academic medical school have led to a variety of academic appointments—tenured, tenure-track, and nontenurable—in which teaching, research, service, clinical practice, and patient care are given different weights and emphases. To the extent that these functions are all designated by traditional academic titles, however modified (e.g., clinical associate professor), they warrant the assumption of faculty status which brings the holders of those titles within the ambit of applicable Association policies and procedures, and hence the protections appropriate to a particular status.

2. Where the configuration of duties is such as to suggest the advisability of an appointment in a non-tenure-track position, a starting point for considering the obligations of the medical school may be found in the Association's 1993 report, *The Status of Non-Tenure-Track Faculty,* for all classes of faculty, full or part time. Where the exigencies of particular kinds of faculty appointments may require exceptions to the standards set forth in that document, those exceptions should be specified after meaningful consultation with the appropriate faculty bodies in the medical school.

3. The Association has never countenanced the creation of large classes of faculty in categories other than tenured, tenure-track, and visiting (or other appointments designated

---

[9] In medical schools, the extent of the inclusion in departmental and faculty governance structures will depend on the extent to which the particular faculty member has responsibility for organizational or instructional matters which go beyond the specific, part-time instructional function for which he or she was appointed. For example, representation on a faculty curriculum committee by a part-time clinical faculty member who has been asked to organize student rotations in primary-care physicians' offices might seem reasonable. Likewise, the inclusion of a full-time non-tenure-track researcher on a faculty research committee might be deemed appropriate.

as short-term with a terminus understood by both parties to the contract). To the extent that a faculty appointment at a medical school resembles a traditional academic appointment, with clearly understood obligations in teaching, research, and service, the burden of proof on the institution is greater to justify making the appointment to a non-tenure-track position.

4. Tenure in a medical school should normally be awarded to a faculty member on the basis of the probationary period as defined in the 1940 *Statement, viz:*

> Beginning with appointment to the rank of full-time instructor or a higher rank, the probationary period should not exceed seven years, including within this period full-time service in all institutions of higher education; but subject to the proviso that when, after a term of probationary service of more than three years in one or more institutions, a teacher is called to another institution, it may be agreed in writing that the new appointment is for a probationary period of not more than four years, even though thereby the person's total probationary period in the academic profession is extended beyond the normal maximum of seven years. Notice should be given at least one year prior to the expiration of the probationary period if the teacher is not to be continued after the expiration of that period [cf. also the Association's *Standards for Notice of Nonreappointment* (1964)].

We note a number of devices in the medical school setting to lengthen the probationary period, for example, by allowing adequate time for persons in clinical positions to seek board certification, time devoted to patient care rather than research. While the complexities with respect to clinical practice may make such arrangements not only useful, but beneficial to the clinical faculty member, we see no reason to consider the extension of such a practice to researchers in the basic sciences when expectations for the award of tenure conform to those extant in connection with appointments elsewhere in the university.

5. The sources of funding for positions in academic medical schools vary perhaps more greatly than in other units of the university, with the faculty member being expected in many cases to make up a designated portion of his or her salary from patient care or research. The 1940 *Statement of Principles* stipulates that tenure is a means not only to academic freedom, but also to "a sufficient degree of economic security to make the profession attractive to men and women of ability." Except, as is sometimes the case, where the reward of rank and tenure is purely honorific, all tenured and tenure-track faculty should be guaranteed an assured minimum salary adequate to the maintenance of support at a level appropriate to faculty members in the basic sciences, and not merely a token stipend, on a formula to be determined by the administration and board of trustees after consultation with a representative body of the faculty. The unilateral administrative abrogation of a portion of that salary, absent a prior understanding as to the extent of its guarantee, may reasonably be interpreted not as an exercise of fiduciary responsibility but as an attack on the principle of tenure. While the same minimum may not apply in the case of non-tenure-track faculty, those faculty should have a clearly understood and contractually enforceable expectation of a stipulated salary which cannot be unilaterally or arbitrarily abridged during the appointment period. Although the extent of economic security may be subject to interpretation, due process must be assured for all faculty regardless of the nature of the appointment.

6. Since medical schools, whether freestanding or part of a larger institution, demonstrably engage many of their faculty in the traditional areas of teaching and research, the participation of the faculty in governance is as essential to educational quality in the medical school context as in any other part of the university. According to the Association's 1966 *Statement on Government of Colleges and Universities,*

> The faculty has primary responsibility for such fundamental areas as curriculum, subject matter and methods of instruction, research, faculty status, and those aspects of student life which relate to the educational process. On these matters the power of review or final decision lodged in the governing board or delegated by it to the president should be exercised adversely only in exceptional circumstances, and for reasons communicated to the faculty.

The level of faculty participation, of course, may be adjusted in individual cases to take into account such considerations as the tenurable or nontenurable nature of the appointment, as well as full- or part-time status, though we suggest that a functional definition of the faculty member's role ought to be the chief determinant. We have seen no compelling argument why the faculty of such schools should exercise a more limited influence in those schools than do faculty elsewhere in higher education, especially since in an academic health center a large portion of the budget may be generated by faculty in the form of clinical income as well as external grants. Key to the role of medical faculty, for the purposes of the present report, is the opportunity to define the terms and conditions of faculty employment, including such appointments as are necessary to meet institutional needs, and procedures for the award of tenure under Association-supported standards.

CONCLUSION

The Association has long held that academic tenure is not merely, or even most importantly, a form of job security, but rather an instrument for the protection of "the common good." In serving that function, a system of tenure, properly applied, is a guarantor of educational quality. We question whether any institution of higher education or one of its components, whether the purpose be undergraduate, graduate, or professional education, can provide such educational quality without that reasonable assurance of stability that helps ensure the commitment of its faculty members to freedom of inquiry in teaching and research and to the preparation of its students.

Academic Freedom in the
Medical School

The statement which follows was adopted by the participants in the Conference on Academic Values in the Transformation of Academic Medicine in May 1999. It was endorsed in June 1999 by the Association's Committee on Academic Freedom and Tenure (Committee A), adopted by the AAUP Council, and approved by the Eighty-fifth Annual Meeting.

The term "academic freedom" refers to the freedom of college and university faculty to teach, to conduct research and publish the results, and to fulfill responsibilities as officers of an educational institution. Academic freedom is a core value in the American community of higher learning. Its protection is a crucial responsibility of university faculties, administrations, and governing boards. While academic freedom clearly safeguards the work of professors and their institutions, its primary purpose is to advance the general welfare. In the words of the seminal 1940 *Statement of Principles on Academic Freedom and Tenure*, "Institutions of higher education are conducted for the common good and not to further the interest of either the individual teacher or the institution as a whole. The common good depends upon the free search for truth and its free expression."[1]

An administrative officer in academic medicine has recently observed that the issue of academic freedom, so central to the academic life of the university, "has rarely been debated within our nation's medical schools."[2] With the major changes that are currently in process in academic health centers—in the teaching of students, in the status of medical school faculty, and in the conditions under which these faculty members work—it is urgent that this topic now be addressed.

The modern medical school has many of the attributes of a complex, market-driven health care system with professors often acting as entrepreneurs in research and in patient care. It is marked by conflicting roles and responsibilities, both academic and nonacademic, for faculty members and administrators alike. The intense competition for private or governmental funding can affect the choice of research subjects, and in some instances, scientists in academic medicine are finding it difficult to secure funding for unorthodox research or research on matters that are politically sensitive. The growing reliance on the clinical enterprise at many medical schools, and the resulting expansion of the number of professors who are engaged mainly in clinical work, may serve to divert the schools from their teaching mission, and may implicitly or explicitly dissuade professors from devoting their attention to such activities as graduate teaching or university service that are not income producing in nature. Further affecting the academic freedom of medical school faculty is the hospital pattern of hierarchical organization, with deans and department chairs—and often professional administrators who lack medical training or academic experience—making decisions that elsewhere in the university would be made collegially or left to individual professors. Academic freedom should be especially nurtured and supported because of the constraints surrounding medical research. Rules governing

---

[1] AAUP, *Policy Documents and Reports*, 9th ed. (Washington, D.C., 2001), 3. For a discussion of problems relating to academic medicine and the importance of tenure as a protection for academic freedom, see "Tenure in the Medical School," *ibid.*, 103–9.

[2] N. Lynn Eckhert, "Time Is Ripe for Dialogue About Academic Freedom," *Academic Physician and Scientist* (July/August 1998): 3.

genetic research and engineering, debates about the beginning and end of human life, and disputes about the use of animals for research and experimentation are examples of matters that can profoundly affect the work of medical school professors. While society may require restraints on the pursuit of knowledge in these and other similarly sensitive areas, basic principles of academic freedom, in the medical school as elsewhere in an institution of higher learning, must be observed.

1. Freedom to Inquire and to Publish

The freedom to pursue research and the correlative right to transmit the fruits of inquiry to the wider community—without limitations from corporate or political interests and without prior restraint or fear of subsequent punishment—are essential to the advancement of knowledge. Accordingly, principles of academic freedom allow professors to publish or otherwise disseminate research findings that may offend the commercial sponsors of the research, potential donors, or political interests, or people with certain religious or social persuasions. As stated in a 1981 AAUP report, however, "Academic freedom does not give its possessors the right to impose any risk of harm they like in the name of freedom of inquiry. It is no violation of any right . . . that falls into the cluster named by 'academic freedom' for a university to prevent a member of its faculty from carrying out research, at the university, that would impose a high risk of serious physical harm on its subjects, and that would in only minimal ways benefit either them or the state of knowledge in the field in question."[3] The pursuit of medical research should proceed with due regard for the rights of individuals as provided by National Institutes of Health and university protocols on the use of human and animal subjects. Any research plan involving such matters should be reviewed by a body of faculty peers or an institutional review board both before research is initiated and while it is being conducted. Any limitations on academic freedom because of the religious or other aims of an institution should be clearly stated in writing at the time of initial appointment.

2. Freedom to Teach

The freedom to teach includes the right of the faculty to select the materials, determine the approach to the subject, make the assignments, and assess student academic performance in teaching activities for which faculty members are individually responsible, without having their decisions subject to the veto of a department chair, dean, or other administrative officer. Teaching duties in medical schools that are commonly shared among a number of faculty members require a significant amount of coordination and the imposition of a certain degree of structure, and often involve a need for agreement on such matters as general course content, syllabi, and examinations. Often, under these circumstances, the decisions of the group may prevail over the dissenting position of a particular individual.

When faculty members are engaged in patient care, they have a special obligation to respect the rights of their patients and to exercise appropriate discretion while on rounds or in other nonclassroom settings.

3. Freedom to Question and to Criticize

According to a 1994 AAUP statement, *On the Relationship of Faculty Governance to Academic Freedom*, faculty members should be free to speak out "on matters having to do with their institution and its policies," and they should be able "to express their professional opinions without fear of reprisal."[4] In speaking critically, faculty members should strive for accuracy and should exercise appropriate restraint. Tolerance of criticism, however, is a crucial component of the academic environment and of an institution's ultimate vitality. No attribute of the modern medical school which may distinguish it from other units within a university should serve as a pretext for abridging the role of the medical faculty in institutional governance, including, but not necessarily confined to, those areas specified in the AAUP's 1966 *Statement on Government of Colleges and Universities* as falling within the faculty's primary responsibility.[5]

---

[3] Regulations Governing Research on Human Subjects," *Academe: Bulletin of the AAUP* 67 (December 1981): 367.
[4] *Policy Documents and Reports*, 224–27.
[5] *Ibid.*, 217–23. See also the derivative statement, "Faculty Participation in the Selection, Evaluation, and Retention of Administrators," *ibid.*, 228–29.

* * * * *

Despite the serious challenges currently facing them, our institutions of academic medicine should respect and foster conditions that are essential to freedom of learning, freedom of teaching, and freedom of expression.

The Assignment of Course Grades and Student Appeals

The statement which follows was approved by the Association's Committee on Academic Freedom and Tenure (Committee A) in June 1997, and further revised by Committee A in June 1998.

The American Association of University Professors regularly receives inquiries concerning the right of instructors to assign course grades to students, the right of students to challenge the assigned grades, and the circumstances and procedures under which student appeals should be made. The Association's Committee A on Academic Freedom and Tenure has approved the issuance of general guidelines on this subject. The following statement is intended to guide faculty members, administrators, and students with respect to the assignment of student grades and student appeals.

THE RIGHT OF AN INSTRUCTOR TO ASSIGN GRADES

The Association's *Statement on Government of Colleges and Universities* places primary responsibility with the faculty "for such fundamental areas as curriculum, subject matter, and methods of instruction."[1] The assessment of student academic performance, it follows, including the assignment of particular grades, is a faculty responsibility. Recognizing the authority of the instructor of record to evaluate the academic performance of students enrolled in a course he or she is teaching is a direct corollary of the instructor's "freedom in the classroom" which the 1940 *Statement of Principles on Academic Freedom and Tenure* assures.[2] The faculty member offering the course, it follows, should be responsible for the evaluation of student course work and, under normal circumstances, is the sole judge of the grades received by the students in that course.

THE RIGHT OF A STUDENT TO APPEAL

According to the Association's *Statement on Professional Ethics*, "professors make every reasonable effort . . . to ensure that their evaluations of students reflect each student's true merit."[3] The academic community proceeds under the strong presumption that the instructor's evaluations are authoritative. At the same time, of course, situations do arise in which a student alleges that a grade he or she has received is wrong, and the *Joint Statement on Rights and Freedoms of Students* provides that "students should have protection through orderly procedures against prejudiced or capricious academic evaluation."[4] A suitable mechanism for appeal, one which respects both the prerogatives of instructors and the rights of students in this regard, should thus be available for reviewing allegations that inappropriate criteria were used in determining the grade or that the instructor did not adhere to stated procedures or grading standards.[5]

---

[1] AAUP, *Policy Documents and Reports*, 9th ed. (Washington, D.C., 2001), 221.

[2] *Ibid.*, 3.

[3] *Ibid.*, 133.

[4] *Ibid.*, 262.

[5] Institutions receiving federal funds are required to provide procedures by which students can challenge grades that they believe may have been tainted by gender or disability discrimination. See, e.g., 34 CFR Sections 106.8 and 104.7 and 28 CFR 35.107. The *Sexual Harassment Guidance*, issued by the Department of Education's Office for Civil Rights (OCR), 62 *Fed. Reg.* 12034, 12044–45, provides information on the necessary components of such procedures. Such grievance procedures are also recommended to address allegations of race and national origin discrimination. See *Protecting Students from Harassment and Hate Crimes: A Guide for Schools*, a joint effort of the OCR and the National Association of Attorneys General.

Under no circumstances should administrative officers on their own authority substitute their judgment for that of the faculty concerning the assignment of a grade. The review of a student complaint over a grade should be by faculty, under procedures adopted by faculty, and any resulting change in a grade should be by faculty authorization.

PROCEDURES FOR APPEAL

Committee A offers the following, not as a single procedure for grade appeals that all should follow, but as recommended procedural considerations.

1. A student who wishes to complain about a grade would be expected to discuss the matter first with the course instructor, doing so as soon as possible after receiving the grade.
2. The instructor should be willing to listen, to provide explanation, and to be receptive to changing the grade if the student provides convincing argument for doing so. (In most cases the discussion between the student and the instructor should suffice and the matter should not need to be carried further.)
3. If, after the discussion with the instructor, the student's concerns remain unresolved, the student might then approach the instructor's department chair or another member of the faculty who is the instructor's immediate administrative superior. That person, if he or she believes that the complaint may have merit, would be expected to discuss it with the instructor. If the matter still remains unresolved, it should be referred to an ad hoc faculty committee.
4. The ad hoc committee would ordinarily be composed of faculty members in the instructor's department or in closely allied fields. The committee would examine available written information on the dispute, would be available for meetings with the student and with the instructor, and would meet with others as it sees fit.
5. If the faculty committee, through its inquiries and deliberations, determines that compelling reasons exist to change the grade, it would request that the instructor make the change, providing the instructor with a written explanation of its reasons. Should the instructor decline, he or she should provide an explanation for refusing.
6. The faculty committee, after considering the instructor's explanation and upon concluding that it would be unjust to allow the original grade to stand, may then recommend to the department head or to the instructor's immediate administrative superior that the grade be changed. That individual will provide the instructor with a copy of the recommendation and will ask the instructor to implement it. If the instructor continues to decline, that individual may then change the grade, notifying the instructor and the student of this action. Only that individual, upon the written recommendation of the faculty committee, should have the authority to effect a change in grade over the objection of the instructor who assigned the original grade.

College and University Policies on Substance Abuse and Drug Testing

The report which follows, prepared by a subcommittee of the Association's Committee on Academic Freedom and Tenure (Committee A), was approved for publication by Committee A in February 1992 and adopted by the Association's Council in November 1994.

INTRODUCTION

Implications of the "war on drugs" for the Association's interest in advancing the cause of higher education and the welfare of the academic profession may not be readily apparent.[1] Federal legislation requiring colleges and universities to enforce anti-drug and -alcohol policies and publicize drug-related incidents at colleges and universities, however, heightens concern over the manner in which substance abuse is handled in higher education. Some institutions have adopted, and others are considering, drug-testing programs, and federal regulations mandate drug testing in some instances.

Substance abuse is not limited to the use of illegal drugs. It includes alcohol abuse, which is likely to have a higher incidence within the academy than abuse of illicit drugs. The obligations federal law imposes on institutions of higher education cover some alcohol-related issues, but their unmistakable focus is on use of illegal drugs.

On a case-by-case basis, abuse of alcohol and other drugs by members of the academy may cause very serious problems. Methods of addressing instances of alcohol and drug abuse within the academy should be developed by institutions. We see no reason, however, to create programs, policies, and systems that combat substance abuse by sacrificing the academy's traditional commitments to self-governance, due process, and professional standards of competence.

The federally mandated means by which institutions of higher education are to participate in the "war on drugs" lack full appreciation for the traditions that serve the academy well. We do not consider it a wise policy for the federal government to compel specific types of actions by institutions of higher education in dealing with substance abuse. But the subcommittee recognizes that refusing to comply with the requirements imposed by federal legislation endangers funding that may be essential to the very existence of academic institutions. We understand, therefore, the need to comply with the federal law, but urge institutions to tailor their compliance activities narrowly in order to avoid dilution of their educational missions and to maintain meaningful commitments to Association-supported policies and practices that are designed to protect academic freedom and tenure.[2]

This report discusses some of the important implications for Association-supported standards of federal requirements for institutional anti-drug and -alcohol policies and drug-testing

---

[1] The Association's policies do not specifically address drug abuse. The Association has, however, addressed other highly charged debates over drugs. See 1968 Annual Meeting resolution, "Legislation on Drugs," *AAUP Bulletin* 54 (1968): 244.

[2] To ensure no misunderstanding, the subcommittee does not assert that, as a *Washington Post* editorial referred to it, "some warped interpretation of academic freedom" requires or encourages institutions to "wink" or to "look the other way when anti-drug laws are violated on campus or by a member of the college or university community." See "Testing for Drugs on Campus," *Washington Post*, 8 April 1991, A16, col. 1. As this report should make clear, effective participation in the "war on drugs" and preservation of academic freedom are neither inconsistent nor irreconcilable. The real challenge is to demonstrate the resolve necessary to combat substance abuse without abandoning institutional structures that promote academic freedom.

programs on campuses. We highlight some of the significant issues that have arisen and dangers posed to traditional standards in the academy when participation in the "war on drugs" obscures the academic character of institutions.

The subcommittee believes that colleges and universities should emphasize education and rehabilitative intervention to address individual substance-abuse problems. They should resist governmental or societal pressures to rely primarily on highly intrusive procedures for discovering drug abuse and punitive sanctions for drug- and alcohol-related conduct.

FEDERAL REQUIREMENTS FOR CAMPUS ANTI-DRUG PROGRAMS

Two federal statutes, the Drug-Free Workplace Act, 40 U.S.C. Sec. 701–702, and the Drug and Alcohol Abuse Prevention Act, 20 U.S.C. Sec. 1011, compel campus-based participation in the "war on drugs." Together they require virtually every college and university to establish, maintain, and enforce substance-abuse policies. Institutions are required to discipline students or employees who violate institutional anti-drug and -alcohol policies. Failure to comply with the requirements of these statutes jeopardizes continued receipt of federal funds.[3]

Some of the federal requirements for substance abuse policies can be summarized as follows:

1. Each institution receiving federal funds must establish, maintain, and enforce drug and alcohol standards of conduct for students and employees.
2. The standards of conduct must prohibit, at a minimum, the illegal use, possession, manufacture, or distribution of drugs or alcohol on campus, on other institutional property, or at institution-sponsored events.
3. Institutional policies must explain that adherence to the standards of conduct is a condition of employment and that sanctions will be imposed for violations of those standards.
4. Sanctions for violating drug and alcohol standards of conduct may include dismissal, referral for prosecution, or referral for rehabilitation. The institutional policy must address sanctions.
5. Institutional policies must provide information on available rehabilitation services, health risks associated with drug and alcohol abuse, and federal, state, and local criminal penalties for drug- and alcohol-related offenses.
6. Institutional policies must require any employee covered by the policy who is convicted of a drug- or alcohol-related offense committed on campus, at the workplace, on other institutional property, or at an institutional function, to report the conviction to the administration.
7. The institutional policy must be distributed to each student and each employee.
8. Institutions must certify to the U.S. Department of Education that they have established a policy complying with federal law.
9. Persons who are the direct recipients of federal funds must individually certify that they will comply with applicable requirements of the statutes.
10. The institution is required to conduct a biennial review of the effectiveness of institutional substance-abuse policies.

Neither statute calls for specific penalties for any offense,[4] and institutions are not required to refer standard-of-conduct violations to law-enforcement officials. Most individuals need not certify their personal adherence to the standards of conduct, and drug testing is not mandated.[5]

---

[3] The two statutes, while addressing the same problem, differ significantly in scope. The Drug and Alcohol Abuse Prevention Act applies to all colleges and universities receiving or applying for any federal funds. They prohibit certain alcohol- and drug-related conduct on any institutional property or at events sponsored by the institution. The Drug-Free Workplace Act is limited to particular programs and individuals receiving federal funds or working on federal contracts, and the focus of prohibited drug-related, although not alcohol-related, conduct is the "workplace."

[4] The Drug-Free Workplace Act requires some adverse personnel action or referral to rehabilitation within thirty days after a covered employee reports a conviction that he or she is required to report. The Drug and Alcohol Abuse Prevention Act requires some sanction any time the institutional anti-drug policy is violated.

[5] Department of Defense regulations implementing the Drug-Free Workplace Act mandate drug testing of all individuals who work on defense contracts and who have access to classified information. 48 C.F.R. Sec. 252.223-7500.

116

Very significantly, neither statute requires institutions to abandon existing procedures and standards for determining whether a standard of conduct has been violated and what the appropriate response to a violation is.

By specifically including referral for rehabilitation services among the available penalties, the federal requirements encourage the enlightened and progressive use of rehabilitative intervention, in lieu of punishment, when violations of anti-drug and -alcohol policies occur. Institutions can and should emphasize the availability of rehabilitation services in response to standard-of-conduct violations. Responsible intervention, exhorting individuals to seek treatment before substance abuse severely affects professional performance or results in standard-of-conduct violations, has the advantage of potentially avoiding later circumstances which may necessitate a resort to punitive sanctions. Rehabilitation should be an institution's first recourse—whether in response to a perceived drug or alcohol problem or in response to a standard-of-conduct violation. Punitive sanctions should be reserved for those instances in which a drug or alcohol problem or drug- or alcohol-related misconduct results in demonstrated professional deficiencies and efforts at rehabilitation have failed.

ANTI-DRUG AND -ALCOHOL POLICIES AND ADHERENCE TO PRINCIPLES OF SHARED GOVERNANCE

The federal requirements intrude on institutional autonomy by requiring that institutional policies mandate punishment for certain illegal conduct. Although a degree of institutional discretion is taken away by the statutorily prescribed minimum standards and the required response to violations, significant discretion to develop the details of a substance-abuse policy is retained. Moreover, the legislation does not require the exclusion of the faculty from the development of substance-abuse policies[6] or the abandonment of the faculty's traditional role in determining whether a violation has occurred and, if so, in recommending an appropriate penalty.[7]

The principles of collegial governance in higher education need not be abandoned in addressing substance abuse. There have, however, been several instances in which anti-drug and -alcohol policies, related standards of conduct, and drug-testing programs have been imposed upon members of the campus community by administrative directive, without consultation with and advice from the faculty and others directly affected by the policies, standards, and programs. Faculty and students should be involved, through the appropriate agencies, in the development of policies, programs, and standards of conduct used to address campus substance abuses.[8] The enforcement of anti-drug and -alcohol policies also raises concerns for collegial governance in terms of the faculty role in determining faculty status. When implementation of a substance-abuse policy threatens any faculty member's status, the ordinary processes for review by faculty peers should be employed.[9]

INSTITUTIONAL ANTI-DRUG AND -ALCOHOL POLICIES AND IMPLICATIONS FOR ASSOCIATION-SUPPORTED STANDARDS AND PRACTICES

Various institutional anti-drug and -alcohol policies have been reviewed by the subcommittee. Most seem to accommodate statutory obligations while affording academic due process protections for those accused of anti-drug and -alcohol policy violations, but there are features in some of them that raise concerns under Association-supported standards.

[6] See "Statement on Government of Colleges and Universities," Part V, AAUP, *Policy Documents and Reports*, 9th ed. (Washington, D.C., 2001), 221–22.
[7] See "1958 Statement on Procedural Standards in Faculty Dismissal Proceedings," *ibid.*, 11–14, and "Recommended Institutional Regulations on Academic Freedom and Tenure," Regulations 5, 6, and 7, *ibid.*, 25–27.
[8] See, generally, "Statement on Government," *ibid.*, 217–23.
[9] See n. 7, above.

1. *Breadth of Prohibited Conduct and the Standard of Professional Fitness*

Two approaches predominate on campuses with respect to identifying the scope of conduct to be prohibited. Some policies codify the minimum requirements of federal legislation and confine their prohibitions to "unlawful" conduct on institutional property or at institutional events. Others exceed statutorily prescribed standards by prohibiting any drug- or alcohol-related conduct and by reaching beyond institutional premises and events.

Policies that are broadly prohibitive and fail to take into account standards of professional fitness and performance are easily subject to overzealous applications. The touchstone for applying penalties under substance-abuse standards of conduct must be the same standard that is employed for other rules of conduct—a demonstrable nexus to professional fitness. An unnecessarily expansive policy proscribes conduct that is purely personal and that may have no bearing on professional fitness. In order to satisfy federal law and to be consistent with policies that fit within the traditional context of institutional standards of conduct, anti-drug and -alcohol standards of conduct must be drafted, interpreted, and applied to recognize that alleged violations shall be judged only in light of the effect of the conduct on professional performance and fitness.[10] Under no circumstances should an individual be punished solely for advocating drug or alcohol use or the liberalization of anti-drug and -alcohol laws. Nor should a policy be so broad that it permits penalties only on the basis of a person's advocacy or maintenance of a lifestyle featuring drug or alcohol use.

Federal substance-abuse statutes require academic institutions to prohibit and punish conduct that is already illegal and punishable through the criminal justice system. The imposition of this law-enforcement type of obligation on institutions of higher education may divert attention from academic standards and direct it toward criminal standards of guilt and innocence. Colleges and universities are not well equipped, by structure or mission, to assume general law-enforcement roles. Their standards of conduct should not mirror criminal law at the expense of educational and academic norms. Institutional anti-drug and -alcohol policies can be consistent with federal law while being narrowly tailored to ensure that traditional standards of professional academic fitness and performance are the determinative standards in applying penalties.

2. *Punitive Sanctions and Standards for Academic Due Process*

The federal requirements leave the issue of appropriate discipline to the discretion of the institution. Referral to rehabilitation, referral for prosecution, or termination of appointment are specified as possible sanctions, but no particular penalties are mandated. Most institutions have not restricted the range of sanctions that may be imposed. Some institutions, however, have established strict progressive systems of discipline or tables of penalties for specific types of violations.

When a standard of conduct is alleged to have been violated, Association-supported policies entitle a faculty member to a hearing on stated charges. If a severe sanction is proposed, a hearing before a body of faculty peers is to determine whether the administration has established its charges and whether the proposed penalty is appropriate.

The federal requirement that any violation of an anti-drug and -alcohol standard of conduct be punished may alter the operation of traditional academic procedures and standards. Nonetheless, regular procedural safeguards should apply in determining whether a standard-of-conduct violation has occurred and in assessing the appropriate penalty. Policies that restrict the range of sanctions, either by prescribing specific penalties for particular offenses or by imposing rigid progressive disciplinary systems, do not allow for discretion to judge individual cases on the basis of individual circumstances against the appropriate professional standard

---

[10] See "1958 Statement on Procedural Standards in Faculty Dismissal Proceedings," *Policy Documents and Reports*, 11–14. Regulation 5(a) of the "Recommended Institutional Regulations" requires that "adequate cause for dismissal" be "related, directly and substantially, to the fitness of faculty members in their professional capacities as teachers or researchers" (*ibid.*, 25).

and to respond in a manner that is proportionate to the offense. Inflexible disciplinary approaches to anti-drug and -alcohol policies are unnecessary for compliance with federal law and are inconsistent with generally accepted standards of academic due process.

3. Potential Prejudice to the Rights of Individuals as Citizens and Relationships with Law Enforcement Agencies

An anti-drug and -alcohol policy necessitates coordination with law-enforcement agencies to the extent that it relates to potentially criminal conduct. Whether or not the prohibitions of a policy are limited to "unlawful" conduct, application of an anti-drug and -alcohol policy to specific individuals can prejudice the right of those individuals to defend themselves against future criminal charges.

The primary mission of colleges and universities is education, not law enforcement. Resources should not be diverted unduly from educational programs to discovering and judging what may be criminal drug- or alcohol-related conduct. A determination that conduct is truly "unlawful" must be adjudicated in a court of law by a judge or jury. For this reason, policies prohibiting "unlawful" or "illegal" conduct, the minimum requirement of the federal law, may be interpreted persuasively as applying only after a criminal conviction. In order to limit the law-enforcement role of colleges and universities, it seems advisable that institutional anti-drug and -alcohol policies expressly state that sanctions for violations do not apply until after a criminal conviction (or after a knowing, clear, and freely offered admission of criminal conduct). In the rare case when "immediate harm to the faculty member or others is threatened" by allowing a faculty member accused of criminal conduct to continue in active service, colleges and universities may consider suspending the faculty member pending the outcome of legal proceedings.[11]

4. Signature Requirements

A significant concern with respect to anti-drug and -alcohol policies is a requirement at some colleges and universities that faculty members sign the institution's policy statement. Federal law does not require individual faculty members, employees, or students to acknowledge their receipt of anti-drug and -alcohol policies. Nonetheless, faculty members have been mistakenly informed that the law requires their signature. Others have been advised that a signature simply acknowledges receipt. There are also faculty members who have been told that their signature constitutes a promise to be bound by the policies in all substantive and procedural respects.

Requiring a recipient of a policy to attest to being bound by a particular standard of conduct may appear to be innocuous to most individuals who have no intention of violating the policy as they understand it. However, anti-drug and -alcohol policies may be overinclusive, may fail to incorporate the appropriate academic standards for judging conduct, may specify strict penalties, and may create procedures for imposing discipline that subvert traditional academic due process. The signature requirement may operate to bind the individual to an overreaching substantive policy and to a relinquishment of academic due process.

Particularly disturbing are instances in which institutions require faculty signatures on copies of substance-abuse policies as a condition of continued appointment. The Association has long opposed the requirement of an oath as a condition of initial or continued appointment. A person's simple refusal to sign a particular policy should not be taken to imply resistance to some or all of the contents of the document. Unwillingness to sign may reflect a prudent degree of caution guarding against potential limitations on the applicability of professional standards and academic due process. Principled objections to signing oaths concerning anti-drug and -alcohol policies, no less than principled objections to political loyalty oaths, must be respected.

---

[11] "Recommended Institutional Regulations," Regulation 5(c)(1), *Policy Documents and Reports*, 26.

5. Drug Testing

Some drug-testing programs exist in higher education. A few faculty members, notably those working with classified defense materials, are required by federal regulations to submit to regular drug tests.[12] Some institutions have adopted faculty and staff drug-testing programs. Increasingly, states are considering drug-testing programs for employees and/or applicants for state employment, including college and university faculty positions.[13] The Association participated in successful litigation challenging Georgia drug-testing legislation, which required applicants for any position of state employment to submit to drug tests. The legislation was susceptible to an interpretation that would have rendered it applicable to faculty members seeking contract renewals and promotion or tenure. The broad sweep of the legislation led a federal court to find it unconstitutional.[14]

Drug testing involves technological and physical intrusions into a person's biological functions to discover whether the person uses drugs. The testing does not discriminate between drug use that impairs performance and drug use that does not impair performance. It does not even determine impairment at the time of the test. It discovers only whether a person's body contains traces of chemicals that may indicate previous drug use. Drug-testing programs at colleges and universities have the potential to erode existing standards for assessing professional fitness, promise, and performance by substituting the results of a chemical analysis for demonstrable academic accomplishments.

Private and public employees have challenged drug-testing programs, meeting with some success and some failure. In the public context, cases ordinarily turn on the Fourth Amendment constitutional guarantee against warrantless and unreasonable searches. Case law currently suggests that some drug screening is constitutionally permissible. Drug-testing policies are most likely to be sustained for safety-sensitive and law-enforcement positions and some positions involving access to classified material. Drug testing of specific individuals has been held to be constitutionally permissible when reasonable cause exists to believe that those persons have used drugs.

In the private sector, where the Fourth Amendment protection against warrantless and unreasonable searches does not apply owing to the absence of state involvement, some challenges to drug-testing programs have relied on privacy rights emanating from state law, state constitutions, public policies, and common law. However, most private-sector drug-testing programs have survived legal challenge.

Drug-testing programs may take the form of mandatory universal testing, mandatory random testing, or "reasonable-cause" testing. Universal drug-testing programs require every person covered by the program to be tested. In random drug-testing programs, which are designed to surprise, some members of a target population are tested for drugs and the procedure is repeated periodically. "Reasonable-cause" testing programs generally require testing when observable events in the course of a person's employment, such as accidents, slurred speech, or violent or erratic behavior, lead to the belief that the individual may be under the influence of drugs. Drug-testing programs typically require submission to a test as a condition of continued employment. Failing or refusing to take a test often results in dismissal.

---

[12] See n. 5, above. Additionally, the Department of Transportation and its component regulatory agencies (e.g., the Federal Aviation Administration and the Federal Highway Administration) require drug tests for some faculty members who teach in transportation-related fields, such as aviation programs.

[13] Hawaii, Iowa, Louisiana, Maine, Maryland, Minnesota, Mississippi, Nebraska, North Carolina, Oklahoma, Oregon, Rhode Island, Texas, and Vermont have adopted legislation or regulations that allow public- and sometimes private-sector employers to conduct drug tests for employees or applicants for employment. Some such measures clearly apply to prospective and/or incumbent faculty members; others may apply to college and university faculty members.

[14] *Georgia Assn. of Educators v. Harris*, 749 F. Supp. 1110 (N.D. Ga. 1990).

Tests are usually conducted through urinalysis, under procedures which attempt to minimize inaccuracies, privacy intrusions, and tampering.[15] The form of urinalysis most frequently used involves the enzyme multiplied immunoassay technique (EMIT). A second and more accurate procedure, gas chromatography mass spectrometry (GC/MS) assessment, is often used to confirm or negate positive results from an EMIT test. Through technological advances, methods of drug testing which are less physically intrusive and more revealing, such as hair sample analysis, are becoming economical and widely available.

Drug abuse, whether in private or in public, at home or at the institution, that adversely affects professional performance and fitness can be cause for action against a faculty member. The overriding issue is impaired professional performance, not simply the abuse of drugs. Since the institution's legitimate interest concerns professional capability, its efforts to discover drug abuse should be limited to addressing its need to identify potential causes for declining professional performance.

A critical issue underlying drug testing at colleges and universities is whether a legitimate interest exists in discovering possible drug abuse that does not appear to impair the performance of professional responsibilities. No inherent conflict exists between academic norms concerned with professional competence and individual privacy rights. Adherence to professional standards guards against undue intrusion on individual privacy, and respect for individual privacy guards against dilution of professional standards by personal behavior lacking a nexus to professional fitness. In this way, academic norms and individual privacy can reinforce each other.

In evaluating the usefulness of drug testing, the subcommittee has found most helpful Alan Westin's construct for analyzing physical intrusions on privacy by technological means.[16] The need for drug testing, its intrusiveness, its reliability, the capacity for controlling abuses of testing methods and results, and the existence of less intrusive methods are evaluated to determine the degree of acceptance the procedure is entitled to claim. The first goal of drug-testing programs is to identify drug abusers. If, as the director of the Office of National Drug Control Policy has remarked, the objective of anti-drug measures on campus "isn't so much how can we discover drug use on our campuses, but what do we do about it when it exists, and how fast do we act,"[17] then routine drug testing will have little or no value beyond possibly frightening a few individuals into not using drugs.

The level of intrusiveness in drug testing is high. The Supreme Court has held that urinalysis is a significant intrusion into a fundamentally private domain. In some limited circumstances, however, courts have held that society's interest in controlling drug abuse overrides individual privacy.[18]

The reliability of current technology for drug screening leaves much to be desired. Reliability depends on many factors, including the sensitivity of the test, the security of testing procedures and samples, and errors in analysis by laboratory personnel. Reliability is also affected by the fact that no drug-testing technology can measure actual physical impairment, let alone impairment of academic capability. The limitations on the reliability of drug screening and the extent of its intrusiveness cannot be eliminated, but may be minimized by carefully constructed procedures for conducting tests, analyzing specimens, and using test results.

Less intrusive methods exist for identifying drug abusers. Observation of conduct may give clues or "reasonable cause" to believe that a person is impaired by drugs. Observation does not

[15] See 53 Fed. Reg. 11970 (April 11, 1988) for the Department of Health and Human Services' Mandatory Guidelines for Federal Workplace Drug-Testing Programs. The "Guidelines" are commonly used in drug-testing programs to guard against both inaccuracies and intrusions on privacy.

[16] See, generally, A.F. Westin, *Privacy and Freedom* (New York: Atheneum, 1967).

[17] Prepared remarks of Governor Bob Martinez, Director, Office of National Drug Control Policy, White House Youth/Education briefing, April 5, 1991.

[18] See, e.g., *Skinner v. Railway Labor Executives Assn.*, 489 U.S. 602 (1989); *National Treasury Employees Union v. von Raab*, 489 U.S. 656 (1989); *Luedtke v. Nabors Alaska Drilling, Inc.*, 768 P.2d 1123 (Alaska 1989); *Vernonia School District 47J v. Acton*, 515 U.S. 646 (1995).

involve physical intrusion and can focus on perceived impairment. It may also provide a vehicle for personal rather than technological intervention when colleagues, students, and administrators detect declining professional performance. Referral for rehabilitation may be more effective when an individual is confronted with concerns over a pattern of observable deficiencies rather than a test result that cannot measure competence or impairment. On the other hand, observation without objective guidelines for interpreting conduct is susceptible to excessive subjectivity and may result in misidentification. A resulting confrontation may be considered offensive, cause resentment, and have an adverse effect on collegiality.

Drug-testing programs themselves do not appear to confront meaningfully the problems that directly involve the academic community in general or the professoriate in particular. There does not seem to be a compelling need for drug-testing programs in the academy, as conventional standards and procedures are more capable of identifying academic deficiencies and lapses in performance.

The subcommittee finds no valid purpose for universal or random drug-testing programs within the academic community.[19] They constitute an excessive intrusion into the private affairs of individuals. No overriding need exists to discover possible drug abuse unless there is reason to suspect that an individual is abusing drugs and is professionally impaired by such abuse. Since the principal interest should be in an individual's professional and academic performance, observation is more effective than drug testing in identifying drug-related performance deficiencies. The subcommittee recognizes, nonetheless, that in some particular circumstances, involving faculty positions so sensitive that margins for error are very thin (for example, a physicist testing nuclear reactions or a microbiologist experimenting with resistant strains of lethal viruses), an institution may have an interest in determining the likelihood that observed performance deficiencies are specifically drug-related. A request that an individual holding such a sensitive position submit to drug testing for the purpose of identifying more definitively whether that individual may need rehabilitation, rather than for the purpose of imposing punitive sanctions, may be appropriate.

An institution may request submission to such a drug test only after observation reveals objective indications of impaired performance related to drug abuse (i.e., "reasonable cause"). The subcommittee believes that a positive test result from a drug test should be used only for the purpose of referring the individual to rehabilitation. A refusal to submit to drug testing should not be considered punishable conduct. The controls on a "reasonable-cause" drug-testing program must be strict. If the testing program is properly structured and disciplinary action is anticipated, the professional deficiency element of the "reasonable-cause" requirement should present the professional and academic basis for initiating proceedings against a particular individual. In short, the first resort should be to rehabilitation, with punitive sanctions reserved for instances of demonstrated professional deficiency and a failure of rehabilitative efforts.

An essential aspect of any "reasonable-cause" testing program is the existence of objective standards for determining "reasonable cause" that can be applied consistently. The subcommittee cannot catalog the variety of physical and behavioral cues that may indicate drug-related impairment. Objective guidelines can be developed, however, through consultation and coordination with rehabilitation and treatment specialists. The standards may differ depending on the nature of an individual's professional duties, but the focus of these standards should always be on identifying behavior which suggests impairment by drug abuse. In no instance should a professional deficiency not accompanied by such behavior be construed as "reasonable cause" to initiate drug testing.

---

[19] Random or universal drug testing mandated by state law or by federal or state regulations is no more consistent with academic norms than are internally developed institutional programs. Such requirements are ill advised, but we appreciate that little recourse may be available, either to the institution or to the affected faculty member. Efforts should be made, however, to ensure that any government-mandated drug-testing program is administered in such a way as to minimize intrusion on individual privacy and limit its adverse effect on existing academic standards and practices.

For those academic institutions that adopt "reasonable-cause" drug-testing procedures, the subcommittee reiterates the importance of controlling technology and processes in order to minimize inaccuracies, errors, and intrusions on individual privacy. Although an EMIT test is relatively inexpensive and may even be conducted on-site through the use of test kits, the reliability of this procedure is quite suspect. False-positive results, incorrectly indicating drug use, are not uncommon.[20] To prevent individuals from being falsely accused of drug abuse based solely upon the results of a questionable EMIT test, a GC/MS assessment should be employed to confirm or negate any positive result obtained from an EMIT test. The chain of specimen custody should be carefully maintained, and only qualified laboratories (those certified by the federal or state government, for instance) should be retained to conduct tests and analyses.

In addition, the confidentiality of test results must be maintained. Rehabilitation records and the results of drug tests are in essence medical records. They should be given the same degree of confidentiality that extends to other medical records. Even the disclosure of a negative assessment may cast unfair suspicion on an innocent person. Positive test results should be disclosed only to those persons with a need to know such information, including counselors and rehabilitation specialists. The confidentiality of records is imperative. If an institution is unable to ensure adequate degrees of confidentiality, it should exercise its discretion not to implement a drug-testing program. Strictly controlled procedures will enhance the likelihood that referral to a rehabilitation program can produce beneficial results.

CONCLUSION

Campus-based efforts to conduct a "war on drugs" should be carefully defined and narrowly circumscribed. Both anti-drug and -alcohol policies and drug-testing programs pose potentially serious threats to academic norms and individual privacy interests. Colleges and universities should direct their policies and practices concerning substance abuse toward education and rehabilitation—goals more compatible with an educational mission—rather than toward punitive action. Punitive sanctions should be reserved for those instances when conduct has a demonstrable nexus to professional fitness and where rehabilitative efforts have not produced beneficial results.

---

[20] See M. Rothstein, "Drug Testing in the Workplace: The Challenge to Employment Regulations and Employment Law," *Chicago-Kent Law Review* 63 (1987): 683–89.

Access to University Records

The report which follows was prepared by a subcommittee of the Association's Committee on Academic Freedom and Tenure (Committee A). It was approved by Committee A and adopted by the Council in November 1996.

"For the great majority of different records the public as a whole
has a *right to know* what its government is doing."

Language of this kind, taken from the legislative history of the federal Freedom of Information Act (FOIA), expresses a view that has been applied in several jurisdictions to college and university documents either under federal law or under similar state statutes. Laws in every state give the public access to records of state government. A wide array of documents from public colleges and universities has been sought under these provisions. While in some states the records of public colleges and universities are largely shielded from public access, in others the laws have broader impact on institutions of higher education. The courts are often called upon to adjudicate claims of access. Among the kinds of documents from public colleges and universities that have been made available by court order are the following:

1. names and addresses of respondents to a research survey about cigarette advertising;
2. filmstrips used in a college course on human sexuality;
3. peer review documents;
4. identity of donors;
5. university legal bills; and
6. copy of an unfunded grant proposal to the National Institutes of Health.[1]

Across the country results even in these categories may vary, depending on the terms and interpretation of different state laws.

There is nothing novel about courts deciding issues of access to information; indeed, it is an essential element in the process of permitting discovery by the parties in litigation. Pre-trial discovery often raises questions about what information must be disclosed to an opposing party. Similarly, labor law compels the sharing of certain information. A union generally has access to information of the employer relevant to satisfaction of the union's responsibilities. On a voluntary basis, members of a college or university community regularly exchange many types of information as they collaborate in advancing the institution's goals. So by court order, by operation of law, and by custom, an academic institution may disclose many of its records for specified purposes. These purposes include litigation, collective bargaining, and shared governance. The information is provided to individuals or groups that stand in defined relationships to the institution whether as litigants, unions, or faculty or student groups.

Public records acts, however, present a broader context because they provide *any* member of the public with access to documents that fall within the terms of the statute. No reason need be stated for requesting the information. FOIA and similar statutes have thus relieved the

---

[1] See Paul M. Fischer, *"Fischer v. The Medical College of Georgia and the R. J. Reynolds Tobacco Company*: A Case Study of Constraints on Research," in *Academic Freedom: An Everyday Concern*, ed. Ernst Benjamin and Donald R. Wagner (San Francisco: Jossey-Bass, Inc., 1994), 33–43 (tobacco advertising); *Russo v. Nassau County Community College*, N. E. 2nd 15 (N.Y. App. 1993) (sexuality teaching materials); *James v. Ohio State University*, 637 N. E. 2nd 911 (Ohio Sup. Ct. 1994) (peer review documents); *Toledo Blade Co. v. University of Toledo Foundation*, 602 N. E. 2nd 1159 (Ohio Sup. Ct. 1992) (donors to private foundation that served as main fundraising arm of public university); "Rutgers Must Show Legal Bills," by Tia Swanson, *Home News and Tribune*, 5 January 1996 (New Brunswick, N.J.); and *Progressive Animal Welfare Society v. University of Washington*, 884 P.2d 592 (Wash. Sup. Co. 1994) (*en banc*) (unfunded grant proposal).

court of balancing the *need to know* of the one requesting access against the other party's desire to keep certain material partially or wholly confidential. Indeed, the assertion of a *right to know* gives conclusive weight to any requester's *want to know* and zero weight to an institution's *want to keep confidential*. This eliminates the distinction between *want* and *need* on the part of each party. FOIA and similar state statutes often contain exceptions. Depending on the state, these might include items such as employee personnel files or strategic materials connected with litigation or real estate transactions. For documents outside such enumerated exceptions, the statutes take no account of possible bases for confidentiality nor dangers of unlimited public access.

We do not address the legal status (state or federal) of requests for access to university documents. Our purpose, in response to a request from the AAUP Council, is to draft a statement of AAUP policy in respect to these matters. While there may be some differences between public and private institutions in this regard—for example, in taxpayers' legitimate interest in the expenditure of public funds—we do not find such differences material to the central issues of AAUP concern.

There are plainly situations in which a compelling case can be made for access by a limited audience to university documents that a university administration may not choose to make available unless compelled to do so. Some obvious examples: a staff member charged with misconduct must be in a position to know the source and nature of the charges made as well as the procedures followed by the administration in response to the complaint; a faculty member denied promotion, reappointment, or a salary increment who believes he or she has been discriminated against on some improper basis must be given access to certain documents with which to test this possibility; a faculty collective bargaining unit negotiating with an administration must have access to certain data with which to confront assertions by the university about its ability to provide salary or fringe benefit improvements; and any individual or group in litigation against the university needs to be able to discover facts with which to press claims.

Although means exist apart from freedom-of-information statutes by which access can be obtained in cases such as these, it is clear that a *generalized right of public access* to all university documents (provided, for example, by an unqualified FOIA) would serve all compelling needs and greatly reduce the efforts and outlays required to compel disclosure in particular situations. If no cost or potential dangers were associated with unqualified access to all university documents, independent of the nature of the request and of the requester's need to know, a general right of access would be both simple and efficient. Regrettably, this is not the case. While access confers benefits, it also carries costs and potential dangers, many of which apply with special force to an academic community by virtue of its essential, perhaps unique, mission to search for and disseminate truth by wide-ranging exploration of inchoate ideas and hypotheses, some of which may be seen as dangerous by others in the society. Sound policy requires a balancing of the benefits and costs of open access.

We believe that such a balancing does not lead to a strong presumption in favor of unlimited public access with respect to university documents.

The nature of the potential benefits and costs has been articulated in many places,[2] but at least a cursory review of some of them will be helpful.

Among the legitimate interests served by open public access to university documents are:

1. The increased ability to expose corrupt, biased, or otherwise improper behavior by institutions.
2. The beneficial pressure exerted on universities to fulfill their intended missions by the knowledge that failure to do so is likely to be exposed.
3. The incentive to university personnel to be more effective because their actions and decisions must survive public scrutiny.

---

[2] For example, see "Access to Faculty Personnel Files," AAUP, *Policy Documents and Reports*, 9th ed. (Washington, D.C., 2001), 41–46.

4. The opportunity provided to a wise public for constructive input into university decisions.[3]
5. The lighter burden on all who seek access to university records.

Among the interests served by restrictions on access to university documents are:

1. The need to create and preserve a climate of academic freedom in the planning and conduct of research, free from harassment, public and political pressure, or premature disclosure of research in process.
2. The need to create a climate in which the university's teaching activities are unimpeded and open to innovation and in which controversial issues may be explored without externally imposed limits on what is said, read, or debated.
3. The gains to be achieved by the ability to collect information available only by assurance of confidentiality. This can apply to research in a variety of contexts. It can also apply to peer review and evaluation of the accomplishments of individuals who are being recruited, evaluated, retained, promoted, rewarded, discontinued, or discharged. Some evaluators require a promise of confidentiality except with respect to persons with a need to know; others will respond, but less helpfully, if confidentiality is not assured.
4. The recruitment of top-level administrators may, in some situations, be aided by assurances to potential candidates that their interest in the appointment will not be disclosed to the public until such time as the candidate has entered the final stages of the search. Absent such assurances, some candidates, perhaps some of the most desirable, will simply refuse to be considered.
5. The need to avoid what has been called the "chilling effect" on what is explored and what is taught. Perceived threats of harassment, pressure, and adverse publicity may result from public disclosure. Teachers and scholars who observe others so treated in the conduct of their careers may modify what they teach and what they study.
6. The need to respect the privacy of teachers and scholars with respect to aspects of their private lives—such as marital status, outside income, sexual preferences, or medical records—that are irrelevant to their performance as teachers and scholars, unless a compelling reason to breach that privacy has been established.

* * * * *

There is ample evidence of both the potential benefits and the potential costs in the academic setting. The balancing of the benefits and costs of open access is not a once-and-for-all matter, because the considerations depend upon the nature of the document requested, the requester's need to know, and the breadth of disclosure to be made. To take easy extreme examples, there can be no question that students' requests for access to an examination that has been prepared but not yet given is without merit. Also lacking in merit would be an institution's refusal to provide anyone requesting it with information about the educational background of a teacher or summary data on the age, sex, and racial composition of its faculty. Few requests are so simply resolved, and thus what is required are some *rebuttable presumptions* that apply to different classes of requests, and an *internal procedure for evaluating competing claims*. We discuss each of these below.

PRESUMPTIONS

Presumptions about the appropriateness of giving access to university documents depend both on the status of the requester and on the nature of the information requested. A great variety of people and groups have at one time or another expressed a desire to know about material

---

[3] The Association has previously addressed the need for faculty involvement in decisions, including decisions on the selection of academic administrators. See the statement on "Faculty Participation in the Selection, Evaluation, and Retention of Administrators" and the "Statement on Government of Colleges and Universities," in *Policy Documents and Reports*, 228–29 and 217–23, respectively.

that universities do not routinely choose to make available. The status of those making the request is not irrelevant to the balancing that we believe to be appropriate. (It is irrelevant under FOIA and similar statutes.) Those requesting information include individual faculty members; faculty committees; faculty unions; students and student organizations; pressure groups from the community eager to influence the nature of what is taught or researched;[4] companies and industry trade associations concerned that what is occurring within the university will adversely (or beneficially) affect them or their competitors; representatives of the media, anxious to build circulation by exposing misbehavior, or merely catering to the curiosity of their clientele; and even lawyers seeking to define potential and profitable litigation against the university. Examples of each of these can be found.

The types of documents that are subject to requests for access are both numerous and varied. They range from simple requests for general information about faculty members' professional backgrounds and activities to the most searching demands for information about individuals' personal lives. Some requests ask for details about promotion or disciplinary files of particular faculty members, and for the records of the deliberations of committees that have evaluated them. Requests may concern current ongoing research or outside activities of university staff. Other requests may seek documents giving detailed information about the origin and the use of university resources, including information about the identity of donors and the amount of payments to outside lawyers in particular cases.

One could conceptually cross-classify the nature of the requester and the nature of the information requested and create a grid with hundreds of "cells." One might then assign a particular presumption of openness or confidentiality to each. While for some cells the appropriate presumption may be self-evident, for many (indeed, we believe most) there is need for a case-specific examination to balance the *need to know* against *the case for confidentiality*. A procedure by which this balancing can occur is also necessary

These are not all matters of first impression for the professoriate and the Association; some of the relevant ground has been covered elsewhere and will not be retraced. The large topic of faculty access to faculty personnel files was the subject of a policy statement adopted by the Association's governing Council in 1992.[5] In addition, the desirability of open-meetings legislation was the subject of a 1986 AAUP report.[6] While the Association has addressed the role of faculty in the selection of academic administrators, it has not analyzed the impact on such search processes of legally compelled disclosure to the public, notably including the media.[7] The Carnegie Commission for the Advancement of Teaching covered the latter subject in its useful report, *Choosing a College President: Opportunities and Constraints* (1990).[8] Further, we shall not discuss the rights of litigants to discovery of relevant documents, nor the requests by officially constituted professional associations or governmental review panels for data relevant to their investigations.

Despite these exclusions, much remains that might be discussed. In respect to the nature of the requester, it is useful to distinguish among four types: (1) regularly constituted internal committees or bodies whose task is to review, evaluate, or adjudicate matters concerning faculty status; (2) other interested persons or groups internal to the university such as faculty unions, AAUP chapters, student governments, or groups with a particular interest, such as a

---

[4] Among these are supporters of animal rights, creationism, right to life, environmental protection, Americanism, and protection from pornography.

[5] That document's principal conclusions were: (1) faculty members should have unrestricted "access to their own files, including unredacted letters, both internal and external"; (2) "for purposes of comparison, files of a faculty complainant and of other faculty members should be available in unredacted form to faculty appeals committees to the extent that such committees deem the information relevant and necessary to the fair disposition of the case before them"; and (3) "a faculty appeals committees should make available to the aggrieved faculty member, in unredacted form and without prejudging the merits of the case, all materials the appeals committee deems relevant to the complaint, including personnel files of other faculty members, having due regard for the privacy of those who are not parties to the complaint" (*Policy Documents and Reports*, 44–46).

[6] "On Open Meetings," *Academe: Bulletin of the AAUP* 72 (January–February 1986): 3a–4a.

[7] See n. 3, above.

[8] The authors of the Carnegie study, Judith Block McLaughlin and David Riesman, served on the Association's subcommittee that addressed open-meetings issues in 1986.

faculty women's caucus; (3) individual faculty members or ad hoc student groups; and (4) outside persons or groups, however motivated.

In respect to the nature of the information requested, for some classes of information the presumption ought to be strong in favor of open access, regardless of the requester's identity. This would include information of the kind contained in a curriculum vitae, information about published research including access to nonconfidential backup data, and summary information about an institution including faculty composition, workloads, curriculum, and salary levels. It would, of course, also include information about fundamental institutional decisions once made and effected, the procedures employed in making these decisions, and the available channels of appeal. At least summary information about sources and uses of the institution's funds is plainly appropriate for public institutions, although perhaps less plainly for private ones.

At the other end of the spectrum are certain kinds of information we believe should be presumed confidential and thus not available to any requester absent a determination of an exceptional and compelling need to know. These include personal information not contained in a curriculum vitae, such as family status, outside income and assets, medical history, records of library use, extramural affiliations, and political or religious affiliations. Similarly, the deliberations, opinions voiced, individual votes, and proceedings of faculty bodies should be presumed to be private, in order not to chill full and candid decision making. Of course, if a charge is made that the decisions resulted from bias or other inappropriate considerations, these matters are the proper domain of a grievance committee.

Even extending these lists of the easy presumptions would leave a vast array of requests for which the extent and purpose of the requester's need to know and the strength of the institution's claim for confidentiality would be essential to evaluating the request. Here, perhaps, some weaker presumptions may be stated.

1. Requests Coming from Regularly Constituted Internal Bodies (Review Committees, Grievance Panels, and Faculty Senates)

We believe that there should be a rebuttable presumption in favor of open and unlimited access to any university records upon a showing by a regularly constituted internal body of a reasonable need to know. Examples include budgetary information, material concerning academic planning, and personnel information. Disclosure may be subject to a pledge of confidentiality with respect to information that is not generally available for which either privacy or confidentiality is claimed. (The redaction of limited private or confidential information can be a useful device.) The processes of shared governance must rest on a premise of shared information. Those arguing for nonrelease in these situations should bear the burden of establishing a reasonable need to keep confidential.

2. Requests from Other (Nonofficial) Internal Groups

We believe that no presumption should exist either way, with the standard being that the specific need to know should be balanced against the specific need for confidentiality and with due concern for the protection of the privacy of individuals. The possibilities of a negotiated agreement on the extent and form of release of requested information should be explored, possibly utilizing the services of an ombudsman or mediator. On some occasions, the parties might agree upon limitations on the use and subsequent dissemination of the information. Narrowly tailored redaction might be considered.

3. Requests from Individual Faculty Members or Student Groups

Requests of these kinds may be substantively similar to those discussed just above, or they may be indistinguishable from those of outsiders, discussed in the next section. For example, the treatment given to a faculty member or a group of students concerned with animal rights ought usually to be no different from that given to an outside group concerned with the same issue. On other issues, the concerns of individual professors or of student groups may be more analogous to the concerns of an official faculty body.[9] Thus, for example, a student group

---

[9] An individual professor seeking information about himself or herself presents, however, different considerations. See "Access to Faculty Personnel Files," n. 2, above.

examining whether the university's curricular decisions were unduly responsive to the wishes of a generous outside benefactor ought generally to be treated no differently with respect to access to data from a faculty committee with the same concerns.

Thus, a first step in resolving such requests involves a determination whether the concern motivating the request is essentially an internal concern or an external one. This decision, rather than the mere fact of university affiliation of the requester, usually ought to be controlling.

4. *Outside Requesters*

We believe that considerations of privacy, academic freedom, and the desirable insulation of the university from outside pressures, as well as considerations of efficient operation of the educational enterprise, argue in favor of a *strong* or even *compelling* presumption against access to university documents for which a reasonable claim of confidentiality has been made. The presumption of confidentiality is strongest with respect to individual privacy rights; the personal notes and files of teachers and scholars; and proposed and ongoing research, where the dangers of external pressures and publicity can be fatal to the necessary climate of academic freedom. This presumption applies as well, but perhaps less conclusively, with respect to many other university records including, but not limited to, promotion and grievance files and disciplinary records.

RESOLVING PRESUMPTIONS

A need exists for a mechanism to do the required balancing. Ultimately, of course, all such decisions are subject to judicial review and final determination under the laws of the relevant jurisdiction. However, we do not believe it is appropriate for universities or academic associations such as AAUP simply to abdicate their responsibility to address the problem. Courts, in exercising judicial discretion, can and do give weight to appropriate internal procedures and findings and also to the standards of respected professional associations.

WE RECOMMEND that academic institutions designate, or create, a joint administration/faculty committee with authority to receive and review requests for access to university records and to make recommendations in writing as to their disposition.

Such a committee should attempt the balancing we believe is required in a large number of cases. While balancing will have to be done within the applicable state and federal laws and internal rules, it may not be inappropriate for the committee to recognize that it might recommend differently if it were free of constraint. Beyond this, the balancing ought to be guided by precedents both of that institution and of the academic community. Considerations of privacy, of academic freedom, and of efficient conduct of the essential functions of an academic institution should not be subordinated to a generalized "right to know."

Institutional Responsibility for Legal Demands on Faculty

The statement which follows, a revision and expansion of a 1984 statement, was approved by the Association's Committee on Academic Freedom and Tenure (Committee A) and adopted by the Association's Council in November 1998.

There has been in recent years a steady growth in lawsuits filed against faculty members over the discharge of their professional responsibilities. Legal actions have been initiated by colleagues, by rejected applicants for faculty positions, by students, and by persons or entities outside the academic community. Litigation has concerned, among numerous issues, admissions standards, grading practices, denial of degrees, denial of reappointment, denial of tenure, dismissals, and allegations of defamation, slander, or personal injury flowing from a faculty member's participation in institutional decisions or from the substance of a faculty member's research and teaching. The increasing number of these lawsuits, which often reflect a lack or misuse of appropriate procedures for evaluation and review within an academic institution, is much to be regretted. The parties concerned are subject not only to damage to reputation but also to significant financial liability, which may include cost of legal representation, loss of time, court costs and expenses, and judgments of the court or out-of-court settlements. Moreover, faculty members have increasingly been summoned by legal process to disclose or account for their research and teaching in lawsuits to which they are not parties. Colleges and universities have a responsibility for ensuring legal representation and indemnification to members of their faculties who are subject to lawsuits stemming from their professional performance in institutional service or their conduct of research and teaching.

STATEMENT

The Association recommends that colleges and universities adopt a comprehensive general policy on legal representation and indemnification for members of their faculties. The policy should ensure effective legal and other necessary representation and full indemnification in the first instance for any faculty member named or included in lawsuits or other extra-institutional legal proceedings arising from an act or omission in the discharge of institutional or related professional duties or in the defense of academic freedom at the institution. It should also include specific provisions as follows:

1. The policy should include all stages of such legal action, threatened or pending, in a judicial or administrative proceeding, and all aspects of the use of compulsory process whether or not the faculty member is a party in the proceeding.
2. The policy should ensure effective legal representation of the faculty member's interests, whether by the institution's regular counsel or by specially retained counsel, with due attention to potential conflicts of interest.
3. The policy should be applicable whether or not the institution is also named or included in the legal action, though the institution might consider joining in the action as a party if it has not been named.
4. The policy should provide for all legal expenses, for all other direct costs, and for court judgments and settlements.
5. The policy may provide for legal representation and indemnification through insurance.
6. The policy may provide for a faculty committee to make recommendations on the application of the policy to extraordinary circumstances not foreseen at the time of promulgating the policy of general application.

PROFESSIONAL ETHICS

From its earliest years, the American Association of University Professors has recognized that the privileges associated with faculty status create a corresponding obligation to observe suitable professional and ethical standards. In his introductory address to the first meeting of the Association in 1915, President John Dewey proclaimed that one of the Association's priorities would be the development of "professional standards . . . which will be quite as scrupulous regarding the obligations imposed by freedom as jealous of the freedom itself." A Committee on University Ethics was one of AAUP's original standing committees, and Professor Dewey served as its first chair.

The 1940 Statement of Principles on Academic Freedom and Tenure declares that academic freedom "carries with it duties correlative with rights." These duties are described in the documents that follow, beginning with the Association's basic Statement on Professional Ethics. Other statements provide guidance on particular ethical situations.

The Association maintains a standing Committee on Professional Ethics. The Association views questions involving propriety of conduct as best handled within the framework of individual institutions by reference to an appropriate faculty body. While its good offices are available for advice and mediation, the Association's function in the area of ethics is primarily educative: to inform members of the higher education community about principles of professional ethics and to encourage their observance.

Statement on Professional Ethics

The statement which follows, a revision of a statement originally adopted in 1966, was approved by the Association's Committee on Professional Ethics, adopted by the Association's Council in June 1987, and endorsed by the Seventy-third Annual Meeting.

INTRODUCTION

From its inception, the American Association of University Professors has recognized that membership in the academic profession carries with it special responsibilities. The Association has consistently affirmed these responsibilities in major policy statements, providing guidance to professors in such matters as their utterances as citizens, the exercise of their responsibilities to students and colleagues, and their conduct when resigning from an institution or when undertaking sponsored research. The *Statement on Professional Ethics* that follows sets forth those general standards that serve as a reminder of the variety of responsibilities assumed by all members of the profession.

In the enforcement of ethical standards, the academic profession differs from those of law and medicine, whose associations act to ensure the integrity of members engaged in private practice. In the academic profession the individual institution of higher learning provides this assurance and so should normally handle questions concerning propriety of conduct within its own framework by reference to a faculty group. The Association supports such local action and stands ready, through the general secretary and the Committee on Professional Ethics, to counsel with members of the academic community concerning questions of professional ethics and to inquire into complaints when local consideration is impossible or inappropriate. If the alleged offense is deemed sufficiently serious to raise the possibility of adverse action, the procedures should be in accordance with the 1940 *Statement of Principles on Academic Freedom and Tenure,* the 1958 *Statement on Procedural Standards in Faculty Dismissal Proceedings,* or the applicable provisions of the Association's *Recommended Institutional Regulations on Academic Freedom and Tenure.*

THE STATEMENT

1. Professors, guided by a deep conviction of the worth and dignity of the advancement of knowledge, recognize the special responsibilities placed upon them. Their primary responsibility to their subject is to seek and to state the truth as they see it. To this end professors devote their energies to developing and improving their scholarly competence. They accept the obligation to exercise critical self-discipline and judgment in using, extending, and transmitting knowledge. They practice intellectual honesty. Although professors may follow subsidiary interests, these interests must never seriously hamper or compromise their freedom of inquiry.
2. As teachers, professors encourage the free pursuit of learning in their students. They hold before them the best scholarly and ethical standards of their discipline. Professors demonstrate respect for students as individuals and adhere to their proper roles as intellectual guides and counselors. Professors make every reasonable effort to foster honest academic conduct and to ensure that their evaluations of students reflect each student's true merit. They respect the confidential nature of the relationship between professor and student. They avoid any exploitation, harassment, or discriminatory treatment of students. They acknowledge significant academic or scholarly assistance from them. They protect their academic freedom.

3. As colleagues, professors have obligations that derive from common membership in the community of scholars. Professors do not discriminate against or harass colleagues. They respect and defend the free inquiry of associates. In the exchange of criticism and ideas professors show due respect for the opinions of others. Professors acknowledge academic debt and strive to be objective in their professional judgment of colleagues. Professors accept their share of faculty responsibilities for the governance of their institution.
4. As members of an academic institution, professors seek above all to be effective teachers and scholars. Although professors observe the stated regulations of the institution, provided the regulations do not contravene academic freedom, they maintain their right to criticize and seek revision. Professors give due regard to their paramount responsibilities within their institution in determining the amount and character of work done outside it. When considering the interruption or termination of their service, professors recognize the effect of their decision upon the program of the institution and give due notice of their intentions.
5. As members of their community, professors have the rights and obligations of other citizens. Professors measure the urgency of these obligations in the light of their responsibilities to their subject, to their students, to their profession, and to their institution. When they speak or act as private persons, they avoid creating the impression of speaking or acting for their college or university. As citizens engaged in a profession that depends upon freedom for its health and integrity, professors have a particular obligation to promote conditions of free inquiry and to further public understanding of academic freedom.

A Statement of the Association's Council: Freedom and Responsibility

The statement which follows was adopted by the Council of the American Association of University Professors in October 1970. In April 1990, the Council adopted several changes in language that had been approved by the Association's Committee on Professional Ethics in order to remove gender-specific references from the original text.

For more than half a century the American Association of University Professors has acted upon two principles: that colleges and universities serve the common good through learning, teaching, research, and scholarship; and that the fulfillment of these functions necessarily rests upon the preservation of the intellectual freedoms of teaching, expression, research, and debate. All components of the academic community have a responsibility to exemplify and support these freedoms in the interests of reasoned inquiry.

The 1940 *Statement of Principles on Academic Freedom and Tenure* asserts the primacy of this responsibility. The *Statement on Professional Ethics* underscores its pertinency to individual faculty members and calls attention to their responsibility, by their own actions, to uphold their colleagues' and their students' freedom of inquiry and to promote public understanding of academic freedom. The *Joint Statement on Rights and Freedoms of Students* emphasizes the shared responsibility of all members of the academic community for the preservation of these freedoms.

Continuing attacks on the integrity of our universities and on the concept of academic freedom itself come from many quarters. These attacks, marked by tactics of intimidation and harassment and by political interference with the autonomy of colleges and universities, provoke harsh responses and counter-responses. Especially in a repressive atmosphere, the faculty's responsibility to defend its freedoms cannot be separated from its responsibility to uphold those freedoms by its own actions.

*   *   *   *   *

Membership in the academic community imposes on students, faculty members, administrators, and trustees an obligation to respect the dignity of others, to acknowledge their right to express differing opinions, and to foster and defend intellectual honesty, freedom of inquiry and instruction, and free expression on and off the campus. The expression of dissent and the attempt to produce change, therefore, may not be carried out in ways which injure individuals or damage institutional facilities or disrupt the classes of one's teachers or colleagues. Speakers on campus must not only be protected from violence, but also be given an opportunity to be heard. Those who seek to call attention to grievances must not do so in ways that significantly impede the functions of the institution.

Students are entitled to an atmosphere conducive to learning and to even-handed treatment in all aspects of the teacher-student relationship. Faculty members may not refuse to enroll or teach students on the grounds of their beliefs or the possible uses to which they may put the knowledge to be gained in a course. Students should not be forced by the authority inherent in the instructional role to make particular personal choices as to political action or their own social behavior. Evaluation of students and the award of credit must be based on academic performance professionally judged and not on matters irrelevant to that performance, whether personality, race, religion, degree of political activism, or personal beliefs.

It is the mastery teachers have of their subjects and their own scholarship that entitles them to their classrooms and to freedom in the presentation of their subjects. Thus, it is improper for an instructor persistently to intrude material that has no relation to the subject, or to fail to present

135

the subject matter of the course as announced to the students and as approved by the faculty in their collective responsibility for the curriculum.

Because academic freedom has traditionally included the instructor's full freedom as a citizen, most faculty members face no insoluble conflicts between the claims of politics, social action, and conscience, on the one hand, and the claims and expectations of their students, colleagues, and institutions, on the other. If such conflicts become acute, and attention to obligations as a citizen and moral agent precludes an instructor from fulfilling substantial academic obligations, the instructor cannot escape the responsibility of that choice, but should either request a leave of absence or resign his or her academic position.

* * * * *

The Association's concern for sound principles and procedures in the imposition of discipline is reflected in the 1940 *Statement of Principles on Academic Freedom and Tenure*, the 1958 *Statement on Procedural Standards in Faculty Dismissal Proceedings*, the *Recommended Institutional Regulations on Academic Freedom and Tenure*, and the many investigations conducted by the Association into disciplinary actions by colleges and universities.

The question arises whether these customary procedures are sufficient in the current context. We believe that by and large they serve their purposes well, but that consideration should be given to supplementing them in several respects:

First, plans for ensuring compliance with academic norms should be enlarged to emphasize preventive as well as disciplinary action. Toward this end the faculty should take the initiative, working with the administration and other components of the institution, to develop and maintain an atmosphere of freedom, commitment to academic inquiry, and respect for the academic rights of others. The faculty should also join with other members of the academic community in the development of procedures to be used in the event of serious disruption, or the threat of disruption, and should ensure its consultation in major decisions, particularly those related to the calling of external security forces to the campus.

Second, systematic attention should be given to questions related to sanctions other than dismissal, such as warnings and reprimands, in order to provide a more versatile body of academic sanctions.

Third, the faculty needs to assume a more positive role as guardian of academic values against unjustified assaults from its own members. The traditional faculty function in disciplinary proceedings has been to ensure academic due process and meaningful faculty participation in the imposition of discipline by the administration. While this function should be maintained, faculties should recognize their stake in promoting adherence to norms essential to the academic enterprise.

Rules designed to meet these needs for faculty self-regulation and flexibility of sanctions should be adopted on each campus in response to local circumstances and to continued experimentation. In all sanctioning efforts, however, it is vital that proceedings be conducted with fairness to the individual, that faculty judgments play a crucial role, and that adverse judgments be founded on demonstrated violations of appropriate norms. The Association will encourage and assist local faculty groups seeking to articulate the substantive principles here outlined or to make improvements in their disciplinary machinery to meet the needs here described. The Association will also consult and work with any responsible group, within or outside the academic community, that seeks to promote understanding of and adherence to basic norms of professional responsibility so long as such efforts are consistent with principles of academic freedom.

Statement on Plagiarism

The statement which follows was approved for publication by the Association's Committee on Professional Ethics, adopted by the Association's Council in June 1990, and endorsed by the Seventy-sixth Annual Meeting.

The main practical activity of the American Association of University Professors, since its founding, has concerned restraints upon the right of faculty members to inquire, to teach, to speak, and to publish professionally. Yet throughout its existence, the Association has emphasized the responsibilities of faculty members no less than their rights. Both rights and responsibilities support the common good served by institutions of higher education which, in the words of the 1940 *Statement of Principles on Academic Freedom and Tenure*, "depends upon the free search for truth and its free exposition."[1]

In its *Statement on Professional Ethics*, the Association has stressed the obligation of professors to their subject and to the truth as they see it, as well as the need for them to "exercise critical self-discipline and judgment in using, extending, and transmitting knowledge."[2] Defending free inquiry by their associates and respecting the opinions of others, in the exchange of criticism and ideas, professors must also be rigorously honest in acknowledging their academic debts.

In the light of recent concerns within and outside of the academic profession, it has seemed salutary to restate these general obligations with respect to the offense of plagiarism.

DEFINITION

The offense of plagiarism may seem less self-evident in some circles now than it did formerly. Politicians, business executives, and even university presidents depend on the ideas and literary skills of committees, aides, and speechwriters in the many communications they are called on to make inside and outside their organizations. When ideas are rapidly popularized and spread abroad through the media, when fashion and the quest for publicity are all around us, a concern with protecting the claims of originality may seem to some a quaint survival from the past or even a perverse effort to deter the spread of knowledge.

Nevertheless, within the academic world, where advancing knowledge remains the highest calling, scholars must give full and fair recognition to the contributors to that enterprise, both for the substance and for the formulation of their findings and interpretations. Even within the academic community, however, there are complexities and shades of difference. A writer of textbooks rests on the labors of hundreds of authors of monographs who cannot all be acknowledged; the derivative nature of such work is understood and even, when it is well and skillfully done, applauded. A poet, composer, or painter may "quote" the creation of another artist, deliberately without explanation, as a means of deeper exploration of meaning and in the expectation that knowledgeable readers, listeners, or viewers will appreciate the allusion and delight in it. There are even lapses—regrettable but not always avoidable—in which a long-buried memory of something read surfaces as a seemingly new thought.

But none of these situations diminishes the central certainty: taking over the ideas, methods, or written words of another, without acknowledgment and with the intention that they be credited as the work of the deceiver, is plagiarism. It is theft of a special kind, for the true author still retains the original ideas and words, yet they are diminished as that author's property

---

[1] AAUP, *Policy Documents and Reports*, 9th ed. (Washington, D.C., 2001), 3.
[2] *Ibid.*, 133.

and a fraud is committed upon the audience that believes those ideas and words originated with the deceiver. Plagiarism is not limited to the academic community but has perhaps its most pernicious effect in that setting. It is the antithesis of the honest labor that characterizes true scholarship and without which mutual trust and respect among scholars is impossible.

PRECEPTS

Every professor should be guided by the following:

1. In his or her own work the professor must scrupulously acknowledge every intellectual debt—for ideas, methods, and expressions—by means appropriate to the form of communication.

2. Any discovery of suspected plagiarism should be brought at once to the attention of the affected parties and, as appropriate, to the profession at large through proper and effective channels—typically through reviews in or communications to relevant scholarly journals. The Association's Committee on Professional Ethics stands ready to provide its good offices in resolving questions of plagiarism, either independently or in collaboration with other professional societies.

3. Professors should work to ensure that their universities and professional societies adopt clear guidelines respecting plagiarism, appropriate to the disciplines involved, and should insist that regular procedures be in place to deal with violations of those guidelines. The gravity of a charge of plagiarism, by whomever it is made, must not diminish the diligence exercised in determining whether the accusation is valid. In all cases the most scrupulous procedural fairness must be observed, and penalties must be appropriate to the degree of offense.[3]

4. Scholars must make clear the respective contributions of colleagues on a collaborative project, and professors who have the guidance of students as their responsibility must exercise the greatest care not to appropriate a student's ideas, research, or presentation to the professor's benefit; to do so is to abuse power and trust.

5. In dealing with graduate students, professors must demonstrate by precept and example the necessity of rigorous honesty in the use of sources and of utter respect for the work of others. The same expectations apply to the guidance of undergraduate students, with a special obligation to acquaint students new to the world of higher education with its standards and the means of ensuring intellectual honesty.

CONCLUSION

Any intellectual enterprise—by an individual, a group of collaborators, or a profession—is a mosaic, the pieces of which are put in place by many hands. Viewed from a distance, it should appear a meaningful whole, but the long process of its assemblage must not be discounted or misrepresented. Anyone who is guilty of plagiarism not only harms those most directly affected but also diminishes the authority and credibility of all scholarship and all creative arts, and therefore ultimately harms the interests of the broader society. The danger of plagiarism for teaching, learning, and scholarship is manifest, the need vigorously to maintain standards of professional integrity compelling.

---

[3] On the question of due process for a faculty member who is the subject of disciplinary action because of alleged plagiarism, see Regulations 5 and 7 of the Association's "Recommended Institutional Regulations on Academic Freedom and Tenure," *Policy Documents and Reports*, 25–27.

Statement on Recruitment and Resignation of Faculty Members

The statement printed below was adopted by the Association of American Colleges (now the Association of American Colleges and Universities) in January 1961 with the following reservations as set forth in a preamble prepared by that association's Commission on Academic Freedom and Tenure:

1. *No set of principles adopted by the Association can do more than suggest and recommend a course of action. Consequently, the present statement in no way interferes with institutional sovereignty.*
2. *The commission realizes that the diversity of practice and control that exists among institutions of higher learning precludes any set of standards from being universally applicable to every situation.*
3. *The statement is concerned only with minimum standards and in no way seeks to create a norm for institutions at which "better" practices already are in force.*
4. *The commission recognizes the fact that "emergency" situations will arise and will have to be dealt with. However, it urges both administration and faculty to do so in ways that will not go counter to the spirit of cooperation, good faith, and responsibility that the statement is seeking to promote.*
5. *The commission believes that the spirit embodied in the proposed statement is its most important aspect.*

In view of these reservations, the Council of the American Association of University Professors in April 1961 voted approval of the statement without adopting it as a binding obligation. Endorsement of the statement in this form was voted by the Forty-seventh Annual Meeting.

The governing bodies of the Association of American Colleges and the American Association of University Professors, acting respectively in January and April 1990, adopted several changes in language in order to remove gender-specific references from the original text.

Mobility of faculty members among colleges and universities is rightly recognized as desirable in American higher education. Yet the departure of a faculty member always requires changes within the institution and may entail major adjustments on the part of faculty colleagues, the administration, and students in the faculty member's field. Ordinarily a temporary or permanent successor must be found and appointed to either the vacated position or the position of a colleague who is promoted to replace the faculty member. Clear standards of practice in the recruitment and in the resignations of members of existing faculties should contribute to an orderly interchange of personnel that will be in the interest of all.

The standards set forth below are recommended to administrations and faculties, in the belief that they are sound and should be generally followed. They are predicated on the assumption that proper provision has been made by employing institutions for timely notice to probationary faculty members and those on term appointments, with respect to their subsequent status. In addition to observing applicable requirements for notice of termination to probationary faculty members, institutions should make provision for notice to all faculty members, not later than March 15 of each year, of their status the following fall, including rank and (unless unavoidable budgetary procedures beyond the institution forbid) prospective salary.

1. Negotiations looking to the possible appointment for the following fall of persons who are already faculty members at other institutions, in active service or on leave of absence and not on terminal appointment, should be begun and completed as early as possible in the academic year. It is desirable that, when feasible, the faculty member who has been approached with regard to another position inform the appropriate officers of his or her institution when such negotiations are in progress. The conclusion of a binding agreement for the faculty member to accept an appointment elsewhere should always be followed by prompt notice to the faculty member's current institution.

2. A faculty member should not resign, in order to accept other employment as of the end of the academic year, later than May 15 or thirty days after receiving notification of the terms of continued employment the following year, whichever date occurs later. It is recognized, however, that this obligation will be in effect only if institutions generally observe the time factor set forth in the following paragraph for new offers. It is also recognized that emergencies will occur. In such an emergency the faculty member may ask the appropriate officials of the institution to waive this requirement; but the faculty member should conform to their decision.

3. To permit a faculty member to give due consideration and timely notice to his or her institution in the circumstances defined in paragraph one of these standards, an offer of appointment for the following fall at another institution should not be made after May 1. The offer should be a "firm" one, not subject to contingencies.

4. Institutions deprived of the services of faculty members too late in the academic year to permit their replacement by securing the members of other faculties in conformity to these standards, and institutions otherwise prevented from taking timely action to recruit from other faculties, should accept the necessity of making temporary arrangements or obtaining personnel from other sources, including new entrants to the academic profession and faculty personnel who have retired.

5. Except by agreement with their institution, faculty members should not leave or be solicited to leave their positions during an academic year for which they hold an appointment.

The Ethics of Recruitment and Faculty Appointments

In 1990, the Council of Colleges of Arts and Sciences (CCAS) established a Commission on Recruitment Ethics to consider the continuing experiences of colleges and universities in recruiting faculty members to their campuses. The commission prepared a draft statement for discussion at the CCAS's national meeting in 1991. Subsequently, the commission asked the American Association of University Professors to review the draft statement and to consider working with it in promulgating a joint statement. In February 1992, a joint committee representing the commission and the Association met in Washington. The commission's original draft statement was revised in the light of comments by the members of the joint committee.

The statement which follows was adopted by the Council of Colleges of Arts and Sciences in November 1992. The statement was approved for publication by the Association's Committee on Professional Ethics in December 1992 and adopted by the Association's Council in June 1993.

The standards set forth below are intended to apply to the recruitment and appointment of faculty members in colleges and universities. They are directed to administrators and faculty members in the belief that they will promote the identification and selection of qualified candidates through a process which promotes candor and effective communication among those who are engaged in recruitment. The standards are offered not as rules to serve every situation, but with the expectation that they will provide a foundation for appropriate practices. The spirit of openness and shared responsibility which these standards are intended to convey is also applicable to considerations of affirmative action in the recruitment of faculty.[1]

THE ANNOUNCEMENT OF A FACULTY POSITION

1. Prior to announcing a faculty vacancy, there should be agreement among all responsible parties on each major element of the position (e.g., rank, salary, and eligibility for tenure), how the position relates to the department's (or the equivalent unit's) likely needs for the future, the expectations concerning the professional work of the faculty member(s) being recruited, and the resources that will be provided to help the faculty member(s) meet those expectations.
2. An institution that announces a search should be genuinely engaged in an open process of recruitment for that position. Descriptions of vacant positions should be published and distributed as widely as possible to reach all potential candidates. The procedure established for reviewing applicants and for selecting final candidates should be consistent with the institution's announced criteria and commitment to a fair and open search.
3. All announcements for faculty positions should be clear concerning rank, the length of the appointment, whether the position is with tenure or carries eligibility for tenure, whether the availability of the position is contingent upon funding or other conditions, teaching and research expectations, and requisite experience and credentials. Criteria and procedures for reappointment, promotion, and tenure at the institution, as well as other relevant information, should be made available to all interested candidates upon request.
4. Interested candidates should have at least thirty days from the first appearance of the announcement to submit their applications.

---

[1] For specific considerations of affirmative action in the recruitment of faculty, see the AAUP's "Affirmative Action Plans: Recommended Procedures for Increasing the Number of Minority Persons and Women on College and University Faculties," AAUP, *Policy Documents and Reports*, 9th ed. (Washington, D.C., 2001), 201–7.

CONFIDENTIALITY, INTERVIEWS, AND THE FINAL DECISION

1. Institutions should respect the confidentiality of candidates for faculty positions. The institution may contact references, including persons who are not identified by the candidate, but it should exercise discretion when doing so. An institution should not make public the names of candidates without having given the candidates the opportunity to withdraw from the search.
2. Those who participate in the interview should avoid any discriminatory treatment of candidates. All communications with the candidates concerning the position should be consistent with the information stated in the announcement for the position.
3. Candidates for faculty positions should disclose in a timely fashion conditions that might materially bear upon the institution's decision to offer the appointment (for example, requirements for research funds, unusual moving costs, a delayed starting date, or the intention to retain an affiliation at the institution with which the candidate is currently associated).
4. If candidates request information about the progress of the search and the status of their candidacy, they should be given the information.
5. The institution's decision about which candidate will be offered the position should be consistent with the criteria for the position and its duties as stated in the announcement of the vacancy. If the selection of the final candidates will be based on significant changes in the criteria for the position or its duties as stated in the original announcement, the institution should start a new search.

THE OFFER AND ACCEPTANCE

1. The institution may wish to provide informal notification to the successful candidate of its intention to offer an appointment, but the formal offer itself should be an unequivocal letter of appointment signed by the responsible institutional officer. "Oral offers" and "oral acceptances" should not be considered binding, but communications between the successful candidate and those representing the institution should be frank and accurate, for significant decisions are likely to be based on these exchanges. The written offer of appointment should be given to the candidate within ten days of the institution's having conveyed an intention to make the offer; a candidate should be informed promptly if the offer is not to be forthcoming within ten days.
2. The terms of an offer to an individual should be consistent with the announcement of the position. Each of the following should be stated clearly in the letter offering an appointment: (a) the initial rank; (b) the length of the appointment; (c) conditions of renewal; (d) the salary and benefits; (e) the duties of the position; (f) as applicable, whether the appointment is with tenure, the amount of credit toward tenure for prior service, and the maximum length of the probationary period; (g) as applicable, the institution's "start-up" commitments for the appointment (for example, equipment and laboratory space); (h) the date when the appointment begins and the date when the candidate is expected to report; (i) the date by which the candidate's response to the offer is expected, which should not be less than two weeks from receipt of the offer; and (j) details of institutional policies and regulations that bear upon the appointment. Specific information on other relevant matters also should be conveyed in writing to the prospective appointee.
3. An offer of appointment to a faculty member serving at another institution should be made no later than May 1, consistent with the faculty member's obligation to resign, in order to accept other employment, no later than May 15.[2] It is recognized that, in special cases, it might be appropriate to make an offer after May 1, but in such cases there should be an agreement by all concerned parties.

---

[2] See the "Statement on Recruitment and Resignation of Faculty Members," issued jointly by the AAUP and the Association of American Colleges, *Policy Documents and Reports*, 139–40.

4. The acceptance of a position is a written, affirmative, and unconditional response sent by the candidate to the institution no later than the date stated in the offer of appointment. If the candidate wishes to accept the offer contingent upon conditions, those conditions should be specified and communicated promptly in writing to the institution which is offering the position.
5. If the candidate wishes to retain an affiliation with his or her current institution, that circumstance should be brought promptly to the attention of the current institution and the recruiting institution.
6. Individuals who accept an appointment should arrive at the institution in sufficient time to prepare for their duties and to participate in orientation programs.

On Preventing Conflicts of Interest in Government-Sponsored Research at Universities

The many complex problems that have developed in connection with the extensive sponsored research programs of the federal government have been of concern to the government, the academic community, and private industry. The American Association of University Professors, through its Council, and the American Council on Education, working in cooperation with the president's science advisor and the Federal Council of Science and Technology, in 1965 developed a statement of principles formulating basic standards and guidelines in this problematic area.

An underlying premise of the statement is that responsibility for determining standards affecting the academic community rests with that community, and that conflict-of-interest problems are best handled by administration and faculty in cooperative effort. In addition to providing guidelines, the statement seeks to identify and alert administration and faculty to the types of situations that have proved troublesome. Throughout, it seeks to protect the integrity of the objectives and needs of the cooperating institutions and their faculties, as well as of sponsoring agencies.

In April 1990, the Council of the American Association of University Professors adopted several changes in language in order to remove gender-specific references from the original text.

The increasingly necessary and complex relationships among universities, government, and industry call for more intensive attention to standards of procedure and conduct in government-sponsored research. The clarification and application of such standards must be designed to serve the purposes and needs of the projects and the public interest involved in them and to protect the integrity of the cooperating institutions as agencies of higher education.

The government and institutions of higher education, as the contracting parties, have an obligation to see that adequate standards and procedures are developed and applied; to inform one another of their respective requirements; and to ensure that all parties to the relationship are informed of and apply the standards and procedures that are so developed.

Consulting relationships between university staff members and industry serve the interests of research and education in the university. Likewise, the transfer of technical knowledge and skill from the university to industry contributes to technological advance. Such relationships are desirable, but certain potential hazards should be recognized.

CONFLICT SITUATIONS

1. Favoring of Outside Interests

When a university staff member (administrator, faculty member, professional staff member, or employee) undertaking or engaging in government-sponsored work has a significant financial interest in, or a consulting arrangement with, a private business concern, it is important to avoid actual or apparent conflicts of interest between government-sponsored university research obligations and outside interests and other obligations. Situations in or from which conflicts of interest may arise are:

(a) the undertaking or orientation of the staff member's university research to serve the research or other needs of the private firm without disclosure of such undertaking or orientation to the university and to the sponsoring agency;

(b) the purchase of major equipment, instruments, materials, or other items for university research from the private firm in which the staff member has the interest without disclosure of such interest;

(c) the transmission to the private firm or other use for personal gain of government-sponsored work products, results, materials, records, or information that are not made generally available (this would not necessarily preclude appropriate licensing arrangements for inventions, or consulting on the basis of government-sponsored research results where there is significant additional work by the staff member independent of the government-sponsored research);

(d) the use for personal gain or other unauthorized use of privileged information acquired in connection with the staff member's government-sponsored activities (the term "privileged information" includes, but is not limited to, medical, personnel, or security records of individuals; anticipated material requirements or price actions; possible new sites for government operations; and knowledge of forthcoming programs or of selection of contractors or subcontractors in advance of official announcements);

(e) the negotiation or influence upon the negotiation of contracts relating to the staff member's government-sponsored research between the university and private organizations with which the staff member has consulting or other significant relationships; and

(f) the acceptance of gratuities or special favors from private organizations with which the university does, or may conduct, business in connection with a government-sponsored research project, or extension of gratuities or special favors to employees of the sponsoring government agency, under circumstances which might reasonably be interpreted as an attempt to influence the recipients in the conduct of their duties.

2. *Distribution of Effort*

There are competing demands on the energies of faculty members (for example, research, teaching, committee work, outside consulting). The way in which a faculty member divides his or her effort among these various functions does not raise ethical questions unless the government agency supporting the research is misled in its understanding of the amount of intellectual effort the faculty member is actually devoting to the research in question. A system of precise time accounting is incompatible with the inherent character of the work of faculty members, since the various functions they perform are closely interrelated and do not conform to any meaningful division of a standard work week. On the other hand, if the research agreement contemplates that a faculty member will devote a certain fraction of effort to the government-sponsored research, or the faculty member agrees to assume responsibility in relation to such research, a demonstrable relationship between the indicated effort or responsibility and the actual extent of the faculty member's involvement is to be expected. Each university, therefore, should—through joint consultation of administration and faculty—develop procedures to ensure that proposals are responsibly made and complied with.

3. *Consulting for Government Agencies or Their Contractors*

When the staff member engaged in government-sponsored research also serves as a consultant to a federal agency, such conduct is subject to the provisions of the Conflict of Interest Statutes (18 U.S.C. 202–209 as amended) and the president's memorandum of May 2, 1963, *Preventing Conflicts of Interest on the Part of Special Government Employees*. When the staff member consults for one or more government contractors, or prospective contractors, in the same technical field as the staff member's research project, care must be taken to avoid giving advice that may be of questionable objectivity because of its possible bearing on the individual's other interests. In undertaking and performing consulting services, the staff member should make full disclosure of such interests to the university and to the contractor insofar as they may appear to relate to the work at the university or for the contractor. Conflict-of-interest problems could arise, for example, in the participation of a staff member of the university in an evaluation for the government agency or its contractor of some technical aspect of the work of another organization with which the staff member has a consulting or employment relationship or a significant financial interest, or in an evaluation of a competitor to such other organization.

UNIVERSITY RESPONSIBILITY

Each university participating in government-sponsored research should make known to the sponsoring government agencies:

1. the steps it is taking to ensure an understanding on the part of the university administration and staff members of the possible conflicts of interest or other problems that may develop in the foregoing types of situations; and
2. the organizational and administrative actions it has taken or is taking to avoid such problems, including:
   (a) accounting procedures to be used to ensure that government funds are expended for the purposes for which they have been provided, and that all services which are required in return for these funds are supplied;
   (b) procedures that enable it to be aware of the outside professional work of staff members participating in government-sponsored research, if such outside work relates in any way to the government-sponsored research;
   (c) the formulation of standards to guide the individual university staff members in governing their conduct in relation to outside interests that might raise questions of conflicts of interest; and
   (d) the provision within the university of an informed source of advice and guidance to its staff members for advance consultation on questions they wish to raise concerning the problems that may or do develop as a result of their outside financial or consulting interests, as they relate to their participation in government-sponsored university research. The university may wish to discuss such problems with the contracting officer or other appropriate government official in those cases that appear to raise questions regarding conflicts of interest.

The above process of disclosure and consultation is the obligation assumed by the university when it accepts government funds for research. The process must, of course, be carried out in a manner that does not infringe on the legitimate freedoms and flexibility of action of the university and its staff members that have traditionally characterized a university. It is desirable that standards and procedures of the kind discussed be formulated and administered by members of the university community themselves, through their joint initiative and responsibility, for it is they who are the best judges of the conditions which can most effectively stimulate the search for knowledge and preserve the requirements of academic freedom. Experience indicates that such standards and procedures should be developed and specified by joint administration-faculty action.

Statement on Conflicts of Interest

The statement which follows was approved for publication by the Association's Committee on Professional Ethics in June 1990.

American universities and colleges have long been engaged with the institutions of the wider society, to their mutual benefit. Universities have trained ministers, teachers, corporate leaders, and public servants, and have taken on wider responsibilities in research and administration for state and federal governments. The years after World War II brought both quantitative and qualitative change in this relationship as a result of the global responsibilities assumed by the United States and of the strikingly new importance attained by science. This change was symbolized and advanced by an immense increase in federal and state funding for higher education and in investment by private foundations. Now, as universities have entered an era of more stringent budgetary limitations, yet another major shift has occurred—to greater reliance on private funding and to a closer symbiosis between universities and industry.

The many opportunities offered to both university researchers and the private sector by sweeping developments in certain areas of science and technology have led to new concerns in both universities and government. One such concern, about freedom to do research and to publish the results, has rightly exercised universities in deliberations about whether or not to undertake such joint efforts and on what terms. More recently, the question of conflict of interest has been raised anew, with regard to the pressures that financial interests of faculty members participating in extra-university enterprises may exert, consciously or not, on the design and the outcome of the research.

The American Association of University Professors has addressed these questions in the past, and we believe it important to reaffirm the 1965 joint statement of the AAUP and the American Council on Education, *On Preventing Conflicts of Interest in Government-Sponsored Research at Universities*, and to commend the 1983 report of an Association subcommittee on *Corporate Funding of Academic Research*.[1] The latter report, avowedly tentative and anticipating a fuller statement at a later time, properly assumed that the initiative must lie with university faculties for drawing up such conflict-of-interest guidelines as are appropriate to each campus, with due regard for the proper disclosure of a faculty member's involvement in off-campus enterprises, in terms of investment, ownership, or consultative status; for the use of university personnel, including students; and for the disposition of potential profits.

Recent developments have suggested the following considerations to be taken into account by faculties involved in developing or revising such guidelines.

Government proposals for policing possible conflicts of interest have been overwhelmingly rejected by the academic community as involving a massive, unneeded enlargement of the government's role on the campus. Faculties must be careful, however, to ensure that they do not defensively propose a similar bureaucratic burden differing only in the locus of administration. Any requirements for disclosure of potential conflicts of interest should be carefully focused on legitimate areas of concern and not improperly interfere with the privacy rights of faculty members and their families.

Because the central business of the university remains teaching and research unfettered by extra-university dictates, faculties should ensure that any cooperative venture between members of the faculty and outside agencies, whether public or private, respects the primacy of the university's principal mission, with regard to the choice of subjects of research and the reaching and publication of results.

---

[1] *Academe: Bulletin of the AAUP* 69 (November–December 1983): 18a–23a.

Faculties should make certain that the pursuit of such joint ventures does not become an end in itself and so introduce distortions into traditional university understandings and arrangements. Private and public agencies have a direct interest in only a few fields of research and in only certain questions within those fields. Accordingly, external interests should not be allowed to shift the balance of academic priorities in a university without thorough debate about the consequences and without the considered judgment of appropriate faculty bodies. So, too, care must be taken to avoid contravening a commitment to fairness by widening disparities—in teaching loads, student supervision, or budgetary allocation—between departments engaged in such outside activity and those not less central to the nature of a university, which have, or can have, no such engagement.

The ability to procure private or government funding may in certain circumstances be an appropriate consideration in making judgments about salaries, tenure, and promotion, but it must be kept in proper proportion and be consistent with criteria established by the faculty. Guidelines concerning intra-university research support should guard against making its availability dependent, solely or predominantly, on the likelihood that the research so supported will result in obtaining outside funding.

Statement on Multiple Authorship

The statement which follows was approved for publication by the Association's Committee on Professional Ethics in June 1990.

Over the years, different scholarly fields have evolved different patterns of research and publication. In some areas, the solitary researcher remains the model, an ideal that draws some of its strength from association with the Romantic conception of the creative artist. Even in those fields, however, genuine collaboration is possible and even inescapable as different analytical skills are called upon to illuminate increasingly complex subjects of inquiry. Elsewhere in the scholarly world, collaboration is the norm. This appears to be particularly true in those sciences where separated disciplines must be brought to bear on a novel question, or where complex, articulated laboratory organizations are essential, or where (as in some areas of physics and astronomy) the scale is so large and the expense so vast that any original contribution is beyond the capacity of a scholar working alone or of even small teams of scholars.

In this varied and constantly shifting situation, disciplines have arrived at certain conventions that govern the listing of names of collaborators. This may seem at first glance a sufficiently equitable arrangement: scholars within the field know what to expect and how to evaluate their colleagues' estimate of their respective contributions. But there are times when the wider academic community must become involved in such questions, as will a still-wider world outside the university. Faculty members and administrators making decisions about appointments, promotion and tenure, and salary increases must try to evaluate individual worth and reckon with the significance of authorship. So, too, must granting agencies, public and private, while the government and the press, seeking expertise, must make repeated judgments about the basis of the authority that individual scholars may claim. A vast list of publications, dazzling to the uninitiated, may conceal as much as it reveals, and the conventions of particular disciplines may give rise to the suspicion, if not the actuality, of questionable ethical practices.

It is well known that actors' agents frequently negotiate hard about the order of credits, placement, and size of type; no such excesses need follow from an expectation that scholars who take part in a collaborative project should explain forthrightly—to disciplinary peers as well as to other academic colleagues and to such members of the public as may have occasion to inquire—the respective contributions of those who put their names to the finished work. This clarification might be accomplished in a preface, an extensive footnote, or an appendix; no one format can serve every scholarly combination. But a candid statement would do much to establish degrees of responsibility and authority, to ensure fair credit to junior or student colleagues, and to avoid unseemly later disputes about priority, real or alleged errors, and plagiarism. Purely formal association with the enterprise (such as the headship of a laboratory where no direct research involvement was present) would be noted for what it is, to the benefit of the participants as much as of those outside the field.

Making plain the actual contribution of each scholar to a collaborative work calls for an equivalent recognition in return. That academic decision makers frequently find themselves in a troubling dilemma when faced with genuine substantive collaboration testifies to the strength of the ideal of individual creativity. While in some scholarly activity carried on in tandem it is possible for contributors to make clear the respective contributions of each (as is often, and should be regularly, done by two or three joint authors of a book), in other cases the collaboration is so intimate as to defy disentangling: the creativity is imbedded in, and consequent upon, constant exchange of ideas and insights. This scholarly and psychological reality must be fully recognized in making academic decisions about the accomplishments and careers of single members of such combinations: what they have done must not be reduced to a second order of merit or, worse, dismissed out of hand. This recognition is particularly important in the case of younger scholars who may take a leading role in a collaboration that at first sight is one of sub-ordination. To insist on individual demonstration of the abilities of a young scholar working on a topic where collaboration is inescapable, and where (as is often the case) immense amounts of time are required for fruitful results, may disrupt a promising career, force unneeded and diversionary publication, put undue emphasis on the vexing question of priority of discovery, and distort perceptions of the creative process.

These are questions of immense complexity and subtlety, not to be resolved by an unimag-inative application of traditional academic myths or by bureaucratic heavy-handedness. Peer judgment alive to these questions, together with a sensible weighing of merely quantitative measures of accomplishment and reputation, will do much to remedy a problem that through parochialism, misplaced egotism, and inadvertence threatens to become steadily worse and to contribute to tarnishing the scholarly enterprise.

RESEARCH AND TEACHING

As an organization of teachers and researchers, the American Association of University Professors has long been concerned with the development and maintenance of effective college and university instruction, including classroom techniques, work with individual students, testing, and the use of library facilities and advanced teaching aids; with the conditions of effective research, creative work, and publication by faculty members; and with the recruitment and training of college and university faculties. The Association's standing Committee on College and University Teaching, Research, and Publication has developed policy statements relating to faculty workload and teaching evaluation and has sponsored occasional studies in these areas.

Statement on Faculty Workload
With Interpretive Comments

The statement which follows was approved by the Association's Committee on College and University Teaching, Research, and Publication in April 1968. It was adopted by the Association's Council in October 1969 and endorsed by the Fifty-sixth Annual Meeting. In April 1990, the Council adopted several changes in language that had been approved by the Committee on College and University Teaching, Research, and Publication in order to remove gender-specific references from the original text.

The Statement on Faculty Workload *is printed below, followed by Interpretive Comments as developed in 2000 by the Committee on College and University Teaching, Research, and Publication.*

INTRODUCTION

No single formula for an equitable faculty workload can be devised for all of American higher education. What is fair and works well in the community college may be inappropriate for the university, and the arrangement thought necessary in the technical institute may be irrelevant in the liberal arts college.

This is not to say, however, that excessive or inequitably distributed workloads cannot be recognized as such. In response to the many appeals received in recent years, therefore, this Association wishes to set forth such guidelines as can be applied generally, regardless of the special circumstances of the institution concerned:

1. A definition of maximum teaching loads for effective instruction at the undergraduate and graduate levels.
2. A description of the procedures that should be followed in establishing, administering, and revising workload policies.
3. An identification of the most common sources of inequity in the distribution of workloads.

MAXIMUM TEACHING LOADS

In the American system of higher education, faculty "workloads" are usually described in hours per week of formal class meetings. As a measurement, this leaves much to be desired. It fails to consider other time-consuming institutional duties of the faculty member, and, even in terms of teaching, it misrepresents the true situation. The teacher normally spends far less time in the classroom than in preparation, conferences, grading of papers and examinations, and supervision of remedial or advanced student work. Preparation, in particular, is of critical importance, and is probably the most unremitting of these demands; not only preparation for specific classes or conferences, but that more general preparation in the discipline, by keeping up with recent developments and strengthening one's grasp on older materials, without which the faculty member will soon dwindle into ineffectiveness as scholar and teacher. Moreover, traditional workload formulations are at odds with significant current developments in education emphasizing independent study, the use of new materials and media, extracurricular and off-campus educational experiences, and interdisciplinary approaches to problems in contemporary society. Policies on workload at institutions practicing such approaches suggest the need for a more sophisticated discrimination and weighting of educational activities.

This Association has been in a position over the years to observe workload policies and faculty performance in a great variety of American colleges and universities, and in its considered judgment the following maximum workload limits are necessary for any institution of higher education seriously intending to achieve and sustain an adequately high level of faculty effectiveness in teaching and scholarship:

For undergraduate instruction, a teaching load of twelve hours per week, with no more than six separate course preparations during the academic year.

For instruction partly or entirely at the graduate level, a teaching load of nine hours per week.

This statement of *maximum* workload presumes a traditional academic year of not more than thirty weeks of classes. Moreover, it presumes no unusual additional expectations in terms of research, administration, counseling, or other institutional responsibilities. Finally, it presumes also that means can be devised within each institution for determining fair equivalents in workload for those faculty members whose activities do not fit the conventional classroom lecture or discussion pattern: for example, those who supervise laboratories or studios, offer tutorials, or assist beginning teachers.

PREFERRED TEACHING LOADS

Even with the reservations just enunciated, however, it would be misleading to offer this statement of maximum loads without providing some guidelines for a preferable pattern. This Association has observed in recent years a steady reduction of teaching loads in American colleges and universities noted for the effectiveness of their faculties in teaching and scholarship to norms that can be stated as follows:

For undergraduate instruction, a teaching load of nine hours per week.

For instruction partly or entirely at the graduate level, a teaching load of six hours per week.

The Association has observed also that in the majority of these institutions further reductions have become quite usual for individuals assuming heavier-than-normal duties in counseling, program development, administration, research, and many other activities. In a smaller number, moreover, even lower teaching loads have been established generally, for all faculty members.

It must be recognized that achievement of nine- or six-hour teaching loads may not be possible at present for many institutions. The Association believes, nevertheless, that the nine- or six-hour loads achieved by our leading colleges and universities, in some instances many years ago, provide as reliable a guide as may be found for teaching loads in any institution intending to achieve and maintain excellence in faculty performance.

PROCEDURES

The faculty should participate fully in the determination of workload policy, both initially and in all subsequent reappraisals. Reappraisal at regular intervals is essential, in order that older patterns of faculty responsibility may be adjusted to changes in the institution's size, structure, academic programs, and facilities. Current policy and practices should be made known clearly to all faculty members, including those new to the institution each year.

The individual may have several quite different duties, some of which may be highly specialized, and the weight of these duties may vary strikingly at different times during the year. It is important, therefore, that individual workloads be determined by, or in consultation with, the department or other academic unit most familiar with the demands involved. Those responsible should be allowed a measure of latitude in making individual assignments, and care should be taken that all of the individual's services to the institution are considered.

COMMON SOURCES OF INEQUITY IN THE DISTRIBUTION OF WORKLOADS

1. Difficulty of Courses

No two courses are exactly alike, and some differences among individual loads are therefore to be expected within a common twelve-hour, nine-hour, or six-hour policy. Serious inequity should be avoided, however, and the most frequent sources of difficulty are easily identified.

    (a) The number of different course preparations should be considered, not only the total class hours per week.

(b) Special adjustments may be appropriate for the faculty member introducing a new course or substantially revising an older course. This is a matter of institutional self-interest as well as of equity; if the new course has been approved as likely to strengthen the institution's program, all appropriate measures should be taken to ensure its success.

(c) Extreme differences in scope and difficulty among courses should not be overlooked merely because contention might be provoked on other less obvious imbalances. The difference in difficulty among some courses is so pronounced that no faculty member concerned would deny the existence of the discrepancy. Such imbalances may occur among courses in different disciplines as well as those within the same discipline. In some subjects the advanced course is the more demanding; in others, the introductory course. One course may entail constant student consultation; another may entail a heavy burden of paperwork. At least the more obvious discrepancies should be corrected.

(d) The size of the classes taught should also be considered. The larger class is not always more demanding than the smaller class; but it does not follow that the question of class size can safely be ignored. In a given institution there will be many generally comparable courses, and for these the difficulty will probably be directly proportionate to the number of students involved. In some institutions aware of this problem, faculty workload is now measured in terms of student-instruction load, or "contact hours," as well as in the conventional classroom or credit hours.

Regardless of the institution's particular circumstances, it should be possible by formal or informal means to avoid serious inequities on these four major points.

2. Research

Increasingly each year undergraduate as well as graduate institutions specify "research" as a major responsibility of the faculty. Lack of clarity or candor about what constitutes such "research" can lead to excessive demands on the faculty generally or on part of the faculty.

If the expectation is only of that "general preparation" already described, no additional reduction in faculty workload is indicated. Usually, however, something beyond that general preparation is meant: original, exploratory work in some special field of interest within the discipline. It should be recognized that if this is the expectation, such research, *whether or not it leads to publication*, will require additional time. It is very doubtful that a continuing effort in original inquiry can be maintained by a faculty member carrying a teaching load of more than nine hours; and it is worth noting that a number of leading universities desiring to emphasize research have already moved or are now moving to a six-hour policy.

If it is original work that is expected, but the institution fails to state candidly whether in practice scholarly publication will be regarded as the only valid evidence of such study, the effect may well be to press one part of the faculty into "publishing research" at the expense of a "teaching research" remainder. Neither faculty group will teach as well as before.

In short, if research is to be considered a *general* faculty responsibility, the only equitable way to achieve it would seem to be a *general* reduction in faculty workload. If the expectation is that some but not all of the faculty will be publishing scholars, then that policy should be candidly stated and faculty workloads adjusted equitably in accordance with that expectation.

3. Responsibilities Other Than Teaching and Research

Although faculty members expect as a matter of course to serve in student counseling, on committees, with professional societies, and in certain administrative capacities, a heavy commitment in any of these areas, or service in too many of these areas at once, will of course impair the effectiveness of the faculty member as teacher and scholar. A reduction in workload is manifestly in order when an institution wishes to draw heavily on the services of an individual in these ways, or when with its approval the individual is engaged in community or government service. No universally applicable rule can be advanced here, but, as suggested earlier, the faculty unit responsible for individual assignments should take all such additional service into full consideration. Often, the determination of an appropriate reduction in workload depends on nothing more complex than an estimate of the hours that these additional duties will require.

2000 INTERPRETIVE COMMENTS

The interpretive comments which follow were approved by the Association's Committee on College and University Teaching, Research, and Publication in March 2000. They were adopted by the Association's Council in June 2000 and endorsed by the Eighty-sixth Annual Meeting.

The world of higher education has changed significantly since the Association issued its *Statement on Faculty Workload* in 1969. While the number of faculty members in the profession has increased considerably, the proportion who hold positions that are with tenure or probationary for tenure has decreased significantly. Colleges and universities are meeting their instructional needs by increasing their reliance on part-time, adjunct, or full-time non-tenure-track faculty members and on new technologies. The increased reliance on various types of non-tenure-track faculty has added to the workload of tenured and tenure-track faculty, who must assume additional administrative and governance responsibilities. In reviewing the 1969 *Statement*, we have looked at how these changes affect the work of faculty in what was already a complex and diversified academic workplace.

The Association's recommendations regarding workload were developed, according to the 1969 *Statement*, in order to ensure and sustain an "adequately high level of faculty effectiveness in teaching and scholarship." That statement recommended *maximum* and *preferred* teaching loads, and offered differing workload recommendations based on whether or not the instruction was offered at the undergraduate or the graduate level. We reaffirm the need to distinguish between *maximum* and *preferred* loads, but we believe that differences in workload should reflect the differing research and instructional expectations for faculty members at different kinds of academic institutions. We believe that institutional expectations concerning the amount of research a faculty member is required to conduct are a more useful determinant than whether instruction is offered at the undergraduate or the graduate level.

The 1969 *Statement* noted that no single formula for an equitable faculty workload could be devised for all of American higher education. Still, we note that the various segments of higher education have all recently undergone similar changes in the pattern of faculty appointments and in the nature of technological innovations.

This committee has also examined the application of the 1969 *Statement* in the context of the rapidly growing community-college segment of American higher education.

MAXIMUM TEACHING LOADS

1. Community Colleges

Community-college teaching loads have typically exceeded the maximum of twelve hours per week that the 1969 *Statement* recommended for undergraduate instruction. We believe that the recommended maximum load should remain the twelve hours recommended in the original statement. The academic and instructional responsibilities and obligations involved in educating the diverse range of students who attend community colleges are no less demanding than those at other institutions of higher education. Although the expectations for research and service in the two-year sector may differ in particulars from those in other sectors of higher education, the professional demands are equivalent.

2. Part-Time Faculty

Many institutions have converted full-time faculty appointments to positions held by part-time faculty or graduate assistants. We observe with concern that recent institutional practice has led to a multi-tier system of appointments that provide part-time faculty members little opportunity to conduct research or to participate in professional development.

We recommend that part-time faculty appointments not be based, as they commonly are, solely on course or teaching hours. Activities that extend well beyond classroom time—including maintaining office hours, participating in collegial curricular discussions, preparing courses, and grading examinations and essays—should be recognized. These faculty duties should be defined, and the part-time faculty members who engage in these activities should be compensated and supported professionally based on pro-rata or proportional performance of an equivalent full-time position.[1]

3. *Graduate Teaching Assistants*

The teaching loads of graduate assistants should permit those who hold these positions to meet their own educational responsibilities as well as to meet the needs of their students. We therefore see merit in an institution's setting a limit on the amount of work it assigns to graduate assistants, generally recommended not to exceed twenty hours per week, so that they are not hindered in completing their own degree requirements.[2]

DISTANCE EDUCATION

No examination of teaching loads today would be complete without consideration of how distance education has affected the work of faculty members who engage in it. Since faculty members have primary responsibility for instruction, the curricular changes needed to implement new technologies—including course design, implementation, review, and revision—require substantial faculty participation. Institutions should provide training as well as support for those faculty members expected to implement new instructional technologies. Consideration should also be given to the matter of increases in contact hours in the real or asynchronous time required to achieve interactive learning and student accessibility.[3] The increased time in course preparation and the demands of interactive electronic communication with individual students call for a reduction in the maximum classroom hour assignment.

[1] See "The Status of Non-Tenure-Track Faculty," AAUP, *Policy Documents and Reports*, 9th ed. (Washington, D.C., 2001), 77–87.
[2] See "Statement on Graduate Students," *ibid.*, 268–70.
[3] For a detailed examination of these issues, see "Statement on Distance Education," *ibid.*, 179–81.

The Work of Faculty: Expectations, Priorities, and Rewards

The statement which follows is excerpted from a longer report of the same title which was approved by the Association's Committee on College and University Teaching, Research, and Publication in December 1993.

INTRODUCTION

What is it that college and university faculty members really do? Much of the confusion surrounding the current debate over faculty workload stems from misconceptions about how faculty spend their time, particularly outside of the classroom. People making policy decisions need to understand the multiple components of faculty work and to take account of the diversity within the American higher education system, a rich variety that militates against the development of simple or uniform standards applicable to all types of institutions.

The purpose of this report is to assess the current state of public discussion regarding the duties and obligations of the professoriate: to look at recent debates about the size and nature of faculty workloads; to offer clarification of the roles of teaching, scholarship, and service for faculty, their institutions, and the public welfare; and to set the problems of the academy against the backdrop of public debates about the costs and benefits of higher education.

In 1969, the Association addressed the question of faculty workloads and the appropriate balance between teaching and research. The statement that was adopted by the AAUP's Council defined maximum and preferred teaching loads in terms of classroom contact hours; advocated collegial procedures for establishing, administering, and revising workload policies; and identified common sources of inequity in the distribution of workloads.

The world changes: the problems of the 1990s differ dramatically from those of 1969. In this report we now address these issues by directing attention to total faculty workload, rather than classroom hours. We approach the question of balance through definitions of teaching, scholarship, and service that emphasize the great variety of activities so embraced; we urge the integration of all the components of academic activity. We do this in the face of external pressures upon the academy and in acknowledgment of the need to reassess our profession and our priorities and to communicate to the general public our understanding of our work and its value, while emphasizing the immense variety of institutions of higher education and the wide range of their problems, resources, and academic and public missions.

*   *   *   *   *

CONCLUSIONS AND RECOMMENDATIONS

We offer these conclusions and recommendations . . . with the forceful reminder that no single answer to any of the complex questions we have examined can possibly fit all institutions in the diverse world of colleges and universities.

1. Faculty workload combines teaching, scholarship, and service; this unity of components is meant to represent the seamless garment of academic life, and it defines the typical scholarly performance and career.

Higher education works best when faculty members teach with enthusiasm, engage in scholarly activities and research, and are deeply committed to collegial, community, and professional service. All of these are vital components of the work of faculty. Ideally they reinforce each other, to the benefit of students and institutions and as major motives and sources of satisfaction in the life and career of each faculty member. We distort the enterprise of higher education if we attempt to separate these endeavors, or to define them as essentially competitive rather than as complementary.

2. *Faculty workload and hours in the classroom are not the same thing.*

The general public tends to equate the number of hours spent in the classroom—the contact-hour teaching load—with a faculty member's workload, which properly should be seen as the aggregate of hours devoted to all the forms and demands of teaching, of scholarship and research and publication, and of the many varieties of professional service. Not only does a mere tally and consideration of "teaching hours" ignore members of the faculty who teach in laboratories, or in settings other than within the traditional classroom (as in studios, small-group tutorials, field work, or clinics); it also distorts the nature of academic work by minimizing the value of the integrated career and the synergistic nature of experience and judgment that comes from engagement in the multiple dimensions of faculty work.

Data show that on average faculty members routinely work somewhere between 45 and 55 hours per week. Workload should be thought of as total professional effort, which includes the time (and energy) devoted to class preparation, grading student work, curriculum and program deliberations, scholarship (including, but not limited to, research and publication), participation in governance activities, and a wide range of community services, both on and off campus.

3. *External mandates of workload and productivity are not an effective or desirable means of enhancing the quality or cost-effectiveness of higher education.*

We believe that nothing of any value, insofar as the quality of higher education is at issue, is likely to result from extramural efforts to define workload or to determine an appropriate mixture among types of professional activity, whether we refer to individuals or to institutions. Many such attempts at external supervision and demands for accountability rest on an unsupported idea that heavier teaching loads are the solution to the current budgetary ills of higher education. We find no reason to think that more hours of student-teacher classroom contact are the road to better higher education. Nor does any convincing logic indicate that closer supervision of faculty performance will raise productivity and cut costs.

It is not difficult to understand why such externally imposed remedies are widely advocated for the problems that beset higher education. However, they neither blend with nor add to higher education's ongoing efforts to improve educational quality and to broaden access to institutions of higher learning.

4. *Teaching is a basic activity of the professoriate, and institutional reward systems should reflect the fundamental importance of effective teaching.*

Teaching—which includes laboratory instruction, academic advising, training graduate students in seminars and individualized research, and various other forms of educational contact in addition to instructing undergraduates in the classroom—should be given very high priority in all institutions of higher education. Surveys and interviews indicate that faculty members derive great satisfaction from teaching well and from working closely with students. Expectations of teaching effectiveness should be high, and those who meet them should be rewarded for their success—as for other noteworthy contributions—as part of the regular reward system of colleges and universities.

We worry that efforts to offer special rewards to a few faculty members for superior teaching may in some instances be substituted for broader and deeper institutional commitment to teaching and to the educational welfare of the students. Such rewards are well earned and come as a welcome signal of institutional concern. But, by themselves, such individualized rewards can become mere tokens and can even detract from efforts to direct scarce and contested resources toward an across-the-board enrichment of education, especially of bread-and-butter undergraduate teaching and student needs. The culture of each institution should expect the vast majority of its faculty—at all ranks—to engage in serious teaching as well as in educational planning, just as it should interpret the many forms of teacher-student interaction as dimensions of its pedagogical mission.

5. *Research, generally understood to mean discovery and publication, should be related to a broader concept of scholarship that embraces the variety of intellectual activities and the totality of scholarly accomplishments. Though discovery and publication are the core of scholarly endeavor, scholarship seen in its many forms offers a wider context within which to weigh individual contributions.*

Innovative and integrative research are essential to research and graduate institutions as well as the capstone of many faculty careers. But scholarship can also mean work done to further the application and integration or synthesis of knowledge, and new directions in pedagogy clearly fall on both sides of the line between what we see as teaching and what can be classified as scholarship. In addition, work in the creative and performing arts, in applied fields of academe, and in areas that demand practical training, is also—by the working definitions of the needs and traditions of such areas—often best classified as research. By enlarging the perspective through which we judge scholarly achievement, we more accurately define the many ways in which intellectual inquiry shapes the path of scholarly pursuits and of our complex and interrelated roles as teachers and researchers in a multitude of institutional and disciplinary settings.

We believe that all faculty members—regardless of institution and regardless of workload—should involve themselves as fully as possible in creative and self-renewing scholarly activities. We enjoin all institutions to commit a suitable share of resources to encourage faculty to engage in the scholarship appropriate to their careers and to each institution's mission. Each institution should create and interpret its system of rewards to reinforce the efforts of all members of its faculty who are striving to contribute. The responsibility of providing opportunities for such creativity falls upon administrators as well as upon faculty members themselves, and we especially point to the responsibility of senior faculty to encourage and support the scholarly development of their junior colleagues.

6. *In a public climate that, in recent years, has posited a competition between teaching and research, and that is inclined to blame the latter for a perceived decline in the quality of the education available to undergraduates, we need to affirm our support for research.*

Eliminating research from the majority of our campuses, and relegating it to an elite few, would cost our country dearly. It would also deal a heavy blow to the morale of the professoriate as well as to the status of higher education as a profession that attracts a stream of gifted and dedicated young men and women.

Major reductions in research would also ultimately lead to a decline in the quality of teaching. We would find it more difficult to prepare a new generation of graduate students and researchers, and our collective loss would extend to the humanistic and social enhancements as well as to the material gains that have come to our society through the advancement of knowledge. The arguments offered against academic research—that if faculty members did less research they could teach more—disregard the quality of teaching that students would receive were professors to become mere transmitters of received information, rather than explorers and discoverers. We must pay tribute to the many ways in which research informs teaching within the world of higher education, just as it serves society beyond the walls of the academy.

7. *The "ratchetting up" of expectations is detrimental to students as well as to faculty.*

Public calls for more faculty time in the classroom have not been balanced by reduced demands, on the part of educational administrators and even by faculty peers, regarding faculty publications and service. The current and highly publicized calls for a "renewed" emphasis on teaching, combined with the long fiscal crisis in the service sectors of our society, have meant that faculty at many institutions—and especially those in the public sector—are being called upon to teach more courses and more students.

At the same time, however, institutions have increasingly urged faculty to publish, and they have shaped the reward system accordingly. Faculty who wish to continue to devote time to scholarship and publication—generally seen as the surest route to tenure and promotion—must often do so while carrying teaching loads that are becoming heavier each year. This is cruel to members of the faculty, as individuals, and it is counterproductive for our students' education. Institutions should define their missions clearly and articulate appropriate and reasonable expectations against which faculty will be judged, rather than simply exercise a managerial prerogative of demanding all things from all their men and women.

8. Service, both institutional and community, is an important component of faculty work.

The institutional service performed by faculty is vital to the functioning of our colleges and universities. We do not urge that the rewards for service be commensurate with those for dedicated teaching and scholarship. On the other hand, we believe that such service is essential to the health of our institutions and can make significant contributions to society. It should be recognized and appropriately rewarded.

Service represents enlightened self-interest on the part of faculty, for whom work on the curriculum, shared governance, academic freedom, and peer review comprise the scholar's and teacher's contributions to the shaping and building of the institution. In addition, it is through service that the professional disciplines communicate and that the exchange of scholarship, by means of conferences and publications, is made feasible. And it is through service that the faculties of our colleges and universities offer their professional knowledge, skills, and advice to their communities. The faculty's commitment to the public welfare, as well as its reinvestment in the health and continuing social and intellectual utility of the academy, is expressed to a considerable extent by what we refer to as service. It is a vital component of our collective lives and of our role in society.

Statement on Teaching Evaluation

The statement which follows was prepared by the Association's Committee on College and University Teaching, Research, and Publication. It was adopted by the Association's Council in June 1975 and endorsed by the Sixty-first Annual Meeting. In April 1990, the Council adopted several changes in language that had been approved by the Committee on College and University Teaching, Research, and Publication in order to remove gender-specific references from the original text.

In response to a chronic need for arriving at fair judgments of a faculty member's teaching, the Association sets forth this statement as a guide to proper teaching evaluation methods and their appropriate uses in personnel decisions. This statement confines itself to the teaching responsibilities of college and university professors and is not intended as the definitive statement on reviewing and weighing all aspects of a faculty member's work. In addressing itself to teaching, the statement has no intention of minimizing the importance of other faculty responsibilities. There is a need for assessment of a teacher's scholarship both more precise and more extensive than commonly employed. There is a need to define service and the value attached to it as well as to review carefully the kind and quality of service performed by faculty members. Additional guidance in the complex task of reviewing faculty service is to be found in other Association documents: the *Statement on Procedural Standards in the Renewal or Nonrenewal of Faculty Appointments*, the *Recommended Institutional Regulations on Academic Freedom and Tenure*, the *Statement on Government of Colleges and Universities*, and the *Statement on Faculty Workload*.

STATEMENT

Colleges and universities properly aspire to excellence in teaching. Institutional aspirations, however, have not often led to practices which clearly identify and reward teaching excellence, and the quality of teaching is not in fact the determining consideration in many decisions on retention, promotion, salary, and tenure. The aspirations of faculty members are often frustrated, because they must wrestle with diverse obligations—commonly identified as *teaching, research*, and *service*—placed upon them by the profession at large, the scholarly discipline, the institution, and their own varied interests. Establishing a positive relationship between the institution's and the department's aspirations and the individual's competencies and aims is one outcome of fair and thorough faculty review procedures.

1. Institutional Values and Policies

Making clear the expectations the institution places upon the teacher and providing the conditions and support necessary to excellent teaching are primary institutional obligations. It is a first order of business that institutions declare their values and communicate them with sufficient clarity to enable colleges and departments to set forth specific expectations as to teaching, research, and service, and to make clear any other faculty obligations. Both institution-wide and college or department policies on promotion, salary, and tenure should be written and subject to periodic review, a process in which faculty members must play a central part.

2. Expectations, Criteria, and Procedures

At the college or department level the expectations as to teaching, the weighting of teaching in relation to other expectations, and the criteria and procedures by which the fulfillment of these expectations is to be judged should be put in writing and periodically reviewed by all members of the college or department. This policy statement should specify the information which is to be gathered for all faculty members, the basic procedures to be followed in gathering it, and the time schedule for various aspects of the review process. Such information should include first-hand data from various sources, including students, and should emphasize the primacy of faculty colleague judgments of teaching effectiveness at the first level of review and recommendation.

3. *Adequate Evaluation Data*

Casual procedures, a paucity of data, and unilateral judgments by department chairs and deans too often characterize the evaluation of teaching in American colleges and universities. Praiseworthy and systematic efforts to improve the processes of teaching evaluation have moved toward identifying characteristics of effective teaching and recognizing and weighting the multiple aspects of an individual teacher's performance. A judicious evaluation of a college professor as teacher should include: (a) an accurate factual description of what an individual does as teacher, (b) various measures of the effectiveness of these efforts, and (c) fair consideration of the relation between these efforts and the institution's and the department's expectations and support.

An important and often overlooked element of evaluating teaching is an accurate description of a professor's teaching. Such a description should include the number and level and kinds of classes taught, the numbers of students, and out-of-class activities related to teaching. Such data should be very carefully considered both to guard against drawing unwarranted conclusions and to increase the possibilities of fairly comparing workloads and kinds of teaching, of clarifying expectations, and of identifying particulars of minimum and maximum performance. Other useful information might include evidence of the ability of a teacher to shape new courses, to reach different levels and kinds of students, to develop effective teaching strategies, and to contribute to the effectiveness of the individual's and the institution's instruction in other ways than in the classroom.

The gathering of such data can promote a careful consideration of both the institution's and the department's values. If a department, for example, places great value upon teaching large numbers of lower-level students, that value should be reflected in the judgments about teachers who perform such tasks effectively. Too often, even at the simple point of numbers and kinds of students taught, departments and institutions operate on value assumptions seldom made clear to the faculty.

Another kind of data which should be systematically gathered and examined by the teacher's colleagues includes course syllabi, tests, materials, and methods employed in instruction. Care should be taken that such scrutiny not inhibit the teacher, limit the variety of effective teaching styles, or discourage purposeful innovation. Evidence of a concern for teaching and teaching competence demonstrated in publications, attendance at meetings, delivery of lectures, and consulting should also be included among the essential information to be reviewed.

4. *Assessing the Effectiveness of Instruction*

Student learning. Evaluation of teaching usually refers to efforts made to assess the effectiveness of instruction. The most valid measure is probably the most difficult to obtain, that is, the assessment of a teacher's effectiveness on the basis of the learning of his or her students. On the one hand, a student's learning is importantly influenced by much more than an individual teacher's efforts. On the other, measures of before-and-after learning are difficult to find, control, or compare. From a practical point of view, the difficulties of evaluating college teaching on the basis of changes in student performance limit the use of such a measure. The difficulties, however, should not rule out all efforts to seek reliable evidence of this kind.

Teaching performance. Evaluating teaching on the basis of teaching performance also presents difficulties in measurement, but the large body of research into the reliability and validity of carefully applied performance measures supports the practical usefulness of these data. Data on teaching performance commonly come from trained observers, faculty colleagues, and students.

Student perceptions. Student perceptions are a prime source of information from those who must be affected if learning is to take place. Student responses can provide continuing insights into a number of the important dimensions of a teacher's efforts: classroom performance, advising, and informal and formal contacts with students outside of class. A variety of ways are available to gather student opinion, ranging from informal questioning of individual students about details of a specific course to campus-wide questionnaires.

Faculty members should be meaningfully involved in any systematic efforts to obtain student opinion. Cooperation among students, faculty, and administration is necessary to secure teaching performance data which can be relied upon. No one questionnaire or method is suitable to every department or institution. Different kinds of questionnaires can be useful in assessing different kinds of courses and subject matters and in meeting the need for information of a particular kind. However, a common instrument covering a range of teachers, departments, and subject matter areas has the great advantage of affording meaningful comparative data. The important consideration is to obtain reliable data over a range of teaching assignments and over a period of time. Evaluations in which results go only to the individual professor may be of use in improving an individual teacher's performance, but they contribute little to the process of faculty review. Student input need not be limited by course evaluations. Exit interviews, questionnaires to alumni, and face-to-face discussion are other ways in which student feedback can be profitably gathered.

Classroom visitation. Because of the usefulness of having first-hand information about an individual's teaching effectiveness, some institutions have adopted a program of classroom visitation. There are various ways of having colleagues visit classrooms, but such visits do not necessarily yield reliable data. Careful observations over a period of time may, however, be useful in evaluating instruction and in fostering effective teaching. Clearly, there must be an understanding among the visitors and the visited upon such matters as who does the visiting, how many visits are made, what visitors look for, what feedback is given to the visited, and what other use is made of the information.

Self-evaluation. Some institutions draw upon self-evaluation as an element in assessing teaching. The limitations on self-evaluation are obvious, and neither the teacher nor the institution should be satisfied with self-evaluation alone. However, faculty members as individuals or as members of committees can assist colleagues in making the kind of self-evaluation which constitutes a contribution to improving and evaluating teaching. Arousing an interest in self-examination, structuring self-evaluations so that they might afford more reliable data, and giving faculty members the opportunity to assess their own teaching effectiveness and to add their own interpretation of student ratings and classroom visitations can increase the usefulness of self-evaluation as a part of the review process.

Outside opinions. Some institutions seek outside opinions and judgments as to a professor's competence. Reliable outside judgments about an individual's teaching, however, are difficult to secure. It would be a mistake to suppose that a college teacher's scholarly reputation is an accurate measure of teaching ability. Visiting teams from the outside, given ample time to observe the teacher, to talk with students, and to examine relevant data, might prove a useful, though expensive, means of improving the quality of evaluation. Information and opinions from faculty members in other departments and from persons outside the university should be sought when an individual's teaching assignment and the informant's first-hand knowledge appear to justify their use.

5. Procedures

The emphasis in evaluation should be upon obtaining first-hand evidence of teaching competence, which is most likely to be found among the faculty of a department or college and the students who receive instruction. Evaluation of teaching in which an administrator's judgment is the sole or determining factor is contrary to policies set forth in the *Statement on Government of Colleges and Universities*.

The institution's commitment to teaching should be manifested in concrete ways. For example, some institutions have adopted policies which make recommendations for promotion unacceptable unless they provide strong and convincing evidence of teaching competence. Combining the systematic evaluation of teaching with direct efforts to assist teachers in developing their effectiveness is another example of institutional commitment. It is the responsibility of the institution and the colleges, departments, or other instructional divisions to establish and maintain written policies and procedures which ensure a sound basis for individual judgments fairly applied to all.

Faculty members should have a primary, though not exclusive, role in evaluating an individual faculty member's performance as teacher. Factual data, student opinion, and colleague judgments should be central in the formal procedures for review which should involve faculty discussion and vote. Those being evaluated should be invited to supply information and materials relevant to that evaluation. If the department does not have final authority, the faculty's considered judgment should constitute the basic recommendation to the next level of responsibility, which may be a college-wide or university-wide faculty committee. If the chair's recommendation is contrary to that of the department faculty, the faculty should be informed of the chair's reasons prior to the chair's submitting his or her recommendation and that of the faculty and should be given an opportunity to respond to the chair's views.

The dean's function, where separate from that of a chair or division head, is typically one of review and recommendation either in the dean's own person or through an official review body at that level. If the recommendation at this level is contrary to that of the department chair or faculty, opportunity should be provided for discussion with the chair or faculty before a formal recommendation is made.

Final decisions should be made in accordance with the *Statement on Government of Colleges and Universities*: "The governing board and president should, on questions of faculty status, as in other matters where the faculty has primary responsibility, concur with the faculty judgment except in rare instances and for compelling reasons which should be stated in detail."[1] Procedures in accordance with the Association's *Recommended Institutional Regulations on Academic Freedom and Tenure* and the *Statement on Procedural Standards in the Renewal or Nonrenewal of Faculty Appointments* should be provided to handle faculty grievances arising from advancement recommendations.

6. Some Further Implications

The responsible evaluation of teaching does not serve advancement procedures alone. It should be wisely employed for the development of the teacher and the enhancement of instruction. Both of these aims can be served by the presence of a faculty committee charged with the overall responsibility of remaining conversant with the research in evaluating teaching and of providing assistance in maintaining sound policies and procedures in reviewing faculty performance. The full dimensions of teaching should not be slighted in the desire to arrive at usable data and systematic practices. Though teaching can be considered apart from scholarship and service, the general recognition of these three professional obligations suggests that the relationships are important. The kind of teaching which distinguishes itself in colleges and universities is integral with scholarship, has a way of getting outside classroom confines, and may exemplify the highest meaning of service. A judicious evaluation system would recognize the broad dimensions of teaching, be sensitive to different kinds and styles of instruction, and be as useful in distinguishing superior teaching from the merely competent as in identifying poor teaching.

---

[1] AAUP, *Policy Documents and Reports*, 9th ed. (Washington, D.C., 2001), 221.

Mandated Assessment of Educational Outcomes

The report which follows was approved by the Association's Committee on College and University Teaching, Research, and Publication and adopted by the Association's Council in June 1991.

BACKGROUND

Toward the end of the 1980s, "state-mandated" assessment of higher education, including attempts to measure learning outcomes for undergraduates, came to the forefront of attention in several states.[1] One recent study indicates that about a dozen states reported "serious efforts" to develop assessment measures in 1987; within two years, twenty-seven states reported either legislative- or board-mandated assessment initiatives in place. Still other states indicated that formal assessment policies were under study at that time, and only eight reported "nothing in place and nothing immediately planned." Of the twenty-seven formal initiatives reported, eighteen were implemented under state board policies requiring institutions separately to develop assessment plans congruent with their own mission, while in others such initiatives involved actual legislation mandating assessment as part of an overall educational reform package, leaving details of implementation to higher education officials. Four states required "across-the-board cognitive-outcomes testing"—that is, statewide mandated assessment instruments—and of these, all but one had been in place for some time. Three states had considered but rejected such tests, and even in the case of previously established basic skills tests for entering college or university students, only four states employed a common measurement instrument.[2]

Although so far only a minority of states has employed common test instruments, the assessment movement itself is generally conceded, by both supporters and critics, to be thriving. The August 1986 report of the Task Force on College Quality, "Time for Results: The Governors' 1991 Report on Education," sets forth six recommendations, calling for: (1) a clear definition of institutional roles and missions in each state; (2) a reemphasis on undergraduate instruction, especially in research universities; (3) the development in both public and private institutions of "multiple measures to assess undergraduate student learning," with the results to be used to evaluate institutional and program quality; (4) the adjustment of funding formulas in the public sector to provide incentives for the improvement of undergraduate education; (5) a renewed commitment to access for all socio-economic groups to higher education; and (6) the requirement by accrediting agencies that information about undergraduate student outcomes be used as one basis for reaccreditation.

Several responses to the governors' report endorse assessment in broad principle while suggesting certain steps for accomplishing its implementation. The National Association of State Universities and Land-Grant Colleges has issued a "Statement of Principles on Student Outcomes Assessment" (November 1, 1988), which stresses the improvement of student learning

---

[1] Throughout this document the word "mandated" usually implies an external mandate, that is, one imposed by an agency outside the college or university. On occasion, however, institutional governing boards (as opposed to a superboard or coordinating board) or even administrative officers may themselves deliver such a mandate. In such instances the roles of the respective parties should be defined in terms of the broad principles of the Association's *Statement on Government of Colleges and Universities*, discussed below.

[2] Statistical information and general commentary on trends are here drawn from Peter Ewell, Joni Finney, and Charles Leath, "Filling in the Mosaic: The Emerging Pattern of State-Based Assessment," *AAHE Bulletin* 42 (April 1990): 3–5.

and performance, reliance on "incentives rather than regulations or penalties" in the process, the importance of faculty involvement, definitions of "quality indicators" appropriate to the diversity of purposes and programs in American higher education, multiple methods of assessment rather than recourse to a standardized test, the need to avoid imposing heavy costs for assessment on either state agencies or institutions, and the linkage of assessment programs to strategic planning and program review. The Commission on Institutions of Higher Education of the North Central Association, at its meeting of October 27, 1989, approved a "Statement on Assessment and Student Academic Achievement," which seems on balance to confirm existing principles of institutional autonomy and the primary responsibility of faculty for assessment. Nonetheless, it appears that no statement has adequately defined the nature of the faculty role in overseeing either the establishment or the subsequent use of an assessment process. This report attempts to accomplish that end.

Public discussion has not always made clear whether assessment instruments are designed simply to provide a diagnostic tool for self-improvement or also to furnish a basis for budgetary allocations. It is worthy of note, however, that, at the time the Committee on College and University Teaching, Research, and Publication undertook its review, at least one state reserved the right, beginning in 1990, to return to the state treasury up to 2 percent of its appropriation for any institution failing to comply with the statute mandating assessment, and that conversely another state promised an additional increment of up to 5 percent in public funds to cooperating institutions, based on indicators of institutional quality as determined through assessment.

The American Association of University Professors has long recognized that the practical difficulties of evaluating student learning do not relieve the academic profession of its obligation to attempt to incorporate such evaluation into measures of teaching effectiveness. The Association's 1975 *Statement on Teaching Evaluation* contains the following comments on "student learning":

> Evaluation of teaching usually refers to the efforts made to assess the effectiveness of instruction. The most valid measure is probably the most difficult to obtain, that is, the assessment of a teacher's effectiveness on the basis of the learning of his or her students. On the one hand, a student's learning is importantly influenced by much more than an individual teacher's efforts. On the other, measures of before-and-after learning are difficult to find, control, or derive comparisons from. From a practical point of view, the difficulties of evaluating college teaching on the basis of changes in student performance limit the use of such a measure. The difficulties, however, should not rule out all efforts to seek reliable evidence of this kind.

It is also important to note that many of the measures proposed by proponents of mandated assessment—examinations of various kinds, essays, student portfolios, senior theses and comprehensive examinations, performances and exhibitions, oral presentations, the use of external examiners—have been in place for many years. So have certain standardized tests that have become widely accepted for specific ends, such as the SAT or ACT for purposes of admission to undergraduate work, or the GRE and the LSAT for admission to post-baccalaureate programs. Other indicators favored by proponents of assessment, such as alumni satisfaction and job placement, have been used in recurring academic program reviews, some of which have been undertaken through institutional initiatives, others of which have been mandated by state agencies. As a general rule it is safe to observe that undergraduates in American postsecondary education, and their academic programs, are more intensively and perhaps more frequently evaluated than are those in postsecondary education anywhere else in the world. If many of the aforementioned measures have long been in place, the question naturally arises: What is different about the call for mandated assessment in its present form, and why is it seen as necessary by many policy makers, including some within the higher education community itself?

The present assessment movement is in part a response to increased demands for public accountability and in part a by-product of various national reports on the state of higher education in the late 1980s which criticized both growing research emphases in the nation's colleges and universities and the quality of undergraduate education. The previously cited governors' report states that, despite "obvious successes and generous funding," "disturbing trends" are evident in both objective and subjective studies of educational effectiveness. The report complains that "not enough is known about the skills and knowledge of the average college graduate," and that the decline in test scores and the frustrations voiced about the readiness of graduates for employment exist in a climate of institutional indifference to educational effectiveness. The opening paragraph of "Time for Results" charges: "Many colleges and universities do not have a systematic way to demonstrate whether student learning is taking place. Rather, learning—and especially developing abilities to utilize knowledge—is *assumed* to take place as long as students take courses, accumulate hours, and progress 'satisfactorily' toward a degree." Such allegations indicate that the call for an increased emphasis on assessment not only will be increasingly linked to subsequent budgetary increments or decrements, but also will, though often inexplicitly, be accompanied by external pressures on the internal academic decision-making processes of colleges and universities.

Critics of mandated assessment have questioned whether the premise of assessment proponents, namely, that higher education has been generously funded in recent years, can withstand the light of scrutiny. Those individuals—board members, administrators, faculty members, students, and staff—who are more directly in touch on a daily basis with the working realities of campus life have noted that support has not kept pace with growth. They see an increased reliance on part-time or short-term faculty, starved scientific and technical laboratories, the deferment of routine maintenance costs, the growth of academic support staffs at a rate that outstrips the number of new tenure-eligible faculty positions, and patterns of funding that follow enrollment trends without regard to the relative priority of subjects in those very liberal arts in which undergraduate unpreparedness has been decried by national study commissions. Under these circumstances, critics question the relevance and importance of assessment when access to higher education has been expanded without a corresponding expansion in the base of support.

In the remainder of this report we examine Association policies that provide a historical context for considering the subject of assessment, and then consider specific issues related to present discussions of mandated assessment. After this review we conclude with a set of recommendations that we believe should govern discussions of the implementation of assessment procedures on particular campuses.

APPLICABLE ASSOCIATION POLICIES

The Association's long-standing principles relating to academic freedom and tenure, and to college and university government, provide a broad and generally accepted context within which to treat the question of assessment in higher education. These principles are embodied in a number of documents from which the earlier-cited *Statement on Teaching Evaluation* derives its own more specific applicability. The joint 1940 *Statement of Principles on Academic Freedom and Tenure* sets forth in its preamble the principle that "academic freedom in its teaching aspect is fundamental to the protection of the rights of the teacher in teaching and of the student to freedom in learning" and goes on to stipulate that "teachers are entitled to freedom in the classroom in discussing their subject."[3] The 1966 *Statement on Government of Colleges and Universities* spells out those areas of institutional life requiring joint effort, and those falling within the primary responsibility of the governing board, the president, and the faculty, respectively. It also contains a concluding section on student status.[4]

The direct implications of mandated assessment for academic freedom and tenure have not yet become a centerpiece of public discussion. Proponents of mandated assessment argue that the impact of assessment instruments on the conduct of individual classes not only has been, but will remain, negligible in the extreme, and that the complaints that such instruments will force individual faculty members to "teach to the test" misrepresent both the purpose and the techniques of assessment in the crudest and most reductive terms. They deny that mandated

---

[3] AAUP, *Policy Documents and Reports*, 9th ed. (Washington, D.C., 2001), 3.
[4] *Ibid.*, 217–23.

assessment would ever be based on a single quantitative instrument. While it is true that, thus far, the assessment movement does not appear to have resulted in any overt infringement of academic freedom as traditionally understood, the question remains whether, in more subtle ways, assessment may begin to shape the planning and conduct of courses. We believe, moreover, that the demand for mandated assessment is related to recent calls for the "post-tenure" review of faculty performance, inasmuch as an increased public demand for "accountability" on the part of colleges and universities, and real or alleged dissatisfaction with their internal processes of decision making, are common themes underlying both movements. This possible interplay between two movements which heretofore have been treated as distinct will be commented upon further below and, in our view, ought to be a continuing subject of discussion and review by the Association.

Our remaining comments in this section focus on the *Statement on Government* as a frame of reference for considering mandated assessment. The statement is premised on the interdependence of governing board, administration, and faculty. It emphasizes the institutional self-definition within which these constituent groups work together, giving recognition to the fact that American higher education is not a unitary system but rather contains many diverse institutions. While unequivocal in its position that "the faculty has primary responsibility for such fundamental areas as curriculum, subject matter and methods of instruction, research, faculty status, and those aspects of student life which relate to the educational process," the statement allows for the possibility that external bodies with jurisdiction over the institution may set "limits to realization of faculty advice." We interpret this proviso to refer to those areas—for example, the allotment of fiscal resources within a statewide system—which are primarily the responsibility of "other groups, bodies, and agencies." It may, for example, be the function of a state agency, and legitimately so, to determine (and provide reasonable grounds to the affected institution for so determining) that the establishment of a new professional school on a particular campus cannot be justified in terms of existing resources. This finding is quite a different matter from external action designed to force particular internal revisions in an existing educational program.[5]

As we see it, the question of most fundamental interest in terms of long-standing Association policy is the extent to which, despite disclaimers by its proponents, the mandatory assessment movement thus far has tended to represent a form of external state intrusion, bypassing the traditional roles of governing board, administration, and faculty, as well as both duplicating and diminishing the role of the independent regional accrediting bodies. A derivative question is whether mandated assessment, to the extent that it is driven by the felt need to compare institutions, requires measures of quantification applicable to all those institutions, and thus tends to diminish the autonomy and discourage the uniqueness of individual campuses. We take up this question as the first of several issues in the section that follows.

SOME SPECIFIC ASSESSMENT ISSUES

1. Institutional Diversity

The manner in which institutional self-identity is defined varies both within and between the private and public sectors, though the historical basis for such distinctions may have been eroded to some extent in recent years. Thus private institutions may seem to have a greater freedom from direct state intrusion, but in states with scholarship or tuition-assistance programs offered without regard to whether the student is attending a public or a private college or university, it is increasingly difficult for all but the most prestigious "independents" to operate without some attention to state policy. Within public systems most state colleges and universities reflect different missions in their degree programs and student clientele. Many of the proponents of

---

[5] Under the heading "Joint Effort," the "Statement on Government" (*Policy Documents and Reports*, 218) adds: "Special considerations may require particular accommodations: (1) a publicly supported institution may be regulated by statutory provisions, and (2) a church-controlled institution may be limited by its charter or bylaws. *When such external requirements influence course content and manner of instruction or research, they impair the educational effectiveness of the institution*" (emphasis added).

assessment link it to this fact and call for clearer and more distinct descriptions of roles and missions: a particular state assessment plan may indeed specify that Campus A is not necessarily expected to follow the same procedure for assessment as Campus B, and the plan may therefore seem to endorse the principle of institutional diversity.

Such lip service to diversity, however, obscures some serious issues. Even a reasoned recognition of institutional differences of the sort that mandated assessment plans claim to recognize may result in the stifling of growth and development at an institution in the process of change, or the favoring of one campus with a particular set of goals over another in the same system. The governors' report makes it clear that "universities that give high priority to research and graduate instruction" will be the object of particularly close scrutiny in the assessment of undergraduate educational outcomes, thus raising the question of whether one implication of institutional definition is the homogenization of different campuses within a particular system, and whether there will not be a de facto ascription of superior value to those institutions that have remained devoted primarily to undergraduate teaching. It is doubtless unwise and undesirable for all institutions in a state system to aspire to research university status, but it is equally unwise and undesirable as a matter of social policy to depreciate, directly or indirectly, the research mission of those campuses capable of carrying it out.

Proponents of mandated assessment have also undercut their own assertions of respect for institutional differences by pointing to specific institutions as exemplars of "good practice." They do not pause to consider whether a model devised at one type of institution, for example, a small Roman Catholic liberal arts college or a middle-sized state institution initially founded for the purpose of teacher training and now embracing an expanded purpose, is necessarily—or properly—transferable to other kinds of institutions. Nor do they pause to note that successful assessment tools may be successful not because of their intrinsic merit, but because the ambience and scale of a particular campus already guarantee those conditions of teaching and learning conducive to such an assessment. The findings and conclusions of a study of student progress at a primarily residential four-year liberal arts college with a high rate of successful degree completion may tell us little or nothing about a large urban campus with significant dropout rates and a greater number of student transfers. Either of these institutions might be more appropriately compared to a peer institution in another state than to another institution that happens to be in the same state. To encourage institutions to develop their own instruments for assessment does not necessarily mean that the outcomes of the various assessment instruments will be properly acknowledged as logical extensions of institutional differences, since, as we have already said, higher education agencies tend to want the kinds of data that facilitate comparisons among institutions.

2. Skills Versus Values

Although any mandated assessment plan might be resisted as an effort to increase external political control over colleges and universities, or dismissed as a cynical public relations ploy, we have no doubt that many supporters and practitioners of mandated assessment are motivated by legitimate and well-intentioned concern for educational quality. But their motivations are diversely grounded and sometimes mutually exclusive. Some educational and political leaders, viewing with alarm the decline in standardized test scores nationwide, tend to focus their attention on the need for colleges and universities to certify that students have attained certain basic educational skills. Others profess primary concern for the student's acquisition of moral values. For them, assessment presents itself as an additional means for achieving curricular change of the sort called for in various books and national reports published in the second half of the 1980s. Though inevitably these goals overlap—indeed, most in either group would probably state their belief in the importance of the purposes espoused by the other—they cannot be reached by similar means or tested by the same instruments. Indeed, as a practical matter, it is not even clear that in a time of budgetary constraints they can both be realized as a part of the same agenda. Given such competing demands, it is likely that mandated assessment will force a change in curriculum, not in order to produce a better-educated student, but to enhance the "measurability" of the outcomes.

As a general rule, those standardized measurement instruments that are the easiest to replicate are the least valid in any context other than the assessment of basic skills. As we have already noted, colleges and universities already employ such standardized tests as the ACT and the SAT to assist them in determining the admissibility of prospective undergraduate students, just as graduate and professional programs employ a variety of other standardized tests to measure undergraduate preparation at their respective entry levels. What lends this process some degree of credibility—despite the well-recognized misuse of these instruments when they are devised without proper regard for persons of varying cultural backgrounds—is that the *interpretation* of results is usually tailored to the mission of the particular institution. Test scores, if they are used in conjunction with other evaluative instruments such as a student's standing as a graduating senior in high school, may argue for admission to one institution if not to another. This capacity to differentiate among students is the particular genius of American higher education: that in its diversity of institutional purposes, it offers a flexible response to different student needs and abilities while ensuring that access to higher education remains a proper part of education for the citizenry of a democratic society. Historically, faculty members and administrators have assumed that test measurements are retrospective, determining admissibility on the basis of the student's demonstrated pre-collegiate or pre-professional skills.

Standardized outcomes testing in general education directed to the acquisition of values as well as facts is another matter, and it is worth noting that neither of the major national testing services has yet succeeded in devising a standardized general education examination that satisfies either the institutions or the test designers themselves. Though proponents of mandated assessment may wish to pay tribute both to the acquisition of skills and to the acquisition of a broadened general education, it is unlikely that the resources that would be required for a basic improvement in skills *alone* at the collegiate level could also be devoted to enhancing the environment necessary for the transmission of diverse content and the development of critical thinking so central to the preparation of students in the liberal arts. The costs of conducting assessment drain funds away from other institutional needs, such as smaller classes, reduced dependence on part-time faculty, and adequate numbers of full-time faculty members to staff both graduate and undergraduate instruction—needs which are at loggerheads, too, with external demands for remediation at the college level. Assessment carried on without proper attention to the incompatibility of the two goals—the attainment of skills and the learning of values—can have only one result: shifting the burden of blame to the faculty, just as in the K–12 system many teachers and principals are operating under a state mandate for reform without adequate funds to implement it and are now under pressure to show measurable results.

Under these conditions, values are likely to be subordinated to skills, and the quality of higher education as *higher* education, rather than as remediation, will suffer. When the mission of a particular institution dictates that scores be used to determine placement in basic skills courses so as to compensate for inadequate prior preparation at the primary and secondary levels, then the funding of such instruction needs to be provided at a level that protects the viability of instruction appropriate to undergraduates who are ready for a college-level curriculum. Under present conditions, such additional resources as are available would be better devoted to remedying inadequate student preparation than to attempting to assess it.

3. Assessment in the Major Field of Study

Most faculty members agree on the importance of assessing systematically a student's competence in the major, as is shown by the multiplicity of forms of assessment that many departments employ. Yet even in this disciplinary context the range of possible student options after graduation makes it unlikely that an externally mandated assessment instrument would do anything more than gauge the lowest common vocational denominator. The major is properly regarded as a vehicle for deepening the student's general education and for sharpening the student's independent research and study skills, and thus standardized assessment of achievement in the major field raises precisely the same objections it does in general education.

Learning for its own end—for the purpose of developing breadth, intellectual rigor, and habits of independent inquiry—is still central to the educational enterprise; it is also one of the least measurable of activities. Whereas professional curricula are already shaped by external agencies, such as professional accrediting bodies and licensing boards, the liberal arts by contrast are far more vulnerable to intrusive mandates from other quarters; for example, the governors' report professes to find evidence of program decline "particularly in the humanities." To be sure, even in the liberal arts a student's accomplishment in the major can be measured with relative objectivity by admissions procedures at the graduate and professional level that include GRE scores as one of the bases for judgment. But a student majoring in English may wish to pursue a career in editing, publishing, journalism, or arts administration (to name only a few); a political science major may have in mind a career in state or local government or in the U.S. State Department. Either of them may have chosen his or her major simply out of curiosity, or perhaps out of a desire to be a well-educated citizen before going to law school or taking over the family business.

For these reasons we suggest that the success of a program in the major field of study is best evaluated not by an additional layer of state-imposed assessment but by the placement and career satisfaction of the student as he or she enters the world of work. Whereas imposed assessment measurements will at best—and rightly—attract faculty cynicism and at worst lead to "teaching to the test," no responsible faculty member will ignore the kinds of informed evaluation of a program available through a candid interchange with a graduating senior or recent graduate.

4. "Value-Added" Measures

Despite their occasional disclaimers, proponents of mandated assessment frequently desire quantifiable outcome data based on a comparison of students' entrance and exit performance at a postsecondary institution, or their performance at entrance and at the beginning of the junior year, before their attention turns primarily to their work in the major. Our concerns are two: (a) whether the data, based on what are sometimes called "value-added" measures, realistically reflect the diverse structures of American higher education and the different kinds of student involvement in it; and (b) whether value-added measures are sound even in narrow quantitative terms.

Perhaps the crudest form of value-added testing involves the administration of an identical general-education examination to the same body of students twice during their college careers. Even if—which we doubt—the acquisition of knowledge could be measured by the mere repetition of an earlier test, the uncritical implementation of value-added measures is quite simply unsustainable in light of the increasingly migratory, part-time, and drop-in–drop-out patterns of many American undergraduates. Like debates over what constitutes the one true curriculum or reading list, value-added measures ignore the fact that any system which presupposes a particular pace or place for student learning is at best applicable to a diminishing, and in some cases relatively elite, proportion of the student population.

We do not believe that the most important, or even useful, kind of learning that takes place at any level of education is readily quantifiable or results from the accumulation of facts by rote. Yet such an emphasis is implied in value-added measures, since the words themselves betray the assumption that one must add something measurable to something else in order to evaluate educational outcomes.

5. Accountability Versus Self-Improvement; or, Does Involving the Faculty in the Process Make It All Right?

Although, as we noted earlier, proponents of assessment have argued that the purpose of assessment is to provide diagnostic tools for self-improvement, both institutional and personal, in some cases direct budgetary consequences may ensue not only from the choice of noncompliance over compliance, but also from the results of the assessment itself. A vivid example of the slippery slope down which higher education could descend can be found in those segments of the K–12 system in which standardized tests have been employed to appraise curricular and teaching effectiveness and to group children by presumed intellectual level. What emerges as the end result of such a process is no longer an educational matter but rather a policy issue external to the schools, with the resulting data being interpreted by persons not necessarily expert in primary and secondary education, and the faculty harboring deep-seated feelings of disenfranchisement in the process.

Proponents of mandated assessment might respond that the historic position of faculties in higher education sufficiently guarantees the continuing primacy of the faculty in the assessment process. If, the argument runs, faculty members develop and administer the assessment instruments, and these are used primarily for pedagogic self-improvement, then what can the objection be?

The second of these points—as to whether pedagogic, curricular, and thus institutional, self-improvement is really the primary reason for mandated assessment—has already been questioned. We have seen sufficient evidence that such a call for self-improvement does not take place in a fiscal or policy vacuum. Most faculty members, in our experience, are perfectly willing to undertake a periodic look at their own effectiveness. Increasing numbers of institutions have been developing programs to devise incentives for such self-examination, which we regard as a continuing faculty responsibility. But self-examination is best conducted in a climate free of external constraint or threats, however vaguely disguised.

The nub of the problem lies, as it has throughout this report, not so much in the noun *assessment* as in the modifier *mandated*. If, indeed, proponents of assessment want to express support for measures of student progress that are based on principles of sound instruction—papers, essay examinations, theses, special projects, or performances or exhibitions—then an informed dialogue between the institution's representatives and the public may be usefully carried on. But if mandated assessment presupposes instruments that move further in the direction of greater standardization and quantification, then the adoption of such instruments requires not only the participation of testing experts, but also an involvement by faculty members and administrators in the development of discipline-specific or general-education versions of such tests.

The fact that faculty members, rather than external agencies, select or even participate in the design of the test instrument does not substantially diminish the problems of standardization and reductionism inherent in the process of developing a reliable test instrument. And in view of the political forces that drive such demands, the assertion that the faculty can oversee or even control the design is of little meaning if the requesting agency wants to accumulate data susceptible of statistical formulation and translatable into budgetary decisions.

We have already implied that one academic, as opposed to budgetary, consequence of mandated assessment is "teaching to the test," a pressure on faculty members to transmit to their students easily testable nuggets of information rather than broader conceptual issues and methods of reasoning. We must also acknowledge that for some faculty members a move toward standardized outcomes measurement might in fact represent a tempting relief from the exigencies of grading papers and essay examinations. An unwelcome result for both higher education and the public would be the exodus of better faculty members to other careers (as has already happened in certain segments of the K–12 system for much the same reason) or at the very least for other campuses not yet infatuated with "value-added" assessment measures.

Furthermore, faculty participation in the development of mandated assessment instruments—a sine qua non if some degree of faculty control were to be exerted over the process—would represent yet one more burden added to the existing teaching, research, and public service responsibilities that faculty members already carry. The added burden might be acceptable if it contributed to furthering the central academic purposes of a college or university, but, as we have sought to show, mandated assessment is not likely to achieve that result.

To reconnect the discussion briefly with the earlier mention of post-tenure reviews, we believe that both mandated systems of post-tenure review and mandated procedures for assessment, even if they involve faculty collaboration, are strikingly similar both in their demands and in their adverse practical outcome. In both cases it can be said that faculty members have been evaluating each other and assessing their students' learning outcomes for many years. In both cases the faculty is informed that it can participate in, or even control, the procedures and thus retain its traditional role of primary responsibility, whether over faculty status or over academic programs. But in both cases the faculty is also being told that the very instruments it has devised in the past are no longer sufficient to ensure either faculty quality or student learning, and that new mandated instruments are needed to satisfy public demands for greater accountability. Thus the logic of mandated assessment requires that faculty judgment be superseded if some agency external to the campus deems the need for public accountability not to have been met.

Proponents of mandated assessment cannot have it both ways. Either the purpose of mandated assessment is the improvement of teaching and learning in an atmosphere of constructive cooperation, or it shifts the responsibility for educational decisions into the hands of political agencies and others not only at a remove from, but by the nature of their own training and biases not versed in, the purposes and processes of higher education.

RECOMMENDED STANDARDS FOR MANDATED ASSESSMENT

American higher education has generally encouraged frequent assessment of student learning. The recent movement to mandate such assessment differs, however, in that it emphasizes evaluation of overall instructional and programmatic performance rather than individual student achievement. The American Association of University Professors recognized in its *Statement on Teaching Evaluation* that assessment of student learning outcomes may provide the most valid measure—though also the most difficult to obtain reliably—for the evaluation of teaching effectiveness. The Association has also recognized that such assessment is the responsibility of the faculty, whose primary role in curriculum and instruction has been set forth in the *Statement on Government of Colleges and Universities*.

Where assessment of student learning is mandated to ensure instructional and programmatic quality, the faculty responsibility for the development, application, and review of assessment procedures is no less than it is for the assessment of individual student achievement. Since the *Statement on Teaching Evaluation* was first formulated, increased public attention has been turned toward various plans for externally mandated assessments of learning outcomes in higher education. Some of the plans have been instituted on short notice and with little or no participation by faculty members who, by virtue of their professional education and experience, are the most qualified to oversee both the details and the implications of a particular plan. Often these plans are the result of external political pressures, and may be accompanied by budgetary consequences, favorable or unfavorable, depending on the actual outcomes the mandated schemes purport to measure.

The Association believes that the justification for developing any assessment plan in a given case, whether voiced by a legislative body, the governing board, or one or more administrative officers, must be accompanied by a clear showing that existing methods of assessing learning are inadequate for accomplishing the intended purposes of a supplementary plan, and that the mandated procedures are consistent with effective performance of the institutional mission. The remaining question involves the principles and derivative policies that should prevail when agencies external to colleges and universities—state legislatures, regional and professional accreditation bodies, and state boards of higher education—insist that assessment take place. We believe that the following standards should be observed:

1. Central to the mission of colleges and universities is the teaching-learning relationship into which faculty members and their students enter. All matters pertinent to curricular design, the method and quality of teaching, and the assessment of the outcome in student learning must be judged by how well they support this relationship.
2. Public agencies charged with the oversight of higher education, and the larger public and the diverse constituencies that colleges and universities represent, have a legitimate stake in the effectiveness of teaching and learning. Their insistence that colleges and universities provide documented evidence of effectiveness is appropriate to the extent that such agencies and their constituencies do not: (a) make demands that significantly divert the energies of the faculty, administration, or governing board from the institution's primary commitment to teaching, research, and public service; or (b) impose additional fiscal and human burdens beyond the capacity of the responding institution to bear.
3. Because experience demonstrates the unlikelihood of achieving meaningful quantitative measurement of educational outcomes for other than specific and clearly delimited purposes, any assessment scheme must provide certain protections for the role of the faculty and for the institutional mission as agreed upon by the faculty, administration, and governing board, and endorsed by the regional accrediting agency. Specifically:

(a) The faculty should have primary responsibility for establishing the criteria for assessment and the methods for implementing it.

(b) The assessment should focus on particular, institutionally determined goals and objectives, and the resulting data should be regarded as relevant primarily to that purpose. To ensure respect for diverse institutional missions, it is important that uniform assessment procedures not be mandated across a statewide system for the purpose of comparing institutions within the system. For a further development of this point, see (f) below.

(c) If externally mandated assessment is to be linked to strategic planning or program review, the potential consequences of that assessment for such planning and review should be clearly stated in advance, and the results should be considered as only one of several factors to be taken into account in budgetary and programmatic planning.

(d) The assessment process should employ methods adequate to the complexity and variety of student learning experiences, rather than rely on any single method of assessment. To prevent assessment itself from making instruction and curriculum rigid, and to ensure that assessment is responsive to changing needs, the instruments and procedures for conducting assessment should be regularly reviewed and appropriately revised by the faculty. We suggest the following considerations with respect to both quantitative and qualitative measures:

    (i) Quantitative performance measures exhibit two specific dangers. First, reliable comparisons between disparate programs, or within individual programs over time, demand narrow and unchanging instruments, and thus may discourage necessary curricular improvement and variety. Second, even where such instruments are ordinarily available or responsive to changing curricula (as with certification and graduate record examinations), they may be unreflective of diverse purposes even within a single discipline or field of study. Thus, such instruments should not be used as the exclusive means of assessment.

    (ii) Qualitative performance measures are often pedagogically superior to quantitative tests. These measures include such devices as capstone courses, portfolios, exhibitions, senior essays, demonstrations and work experiences, and the use of external examiners. The use of these measures, however, is costly and implies a curricular decision to shift additional resources to evaluate outcomes rather than to improve student learning. Hence, adoption of such procedures should include a review of costs and benefits compared to other curricular options such as greater investment in the support of first- and second-year students.

(e) If a state agency mandates assessment, the state should bear the staffing and other associated costs of the assessment procedure, either directly or in the form of a supplemental budgetary allocation to the campus for the purpose.

(f) If comparative data from other institutions are required for purposes of assessment, the faculty should have primary responsibility for identifying appropriate peer units or peer institutions for those purposes, and (as with program planning referred to in [c] above) the results of that assessment should be only one of the several factors in arriving at such comparisons.

(g) Externally mandated assessment procedures are not appropriate for the evaluation of individual students or faculty members and should not be used for that purpose.

DISTANCE EDUCATION AND INTELLECTUAL PROPERTY

The world of higher learning is in the midst of accelerating and sometimes turbulent change. Much of that change is driven by technologies that only a few years ago would have seemed fantastic, yet we can expect ever-newer technologies to permeate and reconfigure higher education in the coming years. These modes of communication are profoundly affecting the work of faculty members; they are reshaping the processes of teaching and learning, redefining the roles and authority of faculty members in organizing and overseeing the curriculum, and altering the bases for evaluating student—and faculty—performance. The implications of these developments extend far beyond teaching and learning, for the new technologies are penetrating many, if not all, major facets of higher education, deeply influencing its organization, governance, and finances. Still further, the emergence of new developers and "brokers" of educational content, often from outside the academy, coupled with arguably looser standards for regional and specialized accreditation, adds considerable complexity to the challenges with which "traditional" higher education must grapple.

Within this context, the roles of faculty members—their authority and responsibilities—are in flux. The situation calls for a close reexamination of the respective rights of faculty members, of the institutions of higher education for which they work, and of third parties who may engage faculty members for specific purposes in this volatile, sometimes highly entrepreneurial environment.

This vital intersection of emergent technologies and the traditional interests of faculty members in their own intellectual products requires scrutiny and the formulation of policies that address the former while preserving the latter. Toward this end, the Council of the American Association of University Professors established in June 1998 a Special Committee on Distance Education and Intellectual Property Issues. Its mandate was to report back to the Council with proposed policy statements in these areas.

The committee prepared two policy statements, the first on distance education and the second on copyright. The statements appear below. Throughout them, the committee refers to "teacher," "faculty," and "faculty member." The terms refer to members of a college or university faculty in either a teaching or a research role.

Statement on Distance Education

The statement which follows was approved in March 1999 by the Association's Special Committee on Distance Education and Intellectual Property Issues. It was adopted by the Association's Council and endorsed by the Eighty-fifth Annual Meeting in June 1999.

PREAMBLE

In distance education (or distance learning) the teacher and the student are separated geographically so that face-to-face communication is absent; communication is accomplished instead by one or more technological media, most often electronic (interactive television, satellite television, computers, and the like).[1] The geographic separation between teacher and student may be considerable (for example, in a course offered over the World Wide Web), or the distance may be slight (for example, from the teacher's computer to the student's in a nearby campus building). Hence distance education may apply to both on- and off-campus courses and programs. For the most part, this statement's focus is on programs and courses offered for credit. It does not, however, exclude noncredit courses, programs of general cultural enrichment, or other programs which support the educational objectives of the institution.

Distance education in its contemporary forms invariably presents administrative, technical, and legal problems usually not encountered in traditional classroom settings. For example, questions arise regarding copyright for materials adapted from traditional classroom settings or created expressly for distance education. In addition, systems of interactive television, satellite television, or computer-based courses and programs are technologically more complex and expensive than traditional classroom instruction, and require a greater investment of institutional resources and more elaborate organizational patterns. These issues not only make more difficult the question who is entitled to claim ownership of materials designed for distance education; they also raise questions about the appropriate distribution of authority and responsibility between the general administration of the college or university, on the one hand, and the separate academic departments or units within a given institution, on the other. The technical and administrative support units responsible for maintaining and operating the means of delivering distance-education courses and programs are usually separate from particular academic departments or units which offer those courses and programs.

More important, the development of distance education technologies has created conditions seldom, if ever, seen in academic life—conditions which raise basic questions about standards for teaching and scholarship. For example, in distance education the teacher does not have the usual face-to-face contact with the student that exists in traditional classroom settings. Thus, special means must be devised for assigning, guiding, and evaluating the student's work. In order to communicate with the student, the teacher frequently utilizes sophisticated and expensive technological devices which are not under the teacher's exclusive control and which often require special technical knowledge that the teacher may not fully possess. The teacher's syllabus, lectures, examinations, and other course materials may be copied or recorded and reused without the teacher's presence. The teacher's academic and legal rights may not be fully or accurately understood or may be in dispute in this new environment. Also in potential dispute are issues regarding the faculty's overall authority in determining appropriate policies and procedures for the use of these new technologies. Finally, the nature of teacher-student interaction and the preparation and teaching of distance education classes often require significantly more

---

[1] For a more comprehensive definition and explanation, see the report, "Distance Learning," *Academe: Bulletin of the AAUP* 84 (May–June 1998): 30–38.

time than that needed for courses offered in traditional classroom settings; consequently, the teacher should receive commensurate compensation.

It is imperative, therefore, that colleges and universities now using or planning to use the new technologies of distance education consider the educational functions these new media are intended to perform and the specific problems they raise. Traditional academic principles and procedures will usually apply to these new media, either directly or by extension, but they will not be applicable in all circumstances. When they are not, new principles and procedures will need to be developed so that the new media will effectively serve the institution's basic educational objectives. The principal purpose of this statement is to offer guidelines to that end.

PRINCIPLES

1. General

The use of new technologies in teaching and scholarship should be for the purpose of advancing the basic functions of colleges and universities to preserve, augment, and transmit knowledge and to foster the abilities of students to learn. The development of appropriate institutional policies concerning these new technologies as instruments of teaching and scholarship is therefore the responsibility of the academic community.

2. Areas of Responsibility

The governing board, administration, faculty, and students all have a continuing concern in determining the desirability and feasibility of utilizing new media as instruments of education. Institutional policies on distance education should define the responsibilities for each group in terms of the group's particular competence. Indeed, a principal role of these groups in devising policies is to find those uses which enhance the institution's performance of its basic functions. These uses will vary depending on (a) the size and complexity of the institution, (b) its academic mission, (c) the potential of the new technological media for scholarship and the delivery of instruction, and (d) the variety and possible combinations of technologies to be employed for education and research.

As with all other curricular matters, the faculty should have primary responsibility for determining the policies and practices of the institution in regard to distance education. The rules governing distance education and its technologies should be approved by vote of the faculty concerned or of a representative faculty body, officially adopted by the appropriate authorities, and published and distributed to all concerned.

The applicable academic unit—usually a department or program—should determine the extent to which the new technologies of distance education will be utilized, and the form and manner of their use. These determinations should conform with established institutional policies.

Before they are offered, all programs and courses for academic credit which utilize distance-education technologies should be considered and approved by the faculties of the department, division, school, college, or university, or by representatives of those bodies that govern curricular matters generally. The procedures for approval should apply to all such courses and programs, including those recorded in some way and thus not requiring the teacher's active presence on a regular basis. The faculty should determine the amount of credit toward a degree that a student may earn in courses utilizing the technologies of distance education.

The faculty of the college or university should establish general rules and procedures for the granting of teaching-load credit in the preparation and the delivery of programs and courses utilizing distance-education technologies, for required outside-of-class student contact (office hours), and for the allocation of necessary supporting resources. Within the general provisions of these governing regulations, specific arrangements should be made within the applicable academic unit (usually the department) for courses offered by its members.

Adequate preparation for a distance-education course, whether one which requires the regular, active presence of the instructor, or one which has been recorded, requires considerable time and effort for the creation or adaptation of materials for the new media, and for the planning of assignments, evaluations, and other course materials and their distribution. The instructor will therefore need to have adequate time to prepare such materials and to become sufficiently familiar with the technologies of instruction prior to delivery of the course. Such preparation—depending on the teacher's training or experience, the extent of the use of these technologies in the course, their complexity and the complexity of the materials to be created or adapted—will usually require significant release time from teaching during an academic term prior to the offering of the new course.

To enable them to carry out their instructional responsibilities, teachers assigned to these courses should be given support in the form of academic, clerical, and technical assistance, as well as means of communicating and conferring with students. Sufficient library resources must also be provided to the students to enable them to benefit from the teaching. Since instruction by distance-education technologies does not allow for the same degree of interaction between students and teacher that is possible in a traditional classroom setting, provision should be made for the students to confer personally with the teacher at designated times.

If the institution prepares courses or programs for use by entities outside the institution, whether for academic credit or not, whether recorded or requiring the regular, active presence of the teacher, the faculty should ensure that the same standards obtain as in courses and programs prepared for use in their own institution.

3. Teaching Appointments

The precise terms and conditions of every appointment should be stated in writing and be in the possession of the faculty member and the institution before the faculty member is assigned to utilize distance-education technologies in the delivery of instructional material in a course for academic credit. No member of the faculty should be required to participate in distance-education courses or programs without adequate preparation and training, and without prior approval of such courses and programs by the appropriate faculty bodies.

4. Academic Freedom

A faculty member engaged in distance education is entitled to academic freedom as a teacher, researcher, and citizen in full accordance with the provisions of the 1940 *Statement of Principles on Academic Freedom and Tenure,* jointly developed by the Association of American Colleges and the American Association of University Professors and endorsed by more than 170 educational and professional organizations.

5. Selection of Materials

Teachers should have the same responsibility for selecting and presenting materials in courses offered through distance-education technologies as they have in those offered in traditional classroom settings. For team-taught or interdisciplinary courses and programs, the faculty involved should share this responsibility.

6. Technical Considerations

The institution is responsible for the technological delivery of the course. Faculty members who teach through distance-education technologies are responsible for making certain that they have sufficient technical skills to present their subject matter and related material effectively, and, when necessary, should have access to and consult with technical support personnel. The teacher, nevertheless, has the final responsibility for the content and presentation of the course.

7. Proprietary Rights and Educational Policies

The institution should establish policies and procedures to protect its educational objectives and the interests of both those who create new material and those who adapt material from traditional courses for use in distance education. The administration should publish these policies and procedures and distribute them, along with requisite information about copyright law, to all concerned persons. The policies should include provisions for compensating those who create new course materials or who adapt course materials originally prepared for traditional classroom usage, including any use or reuse of recorded material.

Provision should also be made for the original teacher-creator, the teacher-adapter, or an appropriate faculty body to exercise control over the future use and distribution of recorded instructional material and to determine whether the material should be revised or withdrawn from use.

A teacher's course presentation should not be recorded without the teacher's prior knowledge and consent. Recordings of course material are academic documents, and thus, as with other works of scholarship, should have their author or creator cited accordingly.

Statement on Copyright

The statement which follows was approved in March 1999 by the Association's Special Committee on Distance Education and Intellectual Property Issues. It was adopted by the Association's Council and endorsed by the Eighty-fifth Annual Meeting in June 1999.

The objective of copyright is, in the words of the U.S. Constitution, to "promote the progress of science and useful arts." To achieve that objective, authors are given exclusive rights under the Copyright Act to reproduce their works, to use them as the basis for derivative works, to disseminate them to the public, and to perform and display them publicly. Institutions of higher learning in particular should interpret and apply the law of copyright so as to encourage the discovery of new knowledge and its dissemination to students, to the profession, and to the public. This mission is reflected in the 1940 *Statement of Principles on Academic Freedom and Tenure:* "Institutions of higher education are conducted for the common good and not to further the interest of either the individual teacher or the institution as a whole. The common good depends upon the free search for truth and its free exposition."

ACADEMIC PRACTICE

Within that tradition, it has been the prevailing academic practice to treat the faculty member as the copyright owner of works that are created independently and at the faculty member's own initiative for traditional academic purposes. Examples include class notes and syllabi; books and articles; works of fiction and nonfiction; poems and dramatic works; musical and choreographic works; pictorial, graphic, and sculptural works; and educational software, commonly known as "courseware." This practice has been followed for the most part, regardless of the physical medium in which these "traditional academic works" appear; that is, whether on paper or in audiovisual or electronic form. As will be developed below, this practice should therefore ordinarily apply to the development of courseware for use in programs of distance education.

UNILATERAL INSTITUTIONAL POLICIES

Some colleges and universities have promulgated policies, typically unenforced, that proclaim traditional academic works to be the property of the institution. Faculty handbooks, for example, sometimes declare that faculty members shall be regarded as having assigned their copyrights to the institution. The Copyright Act, however, explicitly requires that a transfer of copyright, or of any exclusive right (such as the exclusive right to publish), must be evidenced in writing and signed by the author-transferor. If the faculty member is indeed the initial owner of copyright, then a unilateral institutional declaration cannot effect a transfer, nor is it likely that a valid transfer can be effected by the issuance of appointment letters to new faculty members requiring, as a condition of employment, that they abide by a faculty handbook which purports to vest in the institution the ownership of all works created by the faculty member for an indefinite future.

Other colleges and universities instead proclaim that traditional academic works are "works made for hire," with the consequence that the institution is regarded as the initial owner of copyright. This institutional claim is often stated to rest upon the use by the faculty member, in creating such works, of college or university resources, such as office space, supplies, library facilities, ordinary access to computers and networks, and money.

The pertinent definition of "work made for hire" is a work prepared by an "employee within the scope of his or her employment." In the typical work-for-hire situation, the content and purpose of the employee-prepared works are under the control and direction of the employer; the employee is accountable to the employer for the content and design of the work. In the case of traditional academic works, however, the faculty member rather than the institution determines the subject matter, the intellectual approach and direction, and the conclusions. This is the very essence of academic freedom. Were the institution to own the copyright in such works, under a work-made-for-hire theory, it would have the power, for example, to decide where the work is to be published, to edit and otherwise revise it, to prepare derivative works based on it (such as translations, abridgments, and literary, musical, or artistic variations), and indeed to censor and forbid dissemination of the work altogether. Such powers, so deeply inconsistent with fundamental principles of academic freedom, cannot rest with the institution.

COLLEGE OR UNIVERSITY COPYRIGHT OWNERSHIP

Situations do arise, however, in which the college or university may fairly claim ownership of, or an interest in, copyright in works created by faculty (or staff) members. Three general kinds of projects fall into this category: special works created in circumstances that may properly be regarded as "made for hire," negotiated contractual transfers, and "joint works" as described in the Copyright Act.

1. Works Made for Hire

Although traditional academic work that is copyrightable—such as lecture notes, courseware, books, and articles—cannot normally be treated as works made for hire, some works created by college or university faculty and staff members do properly fall within that category, allowing the institution to claim copyright ownership. Works created as a specific requirement of employment or as an assigned institutional duty that may, for example, be included in a written job description or an employment agreement, may be fairly deemed works made for hire. Even absent such prior written specification, ownership will vest with the college or university in those cases in which it provides the specific authorization or supervision for the preparation of the work. Examples are reports developed by a dean or by the chair or members of a faculty committee, or college promotional brochures prepared by a director of admissions. Some institutions appear to treat course examinations as falling within this category, but the stronger case can be made for treating examinations as part of the faculty member's customary instructional materials, with copyright thus owned by the individual.

The Copyright Act also defines as a "work made for hire" certain works that are commissioned from an individual who is not an employee but an "independent contractor." The institution will own the copyright in such a commissioned work when the author is not a college or university employee, or when the author is such an employee but the work to be created falls outside the normal scope of that person's employment duties (such as a professor of art history commissioned by the institution under special contract to write a catalog for a campus art gallery). In such situations, for the work-made-for-hire doctrine to apply there must be a written agreement so stating and signed by both parties; the work must also fall within a limited number of statutory categories, which include instructional texts, examinations, and contributions to a collective work.

2. Contractual Transfers

In situations in which the copyright ownership is held by the faculty (or staff) member, it is possible for the individual to transfer the entire copyright, or a more limited license, to the institution or to a third party. As already noted, under the Copyright Act, a transfer of all of the copyright or of an exclusive right must be reflected in a signed document in order to be valid. When, for example, a work is prepared pursuant to a program of "sponsored research" accompanied by a grant from a third party, a contract signed by the faculty member providing that copyright will be owned by the institution will be enforceable. Similarly, the college or university may reasonably request that the faculty member—when entering into an agreement granting the copyright or publishing rights to a third party—make efforts to reserve to the institution the right to use the work in its internally administered programs of teaching, research, and public service on a perpetual, royalty-free, nonexclusive basis.

3. Joint Works

Under certain circumstances, two or more persons may share copyright ownership of a work, notably when it is a "joint work." The most familiar example of a joint work is a book or article written, fully collaboratively, by two academic colleagues. Each is said to be a "co-owner" of the copyright, with each having all the usual rights of the copyright owner (i.e., to license others to publish, to distribute to the public, to translate, and the like), provided that any income from such uses is shared with the other. In rare situations, an example of which is discussed immediately below, it may be proper to treat a work as a product of the joint authorship of the faculty member and his or her institution, so that both have a shared interest in the copyright.

NEW INSTRUCTIONAL TECHNOLOGIES

The development of new instructional technologies has led to some uncertainties with regard to the respective rights of the institution and its faculty members. For example, courseware prepared for programs of distance education will typically incorporate instructional content authored and presented by faculty members, but the college or university may contribute specialized services and facilities to the production of the courseware that go beyond what is traditionally provided to faculty members generally in the preparation of their course materials. On the one hand, the institution may simply supply "delivery mechanisms," such as videotaping, editing, and marketing services; in such a situation, it is very unlikely that the institution will be regarded as having contributed the kind of "authorship" that is necessary for a "joint work" that automatically entitles it to a share in the copyright ownership. On the other hand, the institution may, through its administrators and staff, effectively determine or contribute to such detailed matters as substantive coverage, creative graphic elements, and the like; in such a situation, the institution has a stronger claim to co-ownership rights.

OWNERSHIP, CONTROL, USE, AND COMPENSATION: THE NEED FOR INFORMED ALLOCATION OF RIGHTS

Given the varying roles possibly played by the institution and the faculty member, and the nascent state of distance-education programs and technologies, it is not likely that a single principle of law can clearly allocate copyright ownership interests in all cases. In some instances, the legal rules may warrant the conclusion that the college or university is a "joint author"; in other instances, that the institution should be compensated with royalties commensurate with its investment; and in yet others, that it has some sort of implied royalty-free "license to use" the copyrighted work. It is therefore useful for the respective rights of individual faculty members and the institution—concerning ownership, control, use, and compensation—to be negotiated in advance and reduced to a written agreement. Although the need for contractual arrangements has become more pressing with the advent of new instructional technologies, such arrangements should be considered even with respect to more traditional forms of authorship when the institution seeks to depart from the norm of faculty copyright ownership. An alternative format—perhaps somewhat less desirable, because less likely to be fully known to and appreciated by individual faculty members—would be detailed and explicit institutional regulations dealing with a variety of pertinent issues, subject to the strictures noted above concerning copyright transfers. Such regulations should of course give great weight to the views of the faculty, and may be reflected either in widely available institutional policy documents or in collective bargaining agreements.

Whoever owns the copyright, the institution may reasonably require reimbursement for any unusual financial or technical support. That reimbursement might take the form of future royalties or a nonexclusive, royalty-free license to use the work for internal educational and administrative purposes. Conversely, when the institution holds all or part of the copyright, the faculty member should, at a minimum, retain the right to take credit for creative contributions, to reproduce the work for his or her instructional purposes, and to incorporate the work in future scholarly works authored by that faculty member. In the context of distance-education courseware, the faculty member should also be given rights in connection with its future uses, not only through compensation but also through the right of "first refusal" in making new versions, or at least the right to be consulted in good faith on reuse and revisions.

DISCRIMINATION

Reflecting positions taken by previous annual meetings, the Association's Council in 1976 adopted a brief formal statement On Discrimination. Primarily through its Committee on the Status of Women in the Academic Profession and the Committee on Academic Freedom and Tenure (Committee A), the Association has developed and issued several policy statements and reports that address potential inequities and discriminatory treatment facing faculty members in colleges and universities. The documents in this section include policy on faculty appointments and family relationships, procedural standards for processing complaints of discrimination, and recommended criteria and procedures for advancing affirmative action and for dealing with sexual harassment. The Recommended Institutional Regulations on Academic Freedom and Tenure, found in an earlier section, provide safeguards of academic due process in responding to allegations of discrimination (see, in particular, Regulations 10 and 15). Additional policy statements and reports on concerns that bear on discrimination (e.g., On Full-Time Non-Tenure-Track Appointments; The Status of Part-Time Faculty; and Senior Appointments with Reduced Loads) are found in other sections of this volume.

On Discrimination

The statement which follows was adopted in October 1976 by the Association's Council. Successive revisions were adopted by the Council in November 1994 and June 1995.

The Association is committed to use its procedures and to take measures, including censure, against colleges and universities practicing illegal or unconstitutional discrimination, or discrimination on a basis not demonstrably related to the job function involved, including, but not limited to, age, sex, disability, race, religion, national origin, marital status, or sexual orientation.

On Processing Complaints of Discrimination

The report which follows, a revision of a report originally adopted in 1977, was approved by the Association's Committee on Academic Freedom and Tenure (Committee A) and adopted by the Association's Council in November 1991. It was endorsed by the Seventy-eighth Annual Meeting in June 1992.

INTRODUCTION

The Association has, through its statement *On Discrimination*, declared its opposition to improper discrimination in colleges and universities and has resolved to work toward correcting inequities:

> The Association is committed to use its procedures and to take measures, including censure, against colleges and universities practicing illegal or unconstitutional discrimination, or discrimination on a basis not demonstrably related to the job function involved, including, but not limited to, age, sex, disability, race, religion, national origin, marital status, or sexual orientation.[1]

With respect to procedures within colleges and universities suitable for identifying and processing complaints of discrimination in a decision against reappointment, the Association, in Regulation 10 of its *Recommended Institutional Regulations on Academic Freedom and Tenure*, sets forth the following provisions:

> If a faculty member on probationary or other nontenured appointment alleges that a decision against reappointment was based significantly on considerations violative of (a) academic freedom or (b) governing policies on making appointments without prejudice with respect to race, sex, religion, national origin, age, disability, marital status, or sexual orientation, the allegation will be given preliminary consideration by the [insert name of committee], which will seek to settle the matter by informal methods. The allegation will be accompanied by a statement that the faculty member agrees to the presentation, for the consideration of the faculty committees, of such reasons and evidence as the institution may allege in support of its decision. If the difficulty is unresolved at this stage, and if the committee so recommends, the matter will be heard in the manner set forth in Regulations 5 and 6, except that the faculty member making the complaint is responsible for stating the grounds upon which the allegations are based, and the burden of proof will rest upon the faculty member. If the faculty member succeeds in establishing a prima facie case, it is incumbent upon those who made the decision against reappointment to come forward with evidence in support of their decision. Statistical evidence of improper discrimination may be used in establishing a prima facie case.[2]

This report examines evidentiary issues of proof of discrimination and provides guidance to faculty, administrators, and the Association's staff on handling complaints raising claims of discrimination. While the report was drafted specifically to address allegations of discrimination on the basis of sex, it has over the years proven useful for complaints of improper discrimination based on other attributes as well.

---

[1] AAUP, *Policy Documents and Reports*, 9th ed. (Washington, D.C., 2001), 185.
[2] *Ibid.*, 28.

THE NATURE OF SEX DISCRIMINATION CLAIMS

Sex discrimination can occur at every stage of decision in an individual's teaching career (e.g., entry, salary, fringe benefits, assignments, academic rank, reappointment, tenure, and retirement). At each stage, some complaints of sex discrimination may be accompanied by supporting evidence of a relatively conventional kind. More often than not, however, sex discrimination claims present the special difficulty of proving motivation.

1. The Importance of Motivation

Most complaints involving sex discrimination require proof of an improper motive for an otherwise proper action. The need to assess motivation in processing complaints is not limited to those alleging sex discrimination. Many other complaints involving a faculty member's status, such as allegations that the faculty member's appointment was not renewed for reasons violative of academic freedom or that a termination for financial exigency was in bad faith, rest upon demonstration of improper motivation. To a significant extent, evidence to support allegations of sex discrimination must be sought in much the same way as in other complaints of violations of Association-supported standards. Proving improper motivation can, however, be more difficult in the area of sex discrimination, because it is the kind of discrimination that often relates to who a person is rather than to what a person says or does.[3] In a complaint involving academic freedom, for example, the complainant will generally assert that the adverse action which allegedly constitutes a violation of academic freedom is in retaliation for something the complainant did or said and that, but for the protected speech or conduct, the adverse action would not have occurred. Sex discrimination, on the other hand, may not result from anything someone says or does. The involuntary characteristic of sex may itself motivate discrimination. It is difficult in such circumstances to point to an "incident" to which the alleged discrimination can be traced, a fact which ordinarily makes proof of discrimination much more elusive.

Principles and standards relating to academic freedom, moreover, have gained more widespread acceptance in the academic community than any analogous principles and standards in the area of sex discrimination in academic life. Consequently, it seems reasonable to anticipate that some faculty members and administrative officers may be less sensitive to, and less supportive of, complaints of sex discrimination than experience has shown them to be concerning complaints raising issues of academic freedom.

2. Evidence of Sex Discrimination

Ascertaining whether improper motive was involved in a given case becomes more manageable when the general search for bias is made more concrete. The categories listed below are intended to specify the types of evidence from which sex discrimination can be inferred. While descriptive, they are not intended to be exhaustive.

These categories consist, in general, of evidence specifically related to sex, and evidence reflecting general institutional deficiencies not specifically related to sex. Direct evidence of sexual bias and unequal application of standards are examples of evidence specifically related to sex. Vague criteria for appointment and promotion, failure to give reasons for nonrenewal upon the faculty member's request, inadequate grievance mechanisms, and deviations from procedures normally employed by an institution are examples of evidence reflecting general deficiencies in procedure. This second type of evidence, while not necessarily as probative of sex discrimination as evidence which is specifically related to sex, might, where there is more direct evidence, be considered part of the totality of circumstances from which sex discrimination can be inferred.

(a) *Direct evidence of sex discrimination.* Criteria which are themselves discriminatory, and sexist statements or conduct, provide direct evidence of sex discrimination. Criteria used for making decisions in colleges and universities are rarely discriminatory on their face. It is highly

---

[3] See the 1972 "Report of the Council Committee on Discrimination," *AAUP Bulletin* 58 (1972): 160.

unlikely that such criteria would be used to select for or against a sexual characteristic.[4] Sexist statements or conduct, whether or not well intentioned, also constitute direct evidence of sex discrimination, and are much more common than obviously discriminatory criteria. Such evidence would be present, for example, if a member of a tenure committee were to state: "Women make bad engineers," or "I will resign if a woman is granted tenure."

(b) *Unequal application of standards.* Unequal treatment of men and women provides one of the most telling forms of evidence of sex discrimination. A criterion might be applied to a member of one sex but not to a similarly situated member of the opposite sex; or the same criterion might be applied more rigorously to a member of one sex than to a similarly situated member of the opposite sex. For example, a woman may be denied tenure (1) for lack of a Ph.D. in a department that has recently granted tenure to a man without one; (2) because of "inadequate teaching" when her teaching evaluations are virtually identical to those of a male faculty member who has been granted tenure; or (3) where standards traditionally considered important by the institution would have strongly suggested a different result.

Because sex discrimination is seldom overt, statistical evidence is an essential tool. Statistics may not, alone, establish discrimination, but they can provide an adequate basis for requesting an explanation from the institution. In approving the "relevance of statistics as a means of shifting the burden to come forward with evidence," the Association's Council Committee on Discrimination pointed to the historically effective application of statistics in detecting and remedying racial discrimination in the composition of juries. The committee noted that, because it was virtually impossible to prove that the persistent absence of blacks from juries was the result of discrimination in each particular case, federal courts came to regard the significant disparity in the proportion of blacks on juries as permitting a prima facie inference that racial discrimination was a contributing element. This inference shifted the burden to the state, even though overt discrimination could not be proved in an individual case.

The following types of statistical data, while not individually or collectively determinative, may be meaningful in cases involving allegations of sex discrimination at the college or university level: (1) salary differentials between men and women (comparisons should, where possible, take into account factors such as institution, department, rank, and years of experience); (2) numerical differentials between men and women (comparisons should, where possible, take into account the same factors as in salary differentials, and also tenured or nontenured status); (3) the proportion of women on the faculty in relation to (i) the number of qualified women available for appointment, and (ii) affirmative action goals; (4) changes in the percentage of women on the faculty; (5) the number and distribution of women on decision-making bodies; and (6) differential promotion and tenuring rates. The Association should intensify its work in gathering and developing such statistical data to the extent that they are not already available from other sources.

(c) *General deficiencies in procedure.* The general deficiencies in procedure summarized above are familiar to the Association's work. The operating assumption that procedural irregularities often indicate substantive violations has guided traditional Committee A work. The Association, when presenting its concern about an academic freedom case to administrative officers, often refers to inadequate evaluation procedures and provisions for due process, the failure to state reasons for nonreappointment, or the statement of vague reasons, as increasing its concern.[5] The Association, on occasion, has also expressed concern over a substantive decision which is an inexplicable departure from results generally reached in similar circumstances. The importance of circumstantial evidence in establishing sex discrimination suggests careful attention to this factor.

It is important to reiterate that these types of evidence from which sex discrimination can be inferred are not exhaustive, and that they cannot be fitted into an abstract formula which

---

[4] An exception would be an improper "anti-nepotism" regulation. See "Faculty Appointment and Family Relationship," *Policy Documents and Reports*, 213.
[5] See "Statement on Procedural Standards in the Renewal or Nonrenewal of Faculty Appointments," *ibid.*, 15–20.

might indicate in advance the precise combination of relevant criteria that would create a presumption of sex discrimination in a particular case. The identification and processing of complaints involving sex discrimination must depend on accumulated precedent and on the sensitivity and judgment of those responsible for seeing them to a conclusion.

THE ASSOCIATION'S PROCESSING OF COMPLAINTS OF SEX DISCRIMINATION

This section of the subcommittee's report, while it may also be applicable in part to review bodies at colleges and universities, discusses particular aspects of the processing by the Association's staff of complaints of sex discrimination. As in the subcommittee's specification of evidence of sex discrimination, this discussion is not intended to be exhaustive.

1. The Complaint

(a) *Complaint evaluation.* The faculty member who believes that his or her rights as an academic have been infringed and who seeks the assistance of the Association is expected to present relevant evidence. Faculty colleagues and members of the Association's staff can often be helpful in clarifying issues and identifying the kind of evidence that may be pertinent. Staff members should help faculty members recognize and develop complaints involving sex discrimination by explaining what constitutes "evidence" and by guiding complainants in collecting such evidence. Inquiries currently made of complainants who allege certain procedural violations (for example, seeking, inter alia, letters of appointment, the faculty handbook, the current contract, and a letter of nonreappointment) provide an appropriate analogy.

(b) *"Mixed" complaints.* Complaints by faculty members will often include the possibility of both sex discrimination and other violations of Association policy. Thus, for example, the complaint may involve late notice or excessive probation as well as sex discrimination. Although the former grounds may more easily be established, any evidence of sex discrimination should be carefully collected and weighed. The more obvious violation, standing alone, may ultimately be deemed an inadequately serious matter to warrant further action. The complaint of sex discrimination, on the other hand, may reflect serious problems which should be pursued. Collecting evidence of sex discrimination is therefore important even when the complaint could be processed on some other, more easily established, ground.

(c) *Multiple jurisdictions.* Complainants should be systematically informed by the staff of their right to go to the Equal Employment Opportunity Commission (EEOC), to other state and federal administrative agencies, and to the courts. The Association in principle is willing to proceed even if an EEOC complaint or a judicial action is also initiated, but it is often more difficult for the Association to pursue a complaint which is simultaneously pending before an administrative or judicial body. College and university officials are less likely to cooperate with representatives of the Association in both the production and assessment of relevant evidence when other proceedings have been instituted.

These facts should be conveyed to complainants, but without any suggestion that the complainant's election of institutional, administrative, and/or judicial remedies would preclude the Association's involvement in a complaint of sex discrimination any more than in a complaint involving academic freedom. In appropriate circumstances, the Association should pursue the complaint and attempt to discover the relevant evidence even though institutional officials may decline to cooperate in the inquiry.

2. Case Status

A "complaint" becomes a "case" in Association terminology when the general secretary, or a staff member acting on behalf of the general secretary, communicates with a college or university administration to express the Association's concern, usually with a recommendation for corrective action.

(a) *Informal assistance.* The Association's staff may, and often should, take a variety of steps before deciding whether the evidence warrants opening a case, including the collection and analysis of data, letters or calls of inquiry, informal efforts to resolve the difficulty, and assistance in helping the complainant pursue remedies through institutional channels. Institutional channels, including hearings before faculty committees as provided by the *Recommended Institutional Regulations*, are in many instances the best forum for an initial review of the range of complaints brought to the attention of the Association. The particular difficulties inherent in proving sex discrimination underline the value of such hearings, which give institutions an opportunity to resolve disputes internally and produce a record upon which the institution's own action can later be reviewed by the Association under a standard of reasonableness. The test for taking any of these steps should be the same for complaints alleging sex discrimination as for any other complaint: whether the action contemplated is an appropriate measure under the circumstances. The complainant need not provide the Association with any specific quantum of proof to gain informal assistance.

(b) *Standards for opening a case.* A case may be opened when the information available to the staff permits a reasonable inference of a significant departure from principles or procedural standards supported by the Association. This is no magical moment, clear to all involved. It is the point at which the staff can reasonably state to the administration that a credible claim appears to exist. The initial approach to the administration should explain that the assessment offered has been based primarily on information received from other sources and should invite the administration to comment and to provide information which might add to the Association's understanding of the matter.

This procedure for opening a case applies to the entire range of Committee A complaints and, in essence, reflects the judgment that an adequate basis exists for asking the college or university to provide a valid explanation. Placing a burden of explanation on the institution can be justified on two grounds: (1) sufficient evidence exists to enable the Association's staff to make a reasonable inference that a lack of adherence to standards supported by the Association may have occurred, and (2) the administration has better access to the reasons for its position.

(c) *The response of the administration.* On some occasions, an administration will respond by accepting the staff's recommendation for corrective action. On other occasions, the administration's explanation of its position will prove, after further discussion with the complainant, to meet the Association's concerns. On still other occasions, an administration may state reasons which appear valid on their face, but are in fact a pretext that camouflages a departure from principles or procedural standards supported by the Association. As in establishing an inference that a departure may have occurred, it will often be necessary to rely on circumstantial evidence to demonstrate that an apparently valid reason is actually a pretext. These determinations are difficult and must be made carefully. The Association does not, for example, substitute its own judgment for the professional judgment of an academic department. Nor does it do so in evaluating a claim of sex discrimination. In an assessment of whether a stated reason is valid, it is not the right to judge that is being questioned, nor the expertise of the judges, but whether the judgment was, in fact, professional and nondiscriminatory. Thus, an administration's apparently valid explanation of an action against a complainant, like the staff's expression of its reasonable inference that sex discrimination was actually a factor in such a decision, is rebuttable rather than conclusive.

3. *Formal Investigation*

(a) *Standards for authorizing an investigation.* The degree of importance of the principles and procedural standards at issue in a particular case, the degree of seriousness of the case itself, and the utility of an investigation and a potential published report, are major factors in a decision by the general secretary to authorize an investigation by an ad hoc committee. The resolutions passed by the 1971 and 1975 Annual Meetings emphasize that the Association has committed itself to use all its applicable procedures and sanctions, including censure, in appropriate cases involving sex discrimination. The importance of clarifying and elaborating Association policy in the area of sex discrimination is an additional factor to consider in a decision to investigate.

(b) *Investigation during litigation.* The 1965 *Report of the Special Committee on Procedures for the Disposition of Complaints under the Principles of Academic Freedom and Tenure* pointed out that the pendency of litigation often makes it difficult for the Association to conduct a formal investigation. Institutional officials may, on the advice of counsel, decline to cooperate. As the 1965 report noted, this position may be justified, or it may unreasonably be used as an obstructive device.[6] Moreover, the importance of such cooperation may vary from case to case. In determining whether to authorize a formal investigation while litigation is pending, the interests of the Association, which are based on its own standards of proper academic practice, may be different from the issues before the courts.

(c) *Composition and briefing of investigating committees.* The Association properly strives to have at least one person on each investigating committee who has previously served on such a committee. The need for experience likewise suggests that an ad hoc committee investigating a case potentially involving sex discrimination have a member adequately experienced and that the committee be well briefed on the nature of such claims and how they are handled by courts and agencies.

(d) *"Mixed" cases.* Investigating committees are likely to be presented with cases involving both sex discrimination and other issues of concern to the Association. In addition, investigating committees may encounter general practices of sex discrimination unrelated to the case that originally prompted the investigation. The question arises whether in these situations the committee should address the sex discrimination issues even though a report might be written without reference to sex discrimination. While decisions on the scope of an investigation rest in the last analysis with the ad hoc committee itself, the 1965 report concluded that reports of investigating committees should not be restricted to the particular issues which prompted the investigation.

> The Association's functions in freedom and tenure cases are not restricted to judging the particular case of the aggrieved professor. We are not merely an academic legal aid society, but a force for academic freedom and tenure throughout American higher education. When that force can be exerted by dealing generally with the health of the institution under investigation or by dealing with issues of a potentially recurrent character, we believe the opportunity should be taken. An investigation should be regarded as an occasion for the advancement of the principles of the Association rather than as a step in a grievance process; while reports of this character may take somewhat longer, they are worth the cost. And where the pursuit of not strictly material issues carries the committee to areas of uncertain and fruitless speculation, the staff and Committee A may be relied upon to reduce the report to its proper dimension.

The subcommittee reaffirms this view, with the caveat that the investigating committee must in each situation determine whether the facts are so unclear that comment might be premature. The inquiries and reports of investigating committees in cases involving claims of sex discrimination, therefore, should address these claims, as they relate both to the individual complainant and to the institution generally, even though other aspects of the complaint could be addressed without reaching them.

GENERAL PATTERNS OF SEX DISCRIMINATION IN THE
ABSENCE OF AN INDIVIDUAL COMPLAINT

Investigations normally are not authorized unless the Association has received an individual complaint. The 1965 report, however, concludes that in certain circumstances investigations should proceed in the absence of an individual complaint. The report points out that conditions in general may be so bad that it would be artificial to dwell on a single offense, that professors may be too intimidated to initiate a complaint, and that severe violations may occur which do not cost anyone a job. It notes with approval a particular investigation that was authorized because of reports of generally poor conditions rather than as a result of a specific complaint and expresses the hope that further investigations will be authorized in this manner.

---

[6] Committee A has periodically reviewed this issue. The difficulties in proceeding with the investigation are noted in "The Report of Committee A, 1971–72," *AAUP Bulletin* 58 (1972): 145. In 1974, the committee "reaffirmed its position that litigation and investigation can be pursued simultaneously under certain circumstances." See *ibid.*, 61 (1975): 16.

The reasons stated in the 1965 report for supporting investigations in the absence of specific cases apply with special force to matters of sex discrimination. Statistical evidence might identify situations that are generally so bad that adequate grounds to justify an investigation already are present. Professors who feel discriminated against, and those who might have evidence of discrimination, seem especially likely to feel intimidated, particularly by the threat of adverse future actions. Further, these cases are more likely than most to place the individual faculty member in opposition to colleagues, rather than only to the administration. In addition, the merits of an individual's case would not be at issue in analyzing a general pattern—a significant consideration given the difficulty of proving discrimination in particular cases. Finally, investigations based on statistical data would enable the Association to focus on the basic source of the problem. The relevant statistical base for a general pattern would often be larger, and might therefore provide more meaningful comparisons than are possible in individual cases.

Investigations based on statistical data, once adequately developed, should be a useful supplement to the case method and, in some respects, could deal with the available evidence more effectively than the case method. Egregious patterns and examples of sex discrimination, as revealed by statistical data and proper investigation and analysis, should be brought to the attention of the profession.

Affirmative Action in Higher Education
A Report by the Council Committee on Discrimination

The report which follows was presented in April 1973 to the Association's Council and to the Fifty-ninth Annual Meeting.

The Council Committee on Discrimination has been directed to formulate a position on the role of affirmative action in the elimination of discriminatory practices in academic recruitment, appointment, and advancement. In doing so, we begin with the premise that discrimination against women and minorities in higher education is both reprehensible and illegal and reaffirm the Association's emphatic condemnation of such practices.

Our concern is directed more particularly to the specific meaning and implications of affirmative action and especially to the question of so-called "preferential" or "compensatory" treatment of women and minorities. Because the phrase "affirmative action" has been assigned such extraordinarily different meanings by different persons and agencies, however, we mean to set the tone for this report at the beginning by stating our own position as to what it must mean consistent with the standards of the AAUP. It is that affirmative-action policies aimed at the improvement of professional opportunities for women and minorities must be (and readily can be) devised so as to be wholly consistent with the highest aspirations of universities and colleges for excellence and outstanding quality, and that affirmative action should in no way use the very instrument of racial or sexual discrimination which it deplores.

The plans that we commend are those which are entirely affirmative, i.e., plans in which "preference" and "compensation" are words of positive connotation rather than words of condescension or noblesse oblige—preference for the more highly valued candidate and compensation for past failures to reach the actual market of intellectual resources available to higher education. The committee believes that the further improvement of quality in higher education and the elimination of discrimination on the basis of race or sex are not at odds with each other, but at one. What is sought in the idea of affirmative action is essentially the revision of standards and practices to ensure that institutions are in fact drawing from the largest marketplace of human resources in staffing their faculties, and a critical review of appointment and advancement criteria to ensure that they do not inadvertently foreclose consideration of the best-qualified persons by untested presuppositions which operate to exclude women and minorities. Further, faculties are asked to consider carefully whether they are requiring a higher standard and more conclusive evidence of accomplishment of those women and minorities who are considered for appointment and advancement. What is asked for in the development of an affirmative-action plan is not a "quota" of women or minorities, but simply a forecast of what a department or college would expect to occur given the nondiscriminatory use of proper appointment standards and recruiting practices—with the expectation that, where the forecast turns out to be wide of the mark as to what actually happens, the institution will at once make proper inquiry as to why that was so. In essence, it is measures such as these that the committee believes to be required by the federal government in the case of universities using federal funds, and we do not see that there is in such requirements anything that the AAUP should find inconsistent with its own goals. Indeed, there may be more reason for concern that affirmative action of this kind, which is critical to the abatement of discrimination, may fail to be pursued with vigor than that it may be pursued too zealously. At the present moment, the politics of reaction are a greater source for concern than is the possibility that affirmative action might lend itself to heavy-handed bureaucratic misapplication.

DEFINING THE CRITERIA OF MERIT

"Excellence" and "quality" are not shibboleths with which institutions of higher learning may turn away all inquiry. Rather, they are aspirations of higher education which are thought to be served by seeking certain attributes and skills in those to be considered for academic positions. Some of these appear almost intuitively to be clearly related to certain standards customarily used by universities, others less obviously so but nonetheless determined by experience to "work," and still others are not infrequently carried along largely by custom and presupposition. Where a long period of time has passed since any serious study has been made to review the effects and the assumptions of stated or unstated standards of appointment and advancement (or where no study was ever made, but the standards were simply adopted on the strength of common custom and plausible hypothesis), it would be reasonable in any case to expect a conscientious faculty to reconsider the matter from time to time. When the use of certain unexamined standards tends to operate to the overwhelming disadvantage of persons of a particular sex or race who have already been placed at a great disadvantage by other social forces (not exclusive of past practices within higher education itself), it is even more reasonable to expect that an institution of higher learning would especially consider its standards in the light of that fact as well: to determine whether it is inadvertently depriving itself of a larger field of potential scholars and teachers than simple economy requires, even while compounding the effects of prior discrimination generally.

We cannot assume uncritically that present criteria of merit and procedures for their application have yielded the excellence intended; to the extent that the use of certain standards has resulted in the exclusion of women and minorities from professional positions in higher education, or their inclusion only in token proportions to their availability, the academy has denied itself access to the critical mass of intellectual vitality represented by these groups. We believe that such criteria must thus be considered deficient on the very grounds of excellence itself.

The rationale for professional advancement in American higher education has rested upon the theoretical assumption that no inherent conflict exists between the principles of intellectual and scholarly merit and of equality of access to the academic profession for all persons. In practice, this access has repeatedly been denied a significant number of persons on grounds related to their membership in a particular group. In part, this denial of access has resulted from unexamined presuppositions of professional fitness which have tended to exclude from consideration persons who do not fall within a particular definition of the acceptable academic person. The matter of access is in part, but only in part, a function of the procedures through which professional academics have been sought out and recognized within the academy. Insofar as few are called, the range of choice must necessarily be a narrow one, and those fewer still who are chosen tend to mirror the profession's image of what it is, not what it should or might be. Beyond procedural defects, however, the very criteria by which professional recognition is accorded have necessarily tended to reflect the prejudices and assumptions of those who set them, and professional recognition and advancement have generally been accorded those who most closely resemble the norm of those who have in the past succeeded in the academy.

It is therefore incumbent upon the academic community, as the first test of equal opportunity, to require something more: that the standards of competence and qualification be set independently of the actual choices made, ostensibly according to these standards; for otherwise, a fatal circularity ensues, in which the very standards of fitness have no independent parameters other than survival itself.

Where a particular criterion of merit, even while not discriminatory on its face or in intent, nonetheless operates to the disproportionate elimination of women and minority-group persons, the burden upon the institution to defend it as an appropriate criterion rises in direct proportion to its exclusionary effect. Where criteria for appointment or promotion are unstated, or so vaguely framed as to permit their arbitrary and highly subjective application in individual cases, the institution's ability to defend its actions is diminished. While we do not mean to suggest that criteria for academic appointment and advancement be reduced to an easily quantifiable set of attributes or credentials, all of which might be possessed uniformly by a large number of persons otherwise wholly unsuited to the position in question, we are convinced that a reluctance or inability to explicate and substantiate the criteria and standards employed generally and in a given instance does nothing to dispel the notion that something more than chance or intuition has been at work.

THE CRITICAL REVIEW AND REVISION OF STANDARDS FOR ACADEMIC APPOINTMENT AND ADVANCEMENT

The range of permissible discretion which has been the norm in reaching professional judgments offers both a hazard and a valuable opportunity to the academic community. The hazard stems from the latitude for the operation of tacit and inadvertent or explicit prejudices against persons because of race or sex, and their consequent exclusion on indefensible grounds when the standards are clearly met; the opportunity stems from the possibility for broadening the internal criteria for choice in accordance with a general notion of excellence, and hence expanding that notion.

As faculty members keenly aware from our own experience that it may not be possible to verify every consideration taken into account or to experiment wildly, we cannot, of course, urge an abandonment of common sense or common experience. Nor, frankly, have we learned of anything in the specifics of federal guidelines which does so. Rather, what is called for is a review to determine whether we have taken too much for granted in ways which have been harmful, to an extent that institutions themselves may not have known, and a consideration of alternatives which would be neither unreasonable nor unduly onerous in the avoidance of inadvertent discrimination and unwarranted exclusion. Specifically, the review and revision of criteria for academic appointment and advancement should be sensitive to the following considerations:

1. The greater the effect of a given standard in diminishing the opportunity of women and minorities for possible appointment, the greater the corresponding responsibility to determine and to defend the particular standard as necessary and proper. The disqualification of larger percentages of women and minorities by standards which are only hypothetically related to professional excellence may, understandably, invite skepticism and inquiry.
2. Standards which may serve valid professional and institutional interests, but which are more exclusionary than alternate standards sufficient to serve those interests, should be reconsidered in light of the less-exclusionary alternatives. For instance, an institution-wide anti-nepotism rule is doubtless connected with a legitimate interest to avoid conflicts of loyalties among faculty members, but its exclusionary effect is far broader than a rule that requires faculty members to excuse themselves from participating in particular decisions involving family members, and in practice the exclusionary effect of overly broad anti-nepotism rules has overwhelmingly disabled a far greater proportion of women than men from consideration for academic appointment. The Association has already called for the curtailment of such rules.
3. Criteria adopted to limit the field of eligible candidates largely (if not exclusively) for reasons of administrative convenience or out of past habits especially need to be reconsidered. For example, candidates may be sought only from those few graduate programs which in the past have provided the majority of the institution's staff; or application may be limited only to those who have had prior teaching experience. To the extent that such a policy of presumed efficiency excludes persons who may be equally excellent, the interest of economy should be carefully weighed against the tendency of the standard to disqualify a disproportionate number of women and minority persons.
4. The overall excellence of a given department may be better assured by considering its existing strengths and weaknesses and, accordingly, varying the emphasis given to different kinds of individual qualification for appointment from time to time, instead of applying a rank-order of standards of fitness identically in every case. The failure to

consider appointments in terms of a balance of qualities within a department may in fact result in less overall excellence than otherwise. Exactly as excellence of a total department is the goal, consideration of different kinds of skills and interests in different persons becomes important in order to maintain that kind of excellence and to liberalize the emphasis given to the appointment of persons stronger in certain respects than those in which the department is already very notable.

We would go further in this observation. An institution which professes to be concerned with many things not only must indicate by its appointment practices that it means what it declares, but also must act consistently with that declaration thereafter in the advancement, salary, and respect for the appointee. It is unacceptable and hypocritical to make an appointment of a candidate based on a belief that that candidate, whose strongest assets are different from those of the existing faculty, is appointed precisely because his or her strengths are valued in what they add to the quality of the department, and thereafter nonetheless treat that person as less valuable when it comes to subsequent consideration relating to salary, tenure, and similar personnel matters.

5. The consideration of diversity of characteristics among the faculty of a given department or institution may be relevant to excellence and to affirmative action in an even larger and more important sense. Ordinarily, an institution would never think to list a narrow range of "age" as a categorical criterion of eligibility for academic appointment, precisely because it is a wholly inappropriate means of categorically eliminating great numbers of people who may be as well qualified as or better qualified than others. To restrict eligible candidates as a general and categorical matter to persons between, say, thirty-five and fifty years old would be thrice wrong: it unduly narrows the field of excellent people by an exclusionary standard which may work against the achievement of the highest quality of faculty obtainable; it is discriminatory and unfair to the well-qualified persons whom it categorically excludes; and it may weaken the faculty in the particular sense of staffing it in a flat and homogeneous manner, depriving it of perspectives and differences among persons of more diverse ages.

It is nonetheless true that a characteristic which may be indefensible when used as a categorical standard of ineligibility is neither inappropriate nor invidious when it is taken into consideration affirmatively in choosing between two or more otherwise qualified persons, when it is related to securing a greater diversity than currently exists within the faculty. As between two otherwise well-qualified persons, a general concern for balance and the subtler values of diversity from the heterogeneity of younger and older faculty members has quite commonly found expression in resolving a preference between two candidates for a given position—never as a reflection upon, or as an "exclusionary" device against, the one, but as a relevant factor in light of the existing composition of the faculty.

The point may be generalized: meeting a felt shortage of tenured professors by preferring a more experienced and senior person; broadening the professional profile within a department, most of whose faculty secured their degrees from the same institution, by preferring in the next several appointments well-qualified persons of a different academic graduate exposure or professional background; leavening a faculty predominantly oriented toward research and publication with others more interested in exploring new teaching methods, and vice versa. It is useless to deny that we believe such considerations are relevant, as indeed we familiarly and unself-consciously take them into account all the time, and rightly so; never in lieu of seeking the "best-qualified person," but as contributing to a sensible decision of what constitutes the best-qualified person in terms of existing needs and circumstances.

We do not think this Association would disapprove conscientious efforts by academic faculties to register an affirmative interest, as they often have, in the positive improvement of their departments in the several ways we have just illustrated, but rather that this Association would (and does) regard those efforts as wholly conducive to fairness and quality. We therefore do not see any sufficient reason to be less approving of the affirmative consideration of race or sex. We would go further to say that special efforts to attract persons whose appointment would serve to improve the overall diversity of a faculty, and to broaden it specifically from its unisex or unirace sameness, seem to us to state a variety of affirmative action which deserves encouragement. A preference in these terms, asserted affirmatively to enrich a faculty in its own experience as well as in what it projects in its example of mutually able men and women, and mutually able blacks and whites, seems to us to state a neutral, principled, and altogether precedented policy of preference.

The argument regarding the special relevance of race and sex as qualifying characteristics draws its strength from a recognition of the richness which a variety of intellectual perspectives and life experiences can bring to the educational program. It is more than simply a matter of providing jobs for persons from groups which have in the past been unfairly excluded from an opportunity to compete for them; it is a matter of reorganizing the academic institution to fulfill its basic commitment to those who are seriously concerned to maintain the academic enterprise as a vital social force. The law now requires the elimination of discriminatory practices and equality of access for all persons regardless of race or sex; moral justice requires an end to prejudice and an increase of opportunities for those who have been denied them in the past by prejudice; enlightened self-interest requires that an institution reexamine its priorities where standards of merit are concerned, to revitalize the intellectual life of the community through the utilization of heretofore untapped resources. Most important, insofar as the university aspires to discover, preserve, and transmit knowledge and experience not for one group or selected groups, but for all people, to that extent it must broaden its perception of who shall be responsible for this discovery, preservation, and transmission. In so doing, it broadens the base of intellectual inquiry and lays the foundation of more humane social practices.

6. It is far from clear that every qualification we may associate with excellence in teaching and research is in fact as important as we are inclined to view it, or that our predisposition to certain qualities we habitually associate with significant scholarship is as defensible as we may earnestly suppose. There is, as we have noted, a certain circularity in the verification of standards insofar as professors may discern "excellence" in others who resemble themselves, and thus, by their appointment and advancement decisions, generate the proof that merit is the function of those resemblances. It is also far from clear that some degree of frank experimentation in academic appointment would not yield significant information in terms of how a faculty decides what is to be taught, or what is an appropriate or interesting subject for research and publication. It is surely not impossible, for instance, to question whether what is not taught and what is not researched is at least as much a function of parochialism and endless circularity of education-and-teaching as it is a function of wise perspective in determining what is truly important. The point need not be labored, however, for the professional literature concerned with higher education has itself repeatedly expressed these same concerns.

Nevertheless, the point has relevance to an affirmative-action plan in the following sense. An institution appropriately concerned with its own continuing development may well wish to involve a component of experimentalism in its own staff policies—deliberately reserving discretion to depart from standards and criteria it generally employs precisely as a means of determining whether there may be important scholarly and educational functions to be served by standards different from those it ordinarily applies. The selection of some faculty "out of the ordinary" is itself very much a part of an institution's continuing concern with excellence in this sense. The preference for candidates who bring to a particular position certain differences of experience and background which the university may very properly be reluctant to adopt as a general matter in advance of any opportunity to determine what kind of difference they may make, but which it needs to take into account in order to have that opportunity, is neither invidious to others nor irrelevant to a university's legitimate aspirations. This consideration, while it exists quite apart from the need for an affirmative action plan in the improvement of equal opportunity for women and minorities, may nevertheless affect and help to broaden the design of that plan.

THE REVIEW AND REVISION OF ACADEMIC RECRUITMENT POLICIES

It must be obvious that even the most conscientious review and revision of eligibility, appointment, and advancement standards can have little effect in the shaping of academic faculties independent of recruiting practices. Even supposing that all of the preceding concerns for excellence, diversity, and experimentalism are nominally composed in the standard of a department or institution, they may yield very little if the manner in which the department goes about the business of finding qualified persons is itself so confined that in fact only a very few qualified persons are likely to turn up, and these not necessarily the best qualified. Additionally, it is now abundantly clear that certain conventional ways of locating possible candidates may operate to the disproportionate exclusion of women and minorities from equal opportunity for consideration—not necessarily as a consequence of willful discrimination but as a practical matter nonetheless. It is natural, for instance, that members of an appointments committee would seek names of possible candidates from acquaintances at other institutions— and that the resulting suggestions may substantially understate the availability of interested, qualified women and minority persons in a number of ways. For example, the institution from which the references are sought may be one which has proportionately fewer women or minority persons among its graduates or graduate students than other institutions. Or, the acquaintances providing the references may act on presuppositions respecting the interest, qualification, or availability of women and minorities, and thus underrepresent them in their references.

Even if we were to assume, therefore, that there is no willful discrimination against women and minorities in the easy custom of recruiting principally by personal inquiry and reference, still the consequence of exclusion by inadvertence is grossly unfair—and altogether inconsistent with the development of excellence in higher education.

The call for affirmative-action plans provides an occasion we believe is long overdue—to reexamine recruiting practices and patterns and to revise them with the specific ambition of broadening the field of persons whose interest and qualifications the institution should want to know of and correspondingly providing them an opportunity to express their interest. In our view, this is an area in which we should be particularly concerned with "underutilization" of qualified women and minority persons, i.e., that customary and unexamined parochialism in recruiting practices seriously understates the availability of persons fully qualified according to an institution's own standards, and that they do so disproportionately with respect to women and minority persons.

The committee does not think it feasible to provide a blueprint of the particular ways in which each discipline, department, or institution can best proceed consistent with reasonable economy—for the means of reaching larger numbers of qualified candidates differs considerably from discipline to discipline. In nearly all cases, however, it may be necessary to assess academic staffing needs more in advance of the time when the appointment is itself to be made, to provide greater lead time in order that new ways of locating additional qualified persons can be given a chance to work successfully. In some disciplines, moreover, it may be feasible through national professional associations to enlist the aid of a national service, readily providing a point of contact between interested candidates and available positions, vastly improving the field of available candidates with very little expense or time to a given department. For more than a decade, the Association of American Law Schools has provided a directory and registry for those interested in law teaching, for instance, and its use by a great number of law schools is now well established. Similarly, many of the disciplinary associations in the humanities and social sciences operate professional registers and employment information bulletins, which provide a mutually satisfactory opportunity for prospective applicants and employers to make themselves known to one another. Far from being regarded as introducing an unhelpful and inefficient element in recruiting, such services should be seen as contributing to the efficiency and quality of academic staffing.

Finally, given the procedural inequity of past recruiting practices, which have not only worked with discriminatory effect against women and minorities but which may well have had an additional effect of discouraging their interest in considering an academic career, we believe that a highly principled argument for preference and compensation may be made which bears on the generation of the pool of candidates to be considered. Since good evidence exists to support the claim that overwhelmingly there has been an initial skewing of the candidate pool in traditional search and recruitment procedures, it may reasonably be argued that equity itself now requires a certain "preference" whose effects are "compensatory" in the special sense that more attention and care shall be paid where little or none was paid before; and this is not to the special advantage of women or blacks, for example, but for the equalization of their opportunity, in the face of prior disadvantage. Such preference and compensation does not discriminate against majority candidates, but puts them on an equal footing for the first time.

STATISTICAL FORECASTS UNDER AN AFFIRMATIVE-ACTION PLAN AND THE MONITORING OF EQUAL PROTECTION

Litigation and governmental inquiry are substantial risks in any case where the observable facts do not seem to support a claim of nondiscrimination. Historically, the relevance of statistics as a means of shifting the burden to come forward with evidence has most frequently been allowed by courts in respect to racial discrimination and the right to trial by jury. As the actual means which may have been used to compose a jury list are often not subject to public view, it proved virtually impossible for black defendants to establish that the persistent absence of blacks from grand juries and trial juries was, in each particular case, the result of willful discrimination. Where a comparison of census figures respecting the proportion of jury-eligible blacks in a given community would give rise to an expectation that over a substantial period of time approximately the same proportion of persons called for jury duty would similarly be black, but where in fact few or none were black, it became familiar that the federal courts would regard the fact of a continuing and significant disparity as yielding a prima facie inference that racial discrimination was a contributing element. The effect of the inference was to shift to the state the duty to come forward with evidence which would explain the result on grounds other than racial discrimination. Without doubt, this development in the law—which now has analogues in many other areas as well, including employment—was important to the effective detection and remedying of racial discrimination. We have thought it important to recall this fragment of civil rights history as a useful way of placing in perspective our several observations about "goals" and "targets," which have become misidentified as "quotas" in the litany of criticism of affirmative-action plans.

In accordance with present requirements of the federal government, a "goal" and the timetable for its fulfillment are to be set by the institution itself. The means of arriving at the "goal" include exactly the kinds of measures we have already discussed in the review and revision of criteria of eligibility and the review and revision of recruiting practices. In this framework, the "goal" is nothing more or less than an expectation of what an institution has reason to suppose will result under conditions of nondiscrimination, given its standards and recruiting practices, in light of the proportion of those within the field of eligibility and recruitment who are women or members of minority groups. Indeed, the word "goal" is itself something of a misnomer insofar as it suggests that the production of percentages is some kind of end in itself. Rather, what is contemplated is the specification of an expectation as to what the institution has reason to believe should appear in the ordinary course of events, given valid criteria of eligibility, proper recruiting practices, and the fair and equal consideration of equally qualified women and minority members in the actual course of selecting among candidates. Essentially, it is an arrangement which leaves open to public review the logic by which the expectation was determined, the general legality of standards which inform the criteria applied in personnel actions, the technical quality of the statistical analyses upon which conclusions are reached, and the degree of integrity with which an institution has adhered to a procedure which it has itself designed. The Council Committee on Discrimination believes that this part of an affirmative-action plan is entirely proper and extremely important in several respects:

1. Depending upon the unit for which the forecast is made, it will enable an institution to continue a policy of decentralized appointments recommended by the faculties of its respective departments and colleges, while simultaneously providing it with a means of ensuring that racial or sexual discrimination is not in fact contributing to those staffing decisions.
2. It provides the governmental agency responsible for making certain that institutions assisted by public funds are not in fact violating executive, statutory, or constitutional requirements of equal protection with a means of fulfilling that responsibility.
3. It provides the institution with a means of rebutting allegations of racial or sexual discrimination, insofar as simplistic impressions of disproportionality might otherwise support an inference of discrimination where, in fact, no such inference is warranted.

Beyond this, conscientious efforts to project personnel needs and to forecast the extent to which affirmative-action plans should tend to make a real difference in the employment opportunities of women and minority persons may serve a broader interest as well. As citizens as well as educators we all have a common interest in attempting to determine how effective our separate and combined efforts are likely to be in the abatement of discrimination and the amelioration of effects from past discrimination. The knowledge these efforts can help to provide is not without significance in assessing whether or not we have done too little in this sensitive area of civil and human rights. It may help, moreover, not only in fortifying the thinking of institutions of higher learning in terms of their own role, but also in considering more knowledgeably what attention needs to be given to other institutions as well—institutions not involved in higher education, but whose existence and operation nonetheless profoundly affect the equal opportunity of women and minorities.

To be effective even in the three respects we have noted, however, it is obvious that additional reports and records must be made and maintained by the university—information to be periodically supplied by the various departments and colleges. An institution's willingness and ability to keep a careful and accurate record of personnel actions are of paramount importance. There is, for example, the requirement that educational institutions collect and analyze personnel statistics by race and sex, so as to determine whether there is cause for inquiry and explanation where actual staffing practices fall short of expectations under a policy of nondiscrimination. The same need to establish reliable information on actual recruiting practices under an affirmative-action plan also holds.

Finally, we think it important to note again the point, purpose, and relationships of the several parts of an affirmative-action plan. It is a plan which is well designed to improve both quality and equal opportunity, but it is a plan which makes an assumption. It assumes that institutions of higher education are what they claim they are—and that all of us as teachers and professors are also what we say we are; that we mean to be fair, that our concern with excellence is not a subterfuge, that we are concerned to be just in the civil rights of all persons in the conduct of our profession. If the assumption is a false one, then it will quickly appear that affirmative-action plans can go the way of other proposals which are intellectually sound but which so frequently fail in their assumptions about the nature of people. For without doubt, the temptation will appear to the indifferent and the cynical to distinguish between the appearance and the substance of such a plan and to opt for the appearance alone: the token production of "adequate" numbers of women and blacks to avoid the likelihood of contract suspensions or federal inquiry, even while disparaging their presence and assigning the "blame" to the government. However, we do not doubt in this respect that institutions of higher learning will thus reveal more about themselves in the manner in which they respond to the call for affirmative action than is revealed about the consistency of such plans with excellence and fairness in higher education. For its own part, the Council Committee on Discrimination believes that plans reflected in the body of this report are entirely sound and congenial to the standards of the Association, and we commend them for the opportunity they provide for the further improvement of higher education as well as for their contribution to the field of civil rights.

Affirmative-Action Plans
Recommended Procedures for Increasing the Number of Minority Persons and Women on College and University Faculties

The report which follows was approved by the Association's Committee on the Status of Women in the Academic Profession and adopted by the Association's Council in June 1983.

What is sought in the idea of affirmative action is essentially the revision of standards and practices to ensure that institutions are in fact drawing from the largest marketplace of human resources in staffing their faculties and a critical review of appointment and advancement criteria to ensure that they do not inadvertently foreclose consideration of the best-qualified persons by untested presuppositions which operate to exclude women and minorities.

Affirmative Action in Higher Education:
A Report by the Council Committee on Discrimination

Since this statement was issued in 1973, the commitment of the American Association of University Professors to affirmative action in higher education has remained strong. Our concern has been heightened, in fact, by a number of worrisome trends:

1. Although some faculty members have vigorously supported affirmative action, faculty members have too often abrogated their traditional role in institutional policy formulation and implementation by allowing administrators to assume major responsibility for affirmative-action requirements.
2. The administrations of many institutions have promulgated rules which not only intrude into the academic decision-making process, but also are counterproductive to the aims of affirmative action.
3. Insufficient progress has been made in removing the vestiges of discrimination and achieving equality.
4. Failure of many universities and colleges to end discriminatory policies and practices or to provide effective internal means of redress has led faculty members to resort to federal agencies and the courts. At the same time, enforcement activities have been viewed as unwarranted interference with institutional autonomy.
5. Criticism of affirmative action—from litigation attacking the use of race as a criterion in student admissions policies to political initiatives restricting the consideration of diversity as a factor in hiring at public institutions—has been widespread. Affirmative action has provided a handy target for the critics of government regulation of academic institutions, although other aspects of government regulation may in fact be far more intrusive and expensive to implement.

AAUP POLICIES

In view of these concerns, now is an appropriate time for the AAUP not only to reaffirm its stand in support of affirmative action, but also to suggest ways that affirmative action might be implemented in such a fashion as to be both effective and consonant with AAUP standards. The AAUP has long endorsed the principle of nondiscrimination, and the 1973 report of the Council Committee on Discrimination saw affirmative action as a necessary corollary to that principle.[1]

---

[1] This committee report endorsed federal guidelines establishing numerical goals and timetables and asked institutions to "review the effects and the assumptions of stated or unstated standards of appointment and advancement, to provide statistical forecasts under an affirmative-action plan, and to monitor equal protection provisions" ("Affirmative Action in Higher Education: A Report by the Council Committee on Discrimination," AAUP, *Policy Documents and Reports*, 9th ed. [Washington, D.C., 2001], 193–200).

Although affirmative action involves the identification of groups, such identification need not and should not imply a remedy which sacrifices individual rights to purported group entitlements. The AAUP has consistently supported the rights of individuals, advocating that an individual receive neither more nor less favorable treatment simply because of his or her race or sex.[2]

We believe that the following forms of affirmative action are consistent with the principle of nondiscrimination in the protection of individual rights:

1. *Examination of policies to be certain that they are scrupulously nondiscriminatory in principle and in practice, followed by corrective action where needed.*

Included would be a review of recruitment practices to ensure all qualified candidates for a position an opportunity to be considered fairly; to eliminate stereotyping assumptions, such as a belief that women with young children will be unable to devote themselves adequately to their profession; and to provide adequate internal grievance procedures for those who perceive that they have been the victims of discrimination.

2. *Examination of policies and procedures that, while facially neutral, have an adverse impact on women or minorities.*

Whenever possible, they should be eliminated or replaced by less exclusionary policies designed to accomplish the same legitimate purpose.[3] The goal is to do away with gratuitous barriers to the fair consideration of women and minorities. Examples would be the narrowing of anti-nepotism policies or the liberalization of child-bearing and child-rearing leave policies. Another, less direct, action might be provision for day-care facilities, the absence of which tends to have a heavier impact on women than on men.

3. *Race- or sex-sensitive selectivity.*

Awareness of race or sex in the appointment and retention process reaches a more difficult concept, but one that we believe was affirmatively addressed by the 1973 committee and by the AAUP's amicus brief in the *Bakke* case.[4] It is contemplated that in the interest of "diversity" a faculty might make the academic judgment that it would be desirable to have more men or more women or more black or more white persons among the faculty or student body. Such a judgment raises a delicate matter in that we must ensure that the call for diversity does not itself lead to a violation of individual rights. It also raises the question of what types of considerations may appropriately be taken into account in the development and application of assessment criteria.

At church-related institutions (although probably not at public institutions), for example, a religious affiliation may be considered in providing a degree of homogeneity in institutional values. With respect to political views, on the other hand, the AAUP would not endorse the right of a faculty to make judgments based on diversity criteria, nor could a public institution do so legally. At the same time there are some considerations that faculty might quite properly

---

[2] This is the basis of the AAUP's position on pension benefits that similarly situated men and women should receive equal periodic benefits. To give each man more in benefits to make up for the fact that more men die early means that men and women who in fact live the same number of years will be treated differently. The Supreme Court in *Los Angeles Department of Water and Power v. Manhart*, 435 U.S. 702 (1978), found this difference in treatment to be an illegal preference for group rights over individual rights. Limited federal legislation guaranteeing group entitlement has been upheld by the Supreme Court in *Fullilove v. Klutznick*, 448 U.S. 448 (1980), but there is no general constitutional provision for group rights, which would, for example, provide for representational voting as is done by some governments. While the AAUP recognizes, as does federal law, the right of religious institutions to formulate appointment policies based on religious affiliation, it has never endorsed a policy of guaranteed representation of certain groups in employment.

[3] See "Affirmative Action in Higher Education," n. 1, above.

[4] The AAUP's amicus curiae brief in *Regents of the University of California v. Bakke*, 438 U.S. 265 (1978). In this brief the AAUP took the position that when (a) a faculty was convinced on the merits that racial heterogeneity was in fact relevant to conditions of its own professional excellence, and when (b) failure to "count" race might necessarily frustrate that possibility to improve its excellence, then it might consider race in deciding on admissions. Justice Powell found this position to be the sole basis on which it was constitutional for a public university to make any use of race. This position has been reiterated subsequently in other amicus briefs filed by the AAUP, including *Gratz v. Bollinger* and *Grutter v. Bollinger*, challenging the admissions policies and practices at the University of Michigan, and *Smith v. University of Washington Law School*, challenging affirmative action in law-school admissions.

take into account in order to achieve a certain heterogeneity they might view as beneficial to the stated purpose of the college or university. Institutional diversity may, in itself, be an appropriate goal. Under certain circumstances it can be sound policy to avoid appointing large numbers of Ph.D.'s from a single institution, apart from the merits of individual candidates, and an age mix may also be sought in a manner consistent with nondiscrimination principles.

Affirmative action may thus permit the inclusion of sex or race among a number of characteristics assessed in a potential candidate—along with his or her publications, area of specialization, academic credentials, etc. Sound academic practice requires that these criteria provide the basis for a complex assessment of relative merit and not merely establish a large pool of minimally qualified candidates. Nonetheless, it is frequently the case that the selection process produces a group of two or more highly rated candidates who are viewed as approximately equivalent. In such circumstances, and in the interests of diversity, affirmative action considerations might control the final selection. This type of selectivity is still consistent with the principle of nondiscrimination in that, as a matter of faculty judgment, the decision may be made that more males are needed in a predominantly female department or more whites at a predominantly black institution.[5] It should be kept in mind, however, that what is permissible or desirable in race- or sex-sensitive selectivity in the appointment process differs from what may be permissible in subsequent personnel decisions.[6]

4. *The establishment of achievable goals for the appointment of women and minority faculty members.*

A "goal is nothing more or less than an expectation of what an institution has reason to suppose will result under conditions of nondiscrimination."[7] The setting of goals in an affirmative-action plan does not guarantee representation for the groups for whom the goals are set, but it does serve as a useful monitoring device consistent with the principle of nondiscrimination and the rights of individuals.

Despite recognition of past and continuing discrimination in higher education and the slow progress in achieving a more diverse faculty in terms of race and sex, the AAUP does not support affirmative action that would set rigid quotas in the appointment of faculty members. We recognize that special efforts may be needed to attract and retain women and minority faculty members. It is our position, however, that if the first three means of implementing affirmative action described above were fully implemented at colleges and universities, there would be no need to mandate appointments from underrepresented groups. Where the principle of nondiscrimination is truly operative, the expectation is that all groups, where large enough units were considered, would achieve adequate representation.[8] The focus of our concern, in light of our equal concern for the rights of individual candidates, must necessarily fall on the decision-making process and how to make it as nondiscriminatory as possible within the academic setting. It is important that faculty members take the initiative in the establishment of numerical goals as well as in other aspects of affirmative action; if, however, individual departments are unwilling to accept responsibility, then there must be effective means within the institution to ensure that provisions are made for equality of opportunity.

The AAUP recognizes that a fundamental commitment to nondiscrimination and equal opportunity requires the careful development and vigorous implementation and monitoring of affirmative-action plans designed to meet the needs and standards of the academic community. In line with the types of affirmative action described above, affirmative-action plans may include a wide range of lawful and academically sound corrective policies and procedures

---

[5] While the body of this statement refers rather consistently to women and minorities, because that is where the problem usually is, it is recognized that, in some cases, affirmative action may be desirable to increase the number of men or whites on the faculty. Again, that would be an academic judgment by the faculty.
[6] See below, 2(e) Professional Advancement (2).
[7] "Affirmative Action in Higher Education," *Policy Documents and Reports*, 199.
[8] We recognize the great difficulties in eliminating the historical effects of discrimination; nonetheless, we believe these historical disabilities can be remedied through a truly nondiscriminatory system without the imposition of mandatory quotas or a double standard which would merely perpetuate the myth of inferiority.

employed to overcome the effects of past or present barriers to equal employment opportunity. We believe that such plans are essential not only to ensure that equal opportunity is realized, but also to remove those vestiges of past discrimination which would otherwise perpetuate indefinitely the disadvantages of unequal treatment.

The second assumption on which these procedures are founded is that primary responsibility for affirmative action should reside within the academic community and especially with the faculty. Members of the academic community frequently regard affirmative action as a bureaucratic intrusion and respond with merely cosmetic formal compliance. We ought instead to recognize that outside pressure, though at times intrusive and insensitive, is sometimes required to stimulate the reform of long-standing discriminatory policies and procedures. We need, in fact, to reexamine long-standing policies to ascertain whether there are some facially neutral policies which have an adverse impact on women or minority persons without providing a substantial contribution to academic excellence. We need to integrate affirmative-action efforts into the routine conduct of personnel decisions through established procedures for peer review and collegial governance. While the primary responsibility lies within the institutions, we recognize that their policies and judgments cannot be exempted from administrative and judicial scrutiny and review. The right to institutional autonomy does not include the right to violate the law. The role of the government should, however, vary inversely with the efforts of the academic community to implement the principles of nondiscrimination.

AFFIRMATIVE-ACTION PLANS

1. Designing the Plan

Consonant with principles of sound academic governance,[9] the faculty should play a major role in formulating an institution's affirmative-action plan. To the extent that persons affected participate in the development and ratification of a plan, the document's acceptability will be enhanced.

The content of affirmative-action plans should be sensitive to classifications requiring academic expertise. Attention must also be paid to institutional policies governing tenure and promotion and fringe benefits and salary, and to any other area of professional life where vestiges of bias may persist. The most difficult aspect of plan development is the formulation of goals and timetables that not only are realistic, but also will serve as an incentive to maximum effort in providing equality of opportunity. Realism requires an honest recognition of diminishing resources, shrinking enrollments, and the limits of the candidate pool available to a specific institution and in specific disciplines or professional fields.

The existence of a formal document which sets forth the institution's commitment to equal opportunity obligations, including goals, timetables, and procedures for the rectification of inequities, should be publicized. Incorporating the plan in faculty, staff, and student handbooks ensures its availability and facilitates its use as a ready reference.

2. Implementing the Plan

    (a) The Affirmative-Action Office

        (1) The institution should establish an affirmative-action office.

        (2) An affirmative-action officer for faculty should be a person selected by a representative committee on which faculty members have a major role; it is preferable that the person selected have had faculty experience in order to ensure an understanding of the role of faculty and to foster cooperation.

        (3) The affirmative-action officer should have power of effective oversight of search and appointment procedures for faculty and academic administrative positions and their

---

[9] See "Statement on Government of Colleges and Universities," *Policy Documents and Reports,* 217–23.

implementation. For example, the affirmative-action officer should have the authority, upon determining that a department's search for candidates has not been adequate, to defer an appointment pending appropriate faculty and administrative review.

(4) The affirmative-action officer should play a role in the normal personnel-action procedures of the institution, including promotion, tenure, and salary determinations. Timely reviews of individual actions should be complemented by public disclosure through periodic reports on the overall situation at the institution with respect to personnel decisions affecting faculty status.

(5) The administration of an institution's affirmative-action program should encourage and provide a mechanism for faculty participation. Support from members of the faculty and the administration is of the utmost importance. A committee established by the appropriate institutional governing body should be responsible for promoting the policies established in the institution's affirmative-action plan and for periodic review of the plan once adopted. An institution-wide committee would be able to see to the integration of the affirmative-action plan into the personnel decision-making process and the coordination of equal-opportunity activities on campus.

(6) A charge for implementation of the affirmative-action plan should be given by the president of the institution to the affirmative-action officer and to the committee that has oversight responsibilities. This charge should be communicated to the faculty, staff, and students.

(b) *Recruitment*

(1) A plan for the recruitment of minority persons and women should be developed by each department and approved by the affirmative-action officer.

(2) Departments should establish search committees which would work in consultation with the department chairperson and other members of the department toward meeting departmental goals in appointing minority persons and women.

(3) Plans for recruitment should include advertising in appropriate professional publications, in newsletters of minority or women's groups, and in publications of minority and women's caucuses or professional organizations. If a search is to be internal only, announcements should be circulated only internally. The deadline for applications should allow for a reasonable period of time after the announcement appears.

(4) Descriptions of vacant positions should be clear concerning teaching load, research expectation, departmental duties, and other responsibilities. Written criteria and procedures for reappointment, promotion, and tenure at the institution should be available for all interested candidates.

(5) Search committees should ask minority and women's caucuses of professional organizations for suggestions of candidates.

(6) Department chairpersons in graduate programs should be asked to call the opening to the attention of their current students or recent graduates.

(7) Search committees should consider going beyond those institutions from which faculty at the institution have been traditionally recruited. Consistent use of the same few institutions may perpetuate a pattern of discrimination in faculty hiring. In addition to broadening the base of sources from which candidates are seriously considered and appointed, the regularly recruited institutions should be asked to submit names of all qualified candidates.

(8) Search committees should contact the minority and women graduates (or men in departments where there are few men) and present and former members of the department for suggestions of possible candidates.

(9) Departments might well consult with the appropriate minority and women's groups on campus to secure their aid in recruitment efforts.

(10) Women and minority candidates who have recently acquired their professional training, after having been absent from formal academic pursuits for some years, should be judged with other recently trained persons for the same positions.

(11) In recruiting for faculty, the standards should be the same for all candidates. White males should not be considered on "promise" and all others, of comparable education

and accomplishments, on "achievement." Search committees should be sensitive in reading letters of reference for indications of bias.

(12) The fact that the pool of minority persons and women candidates for a particular vacancy is small should not be used as an excuse for not attempting to recruit for such candidates.

(c) *Screening of Candidates*

(1) Search committees should make every effort to include among the applicants a diversity of candidates. After receipt of candidates' credentials and accompanying letters of recommendation, search committees should invite applicants—men and women, majority and minority—to the campus for interviews.

(2) When feasible, the affirmative-action officer and/or members of the appropriate minority or women's group on campus should be invited to meet with the minority or women candidates. It is important for the candidates to know that there are current faculty members who are minority persons or women.

(d) *Appointments*

(1) Appointments should be made on the basis of individual merit. Careful consideration should be given to the criteria traditionally used for merit to be certain that they serve to further academic excellence. It is especially important to reconsider any facially neutral policies which have an adverse impact on affirmative-action efforts that is disproportionate to their contribution to the determination of merit. The need for an institution to justify a criterion as appropriate rises in direct proportion to its exclusionary effect.

(2) Offers to minority and women candidates should be made as attractive as possible; for example, appointment to full-time probationary or tenured positions, arranging course assignments in an area of the candidate's specialty, or a part-time appointment when mutually desirable or advantageous. This last item requires special attention because of the tendency to relegate women involuntarily to part-time or irregular positions on the faculty.

(3) Reports on faculty personnel decisions should include information on the department's search for minority and women candidates, interviews held, and the basis for a final choice.

(e) *Professional Advancement*

(1) Criteria for reappointment, promotion, or tenure should have been made clear to the candidate at the time of his or her appointment. They should be reviewed with the appointee on a regular basis afterwards.

(2) Sexual or racial qualifications for reappointment, promotion, or the granting of tenure should not be introduced. Although a decision to seek diversity may be a legitimate factor in the appointment process, denial of retention or advancement because of this consideration is inappropriate and often a breach of stated criteria and expectations. While it is understood that needs of institutions change, a redefinition of criteria and/or the imposition of requirements substantially different from those stated at the time of the initial appointment are suspect and should be carefully examined for their potentially discriminatory impact.

(3) As in the case of all new appointees, care should be taken not to appoint a woman or minority candidate to a position for which she or he is marginally qualified and then to provide no opportunity for professional development, such as a lightened teaching load to enable access to further study or research opportunities. Without support for professional development that is made available to all new appointees equitably, these faculty members often are denied reappointment. The cycle is likely to be repeated with their replacements. Where this occurs, there may be the appearance of a viable affirmative-action program without the reality of one.

(4) Because the number of minority and women faculty members at most institutions is small, it is important that they be made to feel welcome at the institution and educated into practical professional concerns. They should be given advice, if needed,

on appropriate journals for the publication of scholarly papers, on obtaining grant support, and on participation in professional meetings and conferences.

(5) An institution can provide various incentives for the professional development of faculty members in junior academic positions, including postdoctoral opportunities in those fields historically closed to women and minorities, early leaves or sabbaticals, summer research grants, and funds for attendance at professional meetings. Because women and minority persons have traditionally been excluded in disproportionate numbers from such support, special encouragement may be required to ensure their participation.

(f) *Retrenchment*

In those situations where an administration moves to terminate the positions of faculty members on continuous appointment on grounds of financial exigency or discontinuance of program, Regulation 4 of the Association's *Recommended Institutional Regulations on Academic Freedom and Tenure* recognizes that "judgments determining where within the overall academic program termination of appointments may occur involve considerations of educational policy, including affirmative action, as well as of faculty status."[10] That is, special care should be taken that the burden of retrenchment does not fall inequitably on those for whom affirmative action was taken. The same careful scrutiny must be given to retrenchment criteria as to those used in appointment, promotion, and tenure.

3. Monitoring the Plan

Through its governance structure, the faculty is best qualified to ensure that the letter and spirit of affirmative action are followed in the search for new appointees, as well as in promotion, retention, and tenure decisions. Furthermore, it is essential that the faculty, in conjunction with the administration, establishes and implements appropriate grievance procedures. Information regarding nondiscrimination policies, and notice of the recourse available should they not be followed, should be distributed to the faculty. Grievance committees should have access to the files and statements on which disputed decisions have been based, and, upon request, the faculty member should be provided an explanation of decisions affecting his or her status on the faculty.

CONCLUSIONS

Progress in the appointment and professional advancement of women and minority persons in higher education has been exceedingly slow. There are few minority and women faculty members in most academic fields; those there are tend to be concentrated in the lower academic ranks and in part-time and temporary positions. Unequal treatment of the underrepresented groups continues. The AAUP's surveys of faculty compensation consistently show a gap in salary between men and women faculty members.[11] It is clear that discrimination has not been eliminated, and effective affirmative-action plans are necessary. We urge a greater commitment—psychologically, ideologically, and materially—to the basic principles of affirmative action, and to the implementation and monitoring of affirmative-action plans, so as to approach real equality of opportunity.

[10] *Policy Documents and Reports*, 23.
[11] See, e.g., "Annual Report on the Economic Status of the Profession, 1999–2000," *Academe: Bulletin of the AAUP* 86 (2000).

Sexual Harassment
Suggested Policy and Procedures for Handling Complaints

The report which follows, a further revision of a report adopted initially in 1984 and first revised in 1990, was approved by the Association's Committee on the Status of Women in the Academic Profession, adopted by the Association's Council in June 1995, and endorsed by the Eighty-first Annual Meeting.

The American Association of University Professors has traditionally opposed every kind of practice that interferes with academic freedom. In recognition of the profession's own responsibility to protect that freedom, moreover, the Association has frequently spoken to the need for colleges and universities to provide appropriate ethical standards and to provide suitable internal procedures to secure their observance.

Recently, national attention has focused on complaints of sexual harassment in higher education. These particular complaints invoke the Association's more general commitment to the maintenance of ethical standards and the academic freedom concerns these standards reflect. In its *Statement on Professional Ethics*, the Association reiterates the ethical responsibility of faculty members to avoid "any exploitation of students for . . . private advantage." The applicability of this general norm to a faculty member's use of institutional position to seek unwanted sexual relations with students (or anyone else vulnerable to the faculty member's authority) is clear.

Similarly, the Association's *Statement on Freedom and Responsibility* states that "intimidation and harassment" are inconsistent with the maintenance of academic freedom on campus. This statement is no less germane if one is being made unwelcome because of sex, rather than because of race, religion, politics, or professional interests. The unprofessional treatment of students and colleagues assuredly extends to sexual discrimination and sexual harassment, as well as to other forms of intimidation.

It is incumbent upon a university or college to make plain the general policy we have just described, with an established procedure for its implementation. Educational programs about sexual harassment may be very useful in preventing its occurrence.[1]

The institution should also make clear that sexual harassment and attempted sexual duress are included under the heading of unprofessional conduct threatening to the academic freedom of others. At the same time, it is incumbent upon a university or college to provide due process for those accused of harassment.[2]

Not all institutions find it sufficient to treat sexual harassment under existing policy and procedures. Some have developed definitions of exceptional detail. Whatever policy is adopted, it should be made clear that the institution does not condone abuses by faculty members of the academic freedom of others, whether in respect to sexual harassment or otherwise, and that genuine internal recourse is available against such misconduct. It should also be made clear that these procedures will provide due process for those accused. As advice to colleges and universities desiring a separate statement of policy on sexual harassment, the Association proposes the following:

---

[1] The United States Supreme Court has established strong incentives for colleges and universities to create and disseminate policies on sexual harassment. See *Faragher v. City of Boca Raton*, 524 U.S. 775 (1998); *Burlington Industries, Inc. v. Ellerth*, 524 U.S. 742 (1998).

[2] *Federal Register* 62 (13 March 1997): 12034, at 12045.

STATEMENT OF POLICY[3]

It is the policy of this institution that no member of the academic community may sexually harass another. Sexual advances, requests for sexual favors, and other conduct of a sexual nature constitute sexual harassment when:

1. such advances or requests are made under circumstances implying that one's response might affect educational or personnel decisions that are subject to the influence of the person making the proposal;[4] or
2. such speech or conduct is directed against another and is either abusive or severely humiliating, or persists despite the objection of the person targeted by the speech or conduct; or
3. such speech or conduct is reasonably regarded as offensive and substantially impairs the academic or work opportunity of students, colleagues, or co-workers. If it takes place in the teaching context, it must also be persistent, pervasive, and not germane to the subject matter. The academic setting is distinct from the workplace in that wide latitude is required for professional judgment in determining the appropriate content and presentation of academic material.[5]

APPLICABLE PROCEDURES

1. Bringing a Complaint
   (a) Any member of the college or university community who believes that he or she has been the victim of sexual harassment as defined above (the complainant) may bring the matter to the attention of the individual(s) designated to handle complaints of discrimination (such as the grievance officer or another officer on campus sensitive to the issues involved).[6]
   (b) The complainant should present the complaint as promptly as possible after the alleged harassment occurs. One consequence of the failure to present a complaint promptly is that it may preclude recourse to legal procedures should the complainant decide to pursue them at a later date.
   (c) The initial discussion between the complainant and the grievance officer should be kept confidential, with no written record.
   (d) If the complainant, after an initial meeting with the grievance officer, decides to proceed, the complainant should submit a written statement to the grievance officer. Cases involving sexual harassment are particularly sensitive and demand special attention to issues of confidentiality. Dissemination of information relating to the case should be limited, in order that the privacy of all individuals involved is safeguarded as fully as possible.
   (e) The grievance officer should inform the alleged offender of the allegation and of the identity of the complainant. A written statement of the complaint should be given to both parties. Every effort should be made to protect the complainant from retaliatory action by those named in the complaint.

---

[3] For the state of the law as it pertains to sexual harassment in the employment context, see the cases cited in n. 1, as well as *Oncale v. Sundowner Offshore Services, Inc.*, 523 U.S. 75 (1998).
[4] See the Association's 1995 "Consensual Relations Between Faculty and Students," AAUP, *Policy Documents and Reports*, 9th ed. (Washington, D.C., 2001), 211.
[5] See the Association's statement, "On Freedom of Expression and Campus Speech Codes," *ibid.*, 37–38.
[6] The grievance officer at his or her discretion should counsel the complainant about other avenues for pursuing the complaint, such as state or local government human-rights agencies, the federal Equal Employment Opportunity Commission, or the Office of Civil Rights of the U.S. Department of Education. Deadlines for filing complaints with these agencies should be explained. The grievance officer might also suggest that the complainant seek legal advice.

2. *Resolution of a Complaint*
   (a) Promptly after a complaint is submitted, the grievance officer should initiate whatever steps he or she deems appropriate to effect an informal resolution of the complaint acceptable to both parties.
   (b) The complainant, if unsatisfied with the resolution proposed by the grievance officer, should have access to the grievance procedures at the institution upon prompt submission of a written request to the grievance officer.
   (c) *Review by a faculty committee of a complaint against a faculty member.*[7] Members of the faculty review committee should meet to discuss the complaint. Unless the committee concludes that the complaint is without merit, the parties to the dispute should be invited to appear before the committee and to confront any adverse witnesses. The committee may conduct its own informal inquiry, call witnesses, and gather whatever information it deems necessary to assist it in reaching a determination as to the merits of the allegations. Once such a determination has been reached, it should be communicated in writing to both parties and to the grievance officer. A summary of the basis for the determination should be provided to either party upon request.
   (d) *Corrective action and/or disciplinary measures.* If the review committee's findings do not lead to a mutually acceptable resolution, and if the committee believes that reasonable cause exists for seeking sanctions against a faculty offender, the grievance officer should forward the recommendation immediately to the chief administrative officer or his or her designate. The chief administrative officer shall then proceed in the manner set forth in Regulations 5 and 7 of the Association's *Recommended Institutional Regulations on Academic Freedom and Tenure,*[8] except that the need for a preliminary review will be precluded.

Well-publicized procedures such as these will help to create an atmosphere in which individuals who believe that they are the victims of harassment are assured that their complaints will be dealt with fairly and effectively. It is more important still to create an atmosphere in which instances of sexual harassment are discouraged. Toward this end, all members of the academic community should support the principle that sexual harassment represents a failure in ethical behavior and that sexual exploitation of professional relationships will not be condoned.

---

[7] The Association seeks through these guidelines to urge the adoption by colleges and universities of adequate due process provisions for all members of the academic community—students, faculty, and staff—where there has been an allegation of sexual harassment. It has developed specific review procedures to handle complaints involving faculty members. See "Due Process in Sexual Harassment Complaints," *Policy Documents and Reports,* 212.

[8] *Ibid.,* 25–27.

Consensual Relations Between Faculty and Students

The statement which follows was approved by the Association's Committee on the Status of Women in the Academic Profession, adopted by the Association's Council in June 1995, and endorsed by the Eighty-first Annual Meeting.

Sexual relations between students and faculty members with whom they also have an academic or evaluative relationship are fraught with the potential for exploitation. The respect and trust accorded a professor by a student, as well as the power exercised by the professor in an academic or evaluative role, make voluntary consent by the student suspect. Even when both parties initially have consented, the development of a sexual relationship renders both the faculty member and the institution vulnerable to possible later allegations of sexual harassment in light of the significant power differential that exists between faculty members and students.

In their relationships with students, members of the faculty are expected to be aware of their professional responsibilities and to avoid apparent or actual conflict of interest, favoritism, or bias. When a sexual relationship exists, effective steps should be taken to ensure unbiased evaluation or supervision of the student.

Due Process in Sexual Harassment Complaints

The statement which follows was approved by the Association's Committee on Academic Freedom and Tenure (Committee A) in June 1991 and adopted by the Association's Council in November 1994.

The Association's report, *Sexual Harassment: Suggested Policy and Procedures for Handling Complaints*, sets forth specific procedural requirements in processing a complaint against a member of the faculty. If a grievance officer is unable informally to effect a mutually acceptable resolution, the complaint is to be submitted to a faculty committee. That committee, if it decides that the complaint warrants further attention, is to invite the parties to the dispute to appear before it and to confront any adverse witnesses, to gather other information as deemed necessary, and to reach a determination on the merits of the complaint. If the faculty committee's findings do not lead to a mutually acceptable resolution, and if the committee has determined that reasonable cause exists for seeking sanctions against an accused faculty member, the matter is to be submitted to the chief administrative officer. That officer or his or her designate is to proceed in accordance with the applicable provisions in the Association's *Recommended Institutional Regulations on Academic Freedom and Tenure*, assuming the burden, if a severe sanction is sought, of demonstrating adequate cause in an adjudicative proceeding before a faculty hearing body.

Committee A has been informed by the Association's staff of a disturbing number of cases in which a severe sanction has been imposed on a faculty member accused of sexual harassment with no opportunity having been afforded for a hearing before faculty peers. Investigations of complaints of sexual harassment, often conducted by the campus affirmative-action officer or another official appointed to an administrative position, have led in many instances to peremptory administrative action against the accused faculty member without faculty review of the charges and a faculty hearing of record. Accused faculty members, at institutions which purport to adhere to Association-supported standards of academic due process, have been suspended from their responsibilities before any hearing, without any reason to believe that their continuance would threaten immediate harm to themselves or others. Administration-imposed suspensions have been allowed to linger on, with no faculty hearing on cause for suspension in prospect and with the duration of the suspension and the conditions for lifting it equally uncertain.

These instances of avoiding or shortcutting recognized safeguards of academic due process in treating complaints of sexual harassment may be motivated partly by fear of negative publicity or of litigation if prompt and decisive action does not appear to be taken, or they may be motivated by a well-meaning desire to cure a wrong. Nonetheless, sexual harassment—which Committee A certainly does not condone, be the offender a faculty member or anyone else—is not somehow so different from other kinds of sanctionable misconduct as to permit the institution to render judgment and to penalize without having afforded due process. In dealing with cases in which sexual harassment is alleged, as in dealing with all other cases in which a faculty member's fitness is under question, the protections of academic due process are necessary for the individual, for the institution, and for the principles of academic freedom and tenure.

Faculty Appointment
and Family Relationship

The following statement, prepared initially by the Association's Committee on the Status of Women in the Academic Profession, was approved by that committee and by the Committee on Academic Freedom and Tenure (Committee A). The statement was adopted by the Association's Council in April 1971 and endorsed by the Fifty-seventh Annual Meeting. It was endorsed in June 1971 by the board of directors of the Association of American Colleges (now the Association of American Colleges and Universities).

In recent years, and particularly in relation to efforts to define and safeguard the rights of women in academic life, members of the profession have evidenced increasing concern over policies and practices which prohibit in blanket fashion the appointment, retention, or the holding of tenure of more than one member of the same family on the faculty of an institution of higher education or of a school or department within an institution (so-called "anti-nepotism regulations"). Such policies and practices subject faculty members to an automatic decision on a basis wholly unrelated to academic qualifications and limit them unfairly in their opportunity to practice their profession. In addition, they are contrary to the best interests of the institution, which is deprived of qualified faculty members on the basis of an inappropriate criterion, and of the community, which is denied a sufficient utilization of its resources.

The Association recognizes the propriety of institutional regulations which would set reasonable restrictions on an individual's capacity to function as judge or advocate in specific situations involving members of his or her immediate family. Faculty members should neither initiate nor participate in institutional decisions involving a direct benefit (initial appointment, retention, promotion, salary, leave of absence, etc.) to members of their immediate families.

The Association does not believe, however, that the proscription of the opportunity of members of an immediate family to serve as colleagues is a sound method of avoiding the occasional abuses resulting from nepotism. Inasmuch as they constitute a continuing abuse to a significant number of individual members of the profession and to the profession as a body, the Association urges the discontinuance of these policies and practices, and the rescinding of laws and institutional regulations which perpetuate them.

COLLEGE AND UNIVERSITY GOVERNMENT

S ince 1916, the Association has been concerned with ensuring meaningful faculty participation in institutional governance. The Committee on College and University Government (then known as Committee T on the Place and Function of Faculties in University Government and Administration) composed its first statement on the subject in 1920, emphasizing the importance of faculty involvement in personnel decisions, selection of administrators, preparation of the budget, and determination of educational policies. Refinements were introduced in 1938 and 1958–64, and efforts toward a joint statement began in 1963, first with the American Council on Education and then also with the Association of Governing Boards of Universities and Colleges. The culmination of these efforts was the 1966 Statement on Government of Colleges and Universities. This statement, with its call for shared responsibility among the different components of institutional government and its specification of areas of primary responsibility for governing boards, administrations, and faculties, remains the Association's central policy document relating to academic governance. It has been supplemented over the years by a series of derivative policy statements, including those on faculty governance and academic freedom; budgetary and salary matters; financial exigency; the selection, evaluation, and retention of administrators; college athletics; governance and collective bargaining; and the faculty status of college and university librarians, all of which are included in this volume.

Statement on Government of Colleges and Universities

Editorial Note: The statement which follows is directed to governing board members, administrators, faculty members, students, and other persons in the belief that the colleges and universities of the United States have reached a stage calling for appropriately shared responsibility and cooperative action among the components of the academic institution. The statement is intended to foster constructive joint thought and action, both within the institutional structure and in protection of its integrity against improper intrusions.

It is not intended that the statement serve as a blueprint for governance on a specific campus or as a manual for the regulation of controversy among the components of an academic institution, although it is to be hoped that the principles asserted will lead to the correction of existing weaknesses and assist in the establishment of sound structures and procedures. The statement does not attempt to cover relations with those outside agencies which increasingly are controlling the resources and influencing the patterns of education in our institutions of higher learning: for example, the United States government, state legislatures, state commissions, interstate associations or compacts, and other interinstitutional arrangements. However, it is hoped that the statement will be helpful to these agencies in their consideration of educational matters.

Students are referred to in this statement as an institutional component coordinate in importance with trustees, administrators, and faculty. There is, however, no main section on students. The omission has two causes: (1) the changes now occurring in the status of American students have plainly outdistanced the analysis by the educational community, and an attempt to define the situation without thorough study might prove unfair to student interests, and (2) students do not in fact at present have a significant voice in the government of colleges and universities; it would be unseemly to obscure, by superficial equality of length of statement, what may be a serious lag entitled to separate and full confrontation. The concern for student status felt by the organizations issuing this statement is embodied in a note, "On Student Status," intended to stimulate the educational community to turn its attention to an important need.

This statement was jointly formulated by the American Association of University Professors, the American Council on Education (ACE), and the Association of Governing Boards of Universities and Colleges (AGB). In October 1966, the board of directors of the ACE took action by which its council "recognizes the statement as a significant step forward in the clarification of the respective roles of governing boards, faculties, and administrations," and "commends it to the institutions which are members of the Council." The Council of the AAUP adopted the statement in October 1966, and the Fifty-third Annual Meeting endorsed it in April 1967. In November 1966, the executive committee of the AGB took action by which that organization also "recognizes the statement as a significant step forward in the clarification of the respective roles of governing boards, faculties, and administrations," and "commends it to the governing boards which are members of the Association." (In April 1990, the Council of the AAUP adopted several changes in language in order to remove gender-specific references from the original text.)

I. INTRODUCTION

This statement is a call to mutual understanding regarding the government of colleges and universities. Understanding, based on community of interest and producing joint effort, is essential for at least three reasons. First, the academic institution, public or private, often has become less autonomous; buildings, research, and student tuition are supported by funds over which the college or university exercises a diminishing control. Legislative and executive governmental authorities, at all levels, play a part in the making of important decisions in academic policy. If these voices and forces are to be successfully heard and integrated, the academic institution must be in a position to meet them with its own generally unified view. Second, regard for the welfare of the institution remains important despite the mobility and interchange of scholars. Third, a college or university in which all the components are aware of their interdependence, of the usefulness of communication among themselves, and of the force of joint action will enjoy increased capacity to solve educational problems.

II. THE ACADEMIC INSTITUTION: JOINT EFFORT

A. Preliminary Considerations

The variety and complexity of the tasks performed by institutions of higher education produce an inescapable interdependence among governing board, administration, faculty, students, and others. The relationship calls for adequate communication among these components, and full opportunity for appropriate joint planning and effort.

Joint effort in an academic institution will take a variety of forms appropriate to the kinds of situations encountered. In some instances, an initial exploration or recommendation will be made by the president with consideration by the faculty at a later stage; in other instances, a first and essentially definitive recommendation will be made by the faculty, subject to the endorsement of the president and the governing board. In still others, a substantive contribution can be made when student leaders are responsibly involved in the process. Although the variety of such approaches may be wide, at least two general conclusions regarding joint effort seem clearly warranted: (1) important areas of action involve at one time or another the initiating capacity and decision-making participation of all the institutional components, and (2) differences in the weight of each voice, from one point to the next, should be determined by reference to the responsibility of each component for the particular matter at hand, as developed hereinafter.

B. Determination of General Educational Policy

The general educational policy, i.e., the objectives of an institution and the nature, range, and pace of its efforts, is shaped by the institutional charter or by law, by tradition and historical development, by the present needs of the community of the institution, and by the professional aspirations and standards of those directly involved in its work. Every board will wish to go beyond its formal trustee obligation to conserve the accomplishment of the past and to engage seriously with the future; every faculty will seek to conduct an operation worthy of scholarly standards of learning; every administrative officer will strive to meet his or her charge and to attain the goals of the institution. The interests of all are coordinate and related, and unilateral effort can lead to confusion or conflict. Essential to a solution is a reasonably explicit statement on general educational policy. Operating responsibility and authority, and procedures for continuing review, should be clearly defined in official regulations.

When an educational goal has been established, it becomes the responsibility primarily of the faculty to determine the appropriate curriculum and procedures of student instruction.

Special considerations may require particular accommodations: (1) a publicly supported institution may be regulated by statutory provisions, and (2) a church-controlled institution may be limited by its charter or bylaws. When such external requirements influence course content and the manner of instruction or research, they impair the educational effectiveness of the institution.

Such matters as major changes in the size or composition of the student body and the relative emphasis to be given to the various elements of the educational and research program should involve participation of governing board, administration, and faculty prior to final decision.

C. Internal Operations of the Institution

The framing and execution of long-range plans, one of the most important aspects of institutional responsibility, should be a central and continuing concern in the academic community.

Effective planning demands that the broadest possible exchange of information and opinion should be the rule for communication among the components of a college or university. The channels of communication should be established and maintained by joint endeavor. Distinction should be observed between the institutional system of communication and the system of responsibility for the making of decisions.

A second area calling for joint effort in internal operation is that of decisions regarding existing or prospective physical resources. The board, president, and faculty should all seek agreement on basic decisions regarding buildings and other facilities to be used in the educational work of the institution.

A third area is budgeting. The allocation of resources among competing demands is central in the formal responsibility of the governing board, in the administrative authority of the president, and in the educational function of the faculty. Each component should therefore have a voice in the determination of short- and long-range priorities, and each should receive appropriate analyses of past budgetary experience, reports on current budgets and expenditures, and short- and long-range budgetary projections. The function of each component in budgetary matters should be understood by all; the allocation of authority will determine the flow of information and the scope of participation in decisions.

Joint effort of a most critical kind must be taken when an institution chooses a new president. The selection of a chief administrative officer should follow upon a cooperative search by the governing board and the faculty, taking into consideration the opinions of others who are appropriately interested. The president should be equally qualified to serve both as the executive officer of the governing board and as the chief academic officer of the institution and the faculty. The president's dual role requires an ability to interpret to board and faculty the educational views and concepts of institutional government of the other. The president should have the confidence of the board and the faculty.

The selection of academic deans and other chief academic officers should be the responsibility of the president with the advice of, and in consultation with, the appropriate faculty.

Determinations of faculty status, normally based on the recommendations of the faculty groups involved, are discussed in Part V of this statement; but it should here be noted that the building of a strong faculty requires careful joint effort in such actions as staff selection and promotion and the granting of tenure. Joint action should also govern dismissals; the applicable principles and procedures in these matters are well established.[1]

D. External Relations of the Institution

Anyone—a member of the governing board, the president or other member of the administration, a member of the faculty, or a member of the student body or the alumni—affects the institution when speaking of it in public. An individual who speaks unofficially should so indicate. An individual who speaks officially for the institution, the board, the administration, the faculty, or the student body should be guided by established policy.

It should be noted that only the board speaks legally for the whole institution, although it may delegate responsibility to an agent.

The right of a board member, an administrative officer, a faculty member, or a student to speak on general educational questions or about the administration and operations of the individual's own institution is a part of that person's right as a citizen and should not be abridged by the

---

[1] See the "1940 Statement of Principles on Academic Freedom and Tenure," AAUP, *Policy Documents and Reports*, 9th ed. (Washington, D.C., 2001), 3–10, and the "1958 Statement on Procedural Standards in Faculty Dismissal Proceedings," *ibid.*, 11–14. These statements were jointly adopted by the Association of American Colleges (now the Association of American Colleges and Universities) and the American Association of University Professors; the "1940 Statement" has been endorsed by numerous learned and scientific societies and educational associations.

institution.[2] There exist, of course, legal bounds relating to defamation of character, and there are questions of propriety.

III. THE ACADEMIC INSTITUTION: THE GOVERNING BOARD

The governing board has a special obligation to ensure that the history of the college or university shall serve as a prelude and inspiration to the future. The board helps relate the institution to its chief community: for example, the community college to serve the educational needs of a defined population area or group, the church-controlled college to be cognizant of the announced position of its denomination, and the comprehensive university to discharge the many duties and to accept the appropriate new challenges which are its concern at the several levels of higher education.

The governing board of an institution of higher education in the United States operates, with few exceptions, as the final institutional authority. Private institutions are established by charters; public institutions are established by constitutional or statutory provisions. In private institutions the board is frequently self-perpetuating; in public colleges and universities the present membership of a board may be asked to suggest candidates for appointment. As a whole and individually, when the governing board confronts the problem of succession, serious attention should be given to obtaining properly qualified persons. Where public law calls for election of governing board members, means should be found to ensure the nomination of fully suited persons, and the electorate should be informed of the relevant criteria for board membership.

Since the membership of the board may embrace both individual and collective competence of recognized weight, its advice or help may be sought through established channels by other components of the academic community. The governing board of an institution of higher education, while maintaining a general overview, entrusts the conduct of administration to the administrative officers—the president and the deans—and the conduct of teaching and research to the faculty. The board should undertake appropriate self-limitation.

One of the governing board's important tasks is to ensure the publication of codified statements that define the overall policies and procedures of the institution under its jurisdiction.

The board plays a central role in relating the likely needs of the future to predictable resources; it has the responsibility for husbanding the endowment; it is responsible for obtaining needed capital and operating funds; and in the broadest sense of the term it should pay attention to personnel policy. In order to fulfill these duties, the board should be aided by, and may insist upon, the development of long-range planning by the administration and faculty. When ignorance or ill will threatens the institution or any part of it, the governing board must be available for support. In grave crises it will be expected to serve as a champion. Although the action to be taken by it will usually be on behalf of the president, the faculty, or the student body, the board should make clear that the protection it offers to an individual or a group is, in fact, a fundamental defense of the vested interests of society in the educational institution.[3]

---

[2] With respect to faculty members, the "1940 Statement of Principles on Academic Freedom and Tenure" reads: "College and university teachers are citizens, members of a learned profession, and officers of an educational institution. When they speak or write as citizens, they should be free from institutional censorship or discipline, but their special position in the community imposes special obligations. As scholars and educational officers, they should remember that the public may judge their profession and their institution by their utterances. Hence they should at all times be accurate, should exercise appropriate restraint, should show respect for the opinions of others, and should make every effort to indicate that they are not speaking for the institution" (*Policy Documents and Reports*, 4).

[3] Traditionally, governing boards developed within the context of single-campus institutions. In more recent times, governing and coordinating boards have increasingly tended to develop at the multi-campus regional, systemwide, or statewide levels. As influential components of the academic community, these supra-campus bodies bear particular responsibility for protecting the autonomy of individual campuses or institutions under their jurisdiction and for implementing policies of shared responsibility. The American Association of University Professors regards the objectives and practices recommended in the "Statement on Government" as constituting equally appropriate guidelines for such supra-campus bodies, and looks toward continued development of practices that will facilitate application of such guidelines in this new context. [Preceding note adopted by AAUP's Council in June 1978.]

IV. THE ACADEMIC INSTITUTION: THE PRESIDENT

The president, as the chief executive officer of an institution of higher education, is measured largely by his or her capacity for institutional leadership. The president shares responsibility for the definition and attainment of goals, for administrative action, and for operating the communications system which links the components of the academic community. The president represents the institution to its many publics. The president's leadership role is supported by delegated authority from the board and faculty.

As the chief planning officer of an institution, the president has a special obligation to innovate and initiate. The degree to which a president can envision new horizons for the institution, and can persuade others to see them and to work toward them, will often constitute the chief measure of the president's administration.

The president must at times, with or without support, infuse new life into a department; relatedly, the president may at times be required, working within the concept of tenure, to solve problems of obsolescence. The president will necessarily utilize the judgments of the faculty but may also, in the interest of academic standards, seek outside evaluations by scholars of acknowledged competence.

It is the duty of the president to see to it that the standards and procedures in operational use within the college or university conform to the policy established by the governing board and to the standards of sound academic practice. It is also incumbent on the president to ensure that faculty views, including dissenting views, are presented to the board in those areas and on those issues where responsibilities are shared. Similarly, the faculty should be informed of the views of the board and the administration on like issues.

The president is largely responsible for the maintenance of existing institutional resources and the creation of new resources; has ultimate managerial responsibility for a large area of nonacademic activities; is responsible for public understanding; and by the nature of the office is the chief person who speaks for the institution. In these and other areas the president's work is to plan, to organize, to direct, and to represent. The presidential function should receive the general support of board and faculty.

V. THE ACADEMIC INSTITUTION: THE FACULTY

The faculty has primary responsibility for such fundamental areas as curriculum, subject matter and methods of instruction, research, faculty status, and those aspects of student life which relate to the educational process. On these matters the power of review or final decision lodged in the governing board or delegated by it to the president should be exercised adversely only in exceptional circumstances, and for reasons communicated to the faculty. It is desirable that the faculty should, following such communication, have opportunity for further consideration and further transmittal of its views to the president or board. Budgets, personnel limitations, the time element, and the policies of other groups, bodies, and agencies having jurisdiction over the institution may set limits to realization of faculty advice.

The faculty sets the requirements for the degrees offered in course, determines when the requirements have been met, and authorizes the president and board to grant the degrees thus achieved.

Faculty status and related matters are primarily a faculty responsibility; this area includes appointments, reappointments, decisions not to reappoint, promotions, the granting of tenure, and dismissal. The primary responsibility of the faculty for such matters is based upon the fact that its judgment is central to general educational policy. Furthermore, scholars in a particular field or activity have the chief competence for judging the work of their colleagues; in such competence it is implicit that responsibility exists for both adverse and favorable judgments. Likewise, there is the more general competence of experienced faculty personnel committees having a broader charge. Determinations in these matters should first be by faculty action through established procedures, reviewed by the chief academic officers with the concurrence of the board. The governing board and president should, on questions of faculty status, as in other matters where the faculty has primary responsibility, concur with the faculty judgment except in rare instances and for compelling reasons which should be stated in detail.

The faculty should actively participate in the determination of policies and procedures governing salary increases.

The chair or head of a department, who serves as the chief representative of the department within an institution, should be selected either by departmental election or by appointment following consultation with members of the department and of related departments; appointments should normally be in conformity with department members' judgment. The chair or department head should not have tenure in office; tenure as a faculty member is a matter of separate right. The chair or head should serve for a stated term but without prejudice to reelection or to reappointment by procedures which involve appropriate faculty consultation. Board, administration, and faculty should all bear in mind that the department chair or head has a special obligation to build a department strong in scholarship and teaching capacity.

Agencies for faculty participation in the government of the college or university should be established at each level where faculty responsibility is present. An agency should exist for the presentation of the views of the whole faculty. The structure and procedures for faculty participation should be designed, approved, and established by joint action of the components of the institution. Faculty representatives should be selected by the faculty according to procedures determined by the faculty.[4]

The agencies may consist of meetings of all faculty members of a department, school, college, division, or university system, or may take the form of faculty-elected executive committees in departments and schools and a faculty-elected senate or council for larger divisions or the institution as a whole.

The means of communication among the faculty, administration, and governing board now in use include: (1) circulation of memoranda and reports by board committees, the administration, and faculty committees, (2) joint ad hoc committees, (3) standing liaison committees, (4) membership of faculty members on administrative bodies, and (5) membership of faculty members on governing boards. Whatever the channels of communication, they should be clearly understood and observed.

ON STUDENT STATUS

When students in American colleges and universities desire to participate responsibly in the government of the institution they attend, their wish should be recognized as a claim to opportunity both for educational experience and for involvement in the affairs of their college or university. Ways should be found to permit significant student participation within the limits of attainable effectiveness. The obstacles to such participation are large and should not be minimized: inexperience, untested capacity, a transitory status which means that present action does not carry with it subsequent responsibility, and the inescapable fact that the other components of the institution are in a position of judgment over the students. It is important to recognize that student needs are strongly related to educational experience, both formal and informal.

Students expect, and have a right to expect, that the educational process will be structured, that they will be stimulated by it to become independent adults, and that they will have effectively transmitted to them the cultural heritage of the larger society. If institutional support is to have its fullest possible meaning, it should incorporate the strength, freshness of view, and idealism of the student body.

The respect of students for their college or university can be enhanced if they are given at least these opportunities: (1) to be listened to in the classroom without fear of institutional reprisal for the substance of their views, (2) freedom to discuss questions of institutional policy

---

[4] The American Association of University Professors regards collective bargaining, properly used, as another means of achieving sound academic government. Where there is faculty collective bargaining, the parties should seek to ensure appropriate institutional governance structures which will protect the right of all faculty to participate in institutional governance in accordance with the "Statement on Government." [Preceding note adopted by the Council in June 1978.]

and operation, (3) the right to academic due process when charged with serious violations of institutional regulations, and (4) the same right to hear speakers of their own choice as is enjoyed by other components of the institution.

On the Relationship of Faculty Governance to Academic Freedom

The statement which follows was approved in May 1994 by the Association's Committee on College and University Government (Committee T). In June 1994 it was approved by the Committee on Academic Freedom and Tenure (Committee A) and adopted by the Association's Council.

Since its founding in 1915, the AAUP has been actively engaged in developing standards for sound academic practice and in working for their acceptance throughout the community of higher education. Two aspects of an institution's academic practice have been of particular concern to the Association ever since: the rights and freedoms of individual faculty members and the role of the faculty in institutional governance. The fundamental principles describing the rights and freedoms that an institution should accord to its individual faculty members are set forth in the 1940 *Statement of Principles on Academic Freedom and Tenure*; those principles have been further developed in more recent Association statements and reports that bring the principles to bear on specific issues having to do with faculty status. The fundamental principles describing the proper role of faculty members in institutional governance are set forth in the 1966 *Statement on Government of Colleges and Universities*; those principles, too, have been further developed in more recent Association statements and reports.

Although the Association established Committee A in 1915, its initial year, to attend to issues of academic freedom and tenure, and created Committee T the following year to address issues of institutional "government," the AAUP has not spoken explicitly to the links between its principles in these two basic areas. Thus, the 1940 *Statement of Principles* describes faculty members as "officers of an educational institution," but it is silent about the governance role they should carry out in light of their being officers of the institution. The 1966 *Statement* describes the role in institutional government that faculty should be accorded, but it does not speak to the bearing of that role on the rights and freedoms of individual faculty members.[1]

Historical and contemporary links can be clearly seen, however. This statement will suggest that a sound system of institutional governance is a necessary condition for the protection of faculty rights and thereby for the most productive exercise of essential faculty freedoms. Correspondingly, the protection of the academic freedom of faculty members in addressing issues of institutional governance is a prerequisite for the practice of governance unhampered by fear of retribution.[2]

An institution's system of governance is the structure according to which authority and responsibilities are allocated to the various offices and divisions within the institution. How should that authority be allocated? Conducting the academic enterprise requires carrying out a complex array of tasks by the various components of the institution. The 1966 *Statement* singles out three major institutional components—the governing board, the administration, and the faculty—and describes their respective responsibilities, that is, the tasks for which each is primarily responsible. Being responsible for carrying out a task is one thing, however, and having authority over the way in which the task is carried out is quite another. The *Statement on*

---

[1] The "Statement on Government" does, however, quote from the "1940 Statement of Principles" (AAUP, *Policy Documents and Reports*, 9th ed. [Washington, D.C., 2001], 220 n. 2).
[2] Also relevant are the Association's "Statement on Professional Ethics," *ibid.*, 133–34, and "A Statement of the Association's Council: Freedom and Responsibility," *ibid.*, 135–36.

Government connects them in the following general principle, enunciated at the outset: "differences in the weight of each voice, from one point to the next, should be determined by reference to the responsibility of each component for the particular matter at hand...." Thus degrees of authority should track directness of responsibility.

For example, since the faculty has primary responsibility for the teaching and research done in the institution, the faculty's voice on matters having to do with teaching and research should be given the greatest weight. From that idea flow more specific principles regarding the faculty's role, as expressed in the *Statement on Government*. Since such decisions as those involving choice of method of instruction, subject matter to be taught, policies for admitting students, standards of student competence in a discipline, the maintenance of a suitable environment for learning, and standards of faculty competence bear directly on the teaching and research conducted in the institution, the faculty should have primary authority over decisions about such matters—that is, the administration should "concur with the faculty judgment except in rare instances and for compelling reasons which should be stated in detail." Other decisions bear less directly on the teaching and research conducted in the institution; these include, for instance, decisions about the institution's long-range objectives, its physical and fiscal resources, the distribution of its funds among its various divisions, and the selection of its president. But these decisions plainly can have a powerful impact on the institution's teaching and research, and the *Statement on Government*, therefore, declares that the decision-making process must include the faculty, and that its voice on these matters must be accorded great respect.

In short, the 1966 *Statement* derives the weight of the faculty's voice on an issue—that is, the degree to which the faculty's voice should be authoritative on the issue—from the relative directness with which the issue bears on the faculty's exercise of its various institutional responsibilities.

There are at least three reasons why the faculty's voice should be authoritative across the entire range of decision making that bears, whether directly or indirectly, on its responsibilities. For each of these reasons it is also essential that faculty members have the academic freedom to express their professional opinions without fear of reprisal.

In the first place, this allocation of authority is the most efficient means to the accomplishment of the institution's objectives. For example, as the *Statement on Government* maintains, "the educational effectiveness of the institution" is the greater the more firmly the institution is able to protect this allocation of authority against pressures from outside the institution. Moreover, scholars in a discipline are acquainted with the discipline from within; their views on what students should learn in it, and on which faculty members should be appointed and promoted, are therefore more likely to produce better teaching and research in the discipline than are the views of trustees or administrators. More generally, experienced faculty committees—whether constituted to address curricular, personnel, or other matters—must be free to bring to bear on the issues at hand not merely their disciplinary competencies, but also their first-hand understanding of what constitutes good teaching and research generally, and of the climate in which those endeavors can best be conducted.

The second reason issues from the centrality of teaching and research within the array of tasks carried out by an academic institution: teaching and research are the very purpose of an academic institution and the reason why the public values and supports it. This means that the faculty, who are responsible for carrying out those central tasks, should be viewed as having a special status within the institution. The Association has taken this view from its earliest days. Its first statement, the 1915 *Declaration of Principles*,[3] declares that members of a faculty "are the appointees, but not in any proper sense the employees," of the trustees; they are partners with the trustees, and, as the 1915 *Declaration* states, the office of faculty member should be—indeed,

---

[3] See *Policy Documents and Reports*, Appendix I.

it is in the public interest that the office of faculty member should be—"one both of dignity and of independence." Allocation of authority to the faculty in the areas of its responsibility is a necessary condition for the faculty's possessing that dignity and exercising that independence.

The third reason is the most important in the present context: allocation of authority to the faculty in the areas of its responsibility is a necessary condition for the protection of academic freedom within the institution. The protection of free expression takes many forms, but the issue emerges most clearly in the case of authority over faculty status.

The academic freedom of faculty members includes the freedom to express their views (1) on academic matters in the classroom and in the conduct of research, (2) on matters having to do with their institution and its policies, and (3) on issues of public interest generally, and to do so even if their views are in conflict with one or another received wisdom. Association policy documents over the years before and since the adoption of the 1940 *Statement of Principles* have described the reasons why this freedom should be accorded and rights to it protected. In the case (1) of academic matters, good teaching requires developing critical ability in one's students and an understanding of the methods for resolving disputes within the discipline; good research requires permitting the expression of contrary views in order that the evidence for and against a hypothesis can be weighed responsibly. In the case (2) of institutional matters, grounds for thinking an institutional policy desirable or undesirable must be heard and assessed if the community is to have confidence that its policies are appropriate. In the case (3) of issues of public interest generally, the faculty member must be free to exercise the rights accorded to all citizens.[4]

Protecting academic freedom on campus requires ensuring that a particular instance of faculty speech will be subject to discipline only where that speech violates some central principle of academic morality, as, for example, where it is found to be fraudulent (academic freedom does not protect plagiarism and deceit). Protecting academic freedom also requires ensuring that faculty status turns on a faculty member's views only where the holding of those views clearly supports a judgment of competence or incompetence.

It is in light of these requirements that the allocation to the faculty—through appropriate governance processes and structures—of authority over faculty status and other basic academic matters can be seen to be necessary for the protection of academic freedom. It is the faculty—not trustees or administrators—who have the experience needed for assessing whether an instance of faculty speech constitutes a breach of a central principle of academic morality, and who have the expertise to form judgments of faculty competence or incompetence. As AAUP case reports have shown, to the extent that decisions on such matters are not in the hands of the faculty, there is a potential for, and at times the actuality of, administrative imposition of penalties on improper grounds.

A good governance system is no guarantee that academic freedom will flourish. A governance system is merely a structure that allocates authority, and authority needs to be exercised if even the most appropriate allocation of it is to have its intended effects. Faculty members must be willing to participate in the decision-making processes over which a sound governance system gives them authority. As the Association's *Statement on Professional Ethics* says, faculty members must "accept their share of faculty responsibilities for the governance of their institution." If they do not, authority will drift away from them, since someone must exercise it, and if members of the faculty do not, others will.

The second possible source of concern is more subtle. Even with a sound governance system in place and with a faculty active in self-government and operating under rules and regulations protective of academic freedom, dysfunctions that undermine academic freedom may still occur: subtle (or not so subtle) bullying on the part of the faculty itself, a covertly enforced isolation, a disinclination to respect the views of the offbeat and cranky among its members. That is

---

[4] In this connection, several policy statements have particular relevance, including the "Committee A Statement on Extramural Utterances," *Policy Documents and Reports,* 32, and the "Statement on Professors and Political Activity," *ibid.*, 33–34.

to say, given appropriate formal protections, such incivilities may not issue in clear-cut violations of academic freedom, but a faculty member's academic freedom may nevertheless be chilled.[5]

In sum, sound governance practice and the exercise of academic freedom are closely connected, arguably inextricably linked. While no governance system can serve to guarantee that academic freedom will always prevail, an inadequate governance system—one in which the faculty is not accorded primacy in academic matters—compromises the conditions in which academic freedom is likely to thrive. Similarly, although academic freedom is not a sufficient condition, it is an essential one for effective governance. Thus, the earliest principles formulated by the Association, those of 1915 and 1916, are most likely to thrive when they are understood to reinforce one another. Under those conditions, institutions of higher education will be best served and will in turn best serve society at large.

[5] According to "A Statement of the Association's Council: Freedom and Responsibility," "Membership in the academic community imposes on students, faculty members, administrators, and trustees an obligation to respect the dignity of others, to acknowledge their right to express differing opinions, and to foster and defend intellectual honesty, freedom of inquiry and instruction, and free expression on and off the campus" (*Policy Documents and Reports*, 135).

Faculty Participation in the Selection, Evaluation, and Retention of Administrators

The statement which follows, a revision and expansion of the 1974 statement on Faculty Participation in the Selection and Retention of Administrators, *was prepared by the Association's Committee on College and University Government. It was adopted by the Association's Council in June 1981 and endorsed by the Sixty-seventh Annual Meeting.*

The Association's 1966 *Statement on Government of Colleges and Universities* rests largely upon the conviction that interdependence, communication, and joint action among the constituents of a college or university enhance the institution's ability to solve educational problems. As one facet of this interdependence, the *Statement on Government* asserts the expectation that faculty members will have a significant role in the selection of academic administrators, including the president, academic deans, department heads, and chairs.[1] As a corollary, it is equally important that faculty members contribute significantly to judgments and decisions regarding the retention or nonretention of the administrators whom they have helped select.

THE SELECTION OF ADMINISTRATORS

The *Statement on Government* emphasizes the primary role of faculty and board in the search for a president. The search may be initiated either by separate committees of the faculty and board or by a joint committee of the faculty and board or of faculty, board, students, and others, and separate committees may subsequently be joined. In a joint committee, the numbers from each constituency should reflect both the primacy of faculty concern and the range of other groups, including students, that have a legitimate claim to some involvement. Each major group should elect its own members to serve on the committee, and the rules governing the search should be arrived at jointly. A joint committee should determine the size of the majority which will be controlling in making an appointment. When separate committees are used, the board, with which the legal power of appointment rests, should either select a name from among those submitted by the faculty committee or should agree that no person will be chosen over the objections of the faculty committee.

The role of the faculty in the selection of an administrator other than a president should reflect the extent of legitimate faculty interest in the position. In the case of an academic

---

[1] According to the "Statement on Government,"

Joint effort of a most critical kind must be taken when an institution chooses a new president. The selection of a chief administrative officer should follow upon cooperative search by the governing board and the faculty, taking into consideration the opinions of others who are appropriately interested. . . .

The selection of academic deans and other chief academic officers should be the responsibility of the president with the advice of and in consultation with the appropriate faculty. . . .

The chair or head of a department, who serves as the chief representative of the department within an institution, should be selected either by departmental election or by appointment following consultation with members of the department and of related departments; appointments should normally be in conformity with department members' judgment. The chair or department head should not have tenure in office; tenure as a faculty member is a matter of separate right. The chair or head should serve for a stated term but without prejudice to reelection or to reappointment by procedures which involve appropriate faculty consultation (AAUP, *Policy Documents and Reports*, 9th ed. [Washington, D.C., 2001], 218–23).

administrator whose function is mainly advisory to a president or whose responsibilities do not include academic policy, the faculty's role in the search should be appropriate to its involvement with the office. Other academic administrators, such as the dean of a college or a person of equivalent responsibility, are by the nature of their duties more directly dependent upon faculty support. In such instances, the composition of the search committee should reflect the primacy of faculty interest, and the faculty component of the committee should be chosen by the faculty of the unit or by a representative body of the faculty. The person chosen for an administrative position should be selected from among the names submitted by the search committee. The president, after fully weighing the views of the committee, will make the final choice. Nonetheless, sound academic practice dictates that the president not choose a person over the reasoned opposition of the faculty.

THE EVALUATION OF ADMINISTRATORS

Institutions should develop procedures for periodic review of the performance of presidents and other academic administrators. The purpose of such periodic reviews should be the improvement of the performance of the administrator during his or her term of office. This review should be conducted on behalf of the governing board for the president, or on behalf of the appointing administrator for other academic administrators. Fellow administrators, faculty, students, and others should participate in the review according to their legitimate interest in the result, with faculty of the unit accorded the primary voice in the case of academic administrators. The governing board or appointing administrator should publish a summary of the review, including a statement of actions taken as a result of the review.

THE RETENTION OF ADMINISTRATORS

A more intensive review, conducted near the end of a stated term of administrative service, may be an appropriate component of the decision to retain or not to retain an administrator. When used for such a purpose, the review should include such procedural steps as formation of an ad hoc review committee, with different constituencies represented according to their legitimate interest in the result; consideration of such added data as the administrator's self-assessment and interviews with appropriate administrators and faculty and students; and submission of a report and recommendations, after the subject administrator has had an opportunity to comment on the text, to the board or appointing administrator. The board or appointing administrator should accept the recommendations of the review committee, except in extraordinary circumstances and for reasons communicated to the committee with an opportunity for response by the concerned parties prior to a final decision. The report should be made public, except for such sections as the board or appointing administrator and the review committee agree to be confidential, together with an account of actions taken as a result of the review.

All decisions on retention and nonretention of administrators should be based on institutionalized and jointly determined procedures which include significant faculty involvement. With respect to the chief administrative officer, the *Statement on Government* specifies that the "leadership role" of the president "is supported by delegated authority from the board and faculty." No decision on retention or nonretention should be made without an assessment of the level of confidence in which he or she is held by the faculty. With respect to other academic administrators, sound practice dictates that the president should neither retain an administrator found wanting by faculty standards nor arbitrarily dismiss an administrator who meets the accountability standards of the academic community. In no case should a judgment on retention or nonretention be made without consultation with all major constituencies, with the faculty involved to a degree at least co-extensive with its role in the original selection process.

The president and other academic administrators should in any event be protected from arbitrary removal by procedures through which both their rights and the interests of various constituencies are adequately safeguarded.

On Institutional Problems Resulting from Financial Exigency:
Some Operating Guidelines

The guidelines which follow reflect Association policy as set forth in the Recommended Institutional Regulations on Academic Freedom and Tenure, The Role of the Faculty in Budgetary and Salary Matters, *and other policy documents. They were formulated by the Association's staff, in consultation with the Joint Committee on Financial Exigency, the Committee on Academic Freedom and Tenure (Committee A), and the Committee on College and University Government. They were first issued in 1971 and reissued in slightly revised form in 1972. The current text includes revisions approved by Committee A in 1978.*

1. There should be early, careful, and meaningful faculty involvement in decisions relating to the reduction of instructional and research programs. The financial conditions that bear on such decisions should not be allowed to obscure the fact that instruction and research constitute the essential reasons for the existence of the university.
2. Given a decision to reduce the overall academic program, it should then become the primary responsibility of the faculty to determine where within the program reductions should be made. Before any such determination becomes final, those whose life's work stands to be adversely affected should have the right to be heard.
3. Among the various considerations, difficult and often competing, that have to be taken into account in deciding upon particular reductions, the retention of a viable academic program should necessarily come first. Particular reductions should follow considered advice from the concerned departments, or other units of academic concentration, on the short-term and long-term viability of reduced programs.
4. As particular reductions are considered, rights under academic tenure should be protected. The services of a tenured professor should not be terminated in favor of retaining someone without tenure who may at a particular moment seem to be more productive. Tenured faculty members should be given every opportunity, in accordance with Regulation 4(c) of the Association's *Recommended Institutional Regulations on Academic Freedom and Tenure,*[1] to

---

[1] The text of Regulation 4(c) is as follows:
   (c) (1) Termination of an appointment with continuous tenure, or of a probationary or special appointment before the end of the specified term, may occur under extraordinary circumstances because of a demonstrably bona fide financial exigency, i.e., an imminent financial crisis which threatens the survival of the institution as a whole and which cannot be alleviated by less drastic means.
     [NOTE: Each institution in adopting regulations on financial exigency will need to decide how to share and allocate the hard judgments and decisions that are necessary in such a crisis.
     As a first step, there should be a faculty body which participates in the decision that a condition of financial exigency exists or is imminent, and that all feasible alternatives to termination of appointments have been pursued.
     Judgments determining where within the overall academic program termination of appointments may occur involve considerations of educational policy, including affirmative action, as well as of faculty status, and should therefore be the primary responsibility of the faculty or of an appropriate faculty body. The faculty or an appropriate faculty body should also exercise primary responsibility in determining the criteria for identifying the individuals whose appointments are to be terminated. These criteria may appropriately include considerations of length of service.
     The responsibility for identifying individuals whose appointments are to be terminated should be committed to a person or group designated or approved by the faculty. The allocation of this responsibility may vary according to the size and character of the institution, the extent of the terminations to be made, or other considerations of fairness in judgment. The case of a faculty member given notice of proposed termination of appointment will be governed by the following procedure.]
   (2) If the administration issues notice to a particular faculty member of an intention to terminate the appointment because of financial exigency, the faculty member will have the right to a full hearing before a faculty committee.

readapt within a department or elsewhere within the institution; institutional resources should be made available for assistance in readaptation.

5. In some cases, an arrangement for the early retirement of a tenured faculty member, by investing appropriate additional institutional funds into the individual's retirement income (ordinarily feasible only when social-security benefits begin), may prove to be desirable if the faculty member is agreeable to it.

6. In those cases where there is no realistic choice other than to terminate the services of a tenured faculty member, the granting of at least a year of notice should be afforded high financial priority.

7. The granting of adequate notice to nontenured faculty should also be afforded high financial priority. The nonreappointment of nontenured faculty, when dictated by financial exigency, should be a consideration independent of the procedural standards outlined in Regulation 4(c), with one exception: when the need to make reductions has demonstrably emerged after the appropriate date by which notice should be given, financial compensation to the degree of lateness of notice should be awarded when reappointment is not feasible.

8. A change from full-time to part-time service, on grounds of financial exigency, may occasionally be a feature of an acceptable settlement, but in and of itself such a change should not be regarded as an alternative to the protections set forth in Regulation 4(c) or as a substitute for adequate notice.

9. When, in the context of financial exigency, one institution merges with another, or purchases its assets, the negotiations leading to merger or purchase should include every effort to recognize the terms of appointment of all faculty members involved. When a faculty member who has held tenure can be offered only a term appointment following a merger or purchase, the faculty member should have the alternative of resigning and receiving at least a year of severance salary.

10. When financial exigency is so dire as to warrant cessation of operation, the institution should make every effort in settling its affairs to assist those engaged in the academic process so that, with minimal injury, they can continue their work elsewhere.

The hearing need not conform in all respects with a proceeding conducted pursuant to Regulation 5, but the essentials of an on-the-record adjudicative hearing will be observed. The issues in this hearing may include:

(i) The existence and extent of the condition of financial exigency. The burden will rest on the administration to prove the existence and extent of the condition. The findings of a faculty committee in a previous proceeding involving the same issue may be introduced.

(ii) The validity of the educational judgments and the criteria for identification for termination; but the recommendations of a faculty body on these matters will be considered presumptively valid.

(iii) Whether the criteria are being properly applied in the individual case.

(3) If the institution, because of financial exigency, terminates appointments, it will not at the same time make new appointments except in extraordinary circumstances where a serious distortion in the academic program would otherwise result. The appointment of a faculty member with tenure will not be terminated in favor of retaining a faculty member without tenure, except in extraordinary circumstances where a serious distortion of the academic program would otherwise result.

(4) Before terminating an appointment because of financial exigency, the institution, with faculty participation, will make every effort to place the faculty member concerned in another suitable position within the institution.

(5) In all cases of termination of appointment because of financial exigency, the faculty member concerned will be given notice or severance salary not less than as prescribed in Regulation 8.

(6) In all cases of termination of appointment because of financial exigency, the place of the faculty member concerned will not be filled by a replacement within a period of three years, unless the released faculty member has been offered reinstatement and a reasonable time in which to accept or decline it (AAUP, *Policy Documents and Reports*, 9th ed. [Washington, D.C., 2001], 23–24).

The Role of the Faculty in Budgetary and Salary Matters

The statement which follows was approved by the Association's Committee on College and University Government, adopted by the Association's Council in May 1972 and endorsed by the Fifty-eighth Annual Meeting. In April 1990, the Council adopted several changes in language that had been approved by the Committee on College and University Government in order to remove gender-specific references from the original text.

GENERAL PRINCIPLES

The purpose of this statement is to define the role of the faculty in decisions as to the allocation of financial resources according to the principle of shared authority set forth in the 1966 *Statement on Government of Colleges and Universities*,[1] and to offer some principles and derivative guidelines for faculty participation in this area. On the subject of budgeting in general, the *Statement on Government* asserts:

> The allocation of resources among competing demands is central in the formal responsibility of the governing board, in the administrative authority of the president, and in the educational function of the faculty. Each component should therefore have a voice in the determination of short- and long-range priorities, and each should receive appropriate analyses of past budgetary experience, reports on current budgets and expenditures, and short- and long-range budgetary projections. The function of each component in budgetary matters should be understood by all; the allocation of authority will determine the flow of information and the scope of participation in decisions.

Essentially two requirements are set forth in this passage:

1. *Clearly understood channels of communication and the accessibility of important information to those groups which have a legitimate interest in it.*
2. *Participation by each group (governing board, president, and faculty)[2] appropriate to the particular expertise of each.* Thus the governing board is expected to husband the endowment and obtain capital and operating funds; the president is expected to maintain existing institutional resources and create new ones; the faculty is expected to establish faculty salary policies and, in its primary responsibility for the educational function of the institution, to participate also in broader budgetary matters primarily as these impinge on that function. All three groups, the *Statement on Government* makes clear, should participate in long-range planning.

FACULTY PARTICIPATION IN BUDGETING

The faculty should participate both in the preparation of the total institutional budget and (within the framework of the total budget) in decisions relevant to the further apportioning of its specific fiscal divisions (salaries, academic programs, tuition, physical plant and grounds, etc.). The soundness of resulting decisions should be enhanced if an elected representative committee of the faculty participates in deciding on the overall allocation of institutional resources and the proportion to be devoted directly to the academic program. This committee should be

---

[1] AAUP, *Policy Documents and Reports*, 9th ed. (Washington, D.C., 2001), 217–23.
[2] The participation of students in budgetary decisions affecting student programs and student life is taken for granted in this document, but no attempt is made to define the nature of that participation here.

given access to all information that it requires to perform its task effectively, and it should have the opportunity to confer periodically with representatives of the administration and governing board. Such an institution-level body, representative of the entire faculty, can play an important part in mediating the financial needs and the demands of different groups within the faculty and can be of significant assistance to the administration in resolving impasses which may arise when a large variety of demands are made on necessarily limited resources. Such a body will also be of critical importance in representing faculty interests and interpreting the needs of the faculty to the governing board and president. The presence of faculty members on the governing board itself may, particularly in smaller institutions, constitute an approach that would serve somewhat the same purpose, but does not obviate the need for an all-faculty body which may wish to formulate its recommendations independent of other groups. In addition, at public institutions there are legitimate ways and means for the faculty to play a role in the submission and support of budgetary requests to the appropriate agency of government.

Budgetary decisions directly affecting those areas for which, according to the *Statement on Government*, the faculty has primary responsibility—curriculum, subject matter and methods of instruction, research, faculty status, and those aspects of student life which relate to the educational process—should be made in concert with the faculty. Certain kinds of expenditures related to the academic program, such as the allocation of funds for a particular aspect of library development, student projects under faculty sponsorship, or departmental equipment, will require that the decision-making process be sufficiently decentralized to give the various units of the faculty (departments, divisions, schools, colleges, special programs) autonomy in deciding upon the use of their allocations within the broader limits set by the governing board, president, and agencies representative of the entire faculty. In other areas, such as faculty research programs or the total library and laboratory budget, recommendations as to the desirable funding levels for the ensuing fiscal period and decisions on the allocation of university funds within the current budget levels should be made by the university-level, all-faculty committee as well as by the faculty agencies directly concerned.[3] The question of faculty salaries, as an aspect of faculty status, is treated separately below.

Circumstances of financial exigency obviously pose special problems. At institutions experiencing major threats to their continued financial support, the faculty should be informed as early and as specifically as possible of significant impending financial difficulties. The faculty—with substantial representation from its nontenured as well as its tenured members, since it is the former who are likely to bear the brunt of any reduction—should participate at the department, college or professional school, and institution-wide levels in key decisions as to the future of the institution and of specific academic programs within the institution. The faculty, employing accepted standards of due process, should assume primary responsibility for determining the status of individual faculty members.[4] The question of possible reductions in salaries and fringe benefits is discussed in the section below. The faculty should play a fundamental role in any decision which would change the basic character and purpose of the institution, including transformation of the institution, affiliation of part of the existing operation with another institution, or merger, with the resulting abandonment or curtailment of duplicate programs.

Before any decisions on curtailment become final, those whose work stands to be adversely affected should have full opportunity to be heard. In the event of a merger, the faculties from

---

[3] For obvious reasons, the focus here is on funding from the resources of the institution, and not from external agencies such as private contractors or the federal government. Even in these cases, however, it may be possible in certain circumstances for the faculty to play a part in deciding further on the allocation of a particular grant to various purposes related to the project within the institution. There should be careful faculty and administrative scrutiny as to the methods by which these funds are to be employed under the particular contract.

[4] On the question of due process and appropriate terminal settlements for individual faculty members (on tenure or prior to the expiration of a term appointment) whose positions are being abolished, see Regulation 4(c) of the "Recommended Institutional Regulations on Academic Freedom and Tenure," *Policy Documents and Reports*, 23–24.

the two institutions should participate jointly in negotiations affecting faculty status and the academic programs at both institutions. To the extent that major budgetary considerations are involved in these decisions, the faculty should be given full and timely access to the financial information necessary to the making of an informed choice. In making decisions on whether teaching and research programs are to be curtailed, financial considerations should not be allowed to obscure the fact that instruction and research constitute the essential reason for the existence of the university. Among the various considerations, difficult and often competing, that have to be taken into account in deciding upon particular reductions, the retention of a viable academic program necessarily should come first. Particular reductions should follow considered advice from the concerned departments, or other units of academic concentration, on the short-term and long-term viability of reduced programs.

FACULTY PARTICIPATION IN DECISIONS RELATING TO SALARY POLICIES AND PROCEDURES

The *Statement on Government* asserts that "the faculty should actively participate in the determination of policies and procedures governing salary increases." Salaries, of course, are part of the total budgetary picture; and, as indicated above, the faculty should participate in the decision as to the proportion of the budget to be devoted to that purpose. However, there is also the question of the role of the faculty as a body in the determination of individual faculty salaries.

1. The Need for Clear and Open Policy

Many imagined grievances as to salary could be alleviated, and the development of a system of accountability to reduce the number of real grievances could be facilitated, if both the criteria for salary raises and the recommendatory procedure itself were (a) designed by a representative group of the faculty in concert with the administration, and (b) open and clearly understood.[5] Such accountability is not participation per se, but it provides the basis for a situation in which such participation can be more fruitful.

Once the procedures are established, the person or group that submits the initial salary recommendation (usually the department chair, alone or in conjunction with an elected executive committee of the department) should be informed of its status at each further stage of the salary-determination process. As the *Statement on Government* points out, the chief competence for the judgment of a colleague rests in the department, school, or program (whichever is the smallest applicable unit of faculty government within the institution), and in most cases the salary recommendation presumably derives from its judgment. The recommending officer should have the opportunity to defend that recommendation at a later stage in the event of a serious challenge to it.

2. Levels of Decision Making

Not all institutions provide for an initial salary recommendation by the department chair or the equivalent officer; the Association regards it as desirable, for the reasons already mentioned, that the recommendation normally originate at the departmental level. Further review is normally conducted by the appropriate administrative officers; they should, when they have occasion to question or inquire further regarding the departmental recommendation, solicit informed faculty advice by meeting with the department head or chair and, if feasible, the elected body of the faculty. It is also desirable that a mechanism exist for review of a salary recommendation, or of a final salary decision, by a representative elected committee of the faculty above the

---

[5] This section does not take into account those situations in which salaries are determined according to a step system and/or a standard salary is negotiated for each rank. The salary policy and, in effect, individual salaries are public information under such systems.

department level in cases involving a complaint.[6] Such a committee should have access to information on faculty salary levels. Another faculty committee, likewise at a broader level than that of the department, may be charged with the review of routine recommendations.

Of the role of the governing board in college and university government, the *Statement on Government* says: "The governing board of an institution of higher education, while maintaining a general overview, entrusts the conduct of administration to the administrative officers, the president and the deans, and the conduct of teaching and research to the faculty. The board should undertake appropriate self-limitation." The *Statement* adds that "in the broadest sense of the term" the board "should pay attention to personnel policy." The thrust of these remarks is that it is inadvisable for a governing board to make decisions on individual salaries, except those of the chief administrative officers of the institution. Not only do such decisions take time which should be devoted to the board's functions of overview and long-range planning, but such decisions also are in most cases beyond the competence of the board.

When financial exigency leads to a reduction in the overall salary budget for teaching and research, the governing board, while assuming final responsibility for setting the limits imposed by the resources available to the institution, should delegate to the faculty and administration concurrently any further review of the implication of the situation for individual salaries, and the faculty should be given the opportunity to minimize the hardship to its individual members by careful examination of whatever alternatives to termination of services are feasible.

3. Fringe Benefits

The faculty should participate in the selection of fringe benefit programs and in the periodic review of those programs. It should be recognized that of these so-called fringe benefits, at least those included in the definition of total compensation set forth by the Association's Committee on the Economic Status of the Profession, have the same standing as direct faculty salaries and are separated for tax purposes. They should be considered and dealt with in the same manner as direct payment of faculty salary.

---

[6] See Regulation 15 of the "Recommended Institutional Regulations on Academic Freedom and Tenure," *Policy Documents and Reports*, 29.

Governance Standards in Institutional Mergers and Acquisitions

The statement which follows is excerpted from a longer draft statement, On Institutional Mergers and Acquisitions, *which was prepared by a joint subcommittee of the Association's Committee on Academic Freedom and Tenure (Committee A) and the Committee on College and University Government (Committee T) and approved for publication by the parent committees and by the Association's Council in November 1981. Committee T in February 1983 approved the separate publication of the following section of that statement entitled "Procedural Standards in Implementation," which deals with the faculty's role.*

Protection of faculty rights and prerogatives in a merger situation requires early and full faculty involvement in any discussions leading to a merger. The role of the faculty, first in the planning of an institutional merger or acquisition and then in implementing it, derives from the principles of shared responsibility and authority as set forth in the *Statement on Government of Colleges and Universities*. Because, according to the *Statement on Government*, "the faculty has primary responsibility for such fundamental areas as curriculum, subject matter and methods of instruction, research, faculty status, and those aspects of student life which relate to the educational process," and because these areas will inevitably be affected by a merger or acquisition, it is imperative that the faculty of the concerned institutions be afforded a meaningful role in the planning and implementation of mergers and acquisitions. This role is set forth with additional particularity in the Association's statement on *The Role of the Faculty in Budgetary and Salary Matters*:

> The faculty should play a fundamental role in any decision which would change the basic character and purpose of the institution, including transformation of the institution, affiliation of part of the existing operation with another institution, or merger, with the resulting abandonment or curtailment of duplicate programs.
>
> Before any decisions on curtailment become final, those whose work stands to be adversely affected should have full opportunity to be heard. In the event of a merger, the faculties from the two institutions should participate jointly in negotiations affecting faculty status and the academic programs at both institutions.

The essential point is that the faculty of both institutions should be involved before decisions or commitments to affiliate have been made, or before any decisions on curtailment of programs (if such decisions are an aspect of the affiliation) become final. Preliminary or exploratory discussions about the possibility of institutional affiliation may in some instances occur without full faculty involvement, but full involvement of the faculties of both institutions should begin early in any course of discussion which appears likely to eventuate in an affiliation; any final commitment bearing on institutional affiliation made without full faculty involvement would be inimical to the principles set forth in the *Statement on Government* and the statement on *The Role of the Faculty in Budgetary and Salary Matters*.

The possibility for abuse of the merger situation is greatest in those cases in which a condition of imminent or existing financial exigency is offered as the basis for exceptional treatment of the tenure commitment as outlined above. As in any instance in which a condition of financial exigency is offered as a justification for modification of tenure obligations, the decision on the financial situation of the institution is too grave, and its consequences too far-reaching, to be made solely in restricted administrative circles. Any decision to seek merger in a context of financial exigency should be made with the fullest possible participation of the faculty in the institution which would be acquired. The faculty of the institution which is experiencing severe financial difficulties should be informed as early and as specifically as possible of those difficulties, and that faculty should participate fully in any decision to seek merger as an alternative to possible extinction.

Merger of two institutions when one is experiencing financial exigency may present opportunities to preserve faculty positions and protect faculty status. At the same time, care must be taken that merger is not employed as a means of breaching tenure obligations. The Association offers its advice and assistance, as early as possible in the course of merger negotiations, to ensure compliance with the standards set forth in this statement. In all merger situations, the Association is prepared to enforce adherence to these standards, in accordance with its established procedures for processing complaints and cases.

Joint Statement on Faculty Status of College and University Librarians

---

The statement which follows was prepared by the Joint Committee on College Library Problems, a national committee representing the Association of College and Research Libraries, the Association of American Colleges, and the American Association of University Professors. The statement was endorsed by the board and annual meeting of the Association of College and Research Libraries in 1972. It was adopted by the Council of the American Association of University Professors in April 1973 and endorsed by the Fifty-ninth Annual Meeting.

As the primary means through which students and faculty gain access to the storehouse of organized knowledge, the college and university library performs a unique and indispensable function in the educational process. This function will grow in importance as students assume greater responsibility for their own intellectual and social development. Indeed, all members of the academic community are likely to become increasingly dependent on skilled professional guidance in the acquisition and use of library resources as the forms and numbers of these resources multiply, scholarly materials appear in more languages, bibliographical systems become more complicated, and library technology grows increasingly sophisticated. The librarian who provides such guidance plays a major role in the learning process.

The character and quality of an institution of higher learning are shaped in large measure by the nature of its library holdings and the ease and imagination with which those resources are made accessible to members of the academic community. Consequently, all members of the faculty should take an active interest in the operation and development of the library. Because the scope and character of library resources should be taken into account in such important academic decisions as curricular planning and faculty appointments, librarians should have a voice in the development of the institution's educational policy.

Librarians perform a teaching and research role inasmuch as they instruct students formally and informally and advise and assist faculty in their scholarly pursuits. Librarians are also themselves involved in the research function; many conduct research in their own professional interests and in the discharge of their duties.

Where the role of college and university librarians, as described in the preceding paragraphs, requires them to function essentially as part of the faculty, this functional identity should be recognized by the granting of faculty status. Neither administrative responsibilities nor professional degrees, titles, or skills, per se, qualify members of the academic community for faculty status. The *function* of the librarian as participant in the processes of teaching and research is the essential criterion of faculty status.

College and university librarians share the professional concerns of faculty members. Academic freedom, for example, is indispensable to librarians, because they are trustees of knowledge with the responsibility of ensuring the availability of information and ideas, no matter how controversial, so that teachers may freely teach and students may freely learn. Moreover, as members of the academic community, librarians should have latitude in the exercise of their professional judgment within the library, a share in shaping policy within the institution, and adequate opportunities for professional development and appropriate reward.

Faculty status entails for librarians the same rights and responsibilities as for other members of the faculty. They should have corresponding entitlement to rank, promotion, tenure, compensation, leaves, and research funds, and the protection of academic due process. They must go through the same process of evaluation and meet the same standards as other faculty members.[1]

On some campuses, adequate procedures for extending faculty status to librarians have already been worked out. These procedures vary from campus to campus because of institutional differences. In the development of such procedures, it is essential that the general faculty or its delegated agent determine the specific steps by which any professional position is to be accorded faculty rank and status. In any case, academic positions which are to be accorded faculty rank and status should be approved by the senate or the faculty at large before submission to the president and to the governing board for approval.

With respect to library governance, it is to be presumed that the governing board, the administrative officers, the library faculty, and representatives of the general faculty will share in the determination of library policies that affect the general interests of the institution and its educational program. In matters of internal governance, the library will operate like other academic units with respect to decisions relating to appointments, promotions, tenure, and conditions of service.[2]

---

[1] Cf. "1940 Statement of Principles on Academic Freedom and Tenure," AAUP, *Policy Documents and Reports*, 9th ed. (Washington, D.C., 2001), 3–10; "1958 Statement on Procedural Standards in Faculty Dismissal Proceedings," *ibid.*, 11–14; and "Statement of Principles on Leaves of Absence," *ibid.*, 278–80.
[2] Cf. "Statement on Government of Colleges and Universities," *ibid.*, 217–23.

Statement on Intercollegiate Athletics

The statement which follows was prepared by a special committee of the Association's Council. It was adopted by the Council in June 1991.

INTRODUCTION

On many campuses the conduct of intercollegiate athletic programs poses serious and direct conflicts with desired academic standards and goals. The pressure to field winning teams has led to widely publicized scandals concerning the recruitment, exploitation, and academic failure of many athletes.

Expenditures on athletics may distort institutional budgets and can reduce resources available for academic functions. Within some academic programs faculty members have been pressured to give preferential treatment to athletes. Coaches and athletic directors are themselves often trapped in the relentless competitive and financial pressures of the current system, and many would welcome reform.

Not all institutions have problems with athletics of the same type or to the same degree. Nevertheless, we believe that all colleges and universities would benefit from the adoption of a national set of standards that would protect athletes from exploitation and would place expenditures on and administration of athletic programs under the regular governance procedures of the institution.

We urge faculty participation in the cause of reform. We urge our administrators to enter into national efforts to establish new standards through the National Collegiate Athletic Association (NCAA) or other regulatory agencies. We specifically endorse the following proposed reforms and ask faculty colleagues, administrators, and athletic department staff throughout the country to join with us in working to implement them on their campuses, in their athletic conferences, through the NCAA, and nationally.

ADMISSIONS AND ACADEMIC PROGRESS

1. Institutions should not use admissions standards for athletes that are not comparable to those for other students.
2. A committee elected by the faculty should monitor the compliance with policies relating to admissions, the progress toward graduation, and the integrity of the course of study of students who engage in intercollegiate athletics. This committee should report annually to the faculty on admissions, on progress toward graduation, and on graduation rates of athletes by sport. Further, the committee should be charged with seeking appropriate review of cases in which it appears that faculty members or administrators have abused academic integrity in order to promote athletic programs.

AVOIDANCE OF EXPLOITATION

Students who are athletes need time for their academic work. Participation in intercollegiate athletics in the first year of college is ill-advised. Athletes should have at least one day a week without athletic obligations. Overnight absences on weekday evenings should be kept to a maximum of one per week, with rare exceptions. The number of events per season should be periodically reviewed by the faculty. Student athletes should be integrated with other students in housing, food service, tutoring, and other areas of campus life.

FINANCIAL AID

Financial-aid standards for athletes should be comparable to those for other students. The aid should be administered by the financial-aid office of the institution. The assessment of financial need may take account of time demands on athletes which preclude or limit employment during the academic year. Continuation of aid to students who drop out of athletic competition or complete their athletic eligibility should be conditioned only on their remaining academically and financially qualified.

FINANCING ATHLETICS: GOVERNANCE

1. Financial operations of the department of athletics, including all revenues received from outside groups, should be under the full and direct control of the central administration of the campus. Complete budgets of the athletic department for the coming year and actual expenditures and revenues for the past year should be published in full detail. Annual budgets as well as long-term plans should be approved under the regular governance procedures of the campus, with meaningful involvement of elected faculty representatives.
2. Particular scrutiny should be given to use of the institution's general operating funds to support the athletic department. Institutions should establish regulations governing the use of, and the payment of fees for, university facilities by private businesses, such as summer athletic camps. Fees charged to coaches should be assessed on the same basis as those charged to faculty members and other staff engaged in private business on campus. Published budgets should include an accounting of maintenance expenses for sports facilities, activities of booster groups, payments by outsiders for appearances by coaches and other athletic staff, payments by sports-apparel companies, and sources of scholarship funds.
3. Elected faculty representatives should comprise a majority of the campus committee which formulates campus athletic policy, and such a committee should be chaired by an elected faculty member.

CONFLICTS OF INTEREST

Paid-for trips to games, and other special benefits for faculty, administrators, or members of governing boards involved in the oversight of athletics, whether offered by the university or by outside groups, create conflicts of interest and should be eliminated.

IMPLEMENTATION

1. In order to avoid the obstacles to unilateral reform efforts, the university's chief administrative officer should join with counterparts in other institutions to pursue these reforms and report annually to the academic community on the progress of such efforts.
2. Beginning five years from adoption of these principles at an institution, athletic events should be scheduled only with institutions, and within conferences and associations, that commit themselves to the implementation of these principles.

FINAL COMMENT

Institutions should redouble their efforts to enroll and support academically able students from disadvantaged backgrounds regardless of their athletic ability. Athletic programs never should have been considered as a major way of supporting students from disadvantaged backgrounds in institutions of higher education. If these recommendations are adopted, athletes who lack academic skills or interests will no longer be enrolled, and some of those excluded will be from such backgrounds. In the interest of such athletes, institutions and the NCAA should avoid regulations that interfere with the creation of other channels of entry for these athletes into professional athletics.

The Role of the Faculty in the Governance of College Athletics
A Report of the Special Committee on Athletics

The report which follows was prepared by the Special Committee on Athletics, established by the Executive Committee of the Council of the American Association of University Professors. It was approved for publication by the Association's Committee on College and University Government in December 1989.

College athletics in this country is in continuing crisis. Even after several years of proposals and discussions of reform, the gains achieved are quite modest. Earlier inquiries revealed significant educational neglect in major college basketball and football programs, with shockingly low graduation rates at some institutions. Among the dismal revelations were findings that fewer than one in ten basketball players graduated at a large research university in the Midwest, and that no black basketball players graduated in a ten-year period at a southern regional state university. Graduation rates of less than 30 percent were common. Admissions standards often seemed guided solely by athletic concerns. A more recent study revealed that thirty-five of ninety-seven major basketball programs had graduation rates of 0 to 20 percent. These results occurred despite the existence of extensive tutoring efforts. In addition, the integrity of universities was repeatedly compromised when boosters and alumni—and not infrequently members of the institution's staff—improperly paid money to athletes.

Despite the attention given to intercollegiate sports reform in the media and elsewhere, ample evidence exists that the problems in college sports are persistent, substantial, and fundamental. It continues to be true in most major programs that basketball and football players are among the worst students on campus. It is not unusual to find that the median SAT scores for basketball and football players are hundreds of points below those for the general student body. Moreover, while improper payments to athletes appear to have abated from the frenzied level of a few years ago, the practice has not disappeared, as recent investigations have revealed.

It is not surprising that the crisis in intercollegiate sports continues. The fact of the matter is that the economic environment that produced academic and financial improprieties in the past has not substantially changed. The teams that win the most continue to earn the most in college sports. Adherence to rigorous admissions and academic standards is an impediment to winning, and a college that seeks to provide its athletes with a serious academic endeavor runs the risk that its competitors will not. The commercial rewards of athletic success continue to be juxtaposed to rigorous academic pursuits.

The time has come to recognize that intercollegiate athletics poses a major governance problem for American colleges and universities. Athletics is no longer merely an interesting extracurricular activity that occupies the campus on Saturday afternoon. In major programs, athletics often functions as an auxiliary enterprise that generates its own substantial revenues. On many campuses this has led to a suggestion that the intercollegiate athletic program should not be subject to the same governance structure as are more traditional educational endeavors. Moreover, policy making in athletics is greatly affected by decisions that are made far from campus. These include decisions made by the National Collegiate Athletic Association (NCAA), by competing institutions, and by the broadcasting companies that are providing the revenues that have financed the recent expansion of college sports.

Recent experience has shown that the athletic department should not be allowed to function as a separate entity. Such an arrangement ignores the important implications that athletics has for the college's educational program, including the potential for skewing the allocation of institutional resources and impeding the educational development of athletes. Despite the substantial amounts of money earned in athletics at some colleges and universities, almost none of it is used to support academic programs. Indeed, academic programs are often threatened, but seldom benefited, by changes in the fortunes of the athletic program. The impulse toward separateness of the athletic department needs to be curbed. The goal of structural reform in the governance of college sports should be more fully to integrate athletics into the educational mission of the institution.

The policy statement that follows addresses the general allocation of authority in the governance of athletics. This statement is undertaken with a realistic view of the prospects for college sports reform. It is doubtful that faculty efforts alone will be sufficient to refocus the priorities of major athletic programs. On the other hand, faculties are in a unique position to advocate adherence to meaningful academic standards. Faculties, able to speak with independence and candor, can add important balance to the discussion of reform.

The statement emphasizes the obligation of the faculty to ensure academic primacy in an institution's athletic program. An essential message is that the faculty has primary responsibility for ensuring the educational integrity of the student's academic experience. In addition, the faculty has a vital role to play in assessing the educational and budgetary implications of decisions concerning the scope of the athletic program. This statement addresses how responsibility for policy making on athletics should be allocated between the faculty and other components of the university.

GENERAL PRINCIPLES

The basic framework for defining faculty responsibility in the governance of athletics is found in an earlier statement of Association policy. The 1966 *Statement on Government of Colleges and Universities* underscores the need for joint participation in governance by the various constituencies within the university:

> The variety and complexity of the tasks performed by institutions of higher education produce an inescapable interdependence among governing board, administration, faculty, students, and others. The relationship calls for adequate communication among these components, and full opportunity for appropriate joint planning and effort.

The *Statement on Government* recognizes that the faculty has primary responsibility with respect to fundamental areas of educational policy, and that the faculty, along with other components of the institution, should participate in the exchange of information that accompanies long-range planning.

The AAUP's derivative 1972 *Statement on the Role of the Faculty in Budgetary and Salary Matters* elaborates on the faculty's participation in a university's internal budgetary process. An important premise of that statement is that budgetary matters are an appropriate faculty concern:

> The faculty should participate both in the preparation of the total institutional budget and (within the framework of the total budget) in decisions relevant to the further apportioning of its specific fiscal divisions. . . .

Both statements provide that the authority for final decision making is to be allocated among the governing board, the president, and the faculty consistent with the responsibility that each component appropriately claims within the overall governance structure. Even where primary responsibility rests with one component, the other affected parties may have a legitimate participatory role.

1. The Importance of Full Disclosure of Information About the Athletic Program

In the past, the governance of athletics has been made more difficult because administrators and others have treated information about the athletic program as highly secret. Often, information critical of admissions policies, the educational experience of athletes, and financial arrangements with coaches and booster clubs is revealed only as a result of scrutiny by outside agencies, such as the press or the NCAA. Such secretiveness is unacceptable in an intellectual environment that is committed to fostering open and candid discussion. It is also antithetical to effective governance.

For the future, the presumption must be that all aspects of the operation of the athletic department, including the education of athletes and the finances of booster clubs, are open to scrutiny by the university community. A special effort should be made to ensure the confidentiality of information where that is needed to protect the privacy of individual athletes and employees. In general, however, policies with respect to athletics should be subject to the same openness of debate that attends other financial and educational issues within the academic community.

2. *The Primacy of Faculty Responsibility for the Athlete's Educational Experience*

The faculty has primary responsibility for those aspects of an athlete's experience that involve education. Thus, it is the faculty's duty to ensure that the athlete has a full opportunity to participate in the educational process and that a proper balance is achieved between the athletic and educational experiences. Especially in the present era of intensive, highly commercialized college sports, there are often pressures within the athletic program that draw athletes away from the type of preparation, review, and class attendance that are fundamental to a meaningful education. The faculty has the primary obligation to ensure that pressures are tempered and that athletes have adequate opportunity to pursue educational goals. Review of faculty decisions in this area may be allocated to other governing components, but that review is to be exercised with appropriate regard for the primacy of the faculty's role.

3. *The Faculty's Role in Policy Making in Other Aspects of the Athletic Program*

Other issues involving athletic policy have substantial administrative components and thus come within the range of authority of other units of the university. Almost all of these, however, may have important educational implications and thus are legitimately of concern to the faculty. Among the matters warranting attention are questions such as the level of competition at which the university will participate and more specific questions concerning the length of playing seasons and policies with respect to team travel. A decision to move to a higher level of competition, for example, will often mean that athletes face increased pressures on their academic schedules. In the same vein, long playing seasons may present a significant barrier to regular class attendance. Because of their mixed educational and administrative character, such issues of athletic policy will call for joint participation by faculty, administration, and, where appropriate, other components of the university.

In addition to its particular concerns about the impact of athletics on educational programs, the faculty has a shared interest in planning for the long-range development of the university. The faculty should also play an appropriate role in decisions about the allocation of resources within the university. Policy making with respect to athletics affects both of these governance functions and thus the faculty is properly involved.

Faculty involvement is particularly important with respect to the budgetary deliberations undertaken in connection with the athletic program, even with the understanding that ultimate budgetary authority may reside in another body. The allocation of money to and within the athletic program can be a direct determinant of the level of competition that is pursued and hence greatly influences the degree of nonacademic pressure that participants experience. In addition, athletics increasingly involves major decisions on allocation of resources that should properly be viewed in the context of more general institutional needs and goals. A mechanism should exist for meaningful faculty participation in the budgetary decisions that determine the overall size and scope of the athletic program.

4. *The Institution's Relationship with Outside Regulatory Bodies*

Outside regulatory bodies, such as the NCAA and athletic conferences, play an important role in establishing policies that affect the internal functioning of a university's athletic programs. An individual institution's limited influence over such external entities requires special attention in the institution's internal governance structure. The coordination and execution of a university's participation is properly a function of the president or chancellor. On the other hand, the legislative deliberations of the outside body will frequently affect areas over which the faculty has primary internal responsibility.

Each institution should develop mechanisms that recognize the role of the chief executive officer in speaking for the institution, but which also afford an opportunity for faculty participation in the formulation of the institution's response. Consistent with the principles set forth above, responsibility in this area will typically be shared with other components of the university, with the weight given to the faculty's voice dependent on the particular issues and the degree of the faculty's responsibility in the area of concern.

THE MECHANISMS FOR FACULTY PARTICIPATION

1. Oversight of the Educational Experiences of Athletes

The importance of the faculty's role in defining and monitoring the educational experiences of athletes cannot be overstated. A candid appraisal of major intercollegiate athletic programs will reveal that the internal incentives for educational achievement are modest at best. Refinement of the athlete's physical talents requires a commitment of time and a level of attention that can easily become all-consuming. External pressures in athletic programs on coaches often lead to demands that encourage, rather than temper, the heavy emphasis on athletic preparation.

There is ample evidence of the abuses that can result. In some instances coaches have effectively made admissions decisions with respect to athletes, typically without particular regard for the institution's normal admissions standards. Another area of persistent abuse has been special programs for tutoring and counseling athletes. Too often counseling on course selection has concentrated on maintaining the athlete's eligibility rather than on providing a coherent educational program. Requests for favoritism in evaluating an athlete's course performance have been common and persistent.

The faculty must reassert its primary responsibility in monitoring the educational experiences of athletes. The candid goal of this endeavor should be to counterbalance the pressures in college sports that would subvert the athlete's educational effort. Such balance can be achieved only by removing all decision making that relates to academic matters from the commercial incentives that otherwise affect the daily functioning of the athletic department.

Several specific areas warrant faculty attention. These include admissions standards for athletes, where the goal should be to ensure that the educational talents of athletes meet the requirements of the general student body. In addition, programs for tutoring and instruction in study skills should be the same as those offered to non-athletes. Whatever attention may be given to the special needs of athletes, the goal should be to promote the athlete's fuller integration into the student body.

The faculty should also give special attention to ensuring that the athlete's individual curriculum has coherency and reflects normal progress through a recognized degree program. The temptation to elevate maintenance of the athlete's eligibility over substantive academic achievement should specifically be resisted. Because of the uncertainty and changes that can attend any student's movement through the university, ensuring that there is substance to the athlete's educational program will be a particular challenge. However, the goal of the faculty's endeavor in this area is clear: to temper the effects of athletic participation on the student's educational choices.

The mechanisms for faculty monitoring are already in place in many institutions. These take the form of committees and offices that set general academic policy and provide oversight. The issues raised are often of importance to the administration, and it is appropriate that the faculty's primary responsibility in this area be carried out through a structure that utilizes existing administrative entities and involves appropriate administrative participation. As with every other faculty function, the goal of the governing entities in this area is to ensure that relevant information is adequate and that participation is sought from all affected parties.

Coordination of the faculty's role in these endeavors can appropriately be the responsibility of the representative faculty senate or assembly. To the extent that there is a need for a distinctive faculty voice on such educational issues, the faculty senate or assembly is the appropriate body to provide it.

In some situations the faculty will find it necessary to use carefully structured ad hoc inquiries to fulfill its monitoring function. Periodic audits of the athletes' educational experiences will often be appropriate.

2. Institutional Policy Making on Athletics

An internal forum should be available in which the various components of the university, including the faculty, jointly deliberate over the formulation of athletic policy. A university-level athletic committee with representation from those with applicable governance authority would be appropriate. Because of the high degree of faculty responsibility for many of the issues presented, the faculty representation on such a body should be substantial.

An issue of particular importance is the method for selecting the faculty participants. The selection should be undertaken with a view to ensuring the independence of the faculty voice, and thus direct election by the general faculty or its elected governing body is preferable. Such direct election will also serve to define lines of responsibility within the faculty.

The faculty's involvement in the joint policy-making body should be undertaken in furtherance of a governance role that includes heightened responsibility for many of the matters under consideration. Thus, the function of the body is to be more than advisory.

A broad range of matters would be expected to come before such a body. The degree of finality to be accorded to such joint deliberations will be determined by the allocation of responsibility among the various governing components. Because of the mixed nature of many athletics issues, however, the joint deliberative body will often be the most appropriate device for resolving matters that overlap the primary responsibilities of the participating entities. In these instances its deliberations should carry a presumption of finality.

3. Policy Making by Outside Bodies

Because of the significant internal effects of rule making by external associations, a university should take steps to ensure that its voice is heard in whatever deliberations accompany the external decision making. Once the institution has formulated its position on important issues, the president or chancellor or other designated representative should be able to present the institution's position as a unified one.

A structure should be established to allow participation by internal components, including faculty, so that the institution's position is carefully and thoroughly developed before it is advocated to the external body. As with internal governance, the degree of faculty responsibility will vary depending on the nature of the policy in question. The faculty's responsibility, and hence its interest, will be highest with respect to those regulations that have the most significant implications for the educational experiences of athletes. The faculty perspective is also important for issues that have major budgetary implications and those that define the level of importance assigned to athletics within the institution. The same university-level committee that decides internal athletic policy may prove to be the appropriate vehicle for faculty participation. On matters of significant educational importance, full deliberation by the elected faculty senate or assembly may be necessary.

In external organizations that invite the participation of a faculty representative, the person so designated should enjoy the support of the faculty. The importance of the university's speaking with unity suggests that the representative must also have the support of the administration. The goal of mutual acceptance is satisfied by a selection technique that provides for the designation of the faculty representative by the chief administrative officer with the advice and consent of the faculty as expressed through its faculty senate or other representative body.

CONCLUSION

The faculty authority to establish and maintain general academic standards entails faculty responsibility to ensure specific application of these standards in the education of student athletes.

The faculty is responsible for reviewing academic programs for student athletes. The faculty must ensure the primacy of academic concerns in athletics as well as in other student programs. Protection of academic integrity against misplaced internal priorities or external demands in athletic programs, as in other matters, is the essential reason for the faculty's role in institutional governance.

The specific procedural concerns delineated in the body of this report require application and elaboration appropriate to circumstances. The overriding principle, however, is that responsibility for the academic welfare of student athletes is not an extracurricular or departmental obligation of a few faculty members and administrators; it is a fundamental responsibility of the faculty as a whole.

COLLECTIVE BARGAINING

Although collective bargaining in higher education was discussed by the president of the Association in his address to the annual meeting in 1919, the issue was not faced directly by the AAUP until the 1960s, when the policy-making committees of the Association began developing statements of principles on the subject. Since collective negotiations by faculty members constituted a form of governance, the Committee on College and University Government or special subcommittees were usually involved in addressing the issues raised by collective bargaining. In 1970, the Committee on Representation of Economic and Professional Interests was established by the Association's Council. In 1973, the annual meeting adopted the AAUP's first Statement on Collective Bargaining, which recognized formal bargaining as a "major additional way of realizing [the Association's] goals in higher education." Revisions to the statement were adopted in 1984. Ten years later, in 1994, the Committee on Representation of Economic and Professional Interests approved further revisions, affirming that "faculties at public and private institutions are entitled, as professionals, to choose . . . to engage in collective bargaining to ensure effective faculty governance." The revised statement was adopted by the Council in June 1994 and endorsed by the Eightieth Annual Meeting.

The Association's collective bargaining chapters have utilized formal negotiation and enforcement of contractual agreements to advance professional standards and to bring legally binding protections to the rights and prerogatives of faculty members, as collective bodies and as individuals. Committees of the Association have periodically developed policy statements to guide implementation of Association standards in collective bargaining settings. In this regard, the Statement on Academic Government for Institutions Engaged in Collective Bargaining was approved by the Committee on Representation of Economic and Professional Interests and the Committee on College and University Government and adopted by the Council in 1988. The report on Arbitration of Faculty Grievances was approved by the Committee on Academic Freedom and Tenure (Committee A) and the Committee on Representation of Economic and Professional Interests in 1973. The statement on Dismissal Proceedings in a Collective Bargaining Setting Where Arbitration Substitutes for a Faculty Hearing was approved by the same two committees and adopted by the Council in 1991.

Statement on Collective Bargaining

The statement which follows, a further revision of a statement initially adopted in 1973 and revised in 1984, was approved by the Association's Committee on Representation of Economic and Professional Interests, adopted by the Association's Council in November 1993, and endorsed by the Eightieth Annual Meeting.

The basic purposes of the American Association of University Professors are to protect academic freedom, to establish and strengthen institutions of faculty governance, to provide fair procedures for resolving grievances, to promote the economic well-being of faculty and other academic professionals, and to advance the interests of higher education. Collective bargaining is an effective instrument for achieving these objectives.

The presence of institutions of faculty governance does not preclude the need for or usefulness of collective bargaining. On the contrary, collective bargaining can be used to increase the effectiveness of those institutions by extending their areas of competence, defining their authority, and strengthening their voice in areas of shared authority and responsibility. The Association therefore affirms that faculties at both public and private institutions are entitled, as professionals, to choose by an election or comparable informal means to engage in collective bargaining in order to ensure effective faculty governance. Trustees and administrators are of course free publicly to question the desirability of collective bargaining, but they should not resort to litigation or other means having the purpose or effect of restraining or coercing the faculty in its choice of collective bargaining. Where a faculty chooses collective bargaining, the trustees and administration have a corresponding obligation to bargain in good faith with the faculty-selected representative and should not resort to litigation or any other means intended to avoid this obligation.

As a national organization which has historically played a major role in formulating and implementing the principles that govern relationships in academic life, the Association promotes collective bargaining to reinforce the best features of higher education. The principles of academic freedom and tenure, fair procedures, faculty participation in governance, and the primary responsibility of the faculty for determining academic policy will thereby be secured. Moreover, collective bargaining gives the faculty an effective voice in decisions which vitally affect its members' professional well-being, such as the allocation of financial resources and determination of faculty salaries and benefits. For these reasons, the Association supports efforts of local chapters to pursue collective bargaining.

POLICY FOR COLLECTIVE BARGAINING CHAPTERS

1. When a chapter of the Association enters into collective bargaining, it should seek to
   (a) protect and promote the professional and economic interests of the faculty as a whole in accordance with the established principles of the Association;
   (b) maintain and enhance within the institution structures of representative governance which provide full participation by the faculty in accordance with the established principles of the Association;
   (c) obtain explicit guarantees of academic freedom and tenure in accordance with the principles and stated policies of the Association; and
   (d) create orderly and clearly defined procedures for prompt consideration of problems and grievances of members of the bargaining unit, to which procedures any affected individual or group shall have access.
2. In any agency shop or compulsory dues check-off arrangement, a chapter or other Association agency should incorporate provisions designed to accommodate affirmatively asserted conscientious objection to such an arrangement with any representative.
3. The principle of shared authority and responsibility requires a process of discussion, persuasion, and accommodation within a climate of mutual concern and trust. Where that

process and climate exist, there should be no need for any party to resort to devices of economic pressure such as strikes, lockouts, or unilateral changes in terms and conditions of employment by faculty or academic management. Normally, such measures are not desirable for the resolution of conflicts within institutions of higher education.

Therefore, the Association urges faculties and administrations in collective bargaining to seek mutual agreement on methods of dispute resolution, such as mediation, fact-finding, or arbitration. Where such agreement cannot be reached, and where disputes prove themselves resistant to rational methods of discussion, persuasion, and conciliation, the Association recognizes that resort to economic pressure through strikes or other work actions may be a necessary and unavoidable means of dispute resolution.

Participation in a strike or other work action does not by itself constitute grounds for dismissal or for other sanctions against faculty members. Permanent replacement of striking or locked-out faculty members is equivalent to dismissal solely for participation in a strike or other job action. Moreover, if action against a faculty member is proposed on the basis of participation in a strike, as on any ground encompassed by the 1940 *Statement of Principles on Academic Freedom and Tenure*, the proceedings must satisfy the requirements of academic due process supported by the Association. The Association will continue to protect the interests of members of the profession who are singled out for punishment on grounds that are inadequate or unacceptable, or who are not afforded all the protections demanded by the requisites of academic due process.

Statement on Academic Government for Institutions Engaged in Collective Bargaining

The statement which follows was approved by the Association's Committee on Representation of Economic and Professional Interests and the Committee on College and University Government in 1988 and adopted by the Association's Council in June of that year.

The Association's 1966 *Statement on Government of Colleges and Universities* affirms that effective governance of an academic institution requires joint effort based on the community of interest of all parties to the enterprise. In particular, the statement observes that:

> The variety and complexity of the tasks performed by institutions of higher education produce an inescapable interdependence among governing board, administration, faculty, students, and others. The relationship calls for adequate communication among these components and full opportunity for appropriate joint planning and effort.
>
> Joint effort in an academic institution will take a variety of forms appropriate to the kinds of situations encountered.

The various parties engaged in the governance of a college or university bring to higher education differing perspectives based on their differing but complementary roles in the academic effort. Traditional shared governance integrates those differing roles into productive action that will benefit the college or university as a whole. It is in the best interest of all parties to ensure that the institutions of shared governance function as smoothly and effectively as possible. Collective bargaining is one means to that end. As the Association's *Statement on Collective Bargaining* asserts, "collective bargaining can be used to increase the effectiveness of [institutions of faculty governance] by extending their areas of competence, defining their authority, and strengthening their voice in areas of shared authority and responsibility."

Collective bargaining should not replace, but rather should ensure, effective traditional forms of shared governance. The types of governance mechanisms appropriate to a particular college or university are dictated by that institution's needs, traditions, and mission. Since those basic factors are not necessarily affected by the emergence of collective bargaining at a campus, bargaining does not necessarily entail substantive changes in the structure of shared governance appropriate for that institution.

Collective bargaining on a campus usually arises at least in part in response to agencies or forces beyond the scope of institutional governance. When problems in institutional governance do contribute to the emergence of collective bargaining, these problems generally stem less from inadequacy in the structure for shared governance than from a failure in its proper implementation. Bargaining can contribute substantially to the identification, clarification, and correction of such difficulties.

Collective bargaining contributes to problem solving in three primary ways. Formal negotiation can improve communication between the faculty and the administration or governing board. Such communication is essential if the joint planning and effort urged by the *Statement on Government* is to be productive. Collective bargaining can secure consensus on institutional policies and procedures that delineate faculty and administrative participation in shared governance. Finally, collective bargaining can ensure equitable implementation of established procedures.

Collective bargaining should ensure institutional policies and procedures that provide access for all faculty to participation in shared governance. Employed in this way, collective bargaining complements and supports structures of shared governance consistent with the

Statement on Government. From a faculty perspective, collective bargaining can strengthen shared governance by specifying and ensuring the faculty role in institutional decision making. Specification may occur through bargaining of governance clauses that define faculty responsibilities in greater detail; assurance of the faculty's negotiated rights may be provided through a grievance procedure supporting the provisions of the negotiated contract. From an administration perspective, contractual clarification and arbitral review of shared governance can reduce the conflicts occasioned by ill-defined or contested allocation of responsibility and thereby enhance consensus and cooperation in academic governance.

The sharing of authority in the governance of colleges and universities, as the *Statement on Government* asserts, is sound practice for academic institutions to follow. Any process for refining and enforcing proper practice should be viewed by all parties concerned with the welfare of higher education as a welcome addition to academic problem solving. Collective bargaining can be such a process. To be effective, bargaining must allow the parties to confront all aspects of their common problems, without encountering externally imposed barriers to possible solutions. Each party must be free to address matters of legitimate concern, and bargaining should provide an inclusive framework within which the parties will be encouraged to move toward resolution of their differences. For this reason, the scope of bargaining should not be limited in ways that prevent mutual employment of the bargaining process for the clarification, improvement, and assurance of a sound structure of shared governance.

Thus, effective collective bargaining can serve to benefit the institution as a whole as well as its various constituencies. Faculty, administrations, governing boards, and state and federal agencies should cooperate to see that collective bargaining is conducted in good faith. When legislatures, judicial authorities, boards, administrations, or faculty act on the mistaken assumption that collective bargaining is incompatible with collegial governance, they do a grave disservice to the very institutions they seek to serve. The cooperative interaction between faculty and administration that is set forth as a workable ideal in the *Statement on Government* depends on a strong institutional commitment to shared governance. By providing a contractually enforceable foundation to an institution's collegial governance structure, collective bargaining can ensure the effectiveness of that structure and can thereby contribute significantly to the well-being of the institution.

Arbitration of Faculty Grievances

The report which follows, prepared by a joint subcommittee of the Association's Committee on Representation of Economic and Professional Interests and the Committee on Academic Freedom and Tenure (Committee A), was approved by the respective committees in March and April 1973.

INTRODUCTION

Collective bargaining by faculties in higher education has been accompanied by the use of arbitration[1] for the resolution of disputes involving questions of contractual application or interpretation which may include matters of faculty status and rights. It should be noted that the use of arbitration does not wholly depend on the existence of a collective bargaining relationship. It may be provided for in institutional regulations, agreed to between an internal faculty governing body and the administration, or utilized on an ad hoc basis in a particular case. The enforceability of agreements to arbitrate future disputes, however, is a legal question involving both federal and state law. Since arbitration developed in the industrial context, it must be given the closest scrutiny when applied to the needs of higher education. Accordingly, this joint subcommittee was given the task of providing an initial review of that application.

PRELIMINARY CONSIDERATIONS

The Association has been committed, since its founding in 1915, to securing a meaningful role for the faculty in decisions on matters of faculty status, rights, and responsibilities. The Association's *Statement on Government of Colleges and Universities* provides a brief discussion of the bases for this position:

> The primary responsibility of the faculty for such matters is based upon the fact that its judgment is central to general educational policy. Furthermore, scholars in a particular field or activity have the chief competence for judging the work of their colleagues; in such competence it is implicit that responsibility exists for both adverse and favorable judgments. Likewise, there is the more general competence of experienced faculty personnel committees having a broader charge. Determinations in these matters should first be by faculty action through established procedures, reviewed by the chief academic officers with the concurrence of the board. The governing board and the president should, on questions of faculty status, as in other matters where the faculty has primary responsibility, concur with the faculty judgment except in rare instances and for compelling reasons which should be stated in detail.

The *Statement* does not suggest a formal device to resolve disputes between faculty and governing board. Indeed, resort to any body outside the institution, such as the courts, for an official resolution of disputes in matters of faculty status, rights, and responsibilities poses a serious challenge to accepted notions of institutional autonomy. Moreover, a survey of current practices, admittedly limited, reveals that arbitration has been used not solely to break impasses between faculty and governing board but to review the soundness of faculty decisions themselves. This suggests an additional problem of the relationship of arbitration to faculty autonomy.

---

[1] Arbitration is a term describing a system for the resolution of disputes whereby the parties consent to submit a controversy to a third party for decision. The decision may be advisory only but is usually agreed to be binding. The parties participate in the selection of the arbitrator and may shape the procedure to be used; costs are usually borne equally between them.

THE USE OF ARBITRATION

In many situations, administrators are responsive to faculty recommendations and indeed may welcome them. In such cases the resort to arbitration will probably not be perceived as necessary. In some situations, however, administrators or trustees are unresponsive to Association standards and faculty actions, and final legal authority to resolve matters of faculty status usually lies with the governing board concerned. In such cases, outside impartial review may well be useful. It must also be recognized that in many situations faculty members do not enjoy or exercise a degree of independence adequate to the assurance of protections embodied in Association standards. In these situations also, independent impartial review may play a role. For example, disputes regarding the appropriateness of individual salaries, or the imposition of penalties for alleged violations of institutional regulations, or the termination of academic appointments for reason of financial exigency, or decisions affecting a faculty member's teaching duties or programs of instruction are the sorts of controversies resolution of which may be fostered in varying degrees by arbitration.

It seems clear that, where resort to a formal external agency is deemed necessary, arbitration affords some advantages over judicial proceedings. In a court challenge, the procedure and substance are prescribed by federal and state constitutions, statutes, and judicial decisions in whose formulation the profession has almost no role. In contrast, arbitration procedures and substantive rights are largely within the joint power of the administration and the faculty's collective representative to prescribe. Hence the parties to the academic relationship can shape procedures to their special needs, formulate substantive rules embodying the standards of the profession, and select decision makers with special competence in the field. In addition, arbitration may prove a quicker and less expensive remedy.

Thus, where the faculty does not share in the making of decisions or its voice is not accorded adequate weight, arbitration may have particular utility. However, the finality of arbitral review also has its hazards, especially in the present nascent state of arbitral doctrine, and because of the slight experience of arbitrators in academic settings. Accordingly, arbitration may play a useful role in an academic setting to the extent it can foster rather than impair the sound workings of institutional government.

It is suggested that four factors are essential for the effective use of arbitration: (1) sound internal procedures preliminary to arbitration which enjoy the confidence of both faculty and administration; (2) careful definitions of both arbitral subjects and standards to be applied by the arbitrator; (3) the selection of arbitrators knowledgeable in the ways of the academic world, aware of the institutional implications of their decisions, and, of course, sensitive to the meaning and critical value of academic freedom; and (4) the assurance that the hearing will include evidence relating to the standards and expectations of the teaching profession in higher education and that appropriate weight will be given to such evidence.

1. Preliminary Procedures

Arbitration should be used most discriminatingly. It is not a substitute for proper procedures internal to the institution but should serve only as a final stage of that procedure. The availability of this forum should assist in rendering the earlier procedures more meaningful. Indeed, the submission of an inordinate number of grievances to arbitration may be significantly erosive of healthy faculty-administration relations.

The Association has suggested preliminary procedures for the adjustment of general faculty complaints and grievances.[2] With more detail, the Association has crystallized procedures to be utilized in dismissal proceedings,[3] proposed procedures to be used in hearing allegations of violations of academic freedom or discrimination in the nonreappointment of nontenured faculty,[4]

---

[2] Regulation 15, "Recommended Institutional Regulations on Academic Freedom and Tenure," AAUP, *Policy Documents and Reports*, 9th ed. (Washington, D.C., 2001), 29.
[3] "1958 Statement on Procedural Standards in Faculty Dismissal Proceedings," *ibid.*, 11–14.
[4] Regulation 10, "Recommended Institutional Regulations," *ibid.*, 28.

and adopted detailed provisions dealing with decisions on nonreappointment and review therefrom not raising issues of academic freedom or discrimination.[5]

The subcommittee recognizes that a wide variety of institutional practice exists in American higher education, and that the degree to which faculties actually possess the decision-making authority recommended in the foregoing varies accordingly. It may not be possible, then, to propose a single model of arbitration responsive to these varying institutional patterns and the many kinds of issues which could conceivably be presented for an arbitral determination. The subcommittee believes it to be of critical importance, however, that, in the agreement to arbitrate any matter affecting faculty status, rights, and responsibilities, the judgment of the faculty, as the professional body properly vested with the primary responsibility for such determinations, be accorded a strong presumption in its favor.

2. Arbitral Standards

The definition of the arbitral standards requires the most careful attention. In some instances arbitration has been used to correct only procedural departures, while in others arbitral review of the merits of a decision has been afforded. The latter has proceeded under broad standards such as "just cause" for a particular action or more rigorous ones such as determining whether the questioned decision was "arbitrary and capricious."

A tentative review of arbitral decisions under the varying approaches has revealed widely differing results and in some cases a degree of arbitral unresponsiveness to the underlying academic values. Accordingly, the subcommittee believes it to be requisite to the use of arbitration as a means of enhancing internal governance that fairly rigorous arbitral standards be established in those cases in which norms and procedures unique to higher education are implicated.

3. Selection and Education of Arbitrators

Much depends on the qualities of the individual selected to serve as the arbitrator and the degree to which he or she is educated by the parties to the issues for adjudication in the context of professional practice and custom and to the importance of the decision to the life of the institution. Here the Association can make a valuable contribution, whether or not a local affiliate is serving as a collective representative. As the preeminent organization of college and university faculty in the United States, the Association should share its expertise in reviewing the qualifications of proposed arbitrators and should consider, jointly with other organizations, consulting on the establishment of a national panel or regional panels of qualified individuals. Further, the Association may prepare model briefs or other materials dealing with accepted norms of academic practice to be used as educational materials before an arbitrator and should consider sponsoring, again possibly with other organizations, workshops for arbitrators on these issues. The Association should also maintain an up-to-date file of awards and provide detailed comments on their academic implications, perhaps in some published form. Since the use of arbitration in this setting is so novel, it is clear that for higher education, unlike for the industrial sector, no well-defined set of doctrines has been developed. It is incumbent on the Association to assist directly in shaping such doctrines through all available means. Toward this end the Association should establish a joint subcommittee of the national committees having an interest in this area. A detailed study of the actual effects of arbitration under the varying approaches currently practiced and the drafting of model arbitration clauses would fall within the purview of such a body.

Two final issues require attention: the rights of the individual under a collective agreement providing for arbitration as the terminal stage of the grievance procedure; and the Association's role in the event an arbitral award departs significantly from fundamental substantive standards sponsored by it.

---

[5] "Statement on Procedural Standards in the Renewal or Nonrenewal of Faculty Appointments," *Policy Documents and Reports,* 15–20.

Where there is an exclusive collective representative, the agent almost invariably controls access to arbitration. The subcommittee believes that this approach may be inappropriate in an academic setting and recommends that individual faculty members have access to arbitration on their own behalf if the collective representative refuses to press their claims. Because the issue placed before an arbitrator may touch deeply an individual's basic academic rights or freedoms, the individual should have the opportunity of participating in the selection of the arbitrator and have full rights to participate in all phases of the procedure, including all preliminaries, on a parity with the collective representative, if any, and the administration. Experimentation with the allocation of costs of proceedings where the representative does not itself desire to proceed to arbitration would be useful. Costs may be assessed by the arbitrator between the parties according to the gravity of the injury, if one is found, or could be borne equally by the administration and the complaining faculty member.

The Association has traditionally viewed itself as supporting basic standards and has not viewed its processes as being limited because of contrary provisions in an institution's regulations, or, for that matter, an adverse judicial determination. Equally, the Association should continue to challenge significant departures from elemental academic rights, whether or not these departures have warrant in a collective agreement or an arbitrator's award.

SUMMARY

Arbitration can be a useful device for resolving some kinds of disputes and grievances that arise in academic life. Especially when collective bargaining is practiced, resort to arbitrators who are sensitive to the needs and standards of higher education may be the preferred way to avoid deadlocks or administrative domination. But arbitration is not a substitute for careful procedures that respect the autonomy of the faculty and the administration in their respective spheres. A system of collective bargaining that routinely resorts to arbitration is an abdication of responsibility. This is especially true of the faculty's primary responsibility to determine who shall hold and retain faculty appointments.

Dismissal Proceedings in a Collective Bargaining Setting Where Arbitration Substitutes for a Faculty Hearing

The statement which follows was approved for publication by the Association's Committee on Academic Freedom and Tenure (Committee A) and the Committee on Representation of Economic and Professional Interests, and adopted by the Association's Council in June 1991.

In 1973, the Committee on Academic Freedom and Tenure and the Committee on Representation of Economic and Professional Interests approved the publication of a report on *Arbitration of Faculty Grievances*.[1] The committees viewed that report as a first statement on the relationship of arbitration of faculty grievances to established Association policies. A second report, *Arbitration in Cases of Dismissal*, approved for publication by the Council in June 1983, was prepared in response to the increased acceptance of arbitration as a means of resolving disputes in higher education in the intervening ten years.[2]

The 1983 report emphasized the importance "of the faculty as a professional body passing judgment upon its members." The exercise of such judgment forms an essential aspect of the "traditional shared governance" affirmed in the Association's 1988 *Statement on Academic Government for Institutions Engaged in Collective Bargaining*. The responsibility of exercising collective faculty judgment is most importantly present in the goal of faculty participation in proceedings to dismiss faculty members, a goal stressed in the 1940 *Statement of Principles on Academic Freedom and Tenure*.

The Association recognizes, however, that circumstances may arise in which such participation is not feasible. Where circumstances dictate that arbitration substitute for faculty judgment on issues of faculty dismissal, certain key requirements must be met before the procedures can reasonably be regarded as compatible with basic standards of academic freedom and tenure.

These requirements are:

1. Preliminary Procedures

Designated representatives of the faculty should inquire into the situation informally, may attempt mediation, and, if a mutually acceptable adjustment cannot be effected, may advise the administration on whether formal proceedings should be instituted.

The faculty member should not be placed on suspension during the preliminary proceedings or any ensuing formal proceedings unless immediate harm to the faculty member or others is threatened by the faculty member's continuance. Any such suspension should be with pay.

2. Formal Proceedings

Formal proceedings may begin only after the administration has formulated a statement of charges against the faculty member, framed with reasonable particularity.

The process for selecting an arbitrator should ensure the appointment of someone familiar with the standards and practices of the academic community, versed in the meaning of academic freedom, and appreciative of its central value. Tripartite arbitration, in which the arbitrator

---

[1] *AAUP Bulletin* 59 (1973): 168–70.
[2] **AAUP,** *Policy Documents and Reports*, 9th ed. (Washington, D.C., 2001), 92–95.

serves as one member of a hearing panel together with a member of the faculty and a member of the academic administration, may enhance attentiveness to appropriate academic standards.

The arbitration hearing should encourage the inclusion of faculty testimony on disputed matters relating to academic performance and on whether the stated cause, if demonstrated, warrants the penalty of dismissal. The burden of demonstrating adequacy of cause should rest with the administration.

In those dismissal cases where arbitration is the only available forum for a formal proceeding and where the collective bargaining representative decides against going to arbitration, the faculty member should be permitted to proceed to arbitration independently, bearing those costs that the collective bargaining representative would normally assume. The faculty member should have the opportunity to select counsel of his or her choice, at the faculty member's expense.

The proceedings should provide procedural due process as called for in Regulation 5 of the Association's *Recommended Institutional Regulations on Academic Freedom and Tenure,* including the keeping of a verbatim record of the hearing to be made available to the concerned parties and a requirement that the arbitrator's decision be accompanied by a written explanation.

The faculty member's dismissal should not become effective unless and until the arbitrator hands down a decision calling for dismissal.

Whether dismissal proceedings are conducted through a process of faculty hearing or arbitration, cause for dismissal should be decided on the basis of the faculty member's entire record and be related, directly and substantially, to the faculty member's professional fitness as a teacher or researcher; and dismissal after two years of service should, in all cases not involving moral turpitude, be with the affordance of at least one year of terminal notice or severance pay.

STUDENT RIGHTS AND FREEDOMS

Joint Statement on Rights and Freedoms of Students

In June 1967, a committee composed of representatives from the American Association of University Professors, the United States National Student Association (now the United States Student Association), the Association of American Colleges (now the Association of American Colleges and Universities), the National Association of Student Personnel Administrators, and the National Association of Women Deans and Counselors (now the National Association for Women in Education) formulated the Joint Statement. *The document was endorsed by each of its five national sponsors, as well as by a number of other professional bodies. The governing bodies of the Association of American Colleges and the American Association of University Professors acted respectively in January and April 1990 to remove gender-specific references from the original text.*

In September 1990, September 1991, and November 1992, an interassociation task force met to study, interpret, update, and affirm (or reaffirm) the Joint Statement. *Members of the task force agreed that the document has stood the test of time quite well and continues to provide an excellent set of principles for institutions of higher education. The task force developed a set of interpretive notes to incorporate changes in law and higher education that have occurred since 1967. These interpretive notes are referenced within the original text. A list of associations endorsing the annotations appears as an appendix.*

PREAMBLE

Academic institutions exist for the transmission of knowledge, the pursuit of truth, the development of students, and the general well-being of society. Free inquiry and free expression are indispensable to the attainment of these goals. As members of the academic community, students should be encouraged to develop the capacity for critical judgment and to engage in a sustained and independent search for truth. Institutional procedures for achieving these purposes may vary from campus to campus, but the minimal standards of academic freedom of students outlined below are essential to any community of scholars.

Freedom to teach and freedom to learn are inseparable facets of academic freedom. The freedom to learn depends upon appropriate opportunities and conditions in the classroom, on the campus, and in the larger community.[1] Students should exercise their freedom with responsibility.

The responsibility to secure and to respect general conditions conducive to the freedom to learn is shared by all members of the academic community. Each college and university has a duty to develop policies and procedures which provide and safeguard this freedom. Such policies and procedures should be developed at each institution within the framework of general

---

[1] In order to protect the freedom of students to learn, as well as enhance their participation in the life of the academic community, students should be free from exploitation or harassment.

standards and with the broadest possible participation of the members of the academic community. The purpose of this statement is to enumerate the essential provisions for students' freedom to learn.

FREEDOM OF ACCESS TO HIGHER EDUCATION

The admissions policies of each college and university are a matter of institutional choice, provided that each college and university makes clear the characteristics and expectations of students which it considers relevant to success in the institution's program.[2] While church-related institutions may give admission preference to students of their own persuasion, such a preference should be clearly and publicly stated. Under no circumstances should a student be barred from admission to a particular institution on the basis of race.[3] Thus, within the limits of its facilities, each college and university should be open to all students who are qualified according to its admissions standards. The facilities and services of a college or university should be open to all of its enrolled students, and institutions should use their influence to secure equal access for all students to public facilities in the local community.

IN THE CLASSROOM

The professor in the classroom and in conference should encourage free discussion, inquiry, and expression. Student performance should be evaluated solely on an academic basis, not on opinions or conduct in matters unrelated to academic standards.

1. Protection of Freedom of Expression

Students should be free to take reasoned exception to the data or views offered in any course of study and to reserve judgment about matters of opinion, but they are responsible for learning the content of any course of study for which they are enrolled.

2. Protection Against Improper Academic Evaluation

Students should have protection through orderly procedures against prejudiced or capricious academic evaluation.[4] At the same time, they are responsible for maintaining standards of academic performance established for each course in which they are enrolled.

3. Protection Against Improper Disclosure

Information about student views, beliefs, and political associations which professors acquire in the course of their work as instructors, advisers, and counselors should be considered confidential. Protection against improper disclosure is a serious professional obligation. Judgments of ability and character may be provided under appropriate circumstances, normally with the knowledge and consent of the student.

---

[2] In order to enable them to make appropriate choices and participate effectively in an institution's programs, students have the right to be informed about the institution, its policies, practices, and characteristics. Institutions preparing such information should take into account applicable federal and state laws.

[3] The reference to race must not be taken to limit the nondiscrimination obligations of institutions. In all aspects of education, students have a right to be free from discrimination on the basis of individual attributes not demonstrably related to academic success in the institution's programs, including, but not limited to, race, color, gender, age, disability, national origin, and sexual orientation. Under *Regents of the University of California v. Bakke*, 438 U.S. 265 (1978), when colleges and universities determine that achieving diversity within the student body is relevant to their academic mission, their admissions offices may consider, among several stated criteria, individual attributes that otherwise would be prohibited.

[4] The student grievance procedures typically used in these matters are not appropriate for addressing charges of academic dishonesty or other disciplinary matters arising in the classroom. In these instances, students should be afforded the safeguards of orderly procedures consistent with those set forth in "Procedural Standards in Disciplinary Proceedings," below. (In 1997, AAUP's Committee A on Academic Freedom and Tenure approved a statement on "The Assignment of Course Grades and Student Appeals," AAUP, *Policy Documents and Reports*, 9th ed. [Washington, D.C., 2001], 113–14.)

STUDENT RECORDS

Institutions should have carefully considered policy as to the information which should be part of a student's permanent educational record and as to the conditions of its disclosure. To minimize the risk of improper disclosure, academic and disciplinary records should be separate, and the conditions of access to each should be set forth in an explicit policy statement. Transcripts of academic records should contain only information about academic status. Information from disciplinary or counseling files should not be available to unauthorized persons on campus, or to any person off campus without the express consent of the student involved, except under legal compulsion or in cases where the safety of persons or property is involved. No records should be kept which reflect the political activities or beliefs of students. Provision should also be made for periodic routine destruction of noncurrent disciplinary records. Administrative staff and faculty members should respect confidential information about students which they acquire in the course of their work.[5]

STUDENT AFFAIRS

In student affairs, certain standards must be maintained if the freedom of students is to be preserved.[6]

1. Freedom of Association

Students bring to the campus a variety of interests previously acquired and develop many new interests as members of the academic community. They should be free to organize and join associations to promote their common interests.
   (a) The membership, policies, and actions of a student organization usually will be determined by vote of only those persons who hold bona fide membership in the college or university community.
   (b) Affiliation with an extramural organization should not of itself disqualify a student organization from institutional recognition.[7]
   (c) If campus advisers are required, each organization should be free to choose its own adviser, and institutional recognition should not be withheld or withdrawn solely because of the inability of a student organization to secure an adviser. Campus advisers may advise organizations in the exercise of responsibility, but they should not have the authority to control the policy of such organizations.
   (d) Student organizations may be required to submit a statement of purpose, criteria for membership, rules of procedure, and a current list of officers. They should not be required to submit a membership list as a condition of institutional recognition.
   (e) Campus organizations, including those affiliated with an extramural organization, should be open to all students without respect to race, creed, or national origin, except for religious qualifications which may be required by organizations whose aims are primarily sectarian.[8]

2. Freedom of Inquiry and Expression
   (a) Students and student organizations should be free to examine and discuss all questions of interest to them and to express opinions publicly and privately. They should always be free

---

[5] The Family Educational Rights and Privacy Act (FERPA) provides for the protection of student records. Consistent with FERPA, institutions should have a statement of policy on the content of a student's educational record as well as the conditions for its disclosure. Institutions should also have policies and security practices to control access to student records that may be available or transmitted electronically.
[6] As in the case of classroom matters, students shall have protection through orderly procedures to ensure this freedom.
[7] "Institutional recognition" should be understood to refer to any formal relationship between the student organization and the institution.
[8] The obligation of institutions with respect to nondiscrimination, with the exception noted above for religious qualifications, should be understood in accordance with the expanded statement on nondiscrimination in n. 3, above. Exceptions may also be based on gender as authorized by law.

to support causes by orderly means which do not disrupt the regular and essential operations of the institution. At the same time, it should be made clear to the academic and larger community that in their public expressions or demonstrations students or student organizations speak only for themselves.

(b) Students should be allowed to invite and to hear any person of their own choosing. Those routine procedures required by an institution before a guest speaker is invited to appear on campus should be designed only to ensure that there is orderly scheduling of facilities and adequate preparation for the event, and that the occasion is conducted in a manner appropriate to an academic community. The institutional control of campus facilities should not be used as a device of censorship. It should be made clear to the academic and larger community that sponsorship of guest speakers does not necessarily imply approval or endorsement of the views expressed, either by the sponsoring group or by the institution.[9]

3. *Student Participation in Institutional Government*

As constituents of the academic community, students should be free, individually and collectively, to express their views on issues of institutional policy and on matters of general interest to the student body. The student body should have clearly defined means to participate in the formulation and application of institutional policy affecting academic and student affairs.[10] The role of student government and both its general and specific responsibilities should be made explicit, and the actions of student government within the areas of its jurisdiction should be reviewed only through orderly and prescribed procedures.

4. *Student Publications*

Student publications and the student press are valuable aids in establishing and maintaining an atmosphere of free and responsible discussion and of intellectual exploration on the campus. They are a means of bringing student concerns to the attention of the faculty and the institutional authorities and of formulating student opinion on various issues on the campus and in the world at large.

Whenever possible the student newspaper should be an independent corporation financially and legally separate from the college or university. Where financial and legal autonomy is not possible, the institution, as the publisher of student publications, may have to bear the legal responsibility for the contents of the publications. In the delegation of editorial responsibility to students, the institution must provide sufficient editorial freedom and financial autonomy for the student publications to maintain their integrity of purpose as vehicles for free inquiry and free expression in an academic community.

Institutional authorities, in consultation with students and faculty, have a responsibility to provide written clarification of the role of the student publications, the standards to be used in their evaluation, and the limitations on external control of their operation. At the same time, the editorial freedom of student editors and managers entails corollary responsibilities to be governed by the canons of responsible journalism, such as the avoidance of libel, indecency, undocumented allegations, attacks on personal integrity, and the techniques of harassment and innuendo. As safeguards for the editorial freedom of student publications the following provisions are necessary:

(a) The student press should be free of censorship and advance approval of copy, and its editors and managers should be free to develop their own editorial policies and news coverage.

(b) Editors and managers of student publications should be protected from arbitrary suspension and removal because of student, faculty, administration, or public disapproval

---

[9] The events referred to in this section should be understood to include the full range of student-sponsored activities, such as films, exhibitions, and performances.

[10] "Academic and student affairs" should be interpreted broadly to include all administrative and policy matters pertinent to students' educational experiences.

of editorial policy or content. Only for proper and stated causes should editors and managers be subject to removal and then only by orderly and prescribed procedures. The agency responsible for the appointment of editors and managers should be the agency responsible for their removal.

(c) All institutionally published and financed student publications should explicitly state on the editorial page that the opinions there expressed are not necessarily those of the college, university, or student body.

OFF-CAMPUS FREEDOM OF STUDENTS

1. Exercise of Rights of Citizenship

College and university students are both citizens and members of the academic community. As citizens, students should enjoy the same freedom of speech, peaceful assembly, and right of petition that other citizens enjoy and, as members of the academic community, they are subject to the obligations which accrue to them by virtue of this membership. Faculty members and administration officials should ensure that institutional powers are not employed to inhibit such intellectual and personal development of students as is often promoted by their exercise of the rights of citizenship both on and off campus.

2. Institutional Authority and Civil Penalties

Activities of students may upon occasion result in violation of law. In such cases, institutional officials should be prepared to apprise students of sources of legal counsel and may offer other assistance. Students who violate the law may incur penalties prescribed by civil authorities, but institutional authority should never be used merely to duplicate the function of general laws. Only where the institution's interests as an academic community are distinct and clearly involved should the special authority of the institution be asserted. Students who incidentally violate institutional regulations in the course of their off-campus activity, such as those relating to class attendance, should be subject to no greater penalty than would normally be imposed. Institutional action should be independent of community pressure.

PROCEDURAL STANDARDS IN DISCIPLINARY PROCEEDINGS

In developing responsible student conduct, disciplinary proceedings play a role substantially secondary to example, counseling, guidance, and admonition.[11] At the same time, educational institutions have a duty and the corollary disciplinary powers to protect their educational purpose through the setting of standards of scholarship and conduct for the students who attend them and through the regulation of the use of institutional facilities. In the exceptional circumstances when the preferred means fail to resolve problems of student conduct, proper procedural safeguards should be observed to protect the student from the unfair imposition of serious penalties.

The administration of discipline should guarantee procedural fairness to an accused student.[12] Practices in disciplinary cases may vary in formality with the gravity of the offense and the sanctions which may be applied. They should also take into account the presence or absence of an honor code, and the degree to which the institutional officials have direct acquaintance with student life in general and with the involved student and the circumstances of the case in particular. The jurisdictions of faculty or student judicial bodies, the disciplinary responsibilities of institutional officials, and the regular disciplinary procedures, including the student's

---

[11] The student conduct that may be subject to the disciplinary proceedings described in this section should be understood to include alleged violations of standards of student academic integrity.

[12] In addition, student organizations as well as individual students may be subject to institutional disciplinary sanctions, and in those circumstances, student organizations should also be guaranteed procedural fairness.

right to appeal a decision, should be clearly formulated and communicated in advance.[13] Minor penalties may be assessed informally under prescribed procedures.

In all situations, procedural fair play requires that a student charged with misconduct be informed of the nature of the charges and be given a fair opportunity to refute them, that the institution not be arbitrary in its actions, and that there be provision for appeal of a decision. The following are recommended as proper safeguards in such proceedings when there are no honor codes offering comparable guarantees.

1. Standards of Conduct Expected of Students

The institution has an obligation to clarify those standards which it considers essential to its educational mission and its community life. These general behavioral expectations and the resultant specific regulations should represent a reasonable regulation of student conduct, but students should be as free as possible from imposed limitations that have no direct relevance to their education. Offenses should be as clearly defined as possible and interpreted in a manner consistent with the aforementioned principles of relevancy and reasonableness.[14] Disciplinary proceedings should be instituted only for violations of standards of conduct formulated with significant student participation and published in advance through such means as a student handbook or a generally available body of institutional regulations.

2. Investigation of Student Conduct

(a) Except under extreme emergency circumstances, premises occupied by students and the personal possessions of students should not be searched unless appropriate authorization has been obtained. For premises such as residence halls controlled by the institution, an appropriate and responsible authority should be designated to whom application should be made before a search is conducted. The application should specify the reasons for the search and the objects or information sought. The student should be present, if possible, during the search. For premises not controlled by the institution, the ordinary requirements for lawful search should be followed.

(b) Students detected or arrested in the course of serious violations of institutional regulations, or infractions of ordinary law, should be informed of their rights.[15] No form of harassment should be used by institutional representatives to coerce admissions of guilt or disclosure of information about conduct of other suspected persons.

3. Status of Student Pending Final Action

Pending action on the charges, the status of a student should not be altered, or the student's right to be present on the campus and to attend classes suspended, except for reasons relating to the student's physical or emotional safety and well-being, or for reasons relating to the safety and well-being of other students, faculty, or institutional property.

4. Hearing Committee Procedures

When the misconduct may result in serious penalties, and if a penalized student questions the fairness of disciplinary action, that student should be granted, on request, the privilege of a hearing before a regularly constituted hearing committee. The following suggested hearing committee procedures satisfy the requirements of procedural due process in situations requiring a high degree of formality.

---

[13] Like other practices in disciplinary cases, the formality of any appellate procedures should be commensurate with the gravity of the offense and the sanctions that may be imposed.

[14] The institution should state as specifically as possible the sanctions that may be imposed through disciplinary proceedings.

[15] This provision is intended to protect students' rights under both institutional codes and applicable law. Where institutional regulations are violated, students should be informed of their rights under campus disciplinary procedures. Where arrests are made for infractions of the law, students must be informed of their rights by arresting authorities.

(a) The hearing committee should include faculty members or students, or, if regularly included or requested by the accused, both faculty and student members. No member of the hearing committee who is otherwise interested in the particular case should sit in judgment during the proceeding.

(b) The student should be informed, in writing, of the reasons for the proposed disciplinary action with sufficient particularity, and in sufficient time, to ensure opportunity to prepare for the hearing.[16]

(c) The student appearing before the hearing committee should have the right to be assisted in his or her defense by an adviser of the student's choice.

(d) The burden of proof should rest upon the officials bringing the charge.

(e) The student should be given an opportunity to testify, to present evidence and witnesses, and to hear and question adverse witnesses. In no case should the committee consider statements against the student unless he or she has been advised of their content and of the names of those who made them and has been given an opportunity to rebut unfavorable inferences which might otherwise be drawn.

(f) All matters upon which the decision may be based must be introduced into evidence at the proceeding before the hearing committee. The decision should be based solely upon such matters. Improperly acquired evidence should not be admitted.

(g) In the absence of a transcript, there should be both a digest and a verbatim record, such as a tape recording, of the hearing.

(h) The decision of the hearing committee should be final, subject only to the student's right of appeal to the president or ultimately to the governing board of the institution.[17]

APPENDIX

The following associations have endorsed the interpretive footnotes:

American Association of Community Colleges
American Association of University Administrators
American Association of University Professors
American College Personnel Association
Association for Student Judicial Affairs
National Association of Student Personnel Administrators
National Association for Women in Education
National Orientation Directors Association
Southern Association for College Student Affairs
United States Student Association

---

[16] The student should also be informed of the specific sanctions which may be imposed through the disciplinary proceeding.
[17] As a matter of responsible practice, the decision of the hearing committee, as well as grounds and procedures for appeal, should be communicated to the student in writing within a reasonable period of time.

Statement on Graduate Students

The statement which follows was approved by the Association's Committee on College and University Teaching, Research, and Publication in October 1999. It was adopted by the AAUP's Council in June 2000 and endorsed by the Eighty-sixth Annual Meeting.

PREAMBLE

Graduate programs in universities exist for the discovery and transmission of knowledge, the education of students, the training of future faculty, and the general well-being of society. Free inquiry and free expression are indispensable to the attainment of these goals.

In 1967 the American Association of University Professors participated with the National Student Association, the Association of American Colleges, and others in the formulation of the *Joint Statement on Rights and Freedoms of Students*. The *Joint Statement* has twice been revised and updated, most recently in November 1992. The AAUP's Committee on College and University Teaching, Research, and Publication, while supporting the Association's continuing commitment to the *Joint Statement*, believes that the distinctive circumstances of graduate students require a supplemental statement.

The statement which follows has been formulated to reflect the educational maturity and the distinguishing academic characteristics and responsibilities of graduate students. These students not only engage in more advanced studies than their undergraduate counterparts, but often they also hold teaching or research assistantships. As graduate assistants, they carry out many of the functions of faculty members and receive compensation for these duties. The statement below sets forth recommended standards that we believe will foster sound academic policies in universities with graduate programs. The responsibility to secure and respect general conditions conducive to a graduate student's freedom to learn and to teach is shared by all members of a university's graduate community. Each university should develop policies and procedures that safeguard this freedom. Such policies and procedures should be developed within the framework of those general standards that enable the university to fulfill its educational mission. These standards are offered not simply to protect the rights of affected individuals but also to ensure that graduate education fulfills its responsibilities to students, faculty, and society.[1]

RECOMMENDED STANDARDS

1. Graduate students have the right to academic freedom. Like other students, they "should be free to take reasoned exception to the data or views offered in any course of study and to reserve judgment about matters of opinion, but they are responsible for learning the content of any course of study for which they are enrolled."[2] Moreover, because of their advanced education, graduate students should be encouraged by their professors to exercise their freedom of "discussion, inquiry and expression."[3] Further, they should be able to express their opinions freely about matters of institutional policy, and they should have the same freedom of action in the public political domain as faculty members should have.

---

[1] We recognize that the responsibilities of graduate students vary widely among individuals, courses of study, and institutions. Some provisions of this statement may not apply to students in professional schools who may have different types of responsibilities from students in other disciplines.

[2] "Joint Statement on Rights and Freedoms of Students," AAUP, *Policy Documents and Reports*, 9th ed. (Washington, D.C., 2001), 262.

[3] *Ibid.*

Graduate students' freedom of inquiry is necessarily qualified by their still being learners in the profession; nonetheless, their faculty mentors should afford them latitude and respect as they decide how they will engage in teaching and research.

2. Graduate students have the right to be free from illegal or unconstitutional discrimination, or discrimination on a basis not demonstrably related to job function, including, but not limited to, age, sex, disability, race, religion, national origin, marital status, or sexual orientation, in admissions and throughout their education, employment, and placement.[4]

   Graduate students should be informed of the requirements of their degree programs. When feasible, they should be told about acceptance, application, and attrition rates in their fields, but it is also their responsibility to keep themselves informed of these matters. If degree requirements are altered, students admitted under previous rules should be able to continue under those rules. Graduate students should be assisted in making timely progress toward their degrees by being provided with diligent advisers, relevant course offerings, adequate dissertation or thesis supervision, and periodic assessment of and clear communication on their progress. Students should understand that dissertation or thesis work may be constrained by the areas of interest and specialization of available faculty supervisors.

   If a graduate student's dissertation or thesis adviser departs from the institution once the student's work is under way, the responsible academic officers should endeavor to provide the student with alternative supervision, external to the institution if necessary. If a degree program is to be discontinued, provisions must be made for students already in the program to complete their course of study.

3. Graduate students are entitled to the protection of their intellectual property rights, including recognition of their participation in supervised research and their research with faculty, consistent with generally accepted standards of attribution and acknowledgment in collaborative settings. Written standards should be publicly available.

4. Graduate students should have a voice in institutional governance at the program, department, college, graduate school, and university levels.

5. Under the Association's *Recommended Institutional Regulations on Academic Freedom and Tenure*, graduate student assistants are to be informed in writing of the terms and conditions of their appointment and, in the event of proposed dismissal, are to be afforded access to a duly constituted hearing committee.[5] They should be informed of all academic or other institutional regulations affecting their roles as employees. Graduate student employees with grievances, as individuals or as a group, should submit them in a timely fashion and should have access to an impartial faculty committee or, if provided under institutional policy, arbitration. Clear guidelines and timelines for grievance procedures should be distributed to all interested parties. Individual grievants or participants in a group grievance should not be subjected to reprisals. Graduate student employees may choose a representative to speak for them or with them at all stages of a grievance.

6. Good practice should include appropriate training and supervision in teaching, adequate office space, and a safe working environment. Departments should endeavor to acquaint students with the norms and traditions of their academic discipline and to inform them of professional opportunities. Graduate students should be encouraged to seek departmental assistance in obtaining future academic and nonacademic employment. Departments are encouraged to provide support for the professional development of graduate students by such means as funding research expenses and conference travel.

7. Graduate students should have access to their files and placement dossiers. If access is denied, graduate students should be able to have a faculty member of their choice examine their files and, at the professor's discretion, provide the student with a redacted account. Graduate students should have the right to direct that items be added to or removed from their placement dossiers.

---

[4] "On Discrimination," *Policy Documents and Reports*, 185.
[5] "Recommended Institutional Regulations on Academic Freedom and Tenure," Regulation 13, *ibid.*, 29.

8. As the Association's Council affirmed in November 1998, graduate student assistants, like other campus employees, should have the right to organize to bargain collectively. Where state legislation permits, administrations should honor a majority request for union representation. Graduate student assistants must not suffer retaliation from professors or administrators because of their activity relating to collective bargaining.

9. In order to assist graduate students in making steady progress toward their degrees, the time they spend in teaching or research assistantships or other graduate employment at the institution should be limited in amount—a common maximum is twenty hours per week—and should afford sufficient compensation so as not to compel the student to obtain substantial additional employment elsewhere.

10. Graduate student assistants, though they work only part time, should receive essential fringe benefits, and especially health benefits.

COLLEGE AND UNIVERSITY ACCREDITATION

The Role of the Faculty in the Accrediting of Colleges and Universities

The statement which follows was approved by the Association's Committee on Accrediting of Colleges and Universities, adopted by the Association's Council in April 1968, and endorsed by the Fifty-fourth Annual Meeting.

Institutional evaluation is a joint enterprise between institutions of higher education and the accrediting commissions of regional associations. For their most effective work the accrediting commissions require the cooperative effort of qualified faculty members and administrators, who should be encouraged by their colleges and universities to participate in the work of the commissions. Within a college or university, the nature of the accrediting process requires common enterprise among the faculty, the administration, and to some extent the governing board. The appraisal of the academic program should be largely the responsibility of faculty members. They should play a major role in the evaluation of the curriculum, the library, teaching loads and conditions, research, professional activities, laboratories and other academic facilities, and faculty welfare and compensation, all in relation to the institution's objectives and in the light of its financial resources. To higher education generally, faculty members may exercise a special responsibility as the segment of the educational community which is in the best position to recognize and appraise circumstances affecting academic freedom, faculty tenure, the faculty role in institutional government, and faculty status and morale. This statement presents standards for the expression of faculty interest and responsibility in the accreditation process.

RECOMMENDED STANDARDS FOR INSTITUTIONS OF HIGHER EDUCATION

1. Primary responsibility for the preparation of the academic aspects of the self-evaluation should rest with a committee composed largely of faculty members and responsible to the faculty as a whole. Additions or deletions should be made only after consultation with the authors of the sections of the report which are affected.
2. The self-evaluation should include a description of
   (a) conditions of academic freedom and tenure (including provisions for academic due process);
   (b) conditions of faculty participation in institutional government (including provisions for the orderly handling of grievances and disputes); and
   (c) faculty status and morale (including working conditions and total compensation). Significant differences of opinion in these and other areas should be reflected in the self-evaluation.

3. The completed self-evaluation should be made available to the entire faculty prior to its submission to the accrediting commission and should be subject to amendment in the light of faculty suggestions.
4. Representatives of the faculty, including members of appropriate faculty committees, should be available to meet with the visiting committee to discuss questions of faculty concern.
5. The report of the visiting committee should be made available to the entire faculty.
6. The faculty should be fully informed of the accrediting commission's actions after an evaluation and should be kept abreast of all significant developments and issues arising between the accrediting commission and the institution. It should participate, as in the self-evaluation, in any subsequent activities regarding the institution's accreditation.

RECOMMENDED STANDARDS FOR THE REGIONAL ACCREDITING COMMISSIONS

1. Regular visiting committees should include full-time teaching or research faculty members.
2. A formally adopted institutional policy on academic freedom and tenure, consistent with the major provisions of the 1940 *Statement of Principles on Academic Freedom and Tenure,* should be a condition for accreditation.
3. Reports by regular visiting committees should take explicit account of
   (a) conditions of academic freedom and tenure (including provisions for academic due process);
   (b) conditions of faculty participation in institutional government (including provisions for the orderly handling of grievances and disputes); and
   (c) faculty status and morale (including working conditions and total compensation).
   The reports should describe any significant shortcomings in these areas.
4. When significant shortcomings have been found in the areas listed above, the commissions should deal with these as with similar shortcomings in other areas, endeavoring to secure improvement and applying appropriate sanctions in the absence of improvement within a reasonable time.
5. A gross violation of academic freedom, tenure, or due process should, unless promptly corrected, lead to action looking toward withdrawal of accreditation.

COLLATERAL BENEFITS

The Association is concerned with all aspects of the economic welfare of faculties in the setting of proper institutional management and finance, including salaries, tax problems, provision for retirement, and incidental arrangements such as insurance, treatment of outside income or other legal claims of faculty, and education of faculty children and spouses. In addition to sponsoring several studies in these areas, the Association has also adopted, with the Association of American Colleges (now the Association of American Colleges and Universities), two joint statements of policy, one on Academic Retirement and Insurance Plans, the other on Leaves of Absence. The latter document was subsequently supplemented by the AAUP's statement on Faculty Child Care.

The Association's Committee on the Economic Status of the Profession conducts an annual survey of the economic status of college and university faculty members in relation to changing circumstances.

Statement of Principles on Academic Retirement and Insurance Plans

The statement which follows, prepared by a joint committee of the American Association of University Professors and the Association of American Colleges (AAC; now the Association of American Colleges and Universities), represents the most recent revision of a joint statement originally issued in 1950. Subsequent revisions, endorsed by the two organizations, were issued in 1958, in 1969, and in 1980. The present revision, adopted by the Council of the AAUP in November 1987, was adopted by the AAC at its annual meeting in January 1988, and endorsed by the AAUP's Seventy-fourth Annual Meeting.

The purpose of retirement plans and plans for insurance benefits for faculty members and administrators is to help educators and their families maintain their standard of living following retirement and to withstand the financial effects of illness and death. The purpose of such plans for institutions is to increase the educational effectiveness of the college or university. The plans should be designed to attract individuals of the highest abilities to the faculty and administration, to sustain their morale, to permit them to devote their energies to the concerns of the institution and the profession, to provide for their orderly retirement, and thus to afford opportunities for entry and advancement in the profession. In addition, the plans must meet the requirements of current applicable federal and state laws: for example, on the federal level, the Employee Retirement Income Security Act of 1974, the Age Discrimination in Employment Act of 1967, Title VII of the Civil Rights Act of 1964, the Equal Pay Act of 1963, and the Internal Revenue Code have particular relevance.

The following practices are recommended.

1. The institution's retirement and insurance plans should
   (a) be clearly defined;
   (b) take into account, and be coordinated with, old-age, survivor, disability, and medical benefits of federal social security and/or other applicable public programs;
   (c) facilitate mobility among institutions without loss of accrued retirement benefits and with little or no gap in annuity and insurance-plan participation, and, in the case of colleges and universities with defined-benefit plans, seek to offer a plan, or alternative plans, that do not penalize faculty members who leave prior to retirement;
   (d) make available, as a matter of course, both information on all benefits, including an estimation of retirement income, and a program of pre-retirement counseling; and
   (e) be reviewed periodically by a committee representing the faculty and administration of the institution, in consultation with retirees. As appropriate, recommendations should be made to the institution's governing board that ensure that the plans continue to meet and reflect the needs, resources, and objectives of the institution and the participants. Retirement plans that are found to provide retirement income less than, or in excess of, the plans' objectives should be carefully reviewed in relation to the overall allocation of financial resources within the institution.
2. The retirement plan for faculty members and administrative officers of the institution should provide for
   (a) *Normal Retirement.* This term is employed in retirement planning to designate an age for setting retirement income objectives and contribution rates. Plans in which the normal retirement age is set within the age range of sixty-two to seventy-two appear to conform with reasonable practice. The availability of an adequate retirement income at the normal retirement age will encourage timely retirement.

(b) *Early Retirement.* The plan should designate an explicit early retirement age that will enable individuals to retire earlier than the stated normal retirement age and to begin receiving their retirement income at that earlier age.[1] Though plan benefits are generally reduced by early retirement, such reductions may be offset through supplemental benefit arrangements provided by the individual and/or the institution.[2]

(c) *Phased Retirement.* The plan should enable individuals who are approaching retirement to arrange, on their own initiative, reductions in services and salary acceptable both to them and to their institutions.[3]

3. Ordinarily, retirement should occur at the end of the academic year. Each institution should make clear whether the summer period attaches to the preceding or the following academic year. Individuals should notify the administration of their decision to retire as far in advance as possible.

4. At the time of initial appointment and periodically thereafter participants should be both counseled and urged to inform themselves about their retirement options and benefits.

5. The institution should provide for a plan of retirement annuities.

(a) Such a plan should require participation after not more than one year of service by all full-time faculty members and administrators who have attained a specified age, as determined by relevant federal and state law.

(b) It should be financed by regular payments, with the institution contributing as much as or more than each participant. Contributions should continue during leaves of absence with pay. In addition, the retirement plan should permit supplementary contributions from participants (including those on leaves of absence without pay). Individuals should have the opportunity to make both required and voluntary contributions by salary reduction in accordance with relevant tax laws.

(c) It should maintain contributions at a level considered sufficient to give long-term participants at normal retirement age a continuing combined income from the retirement plan and federal social security that is appropriately related to their level of income prior to retirement, with provisions for continuing income to a surviving spouse. The recommended objective for those retiring at the normal retirement age who have participated in the plan for at least thirty-five years is a continuing after-tax income equivalent in purchasing power to approximately two-thirds of the yearly disposable salary (after taxes and other mandatory deductions) during the last few years of full-time employment.[4]

(d) It should ensure that the full accumulations from the participant's and the institution's contributions are fully and immediately vested in the participant, available as a benefit in case of death before annuity payments commence, and with no forfeiture in cases of departure or dismissal from the institution.

(e) It should be such that the participant may receive the accumulated funds only in the form of an annuity. Exceptions might be made for (1) small proportions of the accumulations of retiring participants, or (2) small accumulations in inactive accounts.[5]

---

[1] To conform to the Tax Reform Act of 1986, the plan should explicitly state a minimum early retirement age of fifty-five or later.

[2] In 1998, Congress amended the Age Discrimination in Employment Act to allow institutions to offer supplemental "retirement incentive" benefits to tenured faculty who complete a required number of years of service and attain a specified age. These supplemental benefits may be phased out after a specified maximum age, as long as the supplemental plan allows every faculty member a 180-day opportunity to consider accepting the maximum benefit by retiring within a year. Voluntary Retirement Incentive Plans, Public Law 105–244, Title IX, Part D.

[3] The Tax Reform Act of 1986 makes this approach to early retirement particularly beneficial.

[4] Since current law does not permit age-based discontinuance of retirement contributions, institutions may wish to develop a modified plan that is fully paid when it achieves a specified benefit such as that recommended in item 5(c).

[5] The AAUP's Council, at its meeting in June 1990, adopted changes in this subsection that were discussed with the Association of American Colleges. See the "AAC/AAUP Interim Comment on the Annuitization Provision of the 'Statement of Principles on Academic Retirement and Insurance Plans,'" *Academe: Bulletin of the AAUP* 78 (September–October 1992): 53.

6. Since the abolition of mandatory retirement in 1993, some cases which previously would have resulted in "involuntary retirement" now have to be treated as involuntary termination. Such cases should be considered by representatives of the faculty and administration through appropriate procedures.[6] Reassignment from administrative duties to teaching responsibilities is not considered a retirement.

7. When a retirement plan is initiated or modified, reasonable transition provisions, such as special financial arrangements or the gradual implementation of the new plan, should be made for those who would otherwise be adversely affected, and consideration should be given to the needs of those who are already retired.

8. Each institution should help retired faculty members and administrators remain a part of the academic community, and facilitate timely retirement, by providing, where possible, such amenities as a mail address, library privileges, office space, faculty club membership, the institution's publications, secretarial help, administration of grants, research facilities, faculty dining and parking privileges, and participation in convocations and academic processions. Institutions that confer the emeritus status should do so in accordance with standards determined by the faculty and administration.

9. The institution should maintain a program of group insurance financed in whole or in part by the institution and available to faculty members and administrators promptly after employment commences. The program should continue all coverages during leave of absence with pay, and during leave without pay unless comparable protection is otherwise provided for the individual. At a minimum, the program should include the following:

(a) Life insurance providing a benefit considered sufficient to sustain the standard of living of the faculty member's or administrator's family for at least one year following death. Where additional protection is contemplated, consideration should be given to providing the largest amount of insurance at the younger ages, when the need for insurance often is greater, with coverage decreasing as age advances and the death benefit from the retirement annuity becomes substantial.

(b) Medical-expense insurance providing basic hospital-surgical medical insurance and major-medical insurance, or equivalent protection, for faculty members, administrators, and their dependents. Such insurance should continue to be available through the institution (1) for retired individuals and their spouses, (2) for surviving spouses who do not remarry, and (3) for dependent children of active or retired participants who die while insured. Serious consideration should be given to offering catastrophic medical and long-term health-care insurance.

(c) Disability insurance providing a monthly income for faculty members and administrators who remain totally disabled beyond the period normally covered by salary continuation or sick pay. Provision should also be made to continue payments to the disabled individual's retirement annuity. For a person who has been disabled six months or more, the plan should provide an after-tax income, including federal social security benefits, equivalent in continuing purchasing power to approximately two-thirds of the income realized after taxes and mandatory deductions prior to disability. The plan should be structured so that disability benefits to a disabled individual continue at least until the retirement annuity is greater than the disability benefit or until the age at which the law requires distribution of the annuity, whichever is earlier.

---

[6] See, for example, the joint AAC-AAUP "1958 Statement on Procedural Standards in Faculty Dismissal Proceedings," AAUP, *Policy Documents and Reports*, 9th ed. (Washington, D.C., 2001), 11–14.

Statement of Principles on Leaves of Absence

The statement which follows, prepared by a special committee of the American Association of University Professors and the Association of American Colleges (now the Association of American Colleges and Universities), was adopted by the Association of American Colleges at its annual meeting in January 1972. In May 1972, it was adopted by the Council of the American Association of University Professors and endorsed by the Fifty-eighth Annual Meeting.

The statement, designed to emphasize the value of leaves of absence and to give guidance to institutions in making or improving provisions for them, offers what the two associations believe to be sound standards for flexible and effective leave programs. Though limited financial resources at an individual institution may delay the immediate establishment of an ideal leave policy, careful consideration should be given to possible steps toward the early development of such a policy.

The governing bodies of the Association of American Colleges and the American Association of University Professors, acting respectively in January and April 1990, adopted several changes in language in order to remove gender-specific references from the original text.

PURPOSES

Leaves of absence are among the most important means by which the teaching effectiveness of faculty members may be enhanced, their scholarly usefulness enlarged, and an institution's academic program strengthened and developed. A sound program of leaves is therefore of vital importance to a college or university, and it is the obligation of faculty members to make use of available means, including leaves, to promote their professional competence. The major purpose is to provide opportunity for continued professional growth and new, or renewed, intellectual achievement through study, research, writing, and travel. Leaves may also be provided in appropriate circumstances for projects of direct benefit to the institution and for public or private service outside the institution.[1] Leaves should also be granted for illness, recovery of health, and maternity.

DEVELOPMENT OF LEAVE POLICIES

Leave policies and procedures should be developed with full faculty participation. Faculty members, acting through appropriate representatives, should also have a key role in the selection of the recipients of individual leaves. The institution and the individual faculty member have a common responsibility for endeavoring to achieve the objective of the leave program—the institution by establishing an effective program, the faculty member by making appropriate use of it. Leave policies should be flexible enough to meet the needs of both the individual and the institution.

ELIGIBILITY AND PROCEDURES

The purpose of a leave program is to promote the professional development of all faculty members—those who are likely to stay at the institution for a long period but also, although not necessarily to the same degree, those for whom there is no such assurance.

---

[1] Leave for the purpose of engaging in political activity is discussed in the "Statement on Professors and Political Activity," AAUP, *Policy Documents and Reports*, 9th ed. (Washington, D.C., 2001), 33–34.

Previous service and leaves at other institutions should be taken into consideration in determining eligibility for leave. Persons nearing retirement should be eligible for leave with pay if it is clear that the leave will achieve its purposes both for the individual and for the institution.

For a nontenured faculty member on scholarly leave for one year or less, the period of leave should count as part of the probationary period as if it were prior service at another institution.[2] Exceptions to this policy should be mutually agreed to in writing prior to the leave.

Faculty members should apply for a leave at a reasonable time in advance and through established procedures, so that the institution can more readily care for their work in their absence and so that they can plan to make the best use of the opportunity. All evidence that the leave will increase individual effectiveness or produce academically or socially useful results should be considered in evaluating applications. A leave may either involve specialized scholarly activity or be designed to provide broad cultural experience and enlarged perspective. Administrators and faculty agencies concerned with implementation of leave policies may reasonably require faculty members to submit such advance plans as are likely to ensure productive results.

INDIVIDUAL AND INSTITUTIONAL OBLIGATIONS

Faculty members have an obligation to return for further service following a leave of absence when the circumstances of granting the leave indicate that this is the equitable action, as is often the case when a leave with pay is granted. A faculty member should of course honor an agreement to return to the institution, unless other arrangements are mutually agreed upon. The precise terms of the leave of absence should be in writing and should be given to the faculty member prior to the commencement of the leave.

Even when there is no obligation to return, the faculty member who resigns while on leave should give notice according to accepted standards. Moreover, a college or university should not knowingly invite a person to join its staff at a time when the individual cannot properly accept the invitation. In most instances, an institution which invites a faculty member to accept a new appointment while on leave should feel obliged to pay at least a portion of the cost of the leave.

FREQUENCY AND DURATION OF LEAVES

Leaves should not be considered as deferred compensation to which a faculty member is entitled no matter what other opportunities the faculty member may have had for professional development. They should, however, be provided with reasonable frequency and preferably be available at regular intervals, because they are important to the continuing growth of the faculty member and the effectiveness of the institution.

Ordinarily, leaves of absence, whatever the source of funding, should not be more than one year in length, but exceptions to this rule should be possible in cases involving health, public service, overseas appointments, or other special circumstances.

FINANCIAL ARRANGEMENTS

Leaves of one semester at full salary or an academic year at half salary are commonly provided. The institution is not obliged to assume the financial burden of all types of leaves. It does have the obligation, however, to use its own leave funds in such a manner as to balance the opportunity for professional development among and within academic fields.

---

[2] Credit for prior service toward fulfillment of the probationary period is discussed in the "1940 Statement of Principles on Academic Freedom and Tenure," *Policy Documents and Reports*, 4. Cf. the section on "Academic Tenure," paragraph 2.

Whatever the source of funding, the amount paid to the faculty member on leave should not depend on the cost of caring for the person's work in his or her absence, nor should a leave of absence of a year or less interfere with the opportunity for promotion or increase in salary.

Continuous coverage under various types of insurance programs should be provided while a faculty member is on leave. When the faculty member is on leave with pay, both the institution and the individual should continue contributions toward that person's retirement annuity.

If a faculty member, on leave without pay, takes a temporary but full-time appointment at another institution or organization, it is reasonable to expect the appointing institution or organization to assume the cost of institutional contributions to the individual's retirement annuity and group insurance programs.

Foundations, government agencies, and other organizations supporting leaves for scholarly purposes should include in their grants an amount sufficient to maintain institutional annuity and group insurance contributions as well as salaries.

Faculty Child Care

The statement which follows was approved by the Association's Committee on the Status of Women in the Academic Profession, adopted by the Association's Council in June 1989, and endorsed by the Seventy-fifth Annual Meeting.

The American Association of University Professors has long recognized the problems associated with combining academic careers and family responsibilities. It has developed a body of standards and guidelines to encourage sound institutional practices in this area. These include statements on *Leaves of Absence for Child-bearing, Child-rearing, and Family Emergencies* (1974); *Senior Appointments with Reduced Loads* (1987); and *Anticipated Medical Leaves of Absence* (1987). The Association has supported key legislation in this area.

Consistent with its recommended policies, the AAUP recognizes that, for faculty members with child-rearing responsibilities to participate successfully in teaching, research, and service to their institution, they must have access to quality child-care facilities. Universities and colleges should assume a share of the responsibility for the provision of such services to their faculties. Employers in and out of academe have found that the provision of on-site facilities has led to stronger and more contented families and increased productivity. The ability to reach parents easily in an emergency, the time and money they save in transportation, the opportunity provided them to share an occasional lunch or other daytime activity with their children, the retention and recruitment of faculty—these are just some of the benefits that accrue from child-care arrangements on campus. Faculty members derive peace of mind from knowing that their children are receiving quality care and that the operation has long-term stability. If the institution has an early-childhood-education program, the opportunity to use the facility for training students provides an additional benefit and contributes to high standards of child care.

Some colleges and universities, because of size or other considerations, cannot support on-site child care. There are alternatives: cooperative arrangements with other nearby employers, resource and referral services, and cost sharing, either as a separate benefit or as part of a cafeteria plan. As with other fringe benefits, recommendations on the extent and form of institutional support (whether through subsidized on-campus care or through a fringe-benefit plan) should be sought from an appropriate body of the faculty in consultation with other groups on campus.

The Association strongly recommends an institutional commitment to the provision of quality child care.

CONSTITUTION

The AAUP adopted a Constitution in 1916, the second year of the organization's existence. Then, as now, the document served as the primary governing instrument establishing the organization's officers, membership categories, and structure. While the Constitution has been amended many times since its adoption, it still describes the purpose of the AAUP in terms virtually identical to those used in 1916.

The Constitution establishes categories of membership (Article II) and provides that members at an educational institution may form an AAUP chapter (Article VII). The chapters may join together into state conferences for the purpose of advancing AAUP interests at the state level (Article VIII).

At the national level, the Constitution recognizes the Collective Bargaining Congress (Article IX), composed of representatives of the AAUP chapters that engage in collective bargaining, and the Assembly of State Conferences, composed of representatives of the various state conferences (Article VIII).

The president and other national officers, elected by the membership, serve two-year terms (Articles III, V). Also elected in national balloting are members of the Council, which is the Association's legislative body (Article IV). Three Council members are elected from each of ten geographical districts and serve staggered three-year terms.

The powers of the annual meeting (Article VI) and mechanisms for amending the Constitution (Article X) are described. Because the Constitution is altered from time to time, interested readers are invited to contact the Washington office for a copy of the current text.

Constitution of the Association[1]

ARTICLE I—PURPOSE

The name of this Association shall be the American Association of University Professors. Its purpose shall be to facilitate a more effective cooperation among teachers and research scholars in universities and colleges, and in professional schools of similar grade, for the promotion of the interests of higher education and research, and in general to increase the usefulness and advance the standards, ideals, and welfare of the profession.

ARTICLE II—MEMBERSHIP

1. There shall be five classes of members:
   (a) *Active Members.* Any person who holds a professional position of teacher or researcher, or similar academic appointment, in a college, university, or professional school of similar grade accredited in the United States or Canada may be admitted to active membership in the Association.
   (b) *Graduate Student Members.* Any person who is, or within the past five years has been, a graduate student may be admitted to graduate student membership. Graduate student members shall be transferred to active membership as soon as they become eligible.
   (c) *Associate Members.* Any person in a college, university, or professional school of similar grade accredited in the United States or Canada whose work is primarily administrative shall be eligible for associate membership.
   (d) *Retired Members.* An active member who retires from a full-time teaching or research position may choose to be transferred to retired membership. Retired members retain all rights and privileges accorded to active members under this Constitution, including the right to hold office and to vote in national elections.
   (e) *Public Members.* Any person not eligible for one of the other four classes of membership may be admitted as a public member.
2. The admission of members shall require two steps:
   (a) *Application.* Application for active, graduate student, and public membership shall be made to the secretary-treasurer of the Association.
   (b) *Acceptance and Notification.* When an applicant's eligibility has been determined, it shall be the duty of the secretary-treasurer to inform the applicant promptly of acceptance to membership and to include the applicant's name in the list of new members sent to chapter officers. A person's membership may be protested, on grounds of eligibility, by an active member of the Association. If a majority of the members of the committee on membership and dues votes to sustain the protest, the person in question will be informed that his or her membership has ceased to be effective.
3. A member may resign by notifying the secretary-treasurer, and may be expelled for cause by a two-thirds vote of the Council after opportunity for a hearing. Membership shall be forfeited by nonpayment of dues under conditions to be established by the Council.

[1] Last amended at the Eighty-fifth Annual Meeting of the Association in Washington, D.C., June 13, 1999.

4. Members of chapters which have an approved agreement for fractional memberships in exchange for fractional dues, and the votes of such members, shall be counted fractionally, in the proportion specified in their agreement, wherever specified in the Constitution. Such members shall be eligible for election as officers or members of the Council, or for appointment to the Nominating Committee or standing committees of the Association, only upon payment of full membership dues.

ARTICLE III—OFFICERS

1. The officers of the Association shall be a president, a first vice-president, a second vice-president, and a secretary-treasurer.
2. The terms of office of the foregoing officers shall be two years, and shall expire at the close of the last session of the annual meeting following the election of their successors, or, if a meeting of the Council is held after and in connection with the annual meeting, at the close of the last session of the Council.
3. The foregoing officers shall have the duties usually associated with their respective offices. The president shall preside at meetings of the Association and the Council. The president shall appoint all committees of the Association and shall be ex officio a member of all except the Nominating Committee. The president shall also be a nonvoting ex officio member of the governing bodies of all state conferences.
4. The secretary-treasurer shall be responsible for maintaining the records of the Association. The secretary-treasurer shall also receive all moneys and deposit them in the name of the Association. With the authorization of the Council the secretary-treasurer shall invest any funds not needed for current disbursements. The secretary-treasurer shall pay all bills approved in accordance with procedures determined by the Council, and shall make a report to the Association at the annual meeting and such other reports as the Council may direct. The secretary-treasurer may, with the approval of the Council, authorize one or more assistant secretary-treasurers to exercise the powers of the office. The financial records of the Association shall be audited annually by an external agency, and the report of the audit shall be published.

ARTICLE IV—THE COUNCIL

1. The president, the vice-presidents, the secretary-treasurer, the chair and immediate past-chair of the Assembly of State Conferences, and the chair and immediate past-chair of the Collective Bargaining Congress, together with former presidents for a period of three years immediately following their term as president shall, with thirty elective members, constitute the Council of the Association. Ten members of the Council shall be elected each year in the manner provided in this Constitution, to serve for three-year terms, according to the provision governing the terms of the officers.
2. The Council shall carry out the purposes of the Association and, subject to the authority of a meeting as defined in this Constitution, act for the Association. The Council shall (a) determine the annual dues and regulations governing their payment, subject to ratification at the annual meeting, and may authorize inclusion of conference and/or chapter dues with national dues as a condition of membership in the Association, subject to ratification at the annual meeting; (b) manage the property and financial affairs of the Association, with power to accept gifts to the Association; (c) construe the provisions of this Constitution; (d) provide for the publications of the Association; (e) appoint and determine the salaries of a general secretary, general counsel, and assistant treasurer, members of the professional staff, and such other employees as shall be necessary to administer the affairs of the Association in accordance with the general supervision of the Council; (f) determine the time, place, and program of the annual meeting and convene special meetings of the Association at its discretion; (g) publish a record of its meetings to the membership; (h) authorize the establishment of committees of the Association; (i) authorize the establishment of regional offices of the Association; and (j) authorize reapportionment and redistricting of the membership not less than once each decade.

3. As a representative of both the Association and a district, each member of the Council shall promote the exchange of ideas between the Council and the membership. A Council member may receive and transmit to the Council the proposals of members, chapters, and state conferences within the member's district. A council member shall be a nonvoting ex officio member of the governing committees of those conferences.

4. Meetings of the Council shall be held in connection with the annual meeting of the Association and at least at one other time each year, upon not less than two weeks' notice to the Council. Ten members elected from districts shall constitute a quorum. The Council may also transact business by letter ballot. A special meeting of the Council shall be called by the president on the written request of at least eight members of the Council.

5. There shall be an Executive Committee of the Council, which, between meetings of the Council, may exercise such powers as the Council has delegated to it and, under unforeseen exigencies, exercise other powers subject to prior authorization of the Council. The Executive Committee shall consist of the president, first vice-president, second vice-president, secretary-treasurer, immediate past president, chair of the Collective Bargaining Congress, chair of the Assembly of State Conferences, and four Council members elected for renewable one-year terms from among those elected from the ten geographical districts. Election of these four members to the Executive Committee shall be held after the conclusion of the annual meeting and of any Council meeting held in connection with the annual meeting. Eligible for election to the Executive Committee are the thirty council members elected from districts, including those newly elected and those whose terms are continuing. The electors shall be all the members of the Council, including those newly elected and those whose terms are continuing. The elections will be conducted in a manner determined by Council. The Executive Committee shall meet at least two times a year, with additional meetings to be called as necessary by the president or by a majority of the Executive Committee.

ARTICLE V—ELECTION OF OFFICERS AND COUNCIL

1. Only active members are eligible for election as officers or members of the Council. Nominations for elective offices to be filled and for membership on the Council shall be made by a Nominating Committee of five members, one person to be identified by the executive committee of the Collective Bargaining Congress, one person to be identified by the executive committee of the Assembly of State Conferences, and three persons to be chosen by election from the membership of Council, which election shall take place in the Council at the annual meeting. Service on the Nominating Committee shall bar candidacy for any national elective office or the Council during that year's election cycle. The committee shall seek and receive suggestions from members, chapters, and conferences of the Association with regard to persons to be nominated; meet; and submit its report to the secretary-treasurer for publication to the members not later than a date to be determined by the Council and announced to the membership. No two members of the Nominating Committee may be from the same district.

2. One member of the Council shall be elected each year from each of ten geographical districts formed with regard to the distribution of the Association's membership and to geographical contiguity. Council members shall be elected by vote of active members resident in their respective districts. In preparation for an election, the Nominating Committee shall nominate two active members of the Association from each district for the position on the Council to be filled from the district.

3. Nominations for members of the Council may also be made by petitions signed by at least fifty active members of the Association resident within the district from which the Council member is to be chosen, provided that in determining the required number of signatures not more than ten shall be members at a single institution. Nominations for the presidency, the vice-presidencies, and the secretary-treasurership may also be made by petition, signed by at least 150 active members of the Association, provided that in determining the required number of signatures not more than fifteen of those signing a

petition shall be members at a single institution and not more than ninety shall be members in a single district. No member shall sign more than one petition for the same office. Petitions presenting nominations shall be filed with the secretary-treasurer not later than a date to be determined by the Council and announced to the membership.

4. The secretary-treasurer shall prepare ballots containing the names of all nominees to office and to Council membership, with relevant biographical data and a statement of the method of nomination. Ballots shall be mailed to all active members of the Association at a time to be determined by the Council and announced to the membership, and the polls shall be closed not less than one month nor more than two months after the mailing, the dates to be determined by the Council. The nominee receiving a plurality of votes, counted fractionally pursuant to Article II, section 4, if applicable, shall be declared elected. The president and vice-presidents shall be eligible for election to their respective offices for no more than three consecutive full terms, and retiring elected members of the Council shall be eligible for immediate reelection for one additional term.

5. A vacancy occurring on the Council, in the second vice-presidency, or in the secretary-treasurership shall be filled by a majority vote of the Council for the unexpired term.

ARTICLE VI—MEETINGS OF THE ASSOCIATION

1. The Association shall meet annually except when prevented by war or other national emergency. The secretary-treasurer shall give notice to the membership of a meeting at least thirty days in advance. A quorum shall be a majority of the delegates registered for a meeting. A meeting of the Association shall have authority (a) to amend the Constitution in the manner herein provided; (b) to express its views on professional matters; (c) to act on recommendations presented to it by the Council; (d) to require the Council to report to the ensuing meeting on subjects within the province of the Association; (e) to propose action which, upon concurrence by the Council, shall become the action of the Association; and (f) in the event of disagreement between the Council and a meeting of the Association, to take final action as provided in the following section.

2. If the Council declines to concur in a proposal of a meeting of the Association, it shall report its reasons to the ensuing meeting. If that meeting concurs in the action of the previous meeting, the action shall become that of the Association. An action of the Association reached either (a) by concurrence of the Council in an action of a meeting of the Association or (b) in two successive meetings shall not be changed except by the joint action of the Council and a meeting of the Association or by two successive meetings of the Association.

3. The active members of the Association in each chapter may elect not more than one delegate from that chapter for each twenty-five active members or fraction thereof at the institution, such members counted fractionally pursuant to Article II, section 4, if applicable, to each meeting of the Association. Each of the state conferences may elect two delegates to each meeting of the Association. All members of the Association shall be entitled to the privileges of the floor, but only active members may vote. On request of one-fifth of the delegates present, a proportional vote shall be taken. In a proportional vote, the accredited delegates from each chapter shall be entitled to a number of votes equal to the number of active members at the institution, counted fractionally pursuant to Article II, section 4, if applicable, but any other active member not at an institution thus represented shall be entitled to an individual vote. In case a chapter has more than one delegate, each delegate may cast an equal portion of the votes to which the chapter is entitled.

4. Except as provided in this Constitution or in rules adopted pursuant to it, the meetings of the Association shall be governed by the current edition of *Robert's Rules of Order*.

ARTICLE VII—CHAPTERS

1. Whenever the active members in a given institution number seven or more, they may constitute a chapter of the Association and receive a charter from the Association. More than one chapter may be established in an institution when its parts are geographically separate. Each chapter shall elect, from its active members, at least biannually, a president, a secretary, and a treasurer (or secretary-treasurer), and such other officers as the chapter may determine. It shall be the duty of the secretary of the chapter to report to the secretary-treasurer of the Association the names of the officers of the chapter and to conduct the correspondence of the chapter with the secretary-treasurer.

2. The charter of a chapter may be revoked for financial malpractice, improper performance as a collective bargaining representative, disregard of democratic procedures, or disregard of other principles, policies, or procedures of the Association, in accordance with due process procedures established by the Council, when two-thirds of the Council members present vote in support of the revocation. A chapter whose charter has been revoked by the Council may appeal the Council decision at an annual meeting of the Association. The charter revocation shall remain in effect pending such an appeal. If the meeting sustains the appeal the chapter shall have its charter restored.

3. All active and graduate student members in the institution, but not other members of the faculty, shall be eligible for membership in the chapter. Graduate student members may vote in chapter meetings at the discretion of the chapter. Associate and public members may attend meetings by invitation of the chapter. In collective bargaining chapters, only members of the bargaining unit may vote on matters pertaining to collective bargaining.

4. A chapter may establish local membership dues. It may meet with other chapters and with other local organizations. Its actions shall be in harmony with the principles and procedures of the Association.

ARTICLE VIII—STATE CONFERENCES

Upon approval by the Council, several chapters may organize a conference of the American Association of University Professors which shall be open to all members within the state. The members may be represented through their chapter affiliation. A conference may establish conference dues and may consider and act upon professional matters which are of concern to the members and chapters, but its action shall not bind the members or chapters without their authorization and shall be in harmony with the principles and procedures of the Association. All conferences are entitled to participate in the activities of the Assembly of State Conferences. Formal recommendations on the purposes, structure, and work of the Association from conferences and the Assembly of State Conferences shall go to the Council for consideration and possible transmission to meetings of the Association.

ARTICLE IX—COLLECTIVE BARGAINING CONGRESS

1. Several chapters, which are collective bargaining representatives, or otherwise participate in collective bargaining, may form the Collective Bargaining Congress of the American Association of University Professors. Subject to approval by the Council, the Congress (a) shall adopt bylaws and (b) may establish dues to be paid to the Association by chapters which are members of the Congress.

2. The Congress may consider and act upon professional matters which are of concern to the member chapters, but its action shall not bind the member chapters without their authorization and shall be in harmony with the principles and procedures of the Association. Recommendations adopted by the Congress concerning the purposes, structure, and work of the Association may be submitted by it to the appropriate body of the Association.

ARTICLE X—AMENDMENTS

This Constitution may be amended by a two-thirds vote of a meeting of the Association. The secretary-treasurer shall transmit a proposed amendment to each member of the Association at least one month before the meeting at which it will be proposed.

The Council may initiate and propose an amendment to a meeting of the Association. Also, ten or more active members may initiate an amendment by submitting it in writing to the Council. At the next Council meeting which takes place more than one month after the date of submission, the Council shall approve, modify, or disapprove the submitted amendment and promptly report its action to the proponents. If the Council approves, it will propose the amendment to a meeting of the Association. Upon failure of agreement between the Council and the proponents, the proponents may, with the support of at least five chapters, submit their proposed amendment to a meeting of the Association by communicating it, together with proof of submission to and action by the Council and of support of at least five chapters, to the secretary-treasurer at least three months in advance of the Association meeting at which the amendment is to be proposed.

ARTICLE XI—STATUS OF THE ASSOCIATION

The Association is organized and operated exclusively as a nonprofit charitable and educational organization. No part of its assets, income, or profit shall be distributable to, or inure to the benefit of, any individual, except in consideration for services rendered. In the event of the Association's dissolution, its assets shall be conveyed to one or more organizations exempt from federal income tax under the provisions of the Internal Revenue Code as a charitable, scientific, or educational organization.

APPENDIX I
1915 Declaration of Principles on Academic Freedom and Academic Tenure[1]

PREFATORY NOTE

At the December 1913 meetings of the American Economic Association, the American Political Science Association, and the American Sociological Society, a joint committee of nine faculty members was constituted to consider and report on the questions of academic freedom and academic tenure, so far as these affect university positions in these fields of study. At the December 1914 meeting of these three associations a preliminary report on the subject was presented by the joint committee.

At the meeting of the American Association of University Professors in January 1915, it was decided to take up the problem of academic freedom in general, and the president of the Association was authorized to appoint a committee of fifteen which should include, so far as the members were eligible, this joint committee of nine. The committee was therefore constituted as follows:

Edwin R. A. Seligman, *Chairman*, Columbia University (Economics)
Richard T. Ely, University of Wisconsin (Economics)
Frank A. Fetter, Princeton University (Economics)
James P. Lichtenberger, University of Pennsylvania (Sociology)
Roscoe Pound, Harvard University (Law)
Ulysses G. Weatherly, Indiana University (Sociology)
J. Q. Dealey, Brown University (Political Science)
Henry W. Farnam, Yale University (Political Science)
Charles E. Bennett, Cornell University (Latin)
Edward C. Elliott, University of Wisconsin (Education)
Guy Stanton Ford, University of Minnesota (History)
Charles Atwood Kofoid, University of California (Zoology)
Arthur O. Lovejoy, Johns Hopkins University (Philosophy)
Frederick W. Padelford, University of Washington (English)
Howard C. Warren, Princeton University (Psychology)

In view of the necessity of investigating an incident at the University of Pennsylvania, Professor Lichtenberger resigned in August 1915, and was replaced by Professor Franklin H. Giddings, Columbia University (Sociology). Professor Elliott, having been elected chancellor of the University of Montana, resigned in October. Professor Ford resigned in December, on account of inability to attend the meetings of the committee.

The committee of fifteen had scarcely been constituted when a number of cases of alleged infringement of academic freedom were brought to its attention. These cases were not only numerous, but also diverse in character, ranging from dismissals of individual professors to dismissal or resignation of groups of professors, and including also the dismissal of a university president, and the complaint of another university president against his board of trustees. The total number of complaints laid before the chairman of the committee during the year was

---

[1] *AAUP Bulletin*, Volume I, Part 1 (December 1915): 17–39. The references exclusively to the male gender in this historic document have been left as they were.

eleven. As it was impossible for the committee to command the time or the amount of voluntary service necessary for dealing with all of these cases, those which seemed the most important were selected, and for each of these a subcommittee of inquiry was constituted. In the case of the University of Utah the special committee began work in April and published its report during the summer. In the case of controversies at the University of Colorado, the University of Montana, the University of Pennsylvania, and Wesleyan University, the committees of inquiry have their reports either completed or in an advanced stage of preparation. The general committee has had several meetings and has advised the committees of inquiry upon questions of principle and of method and procedure; but it has not, as a body, participated in the investigations of facts, and the committees of inquiry alone are responsible for their respective findings of fact. The general committee has, however, examined these special reports, and, accepting the findings of the subcommittees upon questions of fact, has approved their conclusions.

Three cases for which the committee was unable to secure investigating committees of this Association have been reported, after some preliminary inquiries, to the appropriate specialist societies; one case, arising at Dartmouth College, to the American Philosophical Association; one at Tulane University, to the American Physiological Society; and one at the University of Oklahoma, to the American Chemical Society.

The committee of fifteen has conceived it to be its duty to consider the problem of academic freedom as a whole and to present a report thereon. Such a report is herewith submitted. The findings of special committees which have not already been printed will be presented in due course.

The safeguarding of a proper measure of academic freedom in American universities requires both a clear understanding of the principles which bear upon the matter, and the adoption by the universities of such arrangements and regulations as may effectually prevent any infringement of that freedom and deprive of plausibility all charges of such infringement. This report is therefore divided into two parts, the first constituting a general declaration of principles relating to academic freedom, the second presenting a group of practical proposals, the adoption of which is deemed necessary in order to place the rules and procedure of the American universities, in relation to these matters, upon a satisfactory footing.

GENERAL DECLARATION OF PRINCIPLES

The term "academic freedom" has traditionally had two applications—to the freedom of the teacher and to that of the student, *Lehrfreiheit* and *Lernfreiheit*. It need scarcely be pointed out that the freedom which is the subject of this report is that of the teacher. Academic freedom in this sense comprises three elements: freedom of inquiry and research; freedom of teaching within the university or college; and freedom of extramural utterance and action. The first of these is almost everywhere so safeguarded that the dangers of its infringement are slight. It may therefore be disregarded in this report. The second and third phases of academic freedom are closely related, and are often not distinguished. The third, however, has an importance of its own, since of late it has perhaps more frequently been the occasion of difficulties and controversies than has the question of freedom of intra-academic teaching. All five of the cases which have recently been investigated by committees of this Association have involved, at least as one factor, the right of university teachers to express their opinions freely outside the university or to engage in political activities in their capacity as citizens. The general principles which have to do with freedom of teaching in both these senses seem to the committee to be in great part, though not wholly, the same. In this report, therefore, we shall consider the matter primarily with reference to freedom of teaching within the university, and shall assume that what is said thereon is also applicable to the freedom of speech of university teachers outside their institutions, subject to certain qualifications and supplementary considerations which will be pointed out in the course of the report.

An adequate discussion of academic freedom must necessarily consider three matters: (1) the scope and basis of the power exercised by those bodies having ultimate legal authority in academic affairs; (2) the nature of the academic calling; and (3) the function of the academic institution or university.

1. Basis of Academic Authority

American institutions of learning are usually controlled by boards of trustees as the ultimate repositories of power. Upon them finally it devolves to determine the measure of academic freedom which is to be realized in the several institutions. It therefore becomes necessary to inquire into the nature of the trust reposed in these boards, and to ascertain to whom the trustees are to be considered accountable.

The simplest case is that of a proprietary school or college designed for the propagation of specific doctrines prescribed by those who have furnished its endowment. It is evident that in such cases the trustees are bound by the deed of gift, and, whatever be their own views, are obligated to carry out the terms of the trust. If a church or religious denomination establishes a college to be governed by a board of trustees, with the express understanding that the college will be used as an instrument of propaganda in the interests of the religious faith professed by the church or denomination creating it, the trustees have a right to demand that everything be subordinated to that end. If, again, as has happened in this country, a wealthy manufacturer establishes a special school in a university in order to teach, among other things, the advantages of a protective tariff, or if, as is also the case, an institution has been endowed for the purpose of propagating the doctrines of socialism, the situation is analogous. All of these are essentially proprietary institutions, in the moral sense. They do not, at least as regards one particular subject, accept the principles of freedom of inquiry, of opinion, and of teaching; and their purpose is not to advance knowledge by the unrestricted research and unfettered discussion of impartial investigators, but rather to subsidize the promotion of opinions held by the persons, usually not of the scholar's calling, who provide the funds for their maintenance. Concerning the desirability of the existence of such institutions, the committee does not wish to express any opinion. But it is manifestly important that they should not be permitted to sail under false colors. Genuine boldness and thoroughness of inquiry, and freedom of speech, are scarcely reconcilable with the prescribed inculcation of a particular opinion upon a controverted question.

Such institutions are rare, however, and are becoming ever more rare. We still have, indeed, colleges under denominational auspices; but very few of them impose upon their trustees responsibility for the spread of specific doctrines. They are more and more coming to occupy, with respect to the freedom enjoyed by the members of their teaching bodies, the position of untrammeled institutions of learning, and are differentiated only by the natural influence of their respective historic antecedents and traditions.

Leaving aside, then, the small number of institutions of the proprietary type, what is the nature of the trust reposed in the governing boards of the ordinary institutions of learning? Can colleges and universities that are not strictly bound by their founders to a propagandist duty ever be included in the class of institutions that we have just described as being in a moral sense proprietary? The answer is clear. If the former class of institutions constitutes a private or proprietary trust, the latter constitutes a public trust. The trustees are trustees for the public. In the case of our state universities this is self-evident. In the case of most of our privately endowed institutions, the situation is really not different. They cannot be permitted to assume the proprietary attitude and privilege, if they are appealing to the general public for support. Trustees of such universities or colleges have no moral right to bind the reason or the conscience of any professor. All claim to such right is waived by the appeal to the general public for contributions and for moral support in the maintenance, not of a propaganda, but of a non-partisan institution of learning. It follows that any university which lays restrictions upon the intellectual freedom of its professors proclaims itself a proprietary institution, and should be so described whenever it makes a general appeal for funds; and the public should be advised that the institution has no claim whatever to general support or regard.

This elementary distinction between a private and a public trust is not yet so universally accepted as it should be in our American institutions. While in many universities and colleges the situation has come to be entirely satisfactory, there are others in which the relation of trustees to professors is apparently still conceived to be analogous to that of a private employer to his employees; in which, therefore, trustees are not regarded as debarred by any moral restrictions, beyond their own sense of expediency, from imposing their personal opinions upon the teaching of the institution, or even from employing the power of dismissal to gratify their private antipathies or resentments. An eminent university president thus described the situation not many years since:

> In the institutions of higher education the board of trustees is the body on whose discretion, good feeling, and experience the securing of academic freedom now depends. There are boards which leave nothing to be desired in these respect; but there are also numerous bodies that have everything to learn with regard to academic freedom. These barbarous boards exercise an arbitrary power of dismissal. They exclude from the teachings of the university unpopular or dangerous subjects. In some states they even treat professors' positions as common political spoils; and all too frequently, in both state and endowed institutions, they fail to treat the members of the teaching staff with that high consideration to which their functions entitle them.[2]

It is, then, a prerequisite to a realization of the proper measure of academic freedom in American institutions of learning, that all boards of trustees should understand—as many already do—the full implications of the distinction between private proprietorship and a public trust.

2. The Nature of the Academic Calling

The above-mentioned conception of a university as an ordinary business venture, and of academic teaching as a purely private employment, manifests also a radical failure to apprehend the nature of the social function discharged by the professional scholar. While we should be reluctant to believe that any large number of educated persons suffer from such a misapprehension, it seems desirable at this time to restate clearly the chief reasons, lying in the nature of the university teaching profession, why it is in the public interest that the professorial office should be one both of dignity and of independence.

If education is the cornerstone of the structure of society and if progress in scientific knowledge is essential to civilization, few things can be more important than to enhance the dignity of the scholar's profession, with a view to attracting into its ranks men of the highest ability, of sound learning, and of strong and independent character. This is the more essential because the pecuniary emoluments of the profession are not, and doubtless never will be, equal to those open to the more successful members of other professions. It is not, in our opinion, desirable that men should be drawn into this profession by the magnitude of the economic rewards which it offers; but it is for this reason the more needful that men of high gift and character should be drawn into it by the assurance of an honorable and secure position, and of freedom to perform honestly and according to their own consciences the distinctive and important function which the nature of the profession lays upon them.

That function is to deal at first hand, after prolonged and specialized technical training, with the sources of knowledge; and to impart the results of their own and of their fellow-specialists' investigations and reflection, both to students and to the general public, without fear or favor. The proper discharge of this function requires (among other things) that the university teacher shall be exempt from any pecuniary motive or inducement to hold, or to express, any conclusion which is not the genuine and uncolored product of his own study or that of fellow specialists. Indeed, the proper fulfillment of the work of the professoriate requires that our universities shall be so free that no fair-minded person shall find any excuse for even a suspicion that the utterances of university teachers are shaped or restricted by the judgment, not of professional scholars, but of inexpert and possibly not wholly disinterested persons outside of their ranks. The lay public is under no compulsion to accept or to act upon the opinions of the scientific experts whom, through the universities, it employs. But it is highly needful, in the interest of society at large, that what purport to be the conclusions of men trained for, and dedicated to, the quest for truth, shall in fact be the conclusions of such men, and not echoes of the opinions of the lay public, or of the individuals who endow or manage universities. To the degree that professional scholars, in the formation and promulgation of their opinions, are, or by the character of their tenure

---

[2] From "Academic Freedom," an address delivered before the New York Chapter of the Phi Beta Kappa Society at Cornell University, May 29, 1907, by Charles William Eliot, LL.D., president of Harvard University.

appear to be, subject to any motive other than their own scientific conscience and a desire for the respect of their fellow experts, to that degree the university teaching profession is corrupted; its proper influence upon public opinion is diminished and vitiated; and society at large fails to get from its scholars, in an unadulterated form, the peculiar and necessary service which it is the office of the professional scholar to furnish.

These considerations make still more clear the nature of the relationship between university trustees and members of university faculties. The latter are the appointees, but not in any proper sense the employees, of the former. For, once appointed, the scholar has professional functions to perform in which the appointing authorities have neither competency nor moral right to intervene. The responsibility of the university teacher is primarily to the public itself, and to the judgment of his own profession; and while, with respect to certain external conditions of his vocation, he accepts a responsibility to the authorities of the institution in which he serves, in the essentials of his professional activity his duty is to the wider public to which the institution itself is morally amenable. So far as the university teacher's independence of thought and utterance is concerned—though not in other regards—the relationship of professor to trustees may be compared to that between judges of the federal courts and the executive who appoints them. University teachers should be understood to be, with respect to the conclusions reached and expressed by them, no more subject to the control of the trustees, than are judges subject to the control of the president, with respect to their decisions; while of course, for the same reason, trustees are no more to be held responsible for, or to be presumed to agree with, the opinions or utterances of professors, than the president can be assumed to approve of all the legal reasonings of the courts. A university is a great and indispensable organ of the higher life of a civilized community, in the work of which the trustees hold an essential and highly honorable place, but in which the faculties hold an independent place, with quite equal responsibilities—and in relation to purely scientific and educational questions, the primary responsibility. Misconception or obscurity in this matter has undoubtedly been a source of occasional difficulty in the past, and even in several instances during the current year, however much, in the main, a long tradition of kindly and courteous intercourse between trustees and members of university faculties has kept the question in the background.

3. The Function of the Academic Institution

The importance of academic freedom is most clearly perceived in the light of the purposes for which universities exist. These are three in number:

(a) to promote inquiry and advance the sum of human knowledge;
(b) to provide general instruction to the students; and
(c) to develop experts for various branches of the public service.

Let us consider each of these. In the earlier stages of a nation's intellectual development, the chief concern of educational institutions is to train the growing generation and to diffuse the already accepted knowledge. It is only slowly that there comes to be provided in the highest institutions of learning the opportunity for the gradual wresting from nature of her intimate secrets. The modern university is becoming more and more the home of scientific research. There are three fields of human inquiry in which the race is only at the beginning: natural science, social science, and philosophy and religion, dealing with the relations of man to outer nature, to his fellow men, and to ultimate realities and values. In natural science all that we have learned but serves to make us realize more deeply how much more remains to be discovered. In social science in its largest sense, which is concerned with the relations of men in society and with the conditions of social order and well-being, we have learned only an adumbration of the laws which govern these vastly complex phenomena. Finally, in the spirit life, and in the interpretation of the general meaning and ends of human existence and its relation to the universe, we are still far from a comprehension of the final truths, and from a universal agreement among all sincere and earnest men. In all of these domains of knowledge, the first condition of progress is complete and unlimited freedom to pursue inquiry and publish its results. Such freedom is the breath in the nostrils of all scientific activity.

The second function—which for a long time was the only function—of the American college or university is to provide instruction for students. It is scarcely open to question that freedom of utterance is as important to the teacher as it is to the investigator. No man can be a successful teacher unless he enjoys the respect of his students, and their confidence in his intellectual integrity. It is clear, however, that this confidence will be impaired if there is suspicion on the part of the student that the teacher is not expressing himself fully or frankly, or that college and university teachers in general are a repressed and intimidated class who dare not speak with that candor and courage which youth always demands in those whom it is to esteem. The average student is a discerning observer, who soon takes the measure of his instructor. It is not only the character of the instruction but also the character of the instructor that counts; and if the student has reason to believe that the instructor is not true to himself, the virtue of the instruction as an educative force is incalculably diminished. There must be in the mind of the teacher no mental reservation. He must give the student the best of what he has and what he is.

The third function of the modern university is to develop experts for the use of the community. If there is one thing that distinguishes the more recent developments of democracy, it is the recognition by legislators of the inherent complexities of economic, social, and political life, and the difficulty of solving problems of technical adjustment without technical knowledge. The recognition of this fact has led to a continually greater demand for the aid of experts in these subjects, to advise both legislators and administrators. The training of such experts has, accordingly, in recent years, become an important part of the work of the universities; and in almost every one of our higher institutions of learning the professors of the economic, social, and political sciences have been drafted to an increasing extent into more or less unofficial participation in the public service. It is obvious that here again the scholar must be absolutely free not only to pursue his investigations but to declare the results of his researches, no matter where they may lead him or to what extent they may come into conflict with accepted opinion. To be of use to the legislator or the administrator, he must enjoy their complete confidence in the disinterestedness of his conclusions.

It is clear, then, that the university cannot perform its threefold function without accepting and enforcing to the fullest extent the principle of academic freedom. The responsibility of the university as a whole is to the community at large, and any restriction upon the freedom of the instructor is bound to react injuriously upon the efficiency and the *morale* of the institution, and therefore ultimately upon the interests of the community.

* * * * *

The attempted infringements of academic freedom at present are probably not only of less frequency than, but of a different character from, those to be found in former times. In the early period of university development in America the chief menace to academic freedom was ecclesiastical, and the disciplines chiefly affected were philosophy and the natural sciences. In more recent times the danger zone has been shifted to the political and social sciences—though we still have sporadic examples of the former class of cases in some of our smaller institutions. But it is precisely in these provinces of knowledge in which academic freedom is now most likely to be threatened, that the need for it is at the same time most evident. No person of intelligence believes that all of our political problems have been solved, or that the final stage of social evolution has been reached. Grave issues in the adjustment of men's social and economic relations are certain to call for settlement in the years that are to come; and for the right settlement of them mankind will need all the wisdom, all the good will, all the soberness of mind, and all the knowledge drawn from experience, that it can command. Toward this settlement the university has potentially its own very great contribution to make; for if the adjustment reached is to be a wise one, it must take due account of economic science, and be guided by that breadth of historic vision which it should be one of the functions of a university to cultivate. But if the universities are to render any such service toward the right solution of the social problems of the future, it is the first essential that the scholars who carry on the work of universities shall not be in a position of dependence upon the favor of any social class or group, that the disinterestedness and impartiality of their inquiries and their conclusions shall be, so far as is humanly possible, beyond the reach of suspicion.

The special dangers to freedom of teaching in the domain of the social sciences are evidently two. The one which is the more likely to affect the privately endowed colleges and universities is the danger of restrictions upon the expression of opinions which point toward extensive social innovations, or call in question the moral legitimacy or social expediency of economic conditions or commercial practices in which large vested interests are involved. In the political, social, and economic field almost every question, no matter how large and general it at first appears, is more or less affected by private or class interests; and, as the governing body of a university is naturally made up of men who through their standing and ability are personally interested in great private enterprises, the points of possible conflict are numberless. When to this is added the consideration that benefactors, as well as most of the parents who send their children to privately endowed institutions, themselves belong to the more prosperous and therefore usually to the more conservative classes, it is apparent that, so long as effectual safeguards for academic freedom are not established, there is a real danger that pressure from vested interests may, sometimes deliberately and sometimes unconsciously, sometimes openly and sometimes subtly and in obscure ways, be brought to bear upon academic authorities.

On the other hand, in our state universities the danger may be the reverse. Where the university is dependent for funds upon legislative favor, it has sometimes happened that the conduct of the institution has been affected by political considerations; and where there is a definite governmental policy or a strong public feeling on economic, social, or political questions, the menace to academic freedom may consist in the repression of opinions that in the particular political situation are deemed ultra-conservative rather than ultra-radical. The essential point, however, is not so much that the opinion is of one or another shade, as that it differs from the views entertained by the authorities. The question resolves itself into one of departure from accepted standards; whether the departure is in the one direction or the other is immaterial.

This brings us to the most serious difficulty of this problem; namely, the dangers connected with the existence in a democracy of an overwhelming and concentrated public opinion. The tendency of modern democracy is for men to think alike, to feel alike, and to speak alike. Any departure from the conventional standards is apt to be regarded with suspicion. Public opinion is at once the chief safeguard of a democracy, and the chief menace to the real liberty of the individual. It almost seems as if the danger of despotism cannot be wholly averted under any form of government. In a political autocracy there is no effective public opinion, and all are subject to the tyranny of the ruler; in a democracy there is political freedom, but there is likely to be a tyranny of public opinion.

An inviolable refuge from such tyranny should be found in the university. It should be an intellectual experiment station, where new ideas may germinate and where their fruit, though still distasteful to the community as a whole, may be allowed to ripen until finally, perchance, it may become a part of the accepted intellectual food of the nation or of the world. Not less is it a distinctive duty of the university to be the conservator of all genuine elements of value in the past thought and life of mankind which are not in the fashion of the moment. Though it need not be the "home of beaten causes," the university is, indeed, likely always to exercise a certain form of conservative influence. For by its nature it is committed to the principle that knowledge should precede action, to the caution (by no means synonymous with intellectual timidity) which is an essential part of the scientific method, to a sense of the complexity of social problems, to the practice of taking long views into the future, and to a reasonable regard for the teachings of experience. One of its most characteristic functions in a democratic society is to help make public opinion more self-critical and more circumspect, to check the more hasty and unconsidered impulses of popular feeling, to train the democracy to the habit of looking before and after. It is precisely this function of the university which is most injured by any restriction upon academic freedom; and it is precisely those who most value this aspect of the university's work who should most earnestly protest against any such restriction. For the public may respect, and be influenced by, the counsels of prudence and of moderation which are given by men of science, if it believes those counsels to be the disinterested expression of the scientific temper and of unbiased inquiry. It is little likely to respect or heed them if it has reason to believe that they are the expression of the interests, or the timidities, of the limited portion of the community which is in a position to endow institutions of learning, or is most likely to be represented upon their boards of trustees. And a plausible reason for this belief is given the public so long as our universities are not organized in such a way as to make impossible any exercise of pressure upon professorial opinions and utterances by governing boards of laymen.

Since there are no rights without corresponding duties, the considerations heretofore set down with respect to the freedom of the academic teacher entail certain correlative obligations. The claim to freedom of teaching is made in the interest of the integrity and of the progress of scientific inquiry; it is, therefore, only those who carry on their work in the temper of the scientific inquirer who may justly assert this claim. The liberty of the scholar within the university to set forth his conclusions, be they what they may, is conditioned by their being conclusions gained by a scholar's method and held in a scholar's spirit; that is to say, they must be the fruits of competent and patient and sincere inquiry, and they should be set forth with dignity, courtesy, and temperateness of language. The university teacher, in giving instruction upon controversial matters, while he is under no obligation to hide his own opinion under a mountain of equivocal verbiage, should, if he is fit for his position, be a person of a fair and judicial mind; he should, in dealing with such subjects, set forth justly, without suppression or innuendo, the divergent opinions of other investigators; he should cause his students to become familiar with the best published expressions of the great historic types of doctrine upon the questions at issue; and he should, above all, remember that his business is not to provide his students with ready-made conclusions, but to train them to think for themselves, and to provide them access to those materials which they need if they are to think intelligently.

It is, however, for reasons which have already been made evident, inadmissible that the power of determining when departures from the requirements of the scientific spirit and method have occurred, should be vested in bodies not composed of members of the academic profession. Such bodies necessarily lack full competency to judge of those requirements; their intervention can never be exempt from the suspicion that it is dictated by other motives than zeal for the integrity of science; and it is, in any case, unsuitable to the dignity of a great profession that the initial responsibility for the maintenance of its professional standards should not be in the hands of its own members. It follows that university teachers must be prepared to assume this responsibility for themselves. They have hitherto seldom had the opportunity, or perhaps the disposition, to do so. The obligation will doubtless, therefore, seem to many an unwelcome and burdensome one; and for its proper discharge members of the profession will perhaps need to acquire, in a greater measure than they at present possess it, the capacity for impersonal judgment in such cases, and for judicial severity when the occasion requires it. But the responsibility cannot, in this committee's opinion, be rightfully evaded. If this profession should prove itself unwilling to purge its ranks of the incompetent and the unworthy, or to prevent the freedom which it claims in the name of science from being used as a shelter for inefficiency, for superficiality, or for uncritical and intemperate partisanship, it is certain that the task will be performed by others—by others who lack certain essential qualifications for performing it, and whose action is sure to breed suspicions and recurrent controversies deeply injurious to the internal order and the public standing of universities. Your committee has, therefore, in the appended "Practical Proposals," attempted to suggest means by which judicial action by representatives of the profession, with respect to the matters here referred to, may be secured.

There is one case in which the academic teacher is under an obligation to observe certain special restraints—namely, the instruction of immature students. In many of our American colleges, and especially in the first two years of the course, the student's character is not yet fully formed, his mind is still relatively immature. In these circumstances it may reasonably be expected that the instructor will present scientific truth with discretion, that he will introduce the student to new conceptions gradually, with some consideration for the student's preconceptions and traditions, and with due regard to character-building. The teacher ought also to be especially on his guard against taking unfair advantage of the student's immaturity by indoctrinating him with the teacher's own opinions before the student has had an opportunity fairly to examine other opinions upon the matters in question, and before he has sufficient knowledge and ripeness of judgment to be entitled to form any definitive opinion of his own. It is not the least service which a college or university may render to those under its instruction, to habituate them to looking not only patiently but methodically on both sides, before adopting any conclusion upon controverted issues. By these suggestions, however, it need scarcely be said that the committee does not intend to imply that it is not the duty of an academic instructor to give to any students old enough to be in college a genuine intellectual awakening and to arouse in them a keen desire to reach personally verified conclusions upon all questions of general concernment to mankind, or of special significance for their own time. There is much truth in some remarks recently made in this connection by a college president:

> Certain professors have been refused reelection lately, apparently because they set their students to thinking in ways objectionable to the trustees. It would be well if more teachers were dismissed because they fail to stimulate thinking of any kind. We can afford to forgive a college professor what we regard as the occasional error of his doctrine, especially as we may be wrong, provided he is a contagious center of intellectual enthusiasm. It is better for students to think about heresies than not to think at all; better for them to climb new trails, and stumble over error if need be, than to ride forever in upholstered ease in the overcrowded highway. It is a primary duty of a teacher to make a student take an honest account of his stock of ideas, throw out the dead matter, place revised price marks on what is left, and try to fill his empty shelves with new goods.[3]

It is, however, possible and necessary that such intellectual awakening be brought about with patience, considerateness, and pedagogical wisdom.

There is one further consideration with regard to the classroom utterances of college and university teachers to which the committee thinks it important to call the attention of members of the profession, and of administrative authorities. Such utterances ought always to be considered privileged communications. Discussions in the classroom ought not to be supposed to be utterances for the public at large. They are often designed to provoke opposition or arouse debate. It has, unfortunately, sometimes happened in this country that sensational newspapers have quoted and garbled such remarks. As a matter of common law, it is clear that the utterances of an academic instructor are privileged, and may not be published, in whole or part, without his authorization. But our practice, unfortunately, still differs from that of foreign countries, and no effective check has in this country been put upon such unauthorized and often misleading publication. It is much to be desired that test cases should be made of any infractions of the rule.[4]

In their extramural utterances, it is obvious that academic teachers are under a peculiar obligation to avoid hasty or unverified or exaggerated statements, and to refrain from intemperate or sensational modes of expression. But, subject to these restraints, it is not, in this committee's opinion, desirable that scholars should be debarred from giving expression to their judgments upon controversial questions, or that their freedom of speech, outside the university, should be limited to questions falling within their own specialties. It is clearly not proper that they should be prohibited from lending their active support to organized movements which they believe to be in the public interest. And, speaking broadly, it may be said in the words of a nonacademic body already once quoted in a publication of this Association, that "it is neither possible nor desirable to deprive a college professor of the political rights vouchsafed to every citizen."[5]

It is, however, a question deserving of consideration by members of this Association, and by university officials, how far academic teachers, at least those dealing with political, economic, and social subjects, should be prominent in the management of our great party organizations, or should be candidates for state or national offices of a distinctly political character. It is manifestly desirable that such teachers have minds untrammeled by party loyalties, unexcited by party enthusiasms, and unbiased by personal political ambitions; and that universities should remain uninvolved in party antagonisms. On the other hand, it is equally manifest that the material available for the service of the state would be restricted in a highly undesirable way,

---

[3] President William T. Foster in *The Nation*, November 11, 1915.
[4] The leading case is *Abernethy v. Hutchison*, 3 L. J., Ch. 209. In this case, where damages were awarded, the court held as follows: "That persons who are admitted as pupils or otherwise to hear these lectures, although they are orally delivered and the parties might go to the extent, if they were able to do so, of putting down the whole by means of shorthand, yet they can do that only for the purpose of their own information and could not publish, for profit, that which they had not obtained the right of selling."
[5] Report of the Wisconsin State Board of Public Affairs, December 1914.

if it were understood that no member of the academic profession should ever be called upon to assume the responsibilities of public office. This question may, in the committee's opinion, suitably be made a topic for special discussion at some future meeting of this Association, in order that a practical policy, which shall do justice to the two partially conflicting considerations that bear upon the matter, may be agreed upon.

It is, it will be seen, in no sense the contention of this committee that academic freedom implies that individual teachers should be exempt from all restraints as to the matter or manner of their utterances, either within or without the university. Such restraints as are necessary should in the main, your committee holds, be self-imposed, or enforced by the public opinion of the profession. But there may, undoubtedly, arise occasional cases in which the aberrations of individuals may require to be checked by definite disciplinary action. What this report chiefly maintains is that such action cannot with safety be taken by bodies not composed of members of the academic profession. Lay governing boards are competent to judge concerning charges of habitual neglect of assigned duties, on the part of individual teachers, and concerning charges of grave moral delinquency. But in matters of opinion, and of the utterance of opinion, such boards cannot intervene without destroying, to the extent of their intervention, the essential nature of a university—without converting it from a place dedicated to openness of mind, in which the conclusions expressed are the tested conclusions of trained scholars, into a place barred against the access of new light, and precommitted to the opinions or prejudices of men who have not been set apart or expressly trained for the scholar's duties. It is, in short, not the absolute freedom of utterance of the individual scholar, but the absolute freedom of thought, of inquiry, of discussion and of teaching, of the academic profession, that is asserted by this declaration of principles. It is conceivable that our profession may prove unworthy of its high calling, and unfit to exercise the responsibilities that belong to it. But it will scarcely be said as yet to have given evidence of such unfitness. And the existence of this Association, as it seems to your committee, must be construed as a pledge, not only that the profession will earnestly guard those liberties without which it cannot rightly render its distinctive and indispensable service to society, but also that it will with equal earnestness seek to maintain such standards of professional character, and of scientific integrity and competency, as shall make it a fit instrument for that service.

PRACTICAL PROPOSALS

As the foregoing declaration implies, the ends to be accomplished are chiefly three:

First: To safeguard freedom of inquiry and of teaching against both covert and overt attacks, by providing suitable judicial bodies, composed of members of the academic profession, which may be called into action before university teachers are dismissed or disciplined, and may determine in what cases the question of academic freedom is actually involved.

Second: By the same means, to protect college executives and governing boards against unjust charges of infringement of academic freedom, or of arbitrary and dictatorial conduct— charges which, when they gain wide currency and belief, are highly detrimental to the good repute and the influence of universities.

Third: To render the profession more attractive to men of high ability and strong personality by insuring the dignity, the independence, and the reasonable security of tenure, of the professorial office. The measures which it is believed to be necessary for our universities to adopt to realize these ends—measures which have already been adopted in part by some institutions—are four:

1. Action by Faculty Committees on Reappointments

Official action relating to reappointments and refusals of reappointment should be taken only with the advice and consent of some board or committee representative of the faculty. Your committee does not desire to make at this time any suggestion as to the manner of selection of such boards.

2. Definition of Tenure of Office

In every institution there should be an unequivocal understanding as to the term of each appointment; and the tenure of professorships and associate professorships, and of all positions above the grade of instructor after ten years of service, should be permanent (subject to the provisions hereinafter given for removal upon charges). In those state universities which are legally incapable of making contracts for more than a limited period, the governing boards should announce their policy with respect to the presumption of reappointment in the several classes of position, and such announcements, though not legally enforceable, should be regarded as morally binding. No university teacher of any rank should, except in cases of grave moral delinquency, receive notice of dismissal or of refusal of reappointment, later than three months before the close of any academic year, and in the case of teachers above the grade of instructor, one year's notice should be given.

3. *Formulation of Grounds for Dismissal*

In every institution the grounds which will be regarded as justifying the dismissal of members of the faculty should be formulated with reasonable definiteness; and in the case of institutions which impose upon their faculties doctrinal standards of a sectarian or partisan character, these standards should be clearly defined and the body or individual having authority to interpret them, in case of controversy, should be designated. Your committee does not think it best at this time to attempt to enumerate the legitimate grounds for dismissal, believing it to be preferable that individual institutions should take the initiative in this.

4. *Judicial Hearings Before Dismissal*

Every university or college teacher should be entitled, before dismissal[6] or demotion, to have the charges against him stated in writing in specific terms and to have a fair trial on those charges before a special or permanent judicial committee chosen by the faculty senate or council, or by the faculty at large. At such trial the teacher accused should have full opportunity to present evidence, and, if the charge is one of professional incompetency, a formal report upon his work should be first made in writing by the teachers of his own department and of cognate departments in the university, and, if the teacher concerned so desires, by a committee of his fellow specialists from other institutions, appointed by some competent authority.

---

[6] This does not refer to refusals of reappointment at the expiration of the terms of office of teachers below the rank of associate professor. All such questions of reappointment should, as above provided, be acted upon by a faculty committee.

APPENDIX II
Association Procedures in Academic Freedom and Tenure Cases

The following procedures were initially approved by the Committee on Academic Freedom and Tenure (Committee A) in August 1957. Subsequent revisions were approved by Committee A in June 1982, November 1999, and June 2000.

1. The general secretary[1] is authorized to receive, on behalf of Committee A, complaints from faculty members at duly accredited colleges and universities about departures from the Association's recommended standards concerned with academic freedom and tenure and related principles and procedures which are alleged to have occurred or to be threatened at their institutions. Incidents coming to the general secretary's attention through other channels may also be subject to examination, if in the general secretary's judgment the incidents in question are likely to be of concern to the Association. In cases where attention by the Association seems justified, the general secretary shall make a preliminary inquiry and, where appropriate, communicate with the administration of the institution concerned in order to secure factual information and comments.

2. The general secretary should attempt to assist the complainant(s) and the institution in arriving at a satisfactory resolution of the situation, if that appears to be possible.

3. If there is substantial reason to believe that a serious departure from applicable Association-supported standards has occurred, and if a satisfactory resolution of the situation does not appear to be possible, the general secretary shall determine, upon the advice of the staff's committee on investigations and of others as appropriate, whether an ad hoc committee should be established to investigate and prepare a written report on the situation. In an exceptional case in which a violation of the 1940 *Statement of Principles on Academic Freedom and Tenure* or related Association standards is clearly established by incontrovertible written evidence, the general secretary may authorize the preparation of a report without an on-site investigation.

4. If a decision is made to establish an investigating committee, the general secretary shall designate a committee of two, three, or occasionally a larger number of members of the Association, depending upon the importance and complexity of the case. One of the members ordinarily shall be designated as chair. In selecting the members, the general secretary shall take account of such relevant factors as their experience and expertise in academic freedom and tenure issues, their subject matter fields in relation to those of the faculty member(s) involved in the incident(s), and the relation of their home institutions to the institution where the investigation will occur.

5. The general secretary shall provide the committee with an advisory briefing on the procedures it will be expected to follow, on the existing information about the situation to be reported upon, and on the issues that appear to call for analysis, accompanied by available documentary evidence relevant to the investigation. The task of the investigating committee is to

---

[1] As used in this statement, "general secretary" means the general secretary or another professional staff member of the Association who may be delegated to perform the duties of the general secretary in relation to a particular matter.

ascertain the facts involved in the incident(s) under investigation and the positions of the principal parties. The committee will determine whether the 1940 *Statement of Principles on Academic Freedom and Tenure* and/or related standards as interpreted by the Association have been violated, whether the institution's own stated policies have been disregarded, and whether conditions for academic freedom and tenure, as well as related conditions, are generally unsatisfactory. The general secretary shall assist the committee so far as possible in making arrangements for its work and in providing it with clerical and editorial services.

6. The investigating committee shall, at Association expense, visit the institution where the incident(s) under investigation occurred, for the purpose of securing information and interviewing the parties concerned and others who may possess relevant information or views.

7. The investigating committee should inquire fully into the violation(s) of AAUP standards alleged to have occurred, into conditions of academic freedom and tenure in the institution that form the background of the particular case(s) or that may have given rise to related incidents, and into relevant subsequent developments. The investigating committee may seek to secure such facts and viewpoints as it may deem necessary for the investigation, through on-site interviews, written documents, or correspondence or interviews both before and after the campus visit. In communications with the principal parties and on its visit to the institution, the investigating committee should make clear that it acts not in partisanship, but as a professional body charged with ascertaining the facts and respective positions as objectively as possible and as related to applicable Association-supported standards.

8. In an institution where a local chapter of the Association exists, the general secretary should consult with the chapter officers when an investigation is being considered, when one is authorized, and when the visit of the investigating committee is being arranged. Either the general secretary or the committee may seek the assistance of these officers in making local arrangements. The appropriate officer of the state conference shall also be consulted.

9. The investigating committee should not accept hospitality or any form of special treatment from the administration, from a faculty member whose case is being investigated, or from anyone else who has had a direct involvement in the case. The AAUP chapter should be alerted to the need to avoid situations, such as social events, which might compromise the integrity of the investigation. If the administration provides a room or other facilities for the committee's interviews, the committee may accept the arrangements if this will serve the convenience of the investigation.

10. The investigating committee may interview any persons who might be able to provide information about the matter(s) under investigation, and it must afford the subject faculty member(s) and the chief administrative officers the opportunity to meet with the committee. The committee should set up personal interviews with individuals who have first-hand information, whether members of the faculty, members of the governing board, or officers of the administration. The committee should also seek meetings with officers of faculty bodies and of the AAUP chapter. Such persons should ordinarily be interviewed separately from each other, but exceptions may be made upon the wishes of those interviewed and at the discretion of the committee. In order for the Association's investigative and mediative processes to be most effective, faculty members, board members, and administrators alike need to be able to communicate freely with the investigating committee. Accordingly, the committee should encourage candor from all interviewees by protecting their confidentiality to the fullest extent possible consistent with the committee's need to prepare its report to Committee A. Information gathered in the course of an investigation should be kept confidential to the maximum extent permitted by law.

11. The function of the investigating committee is to prepare a report for submission to Committee A. The members of the investigating committee should not express opinions upon the matter(s) under investigation, either confidentially to the parties concerned or publicly. If questions about a potential resolution of the situation under investigation should arise, the committee should refer the matter promptly to the general secretary.

12. The investigating committee should determine its plan for the writing of its report. The report should include a sufficiently full statement of the evidence to enable the reader to understand the situation and judge the adequacy of the information in support of the committee's

findings and conclusions. The report should state definite conclusions, either on the issues suggested to the committee by the general secretary or upon its own alternative formulation of the issues involved. The committee should determine whether the administration's actions that were investigated were in procedural and substantive compliance with principles and standards supported by the Association. The committee may set forth recommendations for or against publication of its report and for or against Association censure of the administration concerned; but the decision on these matters will rest with Committee A and, as to censure, with the annual meeting of the Association. Hence any recommendation as to censure will not be published as part of the report. The report should be transmitted in confidence to the general secretary.

13. As soon as possible after receiving the report of the investigating committee, the general secretary shall review it and communicate with the committee regarding any suggestions for revision. The committee's completed draft shall be transmitted to the members of Committee A, who may call for further revisions prior to the report's release to the principal parties and its potential publication. With Committee A's approval, the revised text shall then be transmitted on a confidential basis to the persons most significantly involved in the report, and to the local chapter president, with the request that they provide corrections of any errors of fact that may appear in it and make such comments as they may desire upon the findings and conclusions reached. The appropriate state conference officer shall be provided with the prepublication report on a confidential basis and be invited to offer comments. The general secretary shall invite the investigating committee to revise its report in the light of comments received. If significant revisions are to be made, the general secretary shall seek Committee A's approval. The final text shall be published in *Academe: Bulletin of the American Association of University Professors*. The members of the investigating committee shall be listed as the authors of the published report unless they withhold their names because of disagreement with changes required by Committee A or as a result of comments from the principal parties.

14. At any time during the process described above, the Association remains open to the possibility of a resolution agreeable to all parties that will serve to confirm the administration's acceptance of Association-supported policies and procedures and provide corrective measures for the events which gave rise to the investigation.

APPENDIX III
Standards for Investigations in the Area of College and University Government

---

In 1991, the Association's Council adopted a proposal from the Committee on College and University Government (Committee T) that makes it possible for an AAUP annual meeting to sanction an institution for "substantial non-compliance with standards of academic government." The following procedures, approved by Committee T in May 1994, set out the steps along the path which could lead from an expression of faculty concern at an institution to the imposition and removal of an Association sanction.

1. The general secretary[1] is authorized to receive, on behalf of Committee T, complaints of departures from the Association's recommended standards relating to academic governance at a particular college or university.
2. Such complaints should include a description of the situation and specific information on the past or contemplated use of local remedies. They should be accompanied by supporting documentation.
3. The general secretary shall, in each instance where attention by the Association seems justified, make a preliminary inquiry and, where appropriate, communicate with the administration of the institution to secure information and comments.
4. When feasible, the general secretary should attempt, by correspondence and discussion, to assist the parties to arrive at a resolution compatible with AAUP principles and standards.
5. If there is a substantial reason to believe that a serious departure from applicable Association-supported standards has occurred, and if a satisfactory resolution of the situation does not appear to be possible, the general secretary shall determine, upon the advice of the staff's committee on investigations and of others as appropriate, whether an ad hoc committee should be established to investigate and produce a written report on the situation.
6. In determining whether to proceed to investigation and report on situations related to college or university government, the Association looks to the condition of faculty status and of faculty-administration relations. The Association will investigate when it appears that corporate or individual functions of the faculty, as defined in the 1966 *Statement on Government of Colleges and Universities*, have been seriously threatened or impaired. In reaching a decision on whether or not to undertake an investigation, the general secretary will consider the magnitude of the problem for the faculty involved, for the institution as a whole, and for the Association in its capacity as an organization representing faculty interests in higher education.
7. The Association will ordinarily investigate only after local means for correction—formal as well as informal—have been pursued without satisfactory result. This precondition may not apply where local remedies are inadequate or where recourse to them would worsen the situation or expose individual faculty members to harm.
8. If a decision is made to establish an investigating committee, the general secretary shall appoint the members of the committee, designating one of them as chair. In selecting the members, the general secretary shall consider such relevant factors as their experience and expertise in governance matters.

---

[1] As used in this statement, the "general secretary" may be another member of the Association's professional staff to whom the general secretary has assigned the particular responsibility.

9. The task of the investigating committee is to determine the relevant facts and the positions of the principal parties and to reach findings on whether the standards enunciated in the *Statement on Government* and in derivative Association documents have been violated, and whether unacceptable conditions of academic government prevail. The general secretary shall provide the investigating committee with an advisory briefing on the procedures it will be expected to follow during a campus visit and on the facts, issues, and available documentary evidence relevant to the investigation. The general secretary shall also assist the committee so far as possible in making arrangements for its work and in providing it with clerical and editorial support.

10. The investigating committee's report, to be submitted in confidence to the general secretary, should include sufficient facts for the reader to understand the situation and judge the adequacy of the evidence in support of the committee's findings and conclusions. The committee should determine whether actions by the principal parties were reasonable under the circumstances and consistent with applicable Association-recommended procedural and substantive standards. The committee is welcome to offer advice to Committee T as to whether the Association should impose a sanction on the institution concerned; but it is Committee T's responsibility to determine whether a recommendation to impose a sanction should be presented to the annual meeting of the Association. Hence, any recommendation as to a sanction will not be published as part of the report.

11. As soon as possible after receiving the report of the investigating committee, the general secretary shall review it and communicate any suggestions for revision to the investigating committee. When the report has been satisfactorily revised, the general secretary shall send it to the members of Committee T for comment and a decision concerning its publication. As a condition of approving publication, or by way of suggestion to the authors of the report, the members of Committee T may propose changes in the draft text. After further revision, the text shall then be transmitted confidentially to the persons most significantly affected by or implicated in the report, including the chief administrative officers of the institution, with the request that they provide corrections of any errors of fact that may appear in it and make such comments as they may desire upon the findings and conclusions reached. If their responses indicate a need for significant changes in the report, the text with the resulting revisions may be resubmitted to Committee T. With that committee's concurrence, and after the investigating committee has been consulted as to final revisions, the report will be published in *Academe: Bulletin of the American Association of University Professors*. An advance copy of the published report shall be transmitted to the principal parties.

12. If Committee T judges, based on the published report and any subsequent developments, that the administration and/or governing board of the institution under investigation has seriously infringed standards of college and university government endorsed by the Association, it may recommend to the next annual meeting that the institution be sanctioned for "substantial non-compliance with standards of academic government." If the annual meeting concurs with the recommendation of Committee T, notice of "non-compliance" will be published regularly in *Academe*, for the purpose of informing Association members, the profession at large, and the public that unsatisfactory conditions of academic government exist at the institution in question.

13. After a notice of sanction has been published by the Association, the general secretary, acting on behalf of Committee T, will correspond periodically with the administration and appropriate faculty groups at the institution, seeking to ascertain whether stated policies and procedures have been brought into substantial conformity with standards of college and university government endorsed by the Association, and whether evidence exists of meaningful faculty participation in academic governance. So long as a particular college or university remains under sanction, Committee T will monitor and report on developments at the institution.

14. When evidence has been obtained that a sanctioned institution has achieved substantial compliance with Association-supported governance standards, Committee T will review the information and determine whether to recommend to the annual meeting of the Association that the sanction be removed. Notice of the recommendation and the action will be published in *Academe*.

APPENDIX IV
Selected Judicial Decisions and Scholarly Writings Referring to AAUP Standards

The federal and state courts have, on many occasions, relied on Association policy statements for assistance in resolving academic disputes.[1] Listed below are some examples of judicial decisions referring to AAUP statements in this volume, as well as a few selected scholarly discussions of AAUP policies as a source of "common law" for higher education. Note that this list is merely illustrative and not exhaustive. It is designed only to serve as a useful starting point for further research on the subject.

I. 1940 Statement of Principles on Academic Freedom and Tenure (Pages 3–10)

The Supreme Court and some lower courts have used the 1940 *Statement* in resolving disputes over the eligibility of religious colleges and universities for government support. *Tilton v. Richardson*, 403 U.S. 672, 681–82 (1971)—Adoption of 1940 *Statement* by church-related institutions supports conclusion that "the schools were characterized by an atmosphere of academic freedom rather than religious indoctrination." *Roemer v. Board of Public Works of Maryland*, 426 U.S. 736, 756 (1976)—The fact that "[e]ach college subscribes to, and abides by, the 1940 *Statement* . . ." indicates that the Catholic colleges receiving an annual state subsidy were not pervasively sectarian. *Minnesota Federation of Teachers v. Mammenga*, 485 N.W. 2d 305, 307 (Minn. App. 1992)—Because "the respondent colleges all follow the 1940 *Statement* . . .," they were non-sectarian despite their religious affiliations. *Minnesota Higher Educ. Facilities Auth. v. Hawk*, 305 Minn. 97, 101, 232 N.W.2d 106, 109 (Minn. 1975)—Private colleges benefiting from tax-exempt revenue bonds were nonsectarian, because "the colleges all adhere to the 1940 *Statement*. . . ."

Krotkoff v. Goucher College, 585 F.2d 675, 679 (4th Cir. 1978)—"Probably because it was formulated by both administrators and professors, all of the secondary authorities seem to agree it [1940 *Statement*] is the 'most widely-accepted academic definition of tenure.'"

Barnes v. Washington State Community College Dist. No. 22, 529 P.2d 1102 (Wash. 1975)—The court observes that "[t]he most authoritative source regarding the meaning and purpose of tenure is the American Association of University Professors."

Jiminez v. Almodovar, 650 F.2d 363, 369 (1st Cir. 1981)—When the Puerto Rico legislature enacted a statute concerning dismissal of university personnel with permanent appointments, it presumably was aware of, and intended to preserve, the distinction made in the 1940 *Statement* between a dismissal for cause or for other personal grounds and a dismissal for impersonal institutional reasons such as a change in academic program.

Adamian v. Jacobsen, 523 F.2d 929, 934–35 (9th Cir. 1975)—University regulation on adequate cause for dismissal of tenured faculty member may not be unconstitutionally overbroad if construed by the regents in the same manner as AAUP interprets the 1940 *Statement*.

---

[1] A precursor of this trend is *Cobb v. Howard University*, 106 F.2d 860, 865–66 n. 21 (D.C. Cir. 1939), in which the court noted an increasing emphasis on tenure rights and observed that the AAUP devoted much of its effort toward the protection of tenure.

Bignall v. North Idaho College, 538 F.2d 243, 249 (9th Cir. 1976)—Court of Appeals adopts 1940 *Statement* definition of tenure in financial exigency situation.

McConnell v. Howard University, 818 F.2d 58, 64 n. 7 (D.C. Cir. 1987)—The contractual terms included in the faculty handbook "must be construed in keeping with general usage and custom at the University and within the academic community," citing cases which rely significantly on the 1940 *Statement*.

II. 1958 Statement on Procedural Standards in Faculty Dismissal Proceedings (Pages 11–14)

Lehmann v. Board of Trustees of Whitman College, 576 P.2d 397, 399 (Wash. 1978)—Tenured faculty member's dismissal for misconduct comported with 1958 *Statement on Procedural Standards,* which the institution had adopted.

III. Statement on Procedural Standards in the Renewal or Nonrenewal of Faculty Appointments (Pages 15–20)

Board of Regents of State Colleges v. Roth, 408 U.S. 564, 579 n. 17 (1972)—While concluding that no hearing was constitutionally required on facts of case, Court expressly leaves open the possibility that a hearing or statement of reasons for nonretention may be appropriate or wise in public colleges and universities, citing AAUP's *Statement on Procedural Standards.*

Kunda v. Muhlenberg College, 621 F.2d 532, 545 n. 5 (3rd Cir. 1980)—Decision cites *Statement on Procedural Standards;* the court explains that a university acts unfairly when it deviates from its published standards regarding renewal or nonrenewal of faculty.

IV. Recommended Institutional Regulations on Academic Freedom and Tenure (Pages 21–30)

Beitzell v. Jeffrey, 643 F.2d 870, 872 n. 1 (1st Cir. 1978)—Court notes that University of Massachusetts policies on granting of tenure generally followed AAUP's procedures, and that these policies are followed by numerous universities. The court cites, inter alia, the *Recommended Institutional Regulations.*

Mabey v. Reagan, 537 F.2d 1036, 1043 (9th Cir. 1976)—Court finds useful AAUP's definition of financial exigency, which appears in Regulation 4(c)(1) of the *Recommended Institutional Regulations.*

Browzin v. Catholic University of America, 527 F.2d 843 (D.C. Cir. 1975)—In dismissal of tenured faculty member for reasons of financial exigency, court uses *Recommended Institutional Regulations* as a guide in resolving whether other suitable positions were available, whether replacement was hired soon after dismissal, and upon which party burden of proof lay.

Linn v. Andover Newton Theological School, Inc., 874 F.2d 1, 4–5 (1st Cir. 1989)—Age discrimination and financial exigency contract claim. Discussion of differing standards of financial exigency found in successive revisions of the *Recommended Institutional Regulations.* Both parties agreed that the *Recommended Institutional Regulations* were incorporated by reference into the faculty member's contract.

V. Standards for Notice of Nonreappointment (Page 31)

Greene v. Howard University, 412 F.2d 1128, 1133 n. 7 (D.C. Cir. 1969)—Court takes judicial notice that university handbook incorporates AAUP policy, and quotes *Standards for Notice.*

Mosby v. Webster College, 423 F. Supp. 615 (E.D. Mo. 1976)—Court describes AAUP notice standards and observes that college strictly adheres to them.

VI. Statement on Professional Ethics (Pages 133–34)

Keen v. Penson, 970 F.2d 252, 256 (7th Cir. 1992)—Faculty hearing committee found that professor violated standards for treatment of students established by *Statement on Professional Ethics*, which was incorporated into university rules. Professor had given student unjustified failing grade, demanded that she write letter of apology to him, and failed to treat her with respect.

Korf v. Ball State University, 726 F.2d 1222, 1227 (7th Cir. 1984)—*Statement on Professional Ethics*, which was incorporated into university faculty handbook, prohibits the "exploitation of students for private advantage." The court endorsed the governing board's interpretation of the provision as prohibiting sexual exploitation.

VII. Statement on Government of Colleges and Universities (Pages 217–23)

Barnes v. Washington State Community College Dist. No. 22, 529 P.2d 1102, 1104 (Wash. 1975) (*en banc*) and *Zumwalt v. Trustees of California State Colleges*, 33 Cal. App. 3rd 665, 671 n. 3 (1973)—Both cases quote and follow the *Statement*'s provision that a department chairperson does not have tenure in that office, in contrast to tenure as a faculty member.

VIII. On Institutional Problems Resulting from Financial Exigency: Some Operating Guidelines (Pages 230–31)

Levitt v. Board of Trustees of Nebraska State Colleges, 376 F. Supp. 945, 950 (D. Neb. 1974)—Decision quotes *Operating Guidelines* on retention of viable academic programs in reduction decisions.

IX. Joint Statement on Rights and Freedoms of Students (Pages 261–67)

Stricklin v. Regents of University of Wisconsin, 297 F. Supp. 416, 420 (W.D. Wisc. 1969)—*Joint Statement*'s standard for suspension pending action on disciplinary charges against student is "a fair and reasonable standard, entitled to recognition as an essential ingredient of the procedural due process. . . ."

Soglin v. Kauffman, 295 F. Supp. 978, 990 (W.D. Wisc. 1968), aff'd, 418 F.2d 163 (7th Cir. 1969)—Court quotes with approval predecessor *Statement on the Academic Freedom of Students* for proposition that standards for student misconduct should be clear and explicit.

X. Selected Scholarly Writings on Legal Enforcement of AAUP Policy

Benson, Dena Elliott. "Tenure Rights in Higher Education in the Face of Financial Exigency: The Impact of Private Agreement, Collective Bargaining, the AAUP and the Courts." *Detroit College of Law Review* (fall 1983): 679–707.

Brooks, Brian G. "Adequate Cause for Dismissal: The Missing Element in Academic Freedom." *Journal of College and University Law* 22 (1995): 331–58.

Brown, Ralph S. "Tenure Rights in Contractual and Constitutional Context." *Journal of Law and Education* 6 (1977): 279–318.

Brown, Ralph S., and Matthew W. Finkin. "The Usefulness of AAUP Policy Statements." *Educational Record* 59 (1978): 30–44.

Byrne, J. Peter. "Academic Freedom: A 'Special Concern of the First Amendment.'" *Yale Law Journal* 99 (1989): 251–340.

"Developments in the Law—Academic Freedom." *Harvard Law Review* 81 (1968): 1045–1159.

"Financial Exigency as Cause for Termination of Tenured Faculty Members in Private Post-Secondary Educational Institutions." *Iowa Law Review* 62 (1976): 481–521.

Finkin, Matthew W. "Regulation by Agreement: The Case of Private Higher Education." *Iowa Law Review* 65 (1980): 1119–1200.

Furniss, W. Todd. "The Status of 'AAUP Policy.'" *Educational Record* 59 (1978): 7–29.

Kaplin, William A., and Barbara A. Lee. *The Law of Higher Education: A Comprehensive Guide to Legal Implications of Administrative Decision Making*. 3d ed. San Francisco: Jossey-Bass, Inc., 1995.

Matheson, Scott M., Jr. "Judicial Enforcement of Academic Tenure: An Examination." *Washington Law Review* 50 (1975): 597–622.

Olivas, Michael A. *The Law and Higher Education: Cases and Materials on Colleges in Court*. 2d ed. Durham, N.C.: Carolina Academic Press, 1997.

"The Role of Academic Freedom in Defining the Faculty Employment Contract." *Case Western Reserve Law Review* 31 (1981): 608–55.

"Symposium on Academic Freedom." *Texas Law Review* 66 (1988): 1247–1659.

Van Alstyne, William W., ed. "Freedom and Tenure in the Academy: The Fiftieth Anniversary of the 1940 *Statement of Principles*." *Journal of Law and Contemporary Problems* 53 (summer 1990). Includes nine articles on academic freedom and tenure, many with discussions of AAUP policy.

INDEX

Association of College and Research
Libraries, joint statement with AAUP,
238–39
Association of Governing Boards of Universities and Colleges, 215, 217
joint statements with AAUP, 35–36,
217–23
Association Procedures in Academic Freedom and Tenure Cases, text, 302–4
Athletics, intercollegiate, 240–41
role of faculty in governance of, 242–47
Authorship, multiple, 149–50
copyright and, 183–84
Autonomy, institutional, 135
affirmative action and, 204

B

*Barnes v. Washington State Community College
Dist. No. 22* (1975), 307, 309
Beitzell v. Jeffrey (1978), 308
Benefits, collateral. *See* Collateral benefits
Bignall v. North Idaho College (1976), 308
Board of Regents of State Colleges v. Roth
(1972), 308
Board of trustees. *See* Governing board
Brown, Ralph S., ix
Browzin v. Catholic University of America
(1975), 308
Budgetary matters
faculty role in, 23n, 219, 221, 225, 232–34,
244
and intercollegiate athletics, 241, 244
mandated assessments of educational
outcomes and, 167
students' role in, 232n. 2
Burden of proof in dismissal proceedings,
26, 50, 52, 56, 212, 260
Burlington Industries, Inc. v. Ellerth, 208n. 1

C

Carnegie Commission for the Advancement
of Teaching, 127
Cases and complaints, AAUP processing of,
189–91, 302–4
Censure, AAUP
in academic freedom and tenure cases,
304
in discrimination cases, 185, 186, 190
"limitations" clause and, 99
Chapters, AAUP, ix, 251–52, 289, 303, 304
Charges against faculty
for extramural utterances, 5, 32
written, 4, 12, 26, 118, 212, 259
Children of faculty, 202, 273, 281

Church-related institutions
academic freedom and, 3, 6, 96–99, 293, 307
admission to, 262
appointments to, 202–3
governing boards of, 220
"limitations" clause and, 3, 6, 96–99
Citizens, rights of, 219–20
faculty, 4, 6, 25, 29, 32, 33, 119, 134, 136,
219–20, 226, 292
students, 119, 219–20, 265
Cobb v. Howard University (1939), 307n
Collateral benefits, 273–81
faculty child care, 281
leaves of absence, 278–80
retirement and insurance plans, 275–77
Collective bargaining, 249–60
AAUP history of, 249
and AAUP policy on strikes, 252
academic government and, 222n, 251,
253–54
arbitration in dismissal cases and, 92–95,
259–60
and arbitration of faculty grievances,
255–58
conscientious objection to, 251
by graduate students, 270
non-tenure-track faculty and, 83
part-time faculty and, 63, 82–83, 84
See also Arbitration
Collective Bargaining Congress, AAUP, 289
College and University Policies on Substance
Abuse and Drug Testing, text, 115–23
Collegiality as a Criterion for Faculty Evaluation, On, text, 39–40
Commission on Academic Tenure in Higher
Education, 61, 61n. 13, 84
Committee A on Academic Freedom and
Tenure, 15, 21, 32, 33, 35, 37, 39, 41, 47, 50,
57, 68, 69, 88, 96, 100, 102, 103, 110, 113,
115, 124, 130, 186, 212, 213, 224, 230, 236,
249, 255, 259
complaints and cases, 189–91, 302
discrimination policy and, 185
and extramural utterances, 6, 32, 226n
investigating committee reports, x, 1,
190–91, 302–4
on "limitations" clause, 96–99
Committee A Statement on Extramural
Utterances. *See* Statement on Extramural
Utterances, Committee A
Committee on Accrediting of Colleges and
Universities, 271
Committee on College and University Government (Committee T), 215, 224, 228,
230, 232, 236, 242, 249, 253

of non-tenure-track faculty, 86
of part-time faculty, 62, 63, 86
in post-tenure review, 50–56
of probationary faculty, 7, 16–17, 22
of student performance, 113–14, 133, 135,
  163, 262
of teaching, 162–65
See also Mandated Assessment of Educational Outcomes
Exploitation of athletes, 240
Extramural utterances, 219–20
  academic freedom and, 4, 6, 32, 226, 292,
    299–300
  as grounds for dismissal, 5, 32

F

Faculty
  and accreditation of academic institutions, 271–72
  and administrators' selection, evaluation,
    and retention, 219, 228–29
  affirmative-action plans and, 204
  appointment and family relationship, 213
  arbitration of grievances of, 255–58
  and budgetary and salary matters, 23,
    219, 221–22, 225, 232–35, 244
  as citizens, 4, 6, 25, 29, 32, 33, 119, 134,
    136, 219–20, 226, 292
  collegiality of, 39–40
  course grade assignments and, 113–14
  evaluation by students, 53, 162–65
  evaluation of students, 113–14, 133, 135,
    163, 262
  financial exigency decisions and, 23–24,
    230–31
  fringe benefits selection and, 235
  governance and academic freedom, 42,
    111–12, 224–27, 300
  government-sponsored research and,
    144–46, 147–48
  grievance procedures for, 26–27, 29–30
  hearing committee on dismissal, 4, 13–14,
    25–27, 32, 92, 93–94, 301
  history of role of, 11
  institutional government and, 221–22
  institutional mergers and, 233–34, 236–37
  intercollegiate athletics and, 240–41,
    242–47
  leave policies and, 278–80
  liability, institutional responsibility for, 130
  mandatory retirement of, 4, 102, 277
  nonreappointment review committee,
    19–20, 22–23, 28
  nontenured, evaluation of, 7, 16–17, 22,
    62, 63, 86

part-time, 57–67, 77
personnel files, access to, 41–46
political activities of, 29, 32, 33–34
post-tenure review of, 50–56
probationary rights of, 15–16, 22–23
professional ethics, 6, 43, 113, 131, 133–50,
  208–9, 211, 226
program discontinuance and, 25, 68n
program reduction and, 230–31
rank, 4, 6, 88–91, 139, 141, 142, 238–39
recruitment of, 139–40, 141–43, 197–98,
  205–6
research activities, 3, 135, 144–46, 154,
  155, 156, 158–60, 221
resignation of, 23, 136, 139–40, 279
salary policies/procedures and, 234–35
service responsibilities, 158–59, 161
status of librarians, 238–39
students' educational experience and,
  173, 218, 221, 244, 245–46, 247
teaching evaluation of, 162–65
work of, 158–61
workload, 63–67, 71, 80, 153–57, 158–59
See also Appointments; Non-tenure-track
  appointments; Part-time faculty; Probationary appointments; Promotion;
  Tenure
Faculty Appointment and Family Relationship, text, 213
Faculty Child Care, text, 281
  history, 273
Faculty Participation in the Selection, Evaluation, and Retention of Administrators,
  text, 228–29
Faculty Tenure and the End of Mandatory
  Retirement, text, 102
Family responsibilities, 273, 281
Fargher v. City of Boca Raton, 208n. 1
Federal government
  grants allocation by, 233n. 3
    and artistic expression, 36
  research sponsored by, 144–46, 147–48
  and student appeals of course grade
    assignments, 113n. 5
  substance abuse policy requirements of,
    116–17
Files. *See* Personnel files; University records
Financial aid for athletes, 241
Financial exigency
  affirmative action and, 23–24, 207, 230n
  defined, 23
  faculty responsibility and, 23–24, 230–31,
    233–34, 235, 236–37
  and institutional mergers, 231, 233,
    236–37

judicial decisions referring to, 309
reinstatement after termination for, 24
salary reductions in, 235
and severance salary, 24, 28, 231
tenure rights and, 24, 68n, 230–31, 236–37
termination of faculty appointments in, 4,
    23–24, 230–31
Finkin, Matthew W., ix
Freedom of Expression and Campus Speech
    Codes, On, text, 37–38
Freedom of Information Act, 124–25
Fringe benefits
    child care, 281
    faculty participation in selection of, 235
    for graduate student assistants, 270
    leaves of absence, 278–80
    for non-tenure-track faculty, 72, 82
    for part-time faculty, 64, 66–67, 82, 84, 86
    retirement and insurance plans, 275–77
Fullilove v. Klutznick, 202n. 2
Full-Time Non-Tenure-Track Appointments,
    On, text, 69–76

G

General secretary, AAUP, 302–4, 305–6
Georgia Association of Educators v. Harris
    (1990), 120n. 14
Governance Standards in Institutional Merg-
    ers and Acquisitions, text, 236–37
Governing board
    athletics policy and, 246
    and budgetary matters, 233, 234–35
    dismissal proceedings and, 4, 13–14,
        27, 94
    duties and powers of, 220, 293–94
    faculty representation on, 233
    institutional government and, 220
    presidential selection and, 219, 228–29
    review by, in cases of termination of
        appointment, 25
    students' right of appeal to, 267
    terminal salary/notice and review by, 28
Government, academic, 215–47, 293–94
    agencies for faculty participation in, 222
    athletics financing and, 241
    and budgetary and salary matters, 219,
        232–35, 241
    collective bargaining and, 251, 253–54
    faculty and, 221–22
    faculty role in, and academic freedom,
        42, 111, 224–27
    faculty role in college athletics and, 242–47
    governing board and, 220
    graduate students and, 269
    and intercollegiate athletics, 240–41

investigations relating to, 305–6
joint effort and, 218–20, 228
of medical schools, 108–9, 111
in mergers and acquisitions, 236–37
non-tenure-track faculty role in, 72, 74,
    82–83, 84, 86
part-time faculty role in, 62–63, 82–83,
    84, 86
president and, 221
statement on, 217–23
student participation in, 217, 222–23,
    264, 269
and substance-abuse policies, 117
Government-sponsored research. *See* Federal
    government
Grades. *See* Course grades
Graduate student academic staff
    academic freedom of, 29, 57, 268–69
    appointment and rights of, 29
    and collective bargaining, 270
    part-time faculty status of, 58–59
    at research institutions, 80
    workloads for, 157, 270
Gratz v. Bollinger, 202n. 4
Greene v. Howard University (1969), 308
Grievance procedures
    and access to faculty personnel files, 41,
        42, 44–46
    for graduate students, 269
    for minor sanctions, 27
    in nonreappointment cases, 18–20, 22–23, 28
    recommended standards, 29–30
    in salary disputes, 234–35
    in sexual harassment cases, 209–10
    university records of, 128
Grutter v. Bollinger, 202n. 4

H

Hearing, faculty
    on academic freedom violation com-
        plaints in nonreappointment, 18–19, 28
    on appointment termination
        for financial exigency, 24, 230–31
        for physical or mental disability, 25
        for program discontinuance, 25
    arbitration as substitute for, 259–60
    arbitration following, 93–94
    committee membership and procedures,
        13, 26–27
    on discrimination complaints in nonreap-
        pointment, 18–19, 28
    in dismissal for cause, 4, 13–14, 25–27, 32,
        56, 92, 93–94, 301
    on drug- or alcohol-related charges of
        misconduct, 118–19

for extramural utterances, 32
record of, 4, 26, 27, 260
in sexual harassment complaints, 210, 212
Hearing, student, 266–67

I

Imposition of Tenure Quotas, On the, text, 47–49
Inadequate consideration complaints, non-reappointment and, 19–20, 22–23
Incompetence
hearing on charges of, 4, 27
post-tenure review and, 52–53
Institutional Problems Resulting from Financial Exigency: Some Operating Guidelines, On, text, 2, 30–31
judicial decisions referring to, 309
Institutional Responsibility for Legal Demands on Faculty, text, 130
Institutions, academic
accreditation of, 271–72
autonomy of, 135, 220
budgeting responsibility in, 219, 224, 232–34, 241
child-care arrangements of, 281
church-related, 3, 6, 96–99, 202–3, 220, 262, 307
communication among components of, 222
copyright issues for, 182–84
distance education and, 181
and enforcement of faculty ethical standards, 133
and ethics of faculty recruitment, 141–43
external relations of, 219–20
faculty liability, responsibility for, 130
financial exigency and, 23–24, 207, 231
freedom of artistic expression, responsibility for protecting, 35–36
governance standards in mergers and acquisitions of, 236–37
government of, 217–23
government-sponsored research and, 144–46
mergers of, 231, 233, 236–37
and political activities of faculty, 29, 32, 33–34
recommended regulations on academic freedom and tenure, 21–30
and sexual harassment guidelines, 208–10
speaking officially for, 4, 219–20, 221
and student records, disclosure of, 263
substance-abuse policies and drug testing, 115–23

teaching evaluation procedures, 164–65
and timing of appointment offers, 139–40, 142
Insurance plans, 275–77
coverage during leaves of absence, 280
and faculty liability, 130
Intellectual property
copyright issues, 182–84
distance education and, 177
graduate students' rights to, 269
Interpretations of 1940 Statement of Principles on Academic Freedom and Tenure, 4–7
Investigations, AAUP
committee reports, x, 1, 190–91, 303–4, 306
of discrimination complaints, 190–91
"limitations" clause and, 98
procedures for, in academic freedom and tenure cases, 302–4
standards for, in governance cases, 305–6

J

Jimenez v. Almodovar (1981), 307
Joint effort, in academic government, 218–20
Joint Statement on Faculty Status of College and University Librarians, text, 238–39
Joint Statement on Rights and Freedoms of Students, text, 261–67
judicial decisions referring to, 309
Joint works, 183–84
See also Multiple authorship
Judicial decisions
on drug testing, 120, 121
referring to AAUP standards, x, xi, 307–9
on sexual harassment, 208n. 1, 209n. 3

K

Keen v. Penson (1992), 309
Keyishian v. Board of Regents (1967), 5
Korf v. Ball State University (1984), xi n, 309
Krotkoff v. Goucher College (1978), 307
Kunda v. Muhlenberg College (1980), 308

L

Leaves of absence, 273, 278–80
annuity contributions and, 276
in conflicts of interest, 136
for family responsibility, 281
for librarians, 239
for political activities, 29, 33–34
during probationary period, 22, 279
statement of principles on, 278–80
Legal demands on faculty, institutional responsibility for, 130
Lehmann v. Board of Trustees of Whitman College (1978), 308

professional standards for, 86–87
reasons for use of, 70–71, 77–78
workloads of, 71–74
See also Part-time faculty
Notice
of nonreappointment, standards for, 4, 7, 15n, 22, 31
of renewal of part-time appointments, 62, 84, 85, 86
of resignation, 23, 139–40, 279
terminal, 4, 7, 28, 260
in termination for financial exigency, 24, 231
in termination for program discontinuance, 25

O

Office of Civil Rights, U.S. Department of Education, 133n. 5, 209n. 6
Officers, AAUP, 286–88
Oncale v. Sundowner Offshore Services, Inc., 209n. 3

P

Part-time faculty, 57–67, 77–87
and academic due process, 57, 58–59, 62
academic freedom of, 6, 57, 58–59, 82–83, 88, 90
academic governance role of, 62–63, 82–83, 84, 86
accreditation issues relating to use of, 65, 83, 85
appointment duration for, 80
categories of, 59–61, 68, 77–78
change to status of, in financial exigency, 68n, 231
and collective bargaining, 63, 82–83, 84
compensation for, 62, 63n. 17, 64–66, 79–80, 84, 86
distribution and number of, 57–58, 65, 77–83, 84
evaluation of, 86
fringe benefits, 63–64, 66–67, 82, 84, 86
with full-time employment elsewhere, 60
and grievance procedures, access to, 28, 62, 88
nonteaching duties of, 64–65
and notice of nonreappointment, 62, 84, 85, 86
professional standards for, 86–87
security of employment for, 61–62, 84, 85
senior appointees with reduced loads, 57, 60, 68
tenure for, 61, 65–66, 81, 83, 84, 88
women as, 60–61, 64, 81, 206–7

workloads of, 57–62, 63–67, 80, 156–57
See also Non-tenure-track appointments
Pension benefits, 202n. 2
See also Retirement
Personnel files, faculty, 41–46
confidentiality and, 43–44
openness and, 42–43, 44–46
Plagiarism, 137–38
Policy documents, AAUP
adoption of, by institutions, xi
formation of, x–xi
interpretation of, ix–x
judicial decisions referring to, 307–9
uses of, x
Political activities of faculty, 29, 32, 33–34
Post-tenure review
academic freedom and, 51–54
guidelines for, 54–55
mandated assessment and, 169, 173
minimum good practice standards for, 55–56
Post-Tenure Review: An AAUP Response, text, 50–56
Preferential treatment, affirmative action and, 193, 198
President, academic
budgetary matters and, 232
duties and powers of, 221
evaluation and retention of, 229
in faculty dismissal proceedings, 12, 13, 26, 27, 28, 93–94
governance of athletic programs and, 241, 244–45
selection of, 219, 225, 228–29
students' right of appeal to, 267
Preventing Conflicts of Interest in Government-Sponsored Research at Universities, On, text, 144–46
Prior service elsewhere, crediting of, 4, 6, 100–101
Probationary faculty appointments
academic freedom and, 7, 18–19
automatic termination and, 48
doctorate not prerequisite for, 88
evaluation during, 7, 16–17, 22
leaves of absence during, 22, 279
length of, 4, 22, 48, 100–101
in medical schools, 108
prior service elsewhere and, 4, 6, 100–101
renewal standards and criteria for, 15–16, 22, 162–63, 206
and standards for notice of nonreappointment, 4, 7, 15n, 22, 31
tenure quotas and, 48
terms and conditions of, 4, 6–7, 15–16, 22–23, 142

judicial decisions referring to, 308

Statement on Procedural Standards in the Renewal or Nonrenewal of Faculty Appointments, text, 15–20
judicial decisions referring to, 308

Statement on Professional Ethics, text, 133–34
history, 131
judicial decisions referring to, 309

Statement on Professors and Political Activity, text, 33–34

Statement on Recruitment and Resignation of Faculty Members, text, 139–40

Statement on Teaching Evaluation, text, 162–65

Statistical evidence
and affirmative action, 199–200
and sex discrimination complaints, 28, 29–30, 188, 192

Status of Non-Tenure-Track Faculty, The, text, 77–87

Status of Part-Time Faculty, The, text, 57–67

Stricklin v. Regents of University of Wisconsin (1969), 309

Strikes, faculty, 252

Students, 261–70
academic freedom of, 134, 135, 262, 263–64, 268–69
and appeals of course grades, 113–14
athletic programs and, 240–41, 242–47
and budgetary matters, role in, 232n. 2
at church-related institutions, 262
as citizens, 119, 219–20, 265
in the classroom, 262
conduct of, standards relating to, 266
confidentiality and, 133, 262, 263
consensual relations with faculty, 211
disciplinary proceedings involving, 265–67
discrimination against, 262n. 3, 263n. 8
educational experience of, 135, 173, 218, 221, 244, 245–46, 247
educational records of, 263
evaluation of faculty, 53, 162–65, 167
faculty responsibility for, 133–34, 135, 208, 211, 218, 221, 222–23, 225
governance and, 217, 222–23, 264, 269
graduate, 268–70
institutional authority over, and civil penalties, 265, 266n. 15
judicial decisions on rights and freedoms of, 309
and learning environment, 133, 134, 135, 262
legal counsel for, 265

mandated assessment of educational outcomes and, 166–75
non-tenure-track appointments and effect on, 73–74, 78
organizations, 263–65
performance evaluation of, 113–14, 133, 135, 163, 262
plagiarism and, 138
publications of, 264–65
records of, and conditions of disclosure, 262, 263
rights and freedoms of, 135–36, 261–67
speaker choices of, 223, 264
status of, 222–23
university records and, 128–29
See also Graduate students

Substance-abuse policies, 115–23
academic due process and, 118–19
academic governance and, 117
drug testing, 120–23
federal requirements for, 116–17
potential prejudice to individual rights, 119
professional fitness and, 118, 123
and signature requirements, 119

Suspension
during dismissal proceedings, 7, 12, 26, 259
as severe sanction, 27, 118, 212

T

Teaching, 151–75
academic freedom and, 3, 111
evaluation of, 162–65
expectations, priorities, and rewards, 158–61
faculty workloads and, 153–57
and graduate student assistant workloads, 270
mandated assessment of, 166–75
methods, post-tenure review and, 53
non-tenure-track faculty and, 74–75, 78
See also Workloads

Teaching assistants, 6, 29
See also Graduate student academic staff

Teaching loads. *See* Workloads

Technology, intellectual property rights and, 184

Temporary faculty, 78, 84
See also Non-tenure-track appointments; Part-time faculty

Tenure
academic freedom and, 3, 15, 47–48, 69, 73, 100
academic personnel ineligible for, 88–91